GOING SHOPPING

GOING SHOPPING

Consumer Choices and Community Consequences

Ann Satterthwaite

Yale University Press

New Haven and London

Designed by Bessas & Ackerman
Set in Electra and Officina Sans type by Bessas & Ackerman

Printed in Italy by Conti Tipocolor

Library of Congress Cataloging-in-Publication Data
Satterthwaite, Ann, 1931–
    Going shopping : consumer choices and community consequences /
Ann Satterthwaite.
    p.   cm.
Includes bibliographical references and index.
    ISBN 0-300-08421-8 (alk. paper)
1. Shopping. 2. Consumer education. I. Title.
TX533 .S28 2001
640'.7—dc21   2001003124

A catalogue record for this book is available from the British Library.

The paper in this book meets the guidelines for permanence and durability of
the Committee on Production Guidelines for Book Longevity of the Council
on Library Resources.

10 9 8 7 6 5 4 3 2 1

For Sheafe

Contents

GOING SHOPPING

Introduction

Shopping is an inescapable activity for almost everyone. For some it is a tiresome necessity, for others it is an entertainment and a means of self-fulfillment, and for the poor it is a struggle. Yet shopping has become such an ordinary activity that we rarely think of its influence on our lives and communities, much less its significance in our culture and society at large. Shopping involves our needs and desires; consumes our time and money; and represents a big and growing industry driven by sophisticated marketing and new technology, as well as pervasive economic and social trends. The desire to shop has ballooned with rising aspirations, increased disposable incomes, the changing roles of women, varied ways to shop, and limited leisure time, along with new products and clever advertising. On another level, shopping, now a $3 trillion business employing almost 20 percent of the country's workforce, can been seen as continuing to recharge the engine of capitalism in the twenty-first century, similar to the way that religion, in loosening its rigid strictures, helped to invigorate capitalism in the nineteenth century.

When Alexis de Tocqueville observed in the 1830s that "no Americans are devoid of a yearning desire to rise. . . . Ambition is ardent and continual," he saw the very democratic ability to aspire to a better life.[1] But he also noticed that although "all are seeking to acquire property, power and reputation; few contemplate these things on a grand scale . . . life is generally spent in eagerly coveting small objects which are within reach."[2] Yet seeking goods has become not a means to an end but an end in itself for some—and almost an obsession for stalwarts of the "shop till I drop" school, exceeding the turn-of-the-century American economist Thorstein Veblen's worst fears. Individuals' quests for new and different possessions coupled with the corporate world's need to sell its products and services have created a retailing world of continuous change.

Wal-Mart, a relative newcomer in shopping, symbolizes one recent change in how and where we shop. This superstore, with its vast warehouse buildings, thirty checkout lanes, all sorts of goods, and acres of parking lots, has sparked headline controversies as it tries to locate on the outskirts of towns and cities in every state—and now in downtowns. Many see Wal-Mart and other similar megastores as plundering Main Street and eroding a way of life in their communities. More recently, another newcomer, e-commerce or virtual shopping, has begun revolutionizing how we shop, as it requires no physical stores, only computer Internet connections. This increasingly popular way to shop challenges all types of stores—from superstores and discounters to old-line department stores, specialty shops, and catalogue operations—and it threatens to undermine traditional civil and civic life in real communities dependent on face-to-face encounters.

Such continuous change is embedded in the history of retailing: from the days of Phoenician traders to twentieth-century mail-order houses, chain stores, supermarkets, malls, superstores, and Internet shopping. The intrinsic instability of retailing is clear in Standard and Poor's annual *Industry Surveys of Retailing*, which are sprinkled with such headings as "A New Environment Forces Change," "Losers Left in the Dust," "Competition Intensifying," "The Fickle Consumer Reigns," and "Shake-Out Years Ahead." Some of the more jolting changes in shopping are forcing new, and needed, debates on the role of Main Street and its function in the community, as well as on the role of stores and shopping in our communities and lives today.

Shopping is an increasingly remote experience. We used to shop in stores where we knew the clerks and other customers, and in towns and cities where the stores were part of the nerve center of the community: near the courthouse, banks, movies, barbers, restaurants, and post office. Shopping was part of the public and civic life of a place. Now our shopping is becoming a more and more faceless activity. We patronize superstores and franchised stores with "deskilled" and usually benefitless clerks. These stores, often in vast malls or on highway strips in the no-man's land of suburbia, have an anonymity and a detachment from communities and people. We do not have face-to-face contact with many people in stores—or elsewhere. And now the world of cyberspace, with its Internet shopping, removes us even further from any connections with real places and real people. Remoteness is an accepted part of living. We respond to automatic voices on the telephone, we operate machine keyboards to communicate via e-mail, and we use automatic teller machines instead of dealing with real bank tellers. We have come a long way from the country store–post office where one purchased groceries and necessities—and also met friends and neighbors and learned what was going on. We are not meeting friends for lunch at the local Woolworth, chatting at the drugstore counter, or talking to our seatmates on the commuter bus or train. Instead we drive long distances alone to work, lunch at the cafeteria in our office building off I-95, and live in isolated electronic fortresses where our computers, VCRs, and TVs bring the outside world to us. Indeed, the sociability in many of our day-to-day activities, including shopping, is disappearing.

How, where, and when we shop is closely connected with how we live and how our communities have developed and how they function. The social function of shopping was brought to my attention when I took my eighty-seven-year-old mother to the local supermarket and saw her searching for familiar faces—and even lingering around the meat section hoping to see the one longtime employee she knew, who was assigned to bring out the packaged meat from behind-the-scenes butchers and arrange it in the display cases. I realized that my mother, like many others, viewed shopping as a way of seeing friends and acquaintances. That spurred my interest in investigating what research and writing have been done on the social and civic function of shopping—and I found very little. The activity of shopping aroused the attention of many scholars and observers in the United States only recently, and some interesting books have appeared, including Tom Shachtman's *Around the Block*, on the daily life of the businesses on one block in the Chelsea neighborhood of New York City; William Leach's *Land of Desire*, on merchants and consumer society; Paco Underhill's *Why We Buy*; and George Ritzer's books on McDonaldization. Some of the most searching inquiries have been written by women, like Susan Porter Benson's *Counter Cultures*, on store clerks; Rosalind Williams's *Dream Worlds*, on the sociology of shopping; Rachel Bowlby's *Just Looking* and *Carried Away*, on consumerism; Susan Strasser's *Satisfaction Guaranteed*, on the development of mass marketing; Kristin Ross's introduction to Emile Zola's *The Ladies' Paradise*; and Erika Rappaport's *Shopping for Pleasure* and Lynne Walker's research, both on the Victorian period in England when shopping, particularly in the new department stores, helped to emancipate middle-class women.

So I was launched on this fascinating study of shopping and its social and civic functions through history. Because shopping touches on so many aspects of society, I soon found myself engrossed in research on an array of subjects from history, economics, architecture, sociology, and psychology to planning and beyond. The search for information and ideas was captivating and seemed endless, as each new discovery would lead to yet another. To pull together the diverse data and provide a factual background and overall perspective, I decided to begin the book with a history of shopping. However, in tackling such a broad swath of material, I am well aware that I have missed many things, over- and underestimated others, and could not go into depth on some of the areas I explored. Also, my decision to focus on the interplay of the social and built environments means that some aspects of shopping, like the business side of retailing, and that certain retail activities, like car dealerships and restaurants, and the role of the Jewish merchant/storekeeper, did not receive as much attention as other areas.

Shopping fits in to my long-standing fascination with how economic, social, and cultural history is interwoven and then, as a city planner, with how communities maintain a sense of continuity and civic identity while responding to new and challenging circumstances. Much attention has been directed to the physical losses that occur in our cities and towns—the loss of familiar buildings and landscapes. But my concern has been with the loss of mundane, quotidian, often authentic, and sometimes nitty-gritty services and activities in towns and cities. Such services and activities, which, aside from providing everyday necessities like food, clothing, hardware, drugs, dry cleaning services, shoe repairs, and barbering, can with repeated face-to-face transactions build trust between people and establish a sense of place and time as well as a civic pride in towns and cities.

In the past two decades I have sporadically studied public markets, which over the centuries have served many roles in cities. With a National Endowment for the Arts grant, I investigated the public fish markets in the downtowns of some major American cities; most of these markets have vanished, except for notable exceptions like the Fulton Fish Market in New York and Pike Place Market in Seattle. Some of the old market buildings have been converted into tourist attractions, which led me to explore, also with a National Endowment of the Arts grant, ways to prevent tourism from turning towns and city neighborhoods into stage-sets for outside observers. I have seen my neighborhood, Georgetown in Washington, D.C., lose its diversity of people, activities, and service stores as real estate prices have soared. And along with those losses I have observed that the sense of community has suffered. No doubt my neighborhood, with its tight row houses, where neighbors bump into each other on the sidewalk or at the bus stop, has more opportunities for neighborliness than do sprawled suburban communities, where people move everywhere by car. But as we lose our neighborhood stores in the city, as the suburbs have more and distant malls and workplaces, and as more and more time is spent on the Internet, crowds get lonelier.

Shopping is just one aspect of life in communities, but one that is often overlooked. It touches on many different social, economic, and political functions of our society—and our communities. In this book I try to point out how important the social and civic role of shopping has been throughout history and how major cultural, economic, and demographic forces have influenced the nature of shopping, the aspirations of shoppers, and the ways that shopping areas have developed. In looking at shopping today and speculating on its future, I examine some current retailing trends, from remote ordering on computers to friendly markets and bookstores, as well as new approaches in community planning here and abroad, which encourage sociability in shopping, strengthen community life, and bolster economic vitality.

I recognize that I have concentrated on what appear to me to be mainstream trends, usually powered by upper-income, educated shoppers, and, in focusing on the mainstream, I have slighted some important segments of the population, like the poor, rural, and lower middle class, whose shopping patterns deserve careful attention. Also, because I live in Washington, D.C., and have been closely associated with the East Coast all my life, other sections of the country may have been understudied.

But, for whatever populations in whatever part of the country, the intertwined social and civic functions of shopping deserve more public attention. It is not a matter of embalming out-of-date retailing but of seeing how the centuries-old sociability of shopping can be integrated into contemporary communities to provide accessible and diverse shopping opportunities and to reduce today's remoteness and alienation. New thinking, attitudes, and roles are needed for government, private entrepreneurs, and the general public—that is, citizens and consumers—who can affect the planning and development of their communities and influence policies and legislation.

Although intangible societal pressures, powerful profit-driven corporate strategies, and political development decisions may make the consumer feel powerless, we can influence, through our shopping decisions, what is sold how, where, and when, and through our participation in community planning and the political process we can help to shape our communities. Fresh vegetables, more fat-free products, and hearty breads have been appearing on the shelves of supermarkets, thanks to citizen concerns about health and ecology. Citizens have prevented Wal-Mart from locating in communities like Greenfield, Massachusetts, where it was feared that the life of downtown would be threatened by a nearby superstore. And in places like Bennington, Vermont, citizens backed by state and local support forced Wal-Mart to locate in a community-approved location. Fast-food restaurants have had to conform to local architecture and planning requirements. Friendly, consumer-oriented markets, such as farmers' markets and neighborhood shops, are being found in more places. Conscientious Main Street programs in every corner of the country—from McAllen, Texas, to Baker City, Oregon—are resuscitating these once-vital hubs of communities, creating not quaint anachronisms but new centers meeting current economic and social needs. Countries like England and Norway, worried by the prospect of out-of-town retailing fracturing the economic and social life of their urban centers, have even enacted national legislation to force new stores, especially large shopping centers, to be in or adjacent to cities and towns.

While these citizen- or consumer-driven actions may seem merely refreshing byways in the mainstream of large-scale and remote shopping, they can be critical first steps in altering the ways of mainstream business. Grassroots citizen-consumer political action can influence not only local decisions but also state and federal governments, where many of the laws and regulations affecting retailing are passed. Such grassroots political pressure has accounted for remarkable strides in many arenas, including civil rights and the protection of health and the environment. Fifty years ago one would never have dreamed that citizens could be shielded from the health hazards of corporate toxic wastes or from the life-threatening attacks of assault weapons, or could participate in major environmental decision-making, as is now possible in the environmental impact process, but all that has been made possible by the groundswell of citizen action. Consumer-driven actions can change the way things are done, even in mainstream large-scale and remote shopping.

In looking at the role of shopping in our lives and communities, it is clear that shopping is deeply imbedded in the American character. Back in the 1830s, Tocqueville observed in Americans a "virtuous materialism," which has been a driving force behind the consumption of material goods. Shopping is part of the American dream: freedom of choice, freedom from constraints of class and position, and the ability to improve, transform, and reinvent ourselves. Ever since the earliest trading in Mesopotamia, shopping has had a strain of democratization. Charlemagne's serfs at the medieval regional fairs and the working-class shoppers at the Victorian marble palace department stores were all seen as potential customers. A 1915 report on New York City's public markets in recognizing this democratization noted that "the rich, the middle class, and the poor meet in these markets on an even footing."[3] That intrinsic social leveling has permeated every aspect of shopping in the United States. Yet shopping also mirrors our infatuation with things: our belief that things can change us and that our purchases prove and display our worth. As we enjoy the freedom and opportunities that shopping offers, we find ourselves captured by it and its entrepreneurial manipulations.

This illusion of the freedom in shopping kept reappearing in my studies in different paradoxes: the individual's fantasies and hopes, which are so often dashed by realities, the plethora of choices countered by the lack of money, and the diversity of things to buy, yet their sameness due to ubiquitous franchising. For sociability, the most glaring paradox emerges as today's global village expands the potential for instantaneous communication and "online communities," while at the same time a new isolation reduces face-to-face encounters. With the fax, Internet, e-mail, and the telephone, the world has become a neighborhood—much like William Allen White's observation that electricity made the nation a neighborhood—but today our neighborhood is a figment of electronic circuitry. Such contradictions and the volatility of fashions, stores, retailing techniques, human desires, and needs add excitement and a mercurial quality to shopping. These qualities make shopping an intriguing part of the zestful and optimistic American dream.

Shopping has been a way to share in the better life, to reach for that dream, but it has meant buying in to an economic system selling hope—and making profits by featuring the latest. It is not a marginal activity, as it has been so often viewed by economists, nor is it a function that should be left solely in the hands of private entrepreneurs, as the types and locations of stores, the economic system of retailing itself, and the social and civic functions of shopping have profound effects on our lives and in our communities.

CHAPTER ONE

Shopping Through the Ages

How Rarities Become Commonplace

When Italian designers like Armani, Moschino, and Prada invaded New York City in 1996, their stores, mostly on fashionable Madison Avenue, captured the headlines of not only fashion publications like *Woman's Wear Daily*, but also the *New York Times.* The stores' architecture and interior design were reviewed by newspaper architectural critics, their clothing by fashion editors, and their place in American culture by sociologists. Likewise, the upscale discount store Loehmann's, moving to its first Manhattan location also in 1996, attracted front-page newspaper coverage — not for its architecture but for the popularity of such discount shopping and for its guerilla shoppers seeking Calvin Klein jackets reduced by over 50 percent to $450. The high cost of designers' clothes and accessories — men's suits by Armani can command more than $3,000 — seemed to be accepted as part of the retail excitement ignited by these boutiques. The openings were treated as news events, like the opening of a museum; in fact, Peter Marino, the designer of the Armani stores, compared the opening of his "startling" Madison Avenue store to the opening of the Whitney Museum.[1] But no matter how the architect portrays his design or how the stores project their images, the high-profile coverage of these openings indicates—and almost confirms—the important role of shopping in the United States today, Americans' fascination with fashion, the grip of consumerism in society, and the ability of many to buy extravagant things.

In the succinct statement, "Things that had been rarities to one generation were becoming commonplace to another; luxuries were passing into the category of necessities," Dorothy Davis, an English historian of shopping, sums up a basic theme running through the entire history of shopping.[2] From ancient Mesopotamia to eighteenth-century London or contemporary Los Angeles, rising expectations and the democratization of luxuries have been at the heart of any discussion of shopping. After all, fur coats, gourmet food, jewelry, designer clothes, and yachts, items formerly associated only with Vanderbilts and Rothschilds, are now available to many—through credit cards and installment plans. Such material aspirations and the ability to satisfy them reflect an interplay of broad social, cultural, economic, and political forces. In fact, the history of shopping provides a fascinating glimpse of the sweep of history as seen in the changing nature of the consumer, the institutions serving the consumer, and, most important, the fusions of economic and industrial innovations with supporting societal values, which have produced radical changes in the way people live, work, play—and shop.

Instead of bartering for necessities with an itinerant hawker at a medieval town market or selecting a purchase with the help of a skilled sales clerk in a family-owned early twentieth-century downtown department store, today many order a nationally advertised product by computer, telephone, or fax from a conglomerate company often owned by an international syndicate. The progression from open-air bartering to small and later multiple shops to department stores, chain stores, shopping centers, malls, discount–warehouse–category killer stores to all kinds of remote shopping is yet another indicator of the vast changes in shopping produced by the economic, political, and cultural kaleidoscope.

Changes in shopping, at times dramatic and drastic but usually slow, are part of the long tapestry of history. Some key threads keep reappearing, such as rising material expectations as the middle class grows, the emancipation of women and new interest in style and fashion, an unfettered free enterprise system with the growing specialization and complexity of shopping institutions, new and sophisticated selling and advertising techniques, and the increasing impersonality of the process of shopping and of the shops themselves. The tapestry is interwoven with moral and ethical sanctions, whether from the church or society at large, which throughout history have allowed, and sometimes encouraged, new attitudes toward profit-making, materialism, women, and luxury.

The world of shopping is the world of laissez-faire. Emile Zola's late nineteenth-century Parisian department store tycoon, Octave Mouret, in *The Ladies' Paradise,* told the young girl from the country to warn her draper uncle, about to be swept aside by Mouret's grand Bon Marché department store, that he "will ruin himself if he insists on keeping to his ridiculous old-fashioned ways."[3] Throughout history such ways have succumbed to a parade of new types of selling, stores, and advertising, but since the mid-nineteenth century it seems that those "ridiculous old-fashioned ways" are being pushed aside ever more quickly as the pace of change accelerates, especially with recent technological improvements in communications and electronics.

This free enterprise system, with all its materialistic activities, has required moral sanctions. In the Middle Ages, when the feudal system depended on serfdom and agriculture, the religious and secular authority of the church perpetuated the feudal system, preaching hard work as the way to eternal salvation. To seek riches was to succumb to the sin of avarice. The pope disdained aberrations like Venice, which thrived on maritime trade and displayed the "love of gain." But most of Europe continued in a stratified agricultural society approved by the church, which itself was able to consolidate its power by amassing land and riches. As artisan industries and the early guilds developed, the church's strictures of minimizing the profit motive were still heeded in these new collective organizations. Later, when the Industrial Revolution disrupted the old economic, social, and ethical systems, religious doctrines were crafted to provide the critically needed moral justification for this new era of consumption. Hard work and frugality continued to be valued, but now profit-making was acceptable. At first, accumulation of wealth was permitted only for utilitarian purposes and eventually for more frivolous and even romantic reasons, then with the rationale that it fueled the engine of industry. Today a woman can "shop till she drops" with no guilt—and much debt—while the early nineteenth-century housewife was warned in *The American Frugal Housewife* that extravagance was a treacherous evil and that "expensive habits are productive of much domestic unhappiness, and injurious to public prosperity."[4]

A Lowly Business

Although the origins of retailing and shopping date back to the earliest known settlements in the Mesopotamian valley, where farmers traded their excess produce for other necessities, retailing, whatever its form, has never been viewed as a prestigious economic or social activity. In fact, retailing has usually been regarded as a marginal and disparaged activity of small-time local operators. Even when many shopkeepers achieved middle-class status in nineteenth-century England they constituted a "largely ignored race" treated with "scorn and condescension" by the upper class and lurking resentment by lower classes, according to Michael Winstanley's study of shopkeepers from 1830–1914.[5] After a generation or two of wealth, they had not achieved the reputation of "Gentlemen-tradesmen" that Daniel Defoe anticipated in

1727. In *The Complete English Tradesman* Defoe saw "trade-bred Gentle-men" rising through the ranks to become judges, bishops, "Parliament-men," and statesmen, like Sir William Craven, who became Lord-Mayor of London after a career as a wholesale grocer. Defoe's confidence in the upward mobility of such tradespeople was evident in his advice to young ladies to consider such tradesmen as husbands.[6]

For centuries negative attitudes have been reflected in merchants' views of themselves and their trade. In the United States, even when recognized as "rich men, marked as leading citizens" in midwestern towns in the nineteenth century, merchants "did not regard their occupation as distinguished," according to Lewis Atherton's careful studies of the midwestern settlements.[7] John O'Fallon, a prominent St. Louis merchant, maintained no records of his merchant years but did keep records of his philanthropies and activities with important people. He even advised his brother to choose another trade. Atherton discovered similar views among eastern merchants. The New York City merchant Wynant Van Zandt never discussed his years of trading but kept meticulous notes concerning his public honors.[8] Atherton points out in his studies that the derogatory attitude toward the merchant's trade had existed since the time of the Phoenicians. A more up-to-date example of this attitude is evident in the 1927 withdrawal of Baltimore's Retail Merchants Association from the city's newly organized Association of Commerce—retailers felt that they were playing second fiddle to industry, finance, and transportation.[9]

National governments have traditionally looked with favor at manufacturing, transportation, agriculture, and finance as major economic producers, improving the economic and social welfare of a country. Retailing and other distributive trades, on the other hand, have been considered residual economic activities that, however essential, do not contribute new products—such as cars, steel, and now computers—to society. Retail is "trade" and a service activity. Not until May 1995 were retail companies included among *Fortune's* 500 largest U.S. corporations, and yet at that time they constituted 10 percent of the list, with Wal-Mart holding the number four position and moving into the number two position five years later. Aside from being considered nonproductive, retailing has been viewed as a local matter. In the United States the federal government has usually let state and local governments handle retailing matters, except in cases involving interstate trade. Moreover, this hands-off attitude of the federal government and, indeed, all levels of government, seems to stem from a feeling that retailing represents a laissez-faire system in which competition reigns. "Customers retain the final vote," as Stanley Hollander stated.[10]

Scholars have neglected retailing as a field of study. Few comprehensive surveys of the history of shopping exist, and there are none on the history of American shopping. Economic histories of American eighteenth-century commerce "describe at length the wholesale trade from England but neglect retail trade almost entirely," according to Richard L. Bushman. How the majority of colonial American consumers in the countryside got their goods and provisions from city merchants is not so clear.[11] Even today, despite the interest in consumerism, relatively few scholarly books have been published on different aspects of retailing and consumerism. A great deal of the scholarly work on shopping has been undertaken by women: Susan Benson Porter's *Counter Cultures* on store clerks, Rosalind Williams's *Dream Worlds* on the sociology of consumption, Susan Strasser's *Satisfaction Guaranteed* on the development of mass marketing, Erika Rappaport's *Shopping for Pleasure*, and Pasi Falk and Colin Campbell's edited volume *The Shopping Experience*, with mostly women contributors. However, there have been some important scholarly contributions from men, including the English anthropologist Daniel Miller's work on material culture, the English historian Michael Winstanley's *The Shopkeeper's World, 1830–1914*, and the American architectural historian Richard Longstreth's *Center City to Regional Mall*. Interestingly, many of the significant books as well as innovative research on shopkeeping and consumerism have been either written or published in England, apparently upholding its reputation as a nation of shopkeepers. In the United States much of the research in this field comes from trade organizations, such as the International Council of Shopping Centers, or research organizations for developers—like the Urban Land Institute, which holds conferences and publishes reports on retail developments with a pragmatic eye on how retail developers might do better. Even though retail sales hit $3 trillion in 1999, business schools did not treat retailing seriously until e-commerce came on the scene. For example, the Harvard Business School had only one course on retailing in the early 1990s. Nonetheless, novelists may in fact have contributed the most interesting insights into shopping, such as in Emile Zola's *The Ladies' Paradise*, H. G. Wells's *Mr. Polly*, and short stories by Virginia Woolf and Dorothy Parker.

The fact that retailing and shopping have been neglected and almost disdained by government and academia confirms the longstanding lack of respect for retailing held by the public in general. Attitudes toward and about women no doubt account for some of this neglect, as shopping has been considered a women's activity. New York City's famous shopping avenue in the late nineteenth century, for example, was called Ladies' Mile. The derogatory image of the consumer and shopper as frivolous, trivial, and inconsequential reflects the way women have been seen by many over time. As the English anthropologist Daniel Miller states, this "denigration" of shopping is affected by the "well-established legacy of its gendered nature." He cites such cartoons as "Blondie," which have sneered at the "inconsequential nature of women by detailing their involvement and concern with shopping."[12] Whether shopping for a necessity or just browsing for whatever hits one's fancy, the world of shopping is seen as a woman's world, and, hence, attitudes toward women by society as well as how women view themselves have influenced how shopping has been treated.

The lack of attention to shopping also results from the go-it-alone entrepreneurism of retailing, whether in 4,000 B.C. in the Fertile Crescent or A.D. 1990 in the United States. In less than fifty years the small shops on America's Main Streets were forced out of business by chain stores, then those chain stores were devastated by outlying shopping centers and later malls, and then by Wal-Mart–like warehouses, and now by electronic shopping. These changes have produced crucial yet generally overlooked and understudied social and economic impacts on communities and regions — and on the people who live in them.

Bartering and Its Lingering Reputation

Retailing can trace its roots to bartering and trading, which probably have existed since the cave men. But the discovery of clay tokens recording transactions — presumably between farmers trading excess crops for other produce — indicates that cities like Ur in the Fertile Crescent were bartering around 4,000 B.C. With the Phoenicians' extensive pack-trip forays into the interiors of Asia, Africa, and Europe, their seafaring dominance in the Mediterranean, and the establishment of trading posts, they were not only the earliest trading people, but the major traders until the fifth century B.C. The image of the bustling bazaars of the Middle East persists today, climaxing with Istanbul's Grand Bazaar, covering 2 million square feet, or 125 football fields, which certainly rivals this country's mammoth 4.3 million square-foot Mall of America with 2.5 million square feet for stores.

Yet the disrespect for retailing may stem partly from the nature of those bartering negotiations in which the seller had to peddle his wares so aggressively that their price, quality, and quantity might well have been misrepresented. Egypt had Muhtasibs to protect the buyer from overpricing, fraudulent sales, inaccurate measurement, and adulterated products according to Islamic law. Such inspections indicate that consumer problems existed even then.

For the Greeks, trading was a necessary but low-order activity compared with landowning and agriculture. As a man of culture and leisure, the philosopher king stood at the top of the social ladder; at the bottom were traders, shopkeepers, and bankers—seen by Plato as those "weakest in body . . . unfit for any other work. . . . It is these that provide our cities with a race of shopkeepers, for do we not call those shopkeepers who sit in the market and serve both in selling and buying?"[13] Still, Plato, recognizing the need of trade, urged in his *Republic* the establishment of standards for buying and selling, a money system, and a marketplace. But, in reality, the Greek city governments discouraged the trader with harassing restrictions, heavy taxes, and consumer oversight by the *agoranomoi*, officials ensuring fair consumer deals.

The Greek *agora*, admired for its lively mix of urban activities by contemporary urbanists like William H. Whyte and developers like James Rouse, was indeed an important place in Greek cities from the sixth century B.C. to the fifth century A.D. It was really the "living heart" of the Greek city, according to Richard E. Wycherley's *How the Greeks Built Cities*.[14] Agoras were centrally located, usually on flat open spaces with available water and drainage and often near public buildings and shrines. The agora concentrated a city's daily public activities—political, business, and social. However, for philosophers like Aristotle and other intellectuals, trade was a degrading endeavor, to be segregated from the world of ideas. In Aristotle's hierarchy of activities, the building "appropriated to religious worship" should be on a site

> seen far and wide, which gives elevation to virtue and towers over the neighborhood. Below this spot should be established an agora, such as that which the Thessalians call the "freemen's agora"; from this all trade should be excluded, and no mechanic, husbandman, or any such person allowed to enter, unless he be summoned by the magistrates. There should also be a traders' agora, distinct and apart from the other, in a situation which is convenient for the reception of good both by sea and land. . . . The magistrates who deal with contracts, indictments, summonses, and the like, and those who have the care of the agora and of the city respectively, ought to be established near an agora and some public place of meeting; the neighborhood of the traders' agora will be a suitable spot; the upper agora we devote to the life of leisure, the other is intended for the necessities of trade.[15]

But that segregation did not occur. Instead, the agora mixed trade, civic activities, and socializing, making it the central place for exchanging not just food and wares but also ideas. Callicles reported in *Georgias* that Socrates, ignoring Aristotle's condescending attitude toward the gutsy nature of the democratic agora, enjoyed talking with "cobblers, fullers, and such paltry folk" in the agora.[16]

The conflict between Aristotle's and Plato's disparaging attitudes toward trade and the reality of the agora as a vital place blending trade and ideas that contributed to the prosperity of Greece meant that trading and hawking were viewed ambivalently. "The pursuit of profit was always distrusted as dangerous to the ethical norms and proper social order," according to B. L. Anderson.[17] And that feeling has generally persisted throughout history.

Shops and Shopping Markets in the Early Roman Empire

The Roman Empire was an early exception to the customary ambivalence about commerce. By the second century B.C., Ostia, the port for Rome situated just fifteen miles away at the mouth of the Tiber, had far more shops

1. *Tomb in Ostia depicting a butcher at his trade, c. second century B.C.*

than did Pompeii, and a market economy to serve this concentrated city and its bustling shipping trade. The streets of Ostia were lined with shops as well as small-scale manufacturing workshops for bricks, lamps, and lead pipes; two of these were even owned by women.[18] Retail shops sold the manufactured goods and other necessities like shoes, meat, and tools, as shown in this tomb relief (fig. 1).

The typical shop was a large room facing the street where goods were displayed and sold, a room behind for production, and a staircase leading to an upper floor, or mezzanine, where the family lived. The storefront, which would be open during the day, could be shuttered at night. Some shops were only one room deep, others had no upstairs family quarters, and in many it is difficult to determine from archaeological work which were exclusively retail and which combined production and sales.

Not only is the number of shops in Ostia surprising, but so is its development of shopping markets—a forerunner of today's shopping center. The first of these markets on Via della Foce's south side, one of whose walls can be dated to the second century B.C., had a passageway from the street to an open courtyard lined with eight shops. Later this plan was refined under Hadrian into a larger market, the House of Lararium, with two passageways from two streets and ten shops (fig. 2).

As an active port benefiting from local, Roman, and seafaring business, Ostia's commerce prospered, as confirmed by the number of shops and the amount of manufacturing, warehousing, and wholesale trade in oil and wine. And Ostia's large-scale bakeries indicated that housewives were depending on store-bought rather than homemade bread. Such activities show that the Roman Empire was developing an increasingly sophisticated market economy.

Shops existed in Rome as well, but perhaps most interesting in its early retail history is an urban redevelopment project replacing shops (taber-

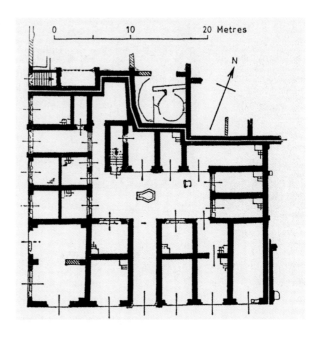

2. Plan of shopping market established in Ostia under Augustus (c. first century A.D.) and restored under Trajan (second century A.D.)

3. The multilevel Trajan Markets, Rome, A.D. 100–110, an early precursor of today's shopping center

4. *The Borgata shopping center, a contemporary translation of a medieval Italian cityscape, in Scottsdale, Arizona, 1997*

nae) and other buildings for the construction of the Forum, the Basilica, and the Trajan Markets. The markets, built in the beginning of the first century A.D. on Quirinal Hill, rose six levels above the street and occupied 110 to 115 meters (fig. 3). Architecturally, this curving building, with no structural columns, displayed the "superbly successful interrelation of design, structure, and function that characterizes Roman vaulted social architecture at its best," according to architectural historian William MacDonald.[19] This complex market, where 170 rooms are still "accessible or visible," is yet another example of Rome's commercial proclivities as well as the development of an early shopping center whose layout does not differ significantly from the 1990s Borgata shopping center in Scottsdale, Arizona, which was inspired by an Italian hilltown's shopping area (fig. 4).

While usually we hear of Roman engineering feats in aqueducts and roads, which are extant in Italy and England, the shops and retailing in early Ostia and Rome show that the Romans were not beset with the doubts about commercial ventures that plagued some prominent Greek philosophers and thus were able to launch their ventures on a scale and with a sophistication of retailing that did not reappear until the late Middle Ages.

Markets and a New Social Leveling

With the ebb and flow of international conflicts in the Mediterranean, Europe regressed to an agricultural state after the Islam irruption in the

5. *The weekly market, which has been operating for 400 years at the same site in the York-shire Dales market town of Leyburn, England, 1996 (post card courtesy Walter Scott Brad-ford, Ltd., Bradford, England)*

Mediterranean. Only a few trading centers, like Rome and Venice, remained for such Eastern products as spices. Itinerant traders wandered from castle to castle peddling wares, many of them Eastern, some smuggled, some boot-legged, and others legitimately purchased. But the growing number of wandering merchants—along with excess local produce or produce insuffi-ciencies brought on by bad weather and poor crops—spurred the develop-ment of a new system of buying and selling: local markets.

These local markets, usually held weekly in the open air, supplied such needed provisions as eggs and vegetables (figs. 5, 6). The markets have survived centuries of change in Europe. One can still attend such weekly markets in small towns and daily markets in large cities throughout England, the Continent, Africa, and South America—and find them operating very much as they did in the fifteenth century. Stallholders, with a canopy sup-ported by a few trestles, set up shop in numbered locations, selling every-thing from cheese, game, straw, hemp, flax, and vegetables to jewelry. The activity, bustle, smells, mess, cries, and laughs of the market remain univer-sal and timeless. These markets bulge with so many merchants and such vari-ety of goods that customers could shop around, checking out the goods to see what was fresh and fairly priced—an early example of comparison shopping. This was a new form of face-to-face shopping—or "auge-in-auge Handel" (eye-to-eye), as the Germans called these immediate exchanges. Everything

6. *Robert Doisneau, Market at the Place Jean-Jaurès, St. Denis, France, 1986 (note the clusters of people talking to one another)*

at these markets was "sold on open market and there it can be seen if they are good and fair or not . . . ; for of things . . . sold on the open market, all may have a share, poor and rich," according to Boileau's *Livres des Metiers*, written in 1270.[20]

Moreover, markets provided opportunities for socializing, as well as for important social leveling. As Boileau states, rich and poor could share the market experience because each customer had the same standing with the merchant, if he or she could pay the prices. In towns and regions, markets became places to see friends, do business, and learn what was going on. "Since people went there on set days, it was a natural focus for social life," states historian Fernand Braudel. "It was at the market that townspeople met, made deals, quarrelled, perhaps came to blows."[21] In fact, Braudel found that more business deals were made on market days. The increasing popularity of this more sophisticated type of shopping indicated a growing demand for retail goods by a population moving away from the era of self-sufficiency. As surpluses and money became available, peasants were being converted into consumers — and townspeople.

7. Map of fairs in France, 1841

Regional Fairs

A larger version of the local market was the regional fair. These fairs, often compared with international expositions, became major exchange centers for both wholesale and retail trade, were held once or twice a year, and attracted vast numbers of people. Goods of every kind were for sale, and entertainment—plays, music, and feasts—were provided, rather like today's county fair midways. The famed Champagne fair, which reached its peak at about the end of the thirteenth century, attracted merchants from all over Europe. Such fairs were really for the trade only, as we would say today. As they expanded they became, in some cases, the basis for permanent commercial centers. Leipzig, for example, knocked down part of its town and rebuilt its buildings and squares to accommodate its expanding fair. These large fairs were at the heart of merchant life, and many continued through the nineteenth century (fig. 7).

The growth of the merchant's world, with its markets, fairs, and shops, reflected some of the pervasive changes in social, economic, and political life of the western world. New commerce and industry were emerging in Flanders, where a flourishing cloth industry attracted international merchants and skilled artisans, making it the foremost cloth center in Europe by the thirteenth century. Its guilds, with their tremendous power, controlled the production and sales of cloth—and even the operation of town market halls, many of which had become regional markets. Specialization, whether in agriculture or commerce, was another critical ingredient in transforming the commercial world; as cities became larger, specialized shopping areas, as well as specialized markets, emerged. London had markets for meat, fish, cloth, vegetables, and countless other goods, some in covered quarters and others sprawling on the streets. The outlying cities in England and Wales were also becoming increasingly specialized, so that 300 of the 800 market towns were devoted to single trades by the seventeenth century.

Shops

One of the most important steps in the history of retailing was the growth of shops. No longer dependent on wandering merchants and periodic fairs and markets, towns and cities were developing distinct shopping areas, which were sometimes guild-controlled. These shops were at first run by artisans like cobblers and bakers, who sold goods from the front of their houses, which also served as their factories. The display space was the bottom half of the front door, while the upper half of the door served as an awning and as a barrier between the house and the street, according to architectural historian Nikolaus Pevsner (fig. 8). In fact, the word "shop" meant porch, vestibule, or lean-to of a residence in old Saxon or German.

While the early development of shops is often associated with the emerging commercial world in Flanders, Lorenzetti's informative mural of good government in Siena's Palazzo Publicco, painted in 1338–39, indicates the existence of shops in Italy in the fourteenth century. In Rome, when the patrician Barberini family started developing its palazzo, Casa Grande, on via dei Giubbonari, they incorporated in 1624 six existing townhouses with ground-floor shops. And their palazzo, which kept expanding to meet the needs of three generations, still has shops on its ground floor lining the street, keeping it "in harmony with its mercantile context," as Patricia Waddy states in her well-documented book *Seventeenth-Century Roman Palaces*.[22] Shops were an urban phenomenon.

In booming cities like Paris and London, different trades clustered their shops in distinct areas, such as London's corn merchants on Corn Hill and goldsmiths in Cheapside or on streets like Milk Street and Bread Street. In Paris, there was the rue de la Lingerie and rue des Boucherie. Such retail trade grew increasingly important in these bustling and expanding cities. London's fivefold population increase in the sixteenth century spurred massive consumer demand, which in turn encouraged development of shops, once again influenced by the rise of guilds, making it a major marketing center. Throughout Europe the medieval pattern of shopping at markets and fairs was being replaced by a new type of guild-controlled urban shopping, producing a new pattern of permanently concentrated shops. In the eighteenth century, shops in many small market towns in the countryside took

8. *Baker's and draper's shops, painting by Jacobus Vrel, seventeenth century (collection of H. A. Wetzlar)*

over the business of collecting farm surpluses and distributing food and goods previously handled by fairs and markets, which were waning in importance. "Shops of all categories came to conquer and devour towns," Braudel wrote. Indeed, the shopkeeper was becoming a small-time capitalist. His shops, said Daniel Defoe, the eighteenth-century writer, were spreading "monstrously."[23]

While this development of shops has been hailed by economic historians as a leap toward more sophisticated retailing, William Cobbett, the early nineteenth-century English social observer and advocate of the benefits of simple, unfettered labor, saw shops creating "those locusts called middlemen who create nothing, who add to the value of nothing, who improve nothing, but who live in idleness, and who live well, too, out of the labour of the producer and the consumer." Cobbett preferred the markets and fairs because they avoided middlemen, were managed carefully, and brought "the producer and the consumer in contact with each other. . . . The fair and the market lay everything open: going to either, you see the state of things at once; and the transactions are fair and just, not disfigured, too, by falsehood, and by those attempts at deception which disfigure traffickings in general."[24] The popularity of today's farmers' and flea markets gives credence to his concerns.

Fashion

At the end of the sixteenth century, fashion was emerging as an important factor in the retailing world. The Middle Ages, with its stagnant economy, survival mentality, and rigid church control, was hardly a time of high fashion. Few changes in styles occurred then, and what changes did occur were in men's costumes, like changes from plate to chain armor. However, by the end of the sixteenth century interest in fashion appeared at court. In England, court became an important style-setter and, really, a parade; Queen Elizabeth I (1558–1603) made material objects symbols of the monarchy, which helped to legitimize her role as a leader. Furthermore, the boredom of court could be broken by a change of dress. And court must have been frightfully boring for Queen Elizabeth, for it is said she had 6,000 "fine garments."[25] To ensure her special place in society, she forbade emulation of her style of dress; compare today's purchasers of expensive designer dresses worrying that others might wear the identical dress to the same party.

Sumptuary laws in the fourteenth and fifteenth centuries restricted ornate and extreme costumes intended to distinguish different classes, so that people could not wear the clothes of higher classes. In France, sumptuary laws under Philip the Fair (fourteenth century) limited the number of costumes to nobles—four, three, or two, depending on their rank. The moral and social reasons for these laws broke down as more people acquired wealth and new lifestyles. Noblemen in England, who tried to emulate the life of the court, soon became big spenders, entertaining in large country houses and sporting vast wardrobes, all of which led to social competition among the nobility and to a new recreation, shopping.

The pleasures of shopping spurred the establishment of new and varied shops, whether in Madrid, Paris, or London. The strolling shopper ambled from one fashionable shop to another on London's Fleet Street, the Strand, and London Bridge. Aside from standing shops and the open-shed shops with awning counters, new shopping precincts, with lock-up shops and shops massed together inside buildings, were becoming commercial and social successes. Fashion in clothes and personal accessories was the main lure for these new shops. The consumers of the new luxurious items were usually women, who now had the time, money, and freedom to shop. Not only did women enjoy the clothes, but they were able to publicize their husband's wealth and their place in society by exhibiting the "show-off and put-down" factor, which has always been a tenet in the fashion world. For men, these growing cities offered opportunities for shopping as well as for new sociability in public taverns and coffee shops.

Due to this new urbanization and rapidly rising expectations, especially in the middle class out to improve and impress, the seventeenth and eighteenth centuries in Europe saw many changes in shopping. As towns and cities expanded with industries and trades, life became increasingly gregarious and sociable, encouraging interest in style, fashion, and consumer goods of all sorts. While London had become a city where many fashionable shops attracted a growing number of moneyed middle- and upper-class people, France was becoming by the seventeenth century the fashion center of Europe, with journals on fashion like *Mercure Gallant,* founded in 1672 and possibly the first fashion journal ever published. Parisian mannequins, called Pandoras or "fashion babies" in English, toured Europe. By the eighteenth century "most people . . . had already . . . crossed the frontier of necessity," Daniel Roche stated in *Culture of Clothing,* his book on French dress and fashion in the seventeenth and eighteenth centuries. In fact, "in Paris, everyone spent more on clothes whilst the difference between the dress of the poor and that of the rich also increased." Provincial towns in France were also getting swept into this new fascination with fashion. "Great finery is the rule in this town," according to reports on seventeenth- and eighteenth-century Montpellier. "The women and girls of the first and second estate have gone overboard for it. The most beautiful silk fabrics, made up of the best of taste, are used for their clothes."[26]

As silks and gold and silver threads became popular in France, the government passed sumptuary legislation based less on social and moral grounds than on hard economics, for France wanted to prevent the continued outflow of money for such imported materials as silk. Recognizing the demand for these fabrics and the possibilities of fattening its treasury, France encouraged the development of its silk industry, eventually making France the foremost producer of luxuries. Later Louis XIV tried to aid France's silk industry and stem the bullion outflow for English printed cotton by outlawing the use of the English fabric. Such laws were enforced; thousands were executed or jailed. But these attempts to regulate clothing gradually collapsed as the bourgeoisie grew and its demands for luxury—and all consumer items—swelled.

Excluded from the glittering new world of fashion and luxury were the poor, for whom shopping remained a search for such affordable basics as bread, ale, and cheese. Fish and especially meat were rare treats, sometimes purchased at London's new major food markets: Billingsgate for fish, Smithfield for meat, and Covent Garden, all of which operated six days a week and provided food for rich and poor and good revenue for the city. The poor, however, had neither the money nor the inclination for more than the bare essentials. Even if they had saved some money they were not tempted to consume more than was actually needed. Not until 1825 did a peasant family who could acquire new possessions feel "compelled to do so," according to Cobbett's *Rural Rides.*

The Industrial Revolution and a New Consumerism

A new dynamic of consumption fueling social change was starting to reshape every aspect of life. While the forces producing this new dynamic had been building for some time, it was not until the late eighteenth and early nineteenth centuries, with the Industrial Revolution and the French Revolution, that the most dramatic changes occurred. At that time the economic machinery, as well as the social, political, and intellectual realms of society, were being transformed. With England's famed spinning jenny and steam-powered printing machines for cotton, which could print up to 500 pieces of cotton a day, mass production took on new meaning. From 1796 to 1840, printing machines increased the annual production of printed textiles from 1 million to 16 million pieces.[27] This ballooning volume of production created the need for mass consumption, which in turn stimulated new demands—and new attitudes toward shopping.

In the United States, many traditional Puritanical and Protestant concerns were being swept aside by a new bourgeois consumer ethic. No longer were housewives warned, as they were in 1832 in *The American Frugal Housewife*, that "if you are about to furnish a house, do not spend all your money, be it much or little. Do not let the beauty of this thing, and the cheapness of that, tempt you to buy unnecessary articles."[28] Benjamin Franklin's advice— "when you incline to have new clothes, look first well over the old ones, and see if you cannot shift with them another year, either by scouring, mending, or even patching if necessary"—did not fit into the new era of rising expectations and increased production stimulating new consumption.[29] By the early nineteenth century Tocqueville observed that Americans were taking "pleasures in material life."[30]

This new era required a radical change in the moral and ethical climate. The Puritans' hard work and frugality, which had helped to fire the Industrial Revolution, had to be converted into a new consumer ethic so that the fruits of their labors, the new material products, could be enjoyed. Utility was the guiding principle for this ethic; for example, toys were acceptable but dancing was not. And those utilitarian and rational tenets of Protestantism not only guided the new ethic but legitimized the bourgeois way of life. The door was being opened to utilitarian consumption and enjoyment of that consumption. But in time new avenues of less utilitarian consumer and more cultural activities like fashion and romance were sanctioned. Luxuries and all their conspicuous consumption were entering the mainstream. "When a society begins to enjoy things of secondary necessity," according to Condillac, "and allows choice in its food, its clothing, its lodging and its weapons, it has more needs, and more wealth."[31] Indeed, the Industrial Revolution spurred a contagious consumer revolution.

The bourgeoisie had been forging the character of the mainstream, but the problems of this new materialism caught the eye of the late nineteenth-century American social and economic critic Thorstein Veblen, whose midwestern Norwegian background endowed him with a severe approach to life and a detachment from the mainstream. This articulate critic feared that the new materialism and obsession with luxuries were diverting material from necessities and thus harming the poor. Samuel Johnson tried to dismiss this concern a century before by arguing that a new world of consumerism and even luxuries would induce the poor to work hard. But for Veblen material competition was not a worthy goal of hard work: "Under the regime of individual ownership the most available means of visibly achieving a purpose is that afforded by the acquisition and accumulation of goods; and as the self-regarding antithesis between man and man reaches fuller consciousness, the propensity for achievement—the instinct of workmanship— tends more and more to shape itself into straining to excel others in pecuniary achievement." And this competitive consumption was primarily an urban phenomenon in Veblen's eyes. "Consumption becomes a larger element in the standard of living in the city than the country," he wrote. "It is also noticeable that the serviceability of consumption as a means of repute, as well as the insistence on it as an element of decency, is at its best in those portions of the community where the human contact of the individual is widest and the mobility of the population is greatest." Even the church's conspicuous consumption, "vicarious consumption," was noted by Veblen. "In all communities, especially in neighbourhoods where the standard of pecuniary decency for dwellings is not high, the local sanctuary is more ornate, more conspicuously wasteful in architecture and decoration, than the dwelling-houses of congregation."[32]

Women

Women took on an increasingly active role in this era of consumption in the late eighteenth and nineteenth centuries. With leisure, money, interest in and societal sanctions to enjoy shopping, women found themselves shopping more and more for nonessentials and sheer luxuries. Romance, whether in novels, theater, marriage, or fashion, became enveloped in romantic love—and was being accepted as part of everyday life. Fashion and the cult of romantic love were intertwined. As with the rising bourgeoisie, women found pleasure in clothes, but their wardrobes were meant to attract the attention of men—and women. For Veblen, an early feminist, women had become pawns in this game of acquisitiveness: "The performance of conspicuous leisure and consumption came to be part of the services required of them." With his perceptive observations about the role of women, especially bourgeois women caught up in the new consumerism, Veblen was well ahead of his time. "The institution of ownership has begun with the ownership of persons, primarily women. The incentives to acquiring such property have been apparently: 1/ a propensity for dominance and coercion; 2/ the utility of these persons as evidence of the prowess of their owner, and 3/ the utility of their services."[33]

Clothing and fashion were a major target of Veblen's venom. Dress had become a status symbol for the mobile middle class. "Our apparel," according to Veblen, "is always in evidence and affords an indication of our pecuniary standing to all observers at the first glance." And women will sacrifice much for this conspicuous consumption. "It is true of dress in even a higher degree than of most other items of consumption, that people will undergo a very considerable degree of privation in the comforts of the necessities of life in order to afford what is considered a decent amount of wasteful consumption."[34] Veblen understood how women's clothing displayed their or their husband's economic values and social worth, but women's absorption with the frivolous and fashionable aspects of dress were unfathomable to Veblen. The interplay between dreams and reality were not a part of this serious, Spartan Norwegian's background. But whether money was misspent on such conspicuous consumption, as Veblen argued, the interest in style and fashion, in material possessions and in the ability to enjoy them, was further evidence of the rising expectations of society, and especially the middle class. There was time, money, and the freedom to shop.

As industry expanded, wealth grew, and values adapted, shopping became increasingly important for the individual—and for the nation's economy. More was being produced and more was being consumed. Whether it was the consumption of production or the production of consumption, the two worked together for each other's benefit. Indeed, "things that had been rarities to one generation were becoming commonplace to another; luxuries were passing into the category of necessities, and nearly all this extra consumption came from outside the home and meant more shopping to make life comfortable and satisfying," as Dorothy Davis stated in her comprehensive history of shopping in England.[35] This was the democratization of luxury. Luxuries were no longer the prerogative of the aristocracy. "One sees little girls dressed as prettily as the rich man's daughter for one hundred dollars," states the Canadian *Welland Times* in 1897 in discussing the "great blessing" of cheap goods resulting from "reduced cost of labor by means of machine."[36]

Consumer goods were becoming plentiful throughout Europe and the United States thanks to marketing, traveling salesmen, and the proliferation of shops and stores in urban centers in the late eighteenth and early nineteenth centuries. In England and France, where the impact of the Industrial Revolution was most pronounced, cities still catered to the upper class and the growing bourgeoisie, while villages had general shops for everyday marketing. Gentry from the country would make semi-annual forays to London to do their shopping in bulk, while others could rely on new roving salesmen, such as Manchester men, Scotch drapers, and Scotch hawkers.

Big Stores, Big Cities

In big cities, the number and size of shops expanded dramatically. Paris developed shops with multiple goods—Bazaar d'Industrie on Boulevard Montmarte and the larger-scale Galeries du Commerce and d'Industrie on Boulevard Bonne Nouvelle, which in 1838 even had shops on several levels. But most shops were still small, specializing in such items as fruit, gloves, toys, tobacco, stationery, or chocolate. By the late eighteenth and early nineteenth centuries in London, shopping districts for all sorts of consumer goods were appearing: the West End for luxury shops, Rosemary Lane's Rag Fair for old clothes shops and pawnshops for the poor. Booksellers clustered by specialty in different areas—Temple and Westminster for law books, the Strand for plays, poetry, and music, the Tower District for technical books. By the early part of the nineteenth century London also boasted fifteen bazaars, many featuring women's dresses and accessories. Soho Bazaar was the first, then Queen's Bazaar on Oxford Street, and later the Pantheon, also on Oxford Street. In these bazaars another giant step in retailing was taken: all goods were visibly priced, whereas in the earlier bazaars bartering was the rule.

In the late eighteenth and early to mid-nineteenth centuries, as the numbers and types of stores increased, the arcade became an increasingly popular way for Europeans to locate multiple commercial establishments in an architectural continuum. Paris had twenty roofed arcades between 1790 and 1860, and Milan's famous shopping arcade Galleria Vittorio Emanuele II was built in 1856–57. London had fewer arcades, but finer ones, than did other European cities, according to Nikolaus Pevsner. London's arcades started with the small Royal Exchange, with stalls leading to four ranges of artisans, then came arcades with two levels in Inigo Jones's New Exchange and the Exeter Exchange near the Strand, and then larger and larger arcades, like Nash and Repton's Royal Opera Arcade and the Burlington Arcade, which had seventy-two shops. London's commercial development, which seemed never-ending, inspired William Moseley to plan and build the two-mile-long Crystal Way, with shop-lined arcades with passageways for carriages, pedestrians, and deliveries at night. Joseph Paxton's plan for his grandiose, but never built, ten-mile arcaded Victorian Way may have climaxed London's interest in arcades.[37]

Not all consumers were the rich and ambitious parading through arcades in grand sections of London, Paris, Milan, or Madrid. But there were retail innovations for regular folk as well. The introduction of chain stores, with standardized and visibly priced goods, as well as credit, was a boon for their marketing needs. Thomas Lipton started a one-man grocery shop in Glasgow in 1872; within twenty-five or so years he had 245 branches all over England. The Lipton's Markets, often in poorer sections of towns and cities (twenty branches in London by 1890), had captured 10 percent of national tea sales by the late 1880s. Lipton, a leading example of a successful retailer expanding his operation into a chain, penetrated the whole country at a time when the working class was growing.[38]

In the latter half of the nineteenth century, shops selling specialized goods, usually with bartered prices, were replaced with stores selling a range of goods with fixed prices. These new stores, precursors of the department store, were not just the melange of shops in arcades, but large shops, like the Parisian *magasins de nouveautes* (novelty stores) as well as major expositions, such as London's 1851 Crystal Palace and the Paris Exposition in 1855, which attracted wealthy tourists from the provinces and abroad. Instead of the goods coming to the buyer via hawkers and peddlers, buyers would go to the products. "Most stores started their big expansions," reported Dorothy Davis, "with a popular custom attracted by genuine bargains of sound quality, and went on to gradually improve their 'tone.'"[39]

The introduction of the department store, while in many ways a natural culmination in the evolution of shops and shopping, did offer dramatic changes in storekeeping—which were occurring simultaneously in Europe and the United States. The multiple departments of this new type of store, with its fixed and clearly displayed prices, represented a radical break from the bartering and haggling over prices that had been a part of shopping from its earliest days.

Most important, the department store had a new philosophy of store-keeping, which marked a new era for the consumer. The customers and the staffs, who were mostly women, were treated with a new respect. Customers could buy on credit, and they could return and exchange merchandise: at the same time the clerks' welfare was considered in some stores, like Paris's Bon Marché, where in 1852 insurance and retirement were available to them. The changing role of women, brought about by their increased leisure, money, freedom of movement, and interest in fashion and style as a direct product of the rising middle class, fueled many changes in retailing, of which the department store is one of the most important.

These stores, housed in grandiose buildings, introduced low mark-up, high volume, and quick turnover. They made shopping thoroughly respectable, as well as pleasurable and almost glamorous. The buildings were designed to make the middle-class woman shopper feel as though she were entering a world of luxe, previously available only to a small elite. Department stores "concentrated on fashion goods," according to Davis, "things shoppers were prepared to come some distance for and to take some time and trouble in choosing."[40] Browsing was encouraged in these new commercial emporia, with artistically displayed merchandise, lunch rooms for tea and meals, and even luxurious rest rooms for lounging. This was a world of fantasy and escape where shoppers could spend the day. It was like the theater. And all that style and gentility lent some class—and much needed respectability—to shopping, erasing some of the lingering image of disreputable bartering and "trade."

9. A. T. Stewart's marble palace, Broadway and Chambers Street, New York, engraving, 1851 (collection of the New-York Historical Society, Prints and Photographs)

Department stores appeared in city after city around Europe and the United States. Most had begun as small stores, but, responding to new consumer desires, expanded into larger stores. Harrod's started out carrying groceries in 1849; John Lewis, now a big chain in England, began as a small shop selling mostly men's goods in Liverpool in 1858 and soon had stores in Manchester and Birmingham. New York's first department store, A. T. Stewart's, started as a small dry goods store in 1823, built a marble palace in 1848, and in 1859 moved to Broadway (fig. 9). Other stores soon followed: Macy's in 1858, Bloomingdale's in 1872, Wanamaker's in 1875, Potter Palmer's Marshall Field in 1881.[41]

The Bon Marché in Paris, created by Aristotle Boucicaut in 1852, developed into the first and one of the most fantastic department stores, setting the example for future stores like Le Printemps, Whitely's, Harrod's, Macy's, Wanamaker's, and Marshall Field. Bon Marché represented the culmination of a long, slow period of growth and change in Paris and the rest of France. Technical developments, such as power looms in the textile industry, new glass and iron technology, and artificial gas illumination made the fantasy architecture of the department store possible. Paris, which was being transformed by Georges Haussmann into a grand and noble city, was also becoming a "pilot plant of mass consumption," and Bon Marché epitomized the new mass consumption.[42]

Ordinary merchandise in Bon Marché was transformed metonymically into enticing goods and the whole store into a spectacle by the theatrical Boucicaut. Window displays, made possible by the introduction of large plate glass, would lure the shopper into the store where entrancing displays, like an Arabian Nights Extravaganza à la latter-day theme parks, would dazzle the shopper. Impulse buying was encouraged even then by a layout designed to disorient customers. As Madame Marty in Zola's *The Ladies' Paradise* found, "Oh dear! What will my husband say? You are right, there is no order in this place. You lose yourself, and commit all sorts of follies." And indeed, "Women now came and spent their leisure time in his establishment, the shivering and anxious hours they formerly passed in churches; a necessary consumption of nervous passion, a growing struggle of the god of dress against the husband, the incessantly renewed religion of the body with the divine future of beauty. If he had closed his doors, there would have been a rising in the street, the despairing cry of worshippers deprived of their confessional and altar."[43] Once the fruits of these commercial wonderlands were tasted, Madame Marty or Zola's innocent heroine, Denise Baudu, became part of the "clientele fidele," as Bon Marché hoped, and bypassed no doubt many of the small shops they had previously frequented.

Bon Marché was part of the commercial bulldozer crushing the city's small shops and shopkeepers, so well described by Zola, who appreciated the sufferings of the small merchants but was fascinated by the new world of retailing. When the draper's niece, fresh from the country and looking for a job at the Ladies' Paradise, was interviewed by Mouret, he said, "They say he [the girl's draper uncle] has a grudge against us. We are people of more liberal minds, and if he can't find employment for his niece in his house, why we will show him that she has only to knock at our door to be received. Just tell him I like him very much, and that he must blame, not me, but the new style of business. Tell him, too, that he will ruin himself if he insists on keeping to his ridiculous old-fashioned ways." The engine of commerce will win over those "rheumatic old brokers shivering in their cellars," an attitude of many entrepreneurs as they trample over the holdouts and leftovers from the past.[44]

American Retailing

In the rapidly growing cities and towns of nineteenth-century America, department and chain stores were changing merchandising as they were in Europe. Especially in cities, the pattern of retailing matched the developments being made in major European cities from the nineteenth century until after World War II, though maybe with less panache. During the postwar period the automobile and suburban development reshaped the American way of living. The United States came to outdistance the rest of the world with innovations in retailing: the shopping center, the enclosed mall, the festival marketplace, interactive shopping, new attitudes toward women, recreational shopping—and credit.

Although early settlers in the United States were unencumbered by centuries of restrictions, regulations, and residue of history and class values, they never completely severed their ties to the Old World. They had brought with them many of the traditions and values of their ancestors. Sumptuary laws, for example, associated with European nobility's effort to protect its status, might seem incongruous in the breakaway colonies, but laws prohibiting fancy clothes and finery such as lace and gold braid were enacted in Boston in 1634. While Boston's aristocracy pretty much ignored these laws, they were revised in 1639, making them applicable only to those "Middling and Inferiour sort" with incomes of less than £200. Such class delineation occurred especially in the emerging cities, a holdover from the Old World, and even increased during the seventeenth century despite criticism from people like John Hull about the "want of subjection of inferiors to superiors."[45]

Some of the strongest ties to the Old World were economic, especially for the elite merchants in Dutch New York or British Boston and the large landowners in the agrarian South. For the upper classes, the Old Country provided many of their clothes, furnishings, and elaborate provisions. George and Martha Washington ordered from their London purchasing agent "only the goods in the last most fashionable taste," according to Robert Dalzell's study of Washington's buying habits.[46] When William Byrd, Sr., built his Virginia plantation in 1690, his curtains, chairs, bedsteads, and porcelain came from Europe. For those few rich who could afford such luxuries, their ties to the mother country allowed them to live in a style becoming to aristocrats. This cultivated gentility allowed the elite "to distance themselves more obviously from their less wealthy neighbors and to impress royal officials and English merchants with their stature and "Englishness."[47]

Trade and commerce were becoming the "all embracing" activities of the colonies, as Bridenbaugh states, and the interdependence that was developing between the colonies and the Old World involved far more than trade for luxuries. New England merchants in the seventeenth century— "towering figures," as historian Bernard Bailyn described them—needed capital, shipping, and established markets, and, in turn, England needed fish and tobacco, which the new country could provide.[48] Towns like Boston, Philadelphia, and New York were evolving from economies based on farming to economies fueled by shipping, then marketing and distributing all with increasing specialization. Early on, these major towns were developing an essentially modern metropolitan economic system, wherein their economic antennae and control stretched far into the backcountry, producing a critical interdependence between central town and nearby hinterland. Boston, for example, was drawing produce from its outlying settlements as well as from Rhode Island, New Hampshire, and Connecticut, and in turn supplying these distant places with goods from Europe and the West Indies. Philadelphia and New York, after being taken over by the English in 1664, followed the same pattern. This exchange between towns and hinterland was helpful to the colonies when imports were cut off from England during the Revolution; the colonies were better able to rely on themselves, thanks to the metropolitan economic system they had developed.

Aside from the major ports, where shipping activities furnished the economic lifeline of the colonies, a thriving—and essential—commercial, trading, and retailing world existed in every town and village. Initially, these communities survived primarily on the daily exchange of goods, crops, and products of their local artisans, farmers, and craftsmen. But as their economic life developed with greater specialization and larger markets, so did their commercial ventures. Mills, cooperies, and tanneries sprang up, as did retail establishments, at first offering wares directly from the house with the help of wives and children, then in true shops, often run by middlemen shopkeepers, and in public markets and fairs, just as in the home country.

Shops for selling the wares of these artisans and craftsmen appeared in the earliest settlements—and they continued to prosper. In 1636, the Dutch West India Company, in what is now Lower Manhattan, built five large stone houses to be used as shops for coopers, hatters, shoemakers, tailors, and armorers, and by 1648 those activities increased to the point that it was necessary to regulate persons who "kept a public or private shop."[49] By 1660, according to the Castello plan of the early Dutch settlement of New York, 11 percent of the population were traders or merchants, the next-to-largest professional category of the new residents, and 32 percent were craftsmen.[50] At the time of the English takeover of New York, there were ten bakers. From 1670 to 1679 bakers had so expanded that the General Court contemplated regulating bakers, and by 1690 seven Master Bakers in Philadelphia were baking thousands of bushels of bread for local and export consumption.[51]

In Boston, a handful of shops operated in the mid-eighteenth century, yet a century later the city was filled with shops, often attended by women and carrying dry goods, groceries, and European products. As towns like Boston grew and prospered, the number of artisans and specializations grew along with the manufacturing of necessities and even luxuries, like silver cups.[52] By 1789, when Boston organized a march in honor of General Washington's visit, the procession included the city's officials, its clergy, doctors, lawyers, and traders—and then forty-six groups of tradesmen and artisans arranged alphabetically—bakers, blacksmiths, block-makers, boat builders, cabinet and chair makers, etc., reports Walter Muir Whitehill.[53]

Unlike in Europe, where markets and fairs preceded the development of shops, in America's early colonial days shops emerged as the prevailing way of buying and selling. It was not until the eighteenth century that markets and fairs became popular in towns and villages throughout the colonies. Following traditions established in England, markets usually were held on one or two set days of the week and fairs once or twice a year. Some, like Dutch New York's, were just for cattle, but they eventually expanded into country produce, while Philadelphia's fair, begun in the city's early days, included all sorts of produce, crafts, and handiworks and continued with entertainments and eventually more merchants' goods than livestock. As cities grew and public markets expanded during the eighteenth century, fairs, although less important in a city's marketing operations, moved from their central locations to nearby county locations, where they attracted "strangers" as well as local citizens and no doubt became the forerunner of today's county fairs.

Public markets, on the other hand, became increasingly popular for both the retail shopper and wholesale buyer—and remained popular in many cities well into the twentieth century. The markets were begun in open areas, as in New York's "Butcher's Shamble" on the Green "under the trees by the Slipp" or near the banks of the Delaware River in Philadelphia. They were later housed in buildings built either by the city, as in Philadelphia, which sheltered its first permanent market in the arcaded ground floor of the 1709 Court House on High Street, or by private developers, like Boston's Peter Faneuil, whose Faneuil Hall had market space on the lower level and meeting space on the second floor.[54] Centrally located in prominent civic institutions following the pattern of English town market halls, with stalls on the ground floor and meeting halls above, these markets, with their rented stalls, soon became important places for town residents to buy their food and goods, as well as major markets in which farmers could sell their produce. Benjamin Franklin found the meat and produce of the Philadelphia markets so satisfactory that he converted his own utilitarian garden "into grass plots and gravel walks, with trees and flowering shrubs."[55]

City after city instituted a public market system. New York had nine markets for produce, including the world's largest food market in 1858, Washington Market, now replaced by skyscrapers, including the nearby World Trade Center towers, and Fulton Fish Market, its best-known twentieth-century market, still operating adjacent to the South Street Seaport. Charleston, South Carolina, had a multi-block public market on its major commercial street, Meeting Street, which functioned as a food and produce market until recently, when T-shirts, antiques, and tourism took over. Philadelphia's Reading Terminal Market has survived as a center city food market, first with a railroad station overhead and now a convention center, but Washington, D.C.'s four public markets, located in each quadrant of the city, have been reduced to one market, Eastern Market on Capitol Hill. Seattle's Pike Place Market outlived an urban renewal threat to continue functioning as a major food market. Aside from providing fresh produce, meat, and fish, these markets have been vital democratic institutions. As Marcus Marks stated in his 1915 report on New York City's market system for the City's Board of Estimate, "the rich, the middle class, and the poor meet in these markets on an even footing, and thus is provided the spirit of democracy, which is essential to the perpetuity of our institutions."[56]

Regulations have always been a part of market operations in America. As early as 1649, Boston saw the need for clerks in the markets to assure fair weights and measures, prevent profiteering, protect local merchants, and assure decent and healthful working conditions. Following English and Dutch regulations, the colonial villages continued controlling market activities, and the economic life of these young villages and towns, with restrictions that the citizens accepted as necessary for the survival of their settlements. They held on to the principle that the individual townsman owed more to the community than the community owed to him—a basic tenet of communities from the Middle Ages on but seemingly forgotten in some current American political circles. Whether artisans or merchants, these colonial townspeople saw their role as serving the whole community, and thus regulation was just one part of civic responsibility.

Commerce and its accompanying prosperity were also recognized as essential ingredients in the welfare and growth of towns and villages, often to the horror of the Puritan leaders of the early colonies, like John Higginson, who preached in 1663 that "New England was originally a plantation of Religion, not a plantation of Trade."[57] But as commerce expanded and profits increased, these new towns—whether run by the Puritans in New England or the Quakers in Philadelphia—flourished with this new mercantilism, which was leading them away from the mores of the Middle Ages into a future of capitalism. Reconciling the needs of the community and the role of religion, these early colonies, like their forebears in the Old World, were able to forge a wily compromise that embraced capitalism and yet constrained it to the overriding ideals of building a better community for everyone.

Rural Retailing

For the rural population, the winds of capitalism and the emerging urbanity of the prospering colonial cities were often remote. The rigors of frontier existence combined with harsh religious tenets meant that life was constrained. Living in cramped quarters, people survived primarily on local produce and products and wore homespun fabrics. Local craftspeople, whether coopers, wheelwrights, or cobblers, provided many of the local necessities, and those not locally available could be found in larger cities or market towns. Coun-

10. *The rural peddler showing his wares.* Peddler's Wagon, *drawing by C. G. Burk for Harper's Magazine, 1886 (Library of Congress, Prints and Photographs Division, Washington, D.C.)*

try folk could purchase from storekeepers those goods they had not grown or raised, and storekeepers in turn purchased their supplies—such as gloves, spices, and buckles—directly from warehouse merchants or from traveling salesmen or traders like the proverbial Yankee peddler.

In the Chesapeake, for example, small clustered settlements formed hamlets with craftsmen's houses and shops, a church, a tavern, and "above all a store," David Hawke writes. The store was stocked with pots and pans, buttons, tea, coffee, hats, and whatever was needed in the hamlet. This forerunner of the general store was hard to describe, for it was not a boutique or magasin. "Neither of these words," according to one Frenchman, "conveys its meaning completely, according to the peculiar character, object, and use of store in America, and especially in places thinly inhabited." The Frenchman continues: "A store is a shop or place where all kinds of commodities intended for consumption are to be found and sold by retail; nothing is excluded from it."[58]

In New England—following the early peddlers, who were known for their "pedestrious tours"—stores like those in the Chesapeake began appearing at rural crossroads in the late eighteenth and the early nineteenth centuries (fig. 10). Selling an array of general merchandise, these stores, often run by ex-peddlers, were located first in the storekeeper's house and later in separate buildings. Their Yankee customers, who tried to live by what they made or produced, used such stores to purchase the many goods, often from

Europe or the West Indies, that they needed but could not grow or manu-facture—such as molasses, sugar, rice, and crockery. Barter was common in these country stores, as their yeoman farmers' produce or crafted goods would be exchanged for store purchases, all accounted for in the stores' leather-bound account book. For centuries such stores have been the mainstay of small-town retailing, flexing with the changing needs, economy, and tastes of the times. As settlers moved westward the general stores followed. In the hin-terland these stores supplied needed goods but also often provided a window to the outside world. "As the bringer of goods," states a Sturbridge Village pamphlet on New England country stores, "the country store brought also—civilization."[59]

As the nation grew and prospered and the severity of Puritanism waned, interest in material goods increased. By the time Tocqueville came to America in the 1830s, the rigid elements of Puritanism had softened. Tocque-ville noted that the "special taste which the men of democratic time entertain for physical enjoyments is not naturally opposed to the principles of public order. . . . Nor is it adverse to regularity or morals, for good morals contribute to public tranquility and are favorable to industry." Once again the pragmatic bent of the Puritan at work. In a country where men, Tocqueville noted, "are stimulated and circumscribed by the obscurity of their birth or the mediocrity of their fortune, I could discover none more peculiarly appropriate to their condition than this love of physical prosperity. The passion for physical com-forts is essentially a passion of the middle classes: with those classes it grows and spreads, with them it preponderates. From them it mounts into the higher orders of society and descends into the mass of the people." And in this democ-racy, interest in gratification—in property and luxuries—depended not on any class rank, but on the ability to pay for them. As Tocqueville noted, "When . . . the distinctions of ranks are confounded together and privileges are destroyed,—when hereditary property is subdivided, and education and free-dom widely diffused, the desire of acquiring the comforts of the world haunts the imagination of the poor, and the dread of losing them that of the rich." The absorbing American drive for physical gratification leads men not to the "pursuit of forbidden enjoyments," Tocqueville suspected, but to a "virtuous materialism . . . which would not corrupt, but enervate the soul, and noise-lessly unbend its springs of action." This "virtuous materialism," possible with America's compelling principles of equality, existed in different degrees depending on the time and money available for such gratification, but its full flowering more likely occurred in the affluent cities.[60]

In the early midwestern border towns, so well described by Lewis Ather-ton, the pioneering settlers in the nineteenth century, while imbued with the democratic principles and the rights to acquire the "comforts of the world," were not haunted by Tocqueville's virtuous materialism, as their needs and conditions were so basic. The merchant, whom Atherton understood, as his

11. Replica of Captain Litch's 1836 store, the first retail store in Davenport, Iowa, constructed for Davenport's centennial in 1936

two brothers-in-law ran stores in Bosworth, Missouri, served a critical role in the life of these early midwestern settlements. By providing manufactured goods and services the merchant could help raise people above the self-sufficient stage of settlement. Jacks-of-all-trades and remarkably self-sufficient, merchants succeeded by not only their own round-the-clock industry but that of all members of their family. Aside from bartering and exchanging crops for dry goods and groceries, these well-educated, well-connected merchants performed innumerable nonmerchandising services, like writing letters or ordering subscriptions. Many were the postmasters in their communities. In the Midwest, Atherton found that some also operated farms on the side—often due to their exposure to scientific farming practices through reading and traveling. Unlike many merchants in the United States and the Western hemisphere, these early midwestern merchants were not Jewish. As the frontier towns, which were established from little more than a tavern and log-cabin store, developed into full-blown towns and often county seats, retail operations would locate on all four sides of the county courthouse square (fig. 11). If the town continued to boom, the stores would spread onto the side streets.[61]

In the South, storekeepers served much the same commercial and social roles in their communities as did midwestern merchants. "In the process of providing these basic economic services the storekeeper naturally contributed to other economic and social activities as well," according to Atherton. "In processing farm crops for market he provided an elementary type of manufacturing by operating subsidiary enterprises such as sawmills and gristmills."[62] Because of his involvement not only in farming but in banking, transportation, and development as well, the storekeeper evolved into one of the more important figures in the villages and towns in the interior before the Civil War.

But even with all the participation in community and regional activities, it seems that there was quite a fallout of southern storekeepers. Many seemed to have been more respected than their western confreres, according to Atherton, and turned to planting staples like cotton because of the lure of greater profits, or they took up enterprises that were less physically taxing and speculative than storekeeping. These shifts to other work—which appear to have been the trend throughout the country—tended toward farming in the agrarian south and toward banking and other commercial activities in the East and West. Reasons for leaving storekeeping behind may include the increasing specialization and competition of retailing, and storekeepers' low self-esteem.

The general store remained an important community fixture until very recently, especially in rural areas, despite the slow but steady parade of merchandising changes, such as department stores, mail-order houses, chain stores, standardized products, and shopping centers, all of which have transformed how people shop. To meet the new competition and the changing times, small stores adapted as best they could to new situations. At the end of the nineteenth century, brand names became retailing necessities for the storekeeper, whose customers now expected the standardization of quality that brand-name products suggested. Everyday customers wanted brand-name goods—Baker's chocolate, Ivory soap, Aunt Jemima's pancake flour, Bissell sweepers, and the National Biscuit Company's Uneeda biscuits. Men's clothes were even bearing names like Hart Schaffner & Marx, whose advertising helped introduce male consumers to new styles.

Rural free delivery, started in 1896, rightfully seen by small-town merchants as a serious threat to their businesses, expanded the possibility of mail-order shopping and eventually converted the rural population into mainstream consumers. Some products, such as Singer sewing machines, could be bought directly from the manufacturer. But by the turn of the century, mail-order shopping through new and large companies, such as Montgomery Ward (founded 1872) and Sears Roebuck (first catalogue in 1891), had become a major way for rural America to shop. Montgomery Ward issued its first one-page catalogue in 1873 with the promise of "satisfaction or your money back" (fig. 12). The next year the catalogue grew to twenty-four pages, and ten years later it featured 10,000 items in 240 pages. By the mid-1890s the catalogue, known as the Great Wish Book, was 544 pages thick and listed 24,000 items. Montgomery Ward targeted the rural population as its market "to meet the wants of the Patrons of Husbandry." To lure the Patrons of Husbandry, Grange members received special privileges, like a ten-day grace period on COD orders. In 1897, Sears Roebuck published its first catalogue, the 786-page Farmer's Friend, which was even larger than Montgomery Ward's. Sears experimented with special premiums for getting new customers. But aside from all the enticements of an incredibly vast array of merchandise and occasional premiums and come-ons, both Sears and Montgomery Ward were able to undercut local stores with low prices, since they bought large lots of merchandise, operated assembly-line warehouses, supposedly an inspiration for Henry Ford, and in the case of Sears, had capital investments in such manufacturing plants.

The tension between the threatened small-town storekeepers and these new mail-order retailers mounted. Sears sent packages in plain wrappers with no return address, and Montgomery Ward in its 1902 catalogue cited a rural newspaper on the tyrannization of farmers by country merchants. But it was the ten-year battle to establish parcel post mail service that brought to a head the conflict between farmers who wanted the service and local storekeepers who saw it as a threat to their livelihood. Parcel post, begun in 1912, understandably was seen by the small rural merchant as a death blow. That year merchants in Cedar Grove, Iowa, expressed their indignation with this new mail service by

12. Montgomery Ward's first catalogue, 1873 (collection of Montgomery Ward Company, American Heritage Center, University of Wyoming, Laramie)

burning mail-order catalogues in the town square. Rural free delivery and parcel post were but two changes in a much larger transportation, communication, accounting, and retail revolution, which challenged the very existence of the old general store.[63]

Self-service and chain stores, also products of this revolution, introduced new steps in industrialized retailing. Featuring cash and carry, no delivery, and racks displaying mostly prepackaged goods, these self-service labor-saving stores proliferated. Nifty Jiffy, Helpy Selfy, Handy Andy, and B.Y.C. (Be Your Own Clerk)—and Clarence Saunders's Piggly Wiggly, alleged to be the first self-service store—were just a few of them (fig. 13). Many were started in the South after the Civil War in response to labor shortages, but others, like Edison's Samaritan Market and Saunders's robotic Keedoozle store, were later attempts to make shopping more efficient.

But it was the successful chain stores that would have the greatest impact on the traditional small general store. The Great Atlantic and Pacific Tea Company, which started in 1859 selling tea and coffee, kept adding other grocery items until the early 1900s, by which time A&P had become a fixture on Main Street providing their own goods thanks to new train and truck access. A&P had 1,726 stores by 1915 and 10,000 by 1923. At the end of the 1920s, chain stores like A&P were gaining a greater foothold in the grocery field with their low prices, low labor costs, high stock turnover, sophisticated accounting, and departmentalization. The stores, managed by out-of-town corporations with the ability to undercut the locally operated store, had captured almost 40 percent of the country's retail trade by 1947.

Another chain competing with the old general store was Woolworth's, which opened stores selling nothing costing more than five cents. The first was in Lancaster, Pennsylvania, in 1879, the second in Utica, New York, in 1899; in 1909 there were 239 stores. By 1919, 1,081 stores were scattered in several states. The company established its main offices in New York's then tallest and splendid skyscraper, the Woolworth Building, designed by Cass Gilbert and built in 1912–13.

13. Piggly Wiggly self-service store near Memphis, 1918 (Library of Congress, Prints and Photographs Division, Washington, D.C.)

As the operation and organization of these complicated and powerful retailing giants like the chain stores and mail-order houses grew, so did an anti–big business movement among the small merchants, whose attempts to impose taxes and restrictions on large-scale retailers were often met by savvy public relations campaigns by the retailing giants.[64]

In the small-town and rural areas, the general store now had competition from national and regional chain stores as well as from mail-order houses. In cities, the department store, the major new development in retailing, was the threat to the small shops, especially in older cities, whether Paris as described by Zola in *The Ladies' Paradise*, or New York, or Philadelphia. Many of the new department stores that were supplanting the smaller stores emerged themselves from smaller operations. A. T. Stewart sold Irish linens in 1823 in New York prior to establishing a wholesale and retail dry goods business, his first step in departmentalizing before he opened in 1862 his renowned department store, which was then the largest retail store in the world. No small store could match the volume of goods, the number of clerks, the breadth of advertising, and the overwhelming scale of the new department store. As Stewart himself put it, "First to lure women shoppers with a store so commodious, pleasant, functional and well stocked that its fascination would not be ignored."[65] This was indeed a new era of shopping.

American Department Stores

These were massive stores. Marshall Field, Chicago's renowned department store begun by Potter Palmer in 1852, when the city was a boom town with soggy planked streets, grew from a simple start on the first floor of a frame building with 200 employees in 1868 to 1,500 employees in 1884 and 6,800 in 1902. Marshall Field himself, a native of Massachusetts' Berkshires, where he apprenticed in a Pittsfield dry goods store for five years, arrived in Chicago in 1856. After a stint in Wardsworth & Company, a leading Chicago dry goods operation where he rose to junior partner in 1862, he joined Potter Palmer in Field, Palmer, and Leiter in 1865, which in 1867 became Field, Leiter and Company, and just Marshall Field and Company in 1881. A key to his success was his motto: "Give the lady what she wants."

The store's most dramatic increase in revenue and employees, however, occurred after Gordon Selfridge, a twenty-one-year-old from Ripon, Wisconsin, hitched up with Marshall Field in 1879. Selfridge began on the wholesale side of Marshall Field as a lace salesman, then eventually became the architect of Marshall Field's explosive success—a true Horatio Alger story. Retail sales jumped from almost $4 million in 1887 to more than $22 million in 1904. Selfridge, like Field, recognized the importance of women in retailing, both as customers and clerks, and he treated them with respect. The store was dominated by a quiet elegance, starting at its entrance, with

14. Marshall Field, 1907 (Courtesy of Marshall Field's archives)

doormen and floormen who brushed snow off coats and checked parcels and umbrellas, to wood-paneled libraries and waiting rooms with maids for service and magazines for entertainment. In 1902, Marshall Field had thirty-nine marble-floored lavatories with three maids in each, as well as soap, talcum powder, hairpins, needles, thread, and scissors (fig. 14). There was a "silence room" for women and children, as well as a children's nursery with a nurse in charge.[66]

The gentility of the department store could be seen in the tearoom. Although Macy's opened one in 1878 and Wanamaker's in 1882, both earlier than Marshall Field, the success of the Marshall Field's tearoom reflected its style of management and the interest of the public in such facilities. Field's tearoom, with gracious touches like linen and silver, was small when it started in 1890: fifteen tables for sixty people served by four maids. In three years the tearoom expanded from a corner of the third floor to the entire fourth floor with 150 tables, and in 1902 to the entire seventh floor, with not only a tea room serving 2,000 people daily, but an "English Room," a dark-oak chop house for men. Four years later the Crystal Buffet, serving 2,000 people daily, was added, and five years after that the seating capacity of the eating facilities was increased by 5,000. A year after that the even larger Walnut Room and South Grill were added, making these eating establishments into what we might call a mega-restaurant.[67]

These early days at Marshall Field were heady. The store's philosophy, in tune with the imaginative retailing in department stores at that time, was generated by its desire to provide shoppers with new conveniences, like a delivery service and, most important, an appealing environment—almost a refuge from the humdrum homes and offices of its customers. Many of

15. London receiving her "Newest Institution," Self-ridge's, 1909 advertisement (Selfridge's archives, History of Advertising Trust, Raveningham, England)

Marshall Field's unique contributions to retailing were made by Selfridge, an amazing innovator in the department store management who left Marshall Field after twenty-five years to explore retailing on his own in London.

Selfridge's store on Oxford Street in London opened in 1909 and allowed him to expand his successful philosophy. He viewed England as a country that knew how to make things but not sell them—and for him selling was the name of the game (fig. 15). Selfridge, dedicated to serving women, saw women as spenders independent of male supervision. He tried to understand them and meet their needs by hiring woman buyers, who could best fathom the desires of other women. He started a cosmetics department as well as a bargain basement, which eventually filled three and a half acres. Organ music was piped throughout the store, and a new showmanship was evident in the store's interior and windows. As at Marshall Field, Selfridge offered good service to his customers and a friendly atmosphere for his clerks. When an eclipse was predicted he invited his clerks to view it from the store's roof.[68]

Soon every city had its centerpiece downtown department store or stores. Whether in Chicago, London, Paris, or Boston, department stores, often locally owned and operated, were popular. When, on September 3, 1912,

Filene's in Boston opened its new Daniel Burnham–designed, eight-floor store on Washington Street, 235,000 people—a third of the city's population—visited the flower-bedecked store. "It seemed . . . that all New England was being poured through the doors," reported the *Boston Globe*.[69] With fixed prices, bargains galore, exchange procedures, delivery service, a myriad of departments, helpful staffs, and a welcoming environment, these stores met the requirements of the growing consumer population. And they continued to fulfill the needs of their customers—and reach new customers. Filene's had traveling trunk shows at hotels, opened branch stores in Providence, Rhode Island, in 1922, Wellesley, Massachusetts, in 1924, Portland, Maine, in 1925, Falmouth on Cape Cod in 1927, and Worcester, Massachusetts, in 1928. It opened summer stores in York Harbor, Maine, and Hyannis on Cape Cod in 1923, and college shops at Smith and Wellesley in 1924. When their customers were leaving the inner cities for the suburbs, department stores, recognizing this expanding new market, opened suburban branches. Between 1940 and 1950, Filene's opened three suburban Massachusetts stores, in Winchester, Belmont, and Chestnut Hill, and converted its Hyannis summer shop into a year-round store. In the next two decades seven suburban stores were built—two out-of-state stores, in Warwick, Rhode Island, and Manchester, New Hampshire—and many of its older suburban stores were renovated or expanded.[70] New York's Arnold Constable had four suburban branches by 1956, and Bloomingdale's had four by 1959. These suburban stores were planned as satellite branches of the center city flagship stores.

The downtown flagship department store was the big store with the largest selection in a prime location for commerce and fashion, like Wanamaker's at Philadelphia's central Penn Square across from City Hall. "Until recently, central cities were almost defined by the locally owned department stores, which dominated local life," observes Kenneth T. Jackson.[71] In fact, the development of a city like New York can be traced by the uptown movement of its department stores to what were considered prime locations for fashionable commerce, including hotels and restaurants, as well as stores. In New York this prime commercial location was on lower Broadway up to Houston Street in the 1850s, but after the Civil War, these fashionable stores moved uptown to 14th Street and 23rd Street along Broadway and Fifth and Sixth Avenues. Then, as the fashionable restaurants, hotels, and shops kept moving up to 34th and 42nd Streets and later to the 50s and 60s, so did most of the major department stores (fig. 16) to keep up with the northerly migration of the city's wealthy class. However, several of New York's best-known stores—Lord & Taylor, Macy's, Gimbel's, and B. Altman—stopped their northward march and remained in the 30s and 40s, where they had located in the early 1900s. But whether on 34th Street or 59th Street, these department stores were considered to be in the heart of the city, as they were in most cities until the 1960s.

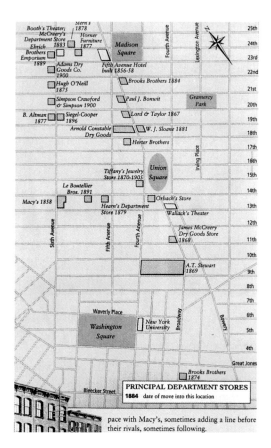

16. *Map of New York showing the uptown march of department stores, 1858–1900*

Suburban Shopping

As population oozed into the outlying sections of cities, into older suburbs and brand-new suburban developments, so did stores—and stores planned intentionally to be part of these new suburban communities. Initially some of the more carefully planned upper-income suburbs experimented with building small shopping facilities in their neighborhoods. Frederick Law Olmsted's 1868 new community, Riverside, west of Chicago, had a central shopping and community building, and Baltimore's Roland Park neighborhood, planned by Kessler and Frederick L. Olmsted, Jr., had a small shopping facility embedded on its main boulevard in 1894.

Riverside's shopping center was one of the country's first arcaded multi-shop commercial buildings. This building, known initially as the Riverside Stores and designed in 1870 by Frederick E. Withers, who manned the Chicago office of Olmsted, Vaux and Company during the development of Riverside, contained all the stores needed in a community—a pharmacy, grocery, and supply stores, as well as the post office. Later known as the Arcade because of its unusual interior glass-walled corridor, this building provided entrances to the stores from the arcade and from the outside. Its central location near the railroad depot and the Des Plaines River has helped to keep it a commercial hub in the town despite many architectural and use changes over the years.[72]

These residentially oriented commercial centers in Riverside and Roland Park were pioneering steps, as most upper-income residential areas prided themselves on the absence of commercial intrusions. Other planned shopping areas grew slowly in the 1920s and 1930s in places like Upper Darby near Philadelphia (1927), Highland Park in Dallas (1931), and River Oaks in Houston (1937).[73]

But it was J. C. Nichols's Country Club Plaza in Kansas City, Missouri, that led the country in a new direction in shopping (fig. 17). Here Nichols planned the country's first regional shopping center as a centerpiece for his suburban Country Club residential development. Nichols had already built the Rockhill Park subdivision in 1919 with a community golf club, open spaces, and Brookside shops, with stores on the first floor and doctors' offices and a community center on the second floor. Four years later Nichols developed the Country Club Plaza shopping center, with its exclusive shops, as a "gateway" to his Country Club District development, which was twenty-five minutes from downtown. These shops were planned to serve not only the

17. *Country Club Plaza, Kansas City, Missouri, 1923 (Western Historical Manuscript Collection—Kansas City, University of Kansas at Kansas City)*

residents of his development but also the "general trade in Kansas City and tributary territory." To accommodate shoppers coming by car, parking lots and garages preceded the shopping center. Although influenced by the English garden city ideal, Nichols turned to the Mediterranean for his shopping center's architectural styling to create "the feeling of an old market place of picturesque Spain in Kansas City."[74] The first tenants moved in in 1923, and by the end of 1924 there were thirty-seven shops, including three Piggly Wiggly stores, a gas station, and six doctors' offices.

This carefully designed and controlled shopping center benefited from an active merchants' association, which organized programs for holidays, and random events, like an annual Spanish fiesta. Both Nichols's residential and commercial developments were amazingly popular. When the overall Nichols development expanded from the initial 10 acres to 5,000 acres, so did its shopping areas, which grew from one shopping center to ten new neighborhood shopping areas "on the English village plan," all contributing to an attractive, profitable, and long-lived development. "Without question, Nichols's shopping centers," according to William Worley, "were the heart of the success of his planned residential communities."[75] In 1958 the Country Club Plaza, with its ninety-two stores, rang up the fifth-largest retail sales of planned shopping centers in the entire country.[76]

For Nichols and shopping center leaders like Victor Gruen and James Rouse, planned shopping centers were more than stores selling merchandise; they were seen for their potential of invigorating community life. They could provide "an environmental climate and atmosphere which in itself becomes an attraction for the inhabitants of a region; . . . they could be shopping towns," according to Gruen.[77] Both Gruen and Rouse hoped that shopping centers would serve as "real community centers."

And this is what Nichols's development and others—like Park Forest, Illinois, Forest Hills Gardens, Long Island, and other new towns like Radburn, New Jersey, and the federal government's model Greenbelt towns— aimed to do in small, controlled communities. Riverside and Roland Park, and Radburn, built right before the Depression and hence never completed, all had a shopping building with community spaces integrally planned with the residential developments (figs. 18–20). However, a study on stores and neighborhood shopping centers for Radburn by Clarence Stein, a key promoter of new towns and a co-sponsor of Sunnyside in the Borough of Queens, New York City, and Radburn, and Catherine Bauer, a leading housing and planning advocate, was instrumental in the planning for the most successful shopping center in the new towns of the 1930s, Greenbelt, Maryland. Here the stores, movie theater, banks, restaurants, community center, school, swimming pool, and town offices were centrally located in a civic core. All community needs could be found in one location within walking distance of all residents.

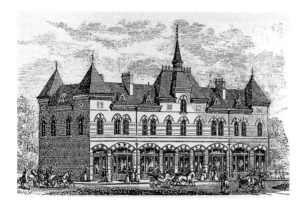

18. *Riverside Stores, Riverside, Illinois, 1871 (courtesy of Riverside Historical Commission)*

19. *Roland Park Building, Baltimore, built 1897 (1996 photograph)*

20. *Radburn Plaza Building, Radburn, New Jersey, built 1928–29 (1996 photograph)*

These neighborhood shopping centers in Greenbelt, Radburn, Roland Park, and Riverside turned out to be aberrations in the mainstream of retail development. Instead, the model for future retailing was the drive-in shopping center, the product of the free enterprise system, the automobile age, and a sprawled scale of development, more typical of California than the East, and certainly not advocated by new town planners. In the 1920s, southern California drive-in markets became increasingly popular and enjoyed what seemed an "overnight success," Richard Longstreth points out.[78] Such one-stop shopping centers, sited in urban fringes on traffic corridors, often on corner lots on the homeward-bound side of the street, attracted the commuter. These were car-oriented centers and destinations in themselves. The right location on the traffic artery became a far more important planning consideration than proximity to residential areas, a prime consideration in the Greenbelt-type of pedestrian-oriented neighborhood shopping center.

The layout of these drive-in shopping centers, with their line-up of stores facing the street with display windows and signs and a forecourt of parking, made them highly visible to their potential customers, the passing motorists. Like the general store, they provided one-stop shopping, but under centralized management with a variety of individually owned stores as well as an increasing number of chain stores. Most significantly, they had off-street parking along main arteries. These shopping centers, built primarily between 1930 and World War II in what have become older suburban areas, were located on the major thoroughfares of a metropolitan area, radiating from the

21. *Park and Shop shopping center, Washington, D.C., 1930 (Library of Congress, Prints and Photographs Division, Washington, D.C.)*

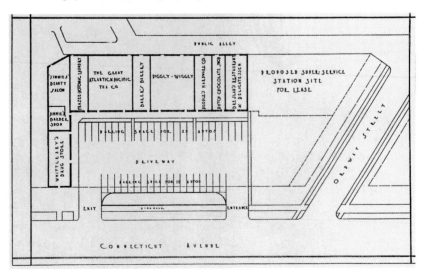

city's center, as in Washington, D.C., along upper Connecticut Avenue and nearby Arlington, Virginia, and Silver Spring, Maryland (fig. 21).[79]

After the War

After World War II the United States experienced sweeping changes in its suburbs and in the role of shopping. With the pent-up demand from the long austerity and the dampened aspirations of both the Depression and the war, mortgages from the Federal Housing Administration (FHA) and Veterans Administration (VA), and federally funded highways, suburbs swelled, as did the interest in shopping. A new consumerism, emerging as a reward for the hardships of the 1930s and 1940s, was translated into a suburban imperative with home ownership at its core. The house itself involved a massive investment, and so did the household appliances, furniture, and, of course, the car. Possessions could now help to provide independence—and personal identity. You were what you owned, and although the costs of this consumerism were high, credit and installment plans were available, along with enslavement to a bank. The thrift and abstinence of the Puritan ethic, so necessary in the hard times of war and depression, were passé in this era of immediate gratification.

While pent-up demands propelled this surge in buying, the introduction of high-powered behavioral scientists in advertising and public relations introduced a new dimension to advertising, which manipulated the consumer in subtle and significant ways. Advertising, which had existed for generations, now was playing upon motivations and the unconscious. Boucicaut and Selfridge had stimulated sales by reaching beyond their customers' rational selves, but they still recognized their customers as primarily rational beings. Now behavioral scientists, who were stretching the reach of advertising into the subconscious, represented a shift in the broader recognition of the power of the irrational nature of human beings. The consumer was a malleable creature.

This opened a new chapter in the Industrial Revolution. Where religion had once been the charge for the productive engine of capitalism, now consumption, driven by these new behavioral manipulative techniques, kept the engine of capitalism running at full steam. "The culture was no longer concerned," wrote sociologist Daniel Bell, "with how to work, and achieve, but with how to spend and enjoy." Despite some continuing use of the language of the Protestant ethic, the fact was that "by the 1950s American culture had become primarily hedonistic, concerned with play, fun, display, and pleasure," according to Bell.[80]

Mass production was churning out consumer goods faster than the old ones could be replaced, but buyers for those consumer products were found, thanks to the "hidden persuaders," as Vance Packard called the advertising manipulators. The advertising of the hidden persuaders delved beyond basic human needs into the realm of perceived and learned needs, thereby creating more needs than the consumer had ever imagined. Advertising and public relations were changing people's habits and desires. They dealt not merely with products but with ideas, images, fantasies, and dreams—which, in turn, required new possessions.

This postwar suburban consumerism meant more dreams and more shopping, as well as new generations of stores: first, the branches of downtown department stores located in upscale suburbs, then those branch stores clustered with smaller shops to form small shopping centers, and then massive centers. The shopping centers were not just being incorporated into new communities, like Nichols's Country Club District, to provide shopping for a nearby population, they were shaping the development of the new suburbs. Instead of population and jobs generating the need for shopping facilities, these postwar shopping centers were actually preceding population and job decentralization. "People are following retail trade to the suburbs," according to urban planner George Sternlieb. "Retail trade is decentralizing independent of population."[81] This new retail determinism was a radical break from the past; formerly, retailing followed residential development, as in New York, where New York's Regional Plan Association reported in 1928 that when the "fashionable residential district moved steadily uptown, it was followed closely by the retail stores."[82]

At the end of World War II there were only several hundred shopping centers in the United States, but by 1958 the number had increased to 2,900; there were 7,100 in 1963, 22,000 in 1980, and 44,426 in 1999. Some of these later shopping centers were massive regional malls. As early as 1954 suburban shopping center retail sales exceeded the retail sales of all metropolitan areas above 1 million population. Between 1954 and 1958 the retail sales in metropolitan areas of all sizes grew 54 percent, compared to a meager 3.5 percent for center city sales. In some metropolitan areas like San Jose, California, center city sales figures actually dropped from 1954 to 1958 as the city's suburban retail sales more than doubled.[83]

Shopping centers of every size were built at major highway intersections on the outskirts of metropolitan areas all over the country with much help from the federal government (fig. 22). The federal highway program and the Internal Revenue Service's tax policies, both legacies from the Eisenhower era (1953–54), spurred the development of shopping centers and malls. Highways provided physical access, and the accelerated-depreciation tax policies on real estate investments encouraged investors seeking tax losses. By making investments in shopping centers attractive with tax shelters that allowed rapid depreciation and created paper losses out of even profitable projects, the government lured new investors into retail development while encouraging rapid turnover as owners/investors exhausted their tax benefits.

22. *Shopping center at highway crossroads in the Maryland suburbs of Washington, D.C., 1960s (collection of the Historical Society of Washington, D.C.)*

Although seemingly private ventures, shopping centers benefited from heavy direct and indirect government support.

The transition to suburban shopping and to the suburban shopping center from traditional downtown shopping was gradual. Initially, the advantages of the shopping centers were seen as proximity to home, easy parking, and convenient hours. In a 1955 study of Columbus, Houston, and Seattle, food was found to be the first commercial need met in the suburbs, followed by movies, medical care, furniture, and clothing. In the mid-1950s the downtown was still appreciated for its greater variety in styles, price, and size, its bargain sales and its being "the best place to meet friends from other parts of the city for a shopping trip together."[84]

As the number and variety of services offered by shopping centers expanded, they took on even more of the old downtown's functions. Surrounded by acres of parking, the centers had major department store anchors at their ends with intervening concourses of shops, movie theaters, and restaurants. Perhaps the most idealistic theorist could hope that these centers in the no-man's land of suburbia would become the centers of commercial and community life, the shopping towns envisioned by architect Victor Gruen, America's early advocate of the social and economic benefits of shopping centers. There were in fact community events, charity fundraisers, dances, and craft shows, as well as public facilities, like army recruiting offices, chapels, post offices, and banks, even though the shopping center was a controlled private space. This was the closest thing to Main Street in many suburban areas. It became the street corner for teenagers; a safe retreat for bored housewives and the elderly, who took over its corridors in early morning hours for exercise walking; and often the only place to purchase clothing and anything not available at the local supermarket. And, of course, as the middle class continued to flee the city for the suburbs, the old downtown department stores moved to the new malls, leaving the inner city for the minorities, the singles, the elderly, and some stalwart remnants of the urban-oriented upper class. "What the railroad had joined together in the nineteenth century, the freeway was tearing asunder in the twentieth-century metropolis," noted Timothy Crimmins and Dana White in their discussion of Atlanta in *The New Georgia Guide*.[85]

The postwar suburban shopping center was yet another seismic change in traditional retailing in the United States and one that separated America from most other countries in the world. Until the 1920s, the advanced countries were progressing at about the same pace in both retailing and consumer spending, as evidenced by the emergence of the department store in England, France, and the United States during the end of the nineteenth century. But from the 1920s, when a new class of consumer durables such as radios, vacuum cleaners, and refrigerators became available, as did electricity and gas, the United States bolted ahead of the rest of the world in consumer goods and retailing. Between 1920 and 1930, Americans were enjoying more and new consumer goods. In that ten-year period, the population with electricity went from 35 percent to 68 percent, with radios from 0 to 40 percent, with vacuum cleaners from 8 to 24 percent, and with mechanized refrigerators from 0 to 8 percent. By 1927, Americans owned 80 percent of the world's cars. America was not only the cradle of democracy, it had become the world capital of democratization of luxury.[86]

A New Crescendo in Shopping

The flowering of this consumer era continued as old forms of shopping, like catalogue and mail order, took on expanded roles, as discount stores evolved into a mainstream type of shopping, as grocery supermarkets turned into 100,000-square-foot superstores with pharmacies, liquor stores, florists, and bank machines, as shopping centers became ever larger malls and even megamalls by the 1990s, like Minnesota's 4.2 million-square foot Mall of America. Then, in the late 1990s, television, fax, and the computer introduced even newer ways to shop. Accompanying all these new kinds of shopping has been a galloping appetite for the acquisition of "stuff," as one mail-order fulfillment center manager labels all the goods on their warehouse pallets. That passion for shopping is aptly expressed in the 1980s bumper-stickers "I shop, therefore I am" and "Shop till I drop."

This is the story of free enterprise at work. It has been an intensely competitive industry that "merchants and the consumer" have been free "to work out . . . through fairly independent, often atomistic decisionmaking," according to Stanley Hollander.[87] Once the province of a few large chain stores, big city department stores, and a host of small, family-owned businesses, retailing has become a vast, concentrated industry dominated by giant corporations, paralleling the changes in manufacturing a generation ago. Retail trade has become industrialized, with concentrated ownership, centralized financial control, a corporatelike hierarchy, lowered skills in the labor force, capital substituting for labor, and big firms buying out or driving out competition. It may be that the retail field will be like other "industries which have experienced waves of consolidation," according to analysis of the transformation of the modern department store by Barry Bluestone and his associates. "When battles for retail turf are resolved, price leadership is likely to develop among the largest firms. This can be expected to result in a rise in consumer prices over the long run. It also will mark the full maturity of the retail sector and will, in many ways, make it indistinguishable from the traditional manufacturing industries that dominate commerce in advanced nations."[88]

These industrialized retail operations affect more than their competitors; they affect communities and regions. "No other property type has the impact on a community that the shopping center does," Alexander and Muhlebach stated in a 1992 Institute of Real Estate Management publication. "In particular, it provides substantial revenue (sales and property taxes to communities), a variety of employment opportunities, the convenience of one-stop shopping and a testing ground for new businesses."[89] However, despite the importance of shopping centers—and really all major retail activities—for communities as well as shoppers, their locations, functions, and operations are determined primarily by market forces, which can be fickle. Shopping centers and malls often have been treated merely as speculations. In the 1960s, when the real estate market for shopping centers was hot, investing in these centers was eagerly promoted; Greenlaw Grupe declared that "a baby shopping center is . . . a good investment" in the Urban Land Institute magazine in 1961.[90] The investment picture remained favorable for several decades, but when tax regulations changed, new competitors appeared, and the real estate market tumbled, many shopping centers failed. Shoppers lost their major emporium and communities an important asset.

By the 1990s, investment prospects for shopping centers and malls of all sizes had soured to the point where a 1996 Urban Land Institute article stated that "retail dons the mantel of the riskiest investment, as its cycle bottoms out in the midst of a protracted merchant shake-out."[91] This radical

23. Christmas crowds—and also many clerks—at Macy's, 1942 (Library of Congress, Prints and Photographs Division, Washington, D.C.)

change in the investment picture for shopping centers points out the irony, inherent in retailing throughout history, that shopping facilities, which have such a profound impact on communities, have been buffeted by unpredictable market forces.

The recent history of department stores also illustrates the role that economic forces have played in molding the new retailing world—and, thereby, in influencing the life of many downtowns and, in the late 1990s, the makeup of suburban malls. Gone are the days of tea rooms, helpful clerks, defined departments, and graciousness (fig. 23). "The customer is always right" philosophy is as old-fashioned as wearing gloves and a hat to church. No longer the locally owned and operated operation, the department store is big business and often part of major national holding corporations like Dayton Hudson and Federated Stores, which alone grossed more than $15 billion in 1997. Subject to rampant competition, new technology, reorganized work/labor processes, and spiraling and collapsing of financial empires, department stores are like many large corporations.

Department stores have become industrialized. High turnover, low-skilled workers load the bottom of the organizational pyramid, and the narrow top is staffed by highly skilled and highly paid professional managers.

Clerks, no longer trained as specialists in particular departments, use "deskilled sales methods," which is code language for processing sales: punching in numbers at the cash register or transacting credit card sales, much like the clerk at the supermarket checkout counter. "Most cashiers in department stores are human modems," as Internet entrepreneur Shikhar Ghoshan bluntly stated at a 1999 Harvard forum on "The Wired Society."[92] And many of those department store cashiers and clerks work only part time. In 1981, 75 percent of New England's department store workers worked part time, and 79 percent worked in their jobs for less than three years; in other words, today's department store clerks are often part-time workers periodically seeking pocket money. And they do not earn much. Twenty percent of the men working in department stores in 1981 earned $15,000 or more compared with only three out of a thousand women workers.[93] Fewer and fewer stores offer commissions, an incentive in the past for clerks to earn more, know their trade, and service the customer. Moreover, today's part-time deskilled workers do not burden the corporation with short-term benefits like medical insurance or long-term benefits like pensions. As for the customer, ever since Clarence Saunders's self-service Piggly Wiggly stores, national advertising and brand recognition have taken the place of the knowledgeable clerks of yesteryear, who provided information on quality and use of products in specific departments.

Automation is behind many of these changes, as fewer clerks are needed for many retailing tasks. Prepricing, for example, eliminated two thousand marking jobs in Detroit, according to the Retail Clerks International Union, which has unionized only a small portion of the clerks. Maintaining inventory and placing orders have been reorganized and sped up by computers. The loyalty of clerks and even managers to particular stores has vanished, as has much of the commitment of the stores to their communities. Department stores have become a part of corporate America, in which economies of scale are the driving forces.

Bloomingdale's on Lexington Avenue in New York highlights the changes in a department store. For many years Bloomingdale's was the local department store for the Upper East Side of New York, where one went for everyday household items. For fashion and clothes there were many much more stylish department stores and many local smaller specialty stores. But this functional and friendly neighborhood department store seemed "drab" to Marvin Traub, who had worked there for nineteen years before he became president in 1969, when he was only forty-four. Traub found that "Bloomingdale's had a reputation for modern furniture, but lacked any other distinction."[94]

So he set about giving Bloomingdale's pizzazz, or, as he put it, "personality," which not only reshaped the store but inspired other department stores to follow suit. A new, theatrical approach to department store operation was introduced. Bold, fresh, and colorful design — of "stage-set quality" — and themed entertainment replaced traditional departments. Towels were arranged in colorful displays, regardless of quality and price; clothes were organized by designer and not by whether they were blouses, skirts, or coats; kitchen items, seen by Traub as "status symbols," were artfully organized.[95] Merchandise was upgraded. Gone was the notions department, traditionally a staple of any department store that came to be considered a low margin or convenience item. Shopping was not meant to be drudgery, where the customer darted in to find a particular item and then fled. Instead, the customer was to be lured through labyrinthian aisles to discover items not on any shopping list.

Shopping as entertainment was not new. Hawkers and traders through history, whether in the agoras, fairs, or markets, aimed to entice potential shoppers with theatrical devices and sometimes even actual plays, but in the mid-nineteenth century Bon Marché in Paris introduced a new level of entertainment in shopping. Boucicaut transformed Bon Marché and its mundane goods into a remarkable spectacle and fantasy world. He was able to "endow metonymically what were essentially nondescript goods with the fascination that was lacking in the merchandise," according to Kristin Ross.[96] Years later Bloomingdale's translated that basic retailing principle of entertaining into a new type of image-making for contemporary department stores. "The image of the store is like a good restaurant: the food or merchandise is a major ingredient," said Marvin Traub in *Like No Other Store.* "The sum total of the shopping experience—the exterior, window display, presentation, service, gift wrapping, logo, shopping bags, delivery, return policy—all create the image." For Traub that image—and the atmospherics— gave him an edge on other department stores. Bloomingdale's, known fondly as Bloomie's, became an in-place to shop for its targeted customer, an "affluent, upwardly mobile, image-conscious twenty-five to fifty-five-year-old who enjoyed a high level of discretionary spending," according to Traub.[97] Soon every department store had the same flexible interior, with dramatic themes and but a few and often invisible clerks. This was a democratization of style.

As in the post–World War II period, the United States once again soared beyond other advanced nations in responding to the new wave of consumer demand. A suburban sprawl dotted with shopping centers and malls frequented by women and teenagers with money and freedom to spend was an American phenomenon in the 1970s. The retail world was leading and responding to this new consumerism. Bloomingdale's and all the other department stores were reshaping their images and reaching for new affluent, mostly suburban, markets as other lines of retailing revamped to meet the growing consumer demand for fashion and products of all kinds.

The story of Sears Roebuck reflects the changes in retailing over a century. Started in 1895 as a mail-order house supplying practical items for men and women, Sears Roebuck responded to the changes in the patterns of development and consumer trends with over-the-counter selling in 1925, first downtown and later in the suburbs. By the 1950s, style became a part of its sales pitch, as designers were hired to create clothes exclusively for Sears. By 1981, Sears was the largest marketer of general merchandise in the world and as of 2000 it was the sixteenth largest corporation on *Fortune*'s 500 list. Although not as secure as in the past, Sears has found a niche, which has helped to ward off some of the economic woes that have killed such stores as Bradlees and even Montgomery Ward.

The 1970s, the 1980s, and the 1990s produced a profusion of retailing activities; new types of retailing as well as recastings of old retailing. The atmospherics and image making that Traub ushered in were adopted by individual stores, shopping centers, and malls—and by festival marketplaces, the new inner-city shopping centers that James Rouse had developed with such skill. Shopping became entertainment, and stores and shopping centers became theme parks.

Yet simultaneous with this profusion of entertainment in retailing, a sameness metastasized both in stores and in their merchandise as a result of contemporary franchising. Like the earlier brand-name products and chain stores, which set the course for the galloping uniformity in retailing today, large corporations have been pushing aside the smaller operations, introducing a new level of standardization, thereby eradicating the diversity of independent, small-scale ventures (fig. 24 and 25). The stores in the mall and on many city streets are mostly the same in Seattle, Boston, and Chicago—and now in Berlin, London, and Paris. In 1993–94, The Limited, which includes Victoria's Secret, had 4,623 stores, The Gap had 1,385 stores in the United States, Canada, and the United Kingdom, Blockbuster Video 3,593 videostores here and 764 in Europe, and Toys "R" Us 798 stores here and 234 in Europe.[98] The same pattern exists for many American fast-food companies.

Another type of retailing, which has grown exponentially, is discount shopping, especially the bare bones, economy-based discount stores, warehouses, membership club stores, factory outlets, and some direct marketers. In contrast to entertainment shopping, discount shopping in its various forms seemed both easier and cheaper for the shopper. Bargain hunting has always been part of shopping. Filene's Basement is a famous Boston institution, started in 1908 in a separate building from Filene's to sell leftover goods at automatic markdowns, beginning at 10 percent, then 25 percent after twelve days, 25 percent after the next six days, 25 percent the following six days. If not sold within thirty days, the item was given to charity. Though not intended as a moneymaker, Filene's Basement moved to the basement of Filene's new building in 1912 and soon became a profitable operation; in fact, the Basement carried the store during the Depression. Now it is a separate store.

Some of the 1990s' largest discount stores were also offshoots of department stores or department store chains: Target from Dayton Hudson, Venture

24. Old retailing, Columbus Avenue, New York, 1998

25. New retailing, Columbus Avenue, New York, 1998

from the May Company, and Gold Circle from Federated Stores. Often items have to be purchased in volume or in slightly imperfect condition, with price tags indicating alleged savings over full price. Some stores, like Loehmann's, have items manufactured solely for them. No longer small outlets near factories or in out-of-the-way places, discount stores have evolved into large operations whose success hinges on lower profit margins than those offered in department stores and, in turn, lower overheads. The expansion of discount stores has depended on modern computer technology that, among other things, has streamlined the entire distribution system. While usually located near cities, often in older strip shopping centers, some have recently ventured into the heart of cities, even to their most fashionable avenues: New York's Fifth and Park Avenues and Boston's Boylston Street, for example (figs. 26 and 27).

26. Old retailing, Fifth Avenue, New York, 1997

27. New retailing, Boylston Street, Boston, 1998

Discount and low-cost outfits have grown and prospered, often spe-cializing in one particular type of product like computers, office equipment, shoes, sports equipment, or hardware (fig. 28). Now known as Category Killers, these large, single-function discount stores—CompUSA, Sports Authority, Home Depot—known for eliminating weaker competitors, can be found either in stand-alone locations, low-rent strip shopping centers, or clustered in Power Centers, shopping centers for such Big Boxes, located on high-traffic thoroughfares in suburban areas. And some Category Killers and Big Boxes have moved into center cities. Costco has been in San Francisco for several years, and right across the Bay Bridge in Emeryville a flat, aban-doned locale became a Power Center. New York City, trying to fill some of its empty manufacturing areas, offered tax breaks and other lures to Category

Killers. Union Square in New York, once the home of Klein's, one of the earliest and most famous discount stores, now has Bradlee's, a new generation of discount store. While the earlier generation of discounters, like Ohrbach's, Loehmann's, and Filene's Basement, originated in cities, now suburban stores like T. J. Maxx and Marshalls are venturing into the hearts of cities. As megamalls developed, so have mega-discount/off-price shopping malls like the massive Potomac Mills, forty minutes south of Washington, D.C., on Interstate 95.

Meanwhile, for many people with little time or inclination for shopping, mail-order retailing has filled a niche. Mail ordering is not just for those who cannot drive to the shopping mall or discount store, but for the growing number of overworked women with a job and family, as well as for the many dissatisfied with available shopping opportunities. Originally Sears was the mail-order house for the isolated rural population; then there were specialty mail-order companies like L. L. Bean and Hammacher Schlemmer, featuring catalogue buying—and now, as the postman knows, the catalogues from large and well-known companies to small and obscure operations have mushroomed into a major retail activity. Census figures confirm this booming business. Between 1987 and 1996, sales from catalogue and mail-order houses more than doubled, from $20 billion to almost $48 billion, and the number of their employees grew from 123,000 to more than 180,000, with the number of the largest firms (those with more than five hundred employees) increasing dramatically, from forty-nine to seventy-three establishments, just from 1991–95.[99] By 1997, twenty-seven of those establishments had more than 1,000 employees each.[100]

Technological advances and indirect shopping offer a myriad of opportunities for those who do not want to or cannot go to stores. In Washington, D.C., meals of any ethnic variety, clothes, appliances, and most necessities can be delivered to one's door in a matter of minutes, and this is possible in most cities in advanced countries in the world. In London, the writer Brenda Maddox gets her gourmet meals ready-made at Marks and Spencer and her household items like paper towels by fax order from an exurban supplier, who delivers them to her doorstep at an appointed time. In the United States, Federal Express can deliver overnight to almost any hamlet, items ordered by catalogue, telephone, fax, or computer. You need never go near a store.

Such shopping and, in fact, much of contemporary shopping, is not related to any community. All you need is a telephone, a television set, a car, and now a computer. You can be anywhere—as long as you have your computer—to order books from Amazon.com or clothes from The Gap. The actual stores can be anywhere. They are not part of the city or of the suburban community, nor part of any community.

The sweep of history has brought the United States to the point where

28. DSW (Discount Shoe Warehouse), Shoppers World, Framingham, Massachusetts, 1998

the cradle of democracy has become the world capital of democratization of luxury. This is also the remarkable tale of the marketplace producing dramatic changes in the way we live, think, and shop. The lone entrepreneur at the market in the Middle East or at the fair in the Middle Ages planted the seeds of the retailing world, which have grown into the marketing of the early twenty-first century. And likewise the well-to-do shopper in the elegant shops in European capitals in the eighteenth century set the course for shopping. Capitalism of the Industrial Revolution, driven by the basic human instinct to succeed within moral and ethical sanctions of pragmatic Protestantism, was driven by consumption, which has been stimulated by all the sophisticated tools of the corporate world. With the growth of consumerism, credit payments, manipulative advertising, and inundation of material goods that we now see as necessary, there is also the possibility that we have come full circle, that instead of face-to-face shopping with an itinerant trader, small storekeeper, druggist, or craftsman, we are now one-on-one with machines. What we are facing is run by complex, specialized, and highly organized remote corporations. But a constant throughout this remarkable history, where "ridiculous old-fashioned ways" have been continuously replaced, is that rarities have become commonplace—and that they can be procured in so many different, and egalitarian, ways.

CHAPTER TWO

Shopping

A Community Activity

"This is not a shop, it's a community centre," Gordon Selfridge declared soon after he opened his department store on Oxford Street in London in 1909.[1] With this statement he expressed an often overlooked fact that local stores—whether large downtown department stores, city corner stores, or country general stores—have often been a social and economic hub in their communities. Not only have stores been community centers and places for repeated encounters among customers and clerks, but the storekeepers themselves have been active participants and often leaders in community affairs. This social dimension of stores and shopping has rarely been adequately discussed or understood, yet through history it has been one of the most enduring features of shopping, from the time of the Phoenicians to today's farmers' markets. These community and social functions enlarge the public concern for shopping beyond the economic realm and show that shopping affects not only our pocketbooks but the civic life of our communities.

The corner store at 35th and Greenfield Avenue in Southside Milwaukee was "the center of all neighborhood activities. . . . It was like a Town Hall," recalled Catherine Otten, whose father ran the store.[2] In Stamps,

29. *Christmas shopping crowds in Gadsden, Alabama, 1940 (Library of Congress, Prints and Photographs Division, Washington, D.C.)*

Arkansas, where Maya Angelou grew up in the rear of the Wm. Johnson General Merchandise Store that her grandmother and uncle owned, the Store (always "spoken of with a capital *s*," she said) "became the lay center of activities in town."[3] In large cities the major department store was where one shopped for everything from notions to clothing, and where one met friends for lunch and tidied up in the capacious and staffed restrooms. These stores were part of their communities, whether through participation in local Chambers of Commerce, planning and redevelopment boards, or events and charities, like Macy's Thanksgiving Day parade, health fairs, Little League, war bond drives, and literacy programs. In times of crises, when fires, floods, and economic calamities hit their cities, leading department stores, like Rich's in Atlanta, offered their help. They had become community institutions.

Going to the store, aside from purchasing provisions, provided a way of getting out of the house, off the farm, or in from the country, as well as a way of seeing acquaintances and neighbors, sometimes on a daily basis (fig. 29). It was a social occasion. When one went to the high street in an English town or to the baker for the daily baguette in a French village or to the drugstore on Main Street in America, he or she could catch up on what was going on. This is centuries old. In Charlemagne's time, in the late eighth and early ninth centuries, small weekly markets were held for purchasing local produce as well as "satisfying that instinct of sociability in all men," according to Henri Pirenne, noted scholar of medieval Europe. These markets were the "sole distraction offered by a society settled in work on the land," he states. For agrarian peasants, the distractions of socializing at the markets were evidently so enjoyable and time-consuming that Charlemagne ordered the serfs on his estates not to "run about to markets."[4]

This timeless sociability of shopping and the stabilizing role of stores in neighborhoods, towns, and cities, however, have been threatened throughout history, however, by constant and often disruptive changes in urban life and new efficiencies in retailing, so well described by Emile Zola and, more recently, by Philip Nord in *Paris Shopkeepers and the Politics of Resentment*. In the late nineteenth century, Parisians bemoaned the impact of the new department stores and Georges Haussmann's dramatic redesign of their city. They saw whole neighborhoods devoured, smaller shops eradicated, and "bonds of social solidarity" sundered "in the name of efficiency." Many Parisians feared that the loss of the small shopkeeper spelled the disintegration of neighborhood life, as the shopkeeper was seen occupying a "strategic position in the moral life of the community. His enterprise and authority assured the continued existence of the quartier, workshop, and family," Nord noted.[5] The threat of new types of retailing, as well as the changes in urban life, have been constants in the history of retailing.

In the past fifty years those threats to the traditional sociability of shopping and to the role of stores in community life have accelerated as the ways we live and shop have undergone drastic changes. As stores have become part of larger and distant corporations, as their size and complexity have grown, automation has intruded itself and ever greater economy of scale has taken over, making shopping an increasingly impersonal experience. Shopping online or at the regional mall, with its tens of franchised stores at the interchange off Interstate 66, is a very different experience from ambling along Main Street and darting into locally owned stores or going to a city's downtown department store. This increase in impersonality in shopping parallels massive changes in how people live, work, and play; the role of the car; and the death of older cities and the dominance of suburbanization; the influence of automation, advertising, and megacorporations; as well as the changing values and attitudes involved with mass culture. Shopping is indeed a mirror of social, cultural, and economic changes.

Small-Time Shopping

Tree-lined Main Street, with its small, independent stores, is now mythic Americana. It can be seen in Disney's theme parks, where yesteryear's small shops on its Main Street are the first sights to greet visitors, in gentrified villages in New England and the Midwest, and more recently in developments like Mashpee Commons on Cape Cod, designed by the Duany Plater-Zybert team, the currently popular neotraditionalists. The many permutations of this Norman Rockwell–Main Street image attempt to counter the dominant store configuration of a sprawling, low-slung concrete complex surrounded by acres of asphalt parking lots, or the strips of stores, car sales lots, fast-food restaurants, movie theaters, and sundry insurance, real estate, and accountant offices and their parking that line highways. That the myth of small-town America's Main Street persists, and its imitations proliferate, indicate a nostalgia for what seem to be simpler times and comfortable values.

The small, independent store, the type pictured in the mythic Main Street, belongs to the past. Hardware and general merchandise stores, once Main Street anchors, have either disappeared or become franchised stores. In the past fifty years the number of hardware stores has shrunk by 60 percent.[6] Likewise, the number of general merchandise stores, a type of store probably unknown to most current teenagers, is less than half what it was fifty years ago, yet the number of employees in these stores has more than doubled in the same period. Fifty years ago, 90 percent of these general merchandise stores had fewer than ten employees, but only 60 percent of these small stores have survived; while fifty years ago the large general merchandise stores with 100 or more employees numbered fifty-four, by 1997 there were almost one hundred such stores.[7]

The disappearance of the small functional store, which sells everything from safety pins to sandpaper, is noticeable in every village, town, and city. The remaining stores are larger and often multipurpose. With new marketing skills, inventory, and production technology made possible by automation, the high-volume, fast-turnover stores are the winners. For the Mom and Pop, or for small, family-run hardware stores, it is a struggle to cope with rising rents, insurance, pricing, and the large Deep Discounter competitors, whose volume allows them to work out all sorts of cooperative advertising, pricing, and ticketing deals with manufacturers. Even the supermarket, with new—and expensive—software analyzing purchases through checkout scanners, knows just what and why items have been selling, information that in turn can help these stores hone their inventory, bolster their bottom line, and influence consumer decisions.

Statistics tell the story of the disappearance of the small stores. Variety stores, Main Street mainstays that sold pencils, dress shields, plastic pails, or cheap picture frames—items in "low and popular price ranges on a cash and carry basis," according to the Census definition—have shrunk. Their

311,622 employees in 1948 in 14,489 stores shriveled to 95,805 employees in 12,597 stores by 1997. Yet along with this reduction in the number of stores and employees, the volume of business in that same time period more than doubled.[8]

Hardware Stores

It's the same story with hardware stores. Overall, the number of such stores, especially small ones, has dwindled while sales have surged. Whopping hardware Big Boxes like Home Depot account for some of this increase. In 1948, 32,088 hardware stores hired 153,868 employees, and by 1997 only half of those stores, 15,852, remained, with 140,172 employees. However, in that fifty-year period only about a third of the small stores with fewer than ten employees were left, while the larger stores increased by more than 50 percent, a pattern seen throughout the country.[9]

In Bergen County, New Jersey, across the George Washington Bridge from New York City, population more than doubled from 1940 to 1959, and since then it has held at 825,000 to 850,000. At the same time, the number of hardware stores shrank from ninety-one in 1959 to fifty by 1997, with no appreciable increase in the number of employees. The small hardware store with fewer than ten employees was hit hardest in this fifty-year period—only half remained. On the other side of the country, in the exploding California county of Santa Clara—where the population ballooned from 175,000 to 1.65 million between 1940 and 1998—the number of people employed in hardware stores more than tripled even as the number of stores shrank by more than a third. In 1959, Santa Clara County had three hardware stores with more than twenty employees and none with a hundred or more employees. By 1997 there were sixteen stores with more than twenty employees, six of which hired between 100 and 249 people. That pattern of the big getting bigger and the small disappearing appears to be continuing as the Wal-Marts, Home Depots, and other Big Boxes and Category Killers penetrate new markets. The small independent store is, indeed, a vanishing breed.[10]

Drugstores

The public's trust in the individual druggist should make independent drugstores a tough target for Deep Discounters, one-stop supermarkets, and online pharmacies. Druggists invariably rise to the top of Gallup's Honesty and Ethics Poll. They were number 1 in the poll for many years, slipped to number 2 in 1999 behind nurses, but edged out veterinarians, teachers, and clergy. Insurance salesmen, HMO managers, advertising practitioners, telemarketers, and car salesmen took the poll's bottom five slots—numbers 41, 42, 43, 44, and 45.[11]

Druggists have been respected, accessible medical advisers in every town and city neighborhood in the United States. If you had questions that did not warrant a visit to the doctor, the druggist was your adviser. He or she knew you, knew your doctor, knew about your ailments—and your drugs. The local druggist, the symbol of the best of small-town American shopkeepers—decency, intelligence, hard work, kindness, and professionalism—and his or her pharmacy have been Main Street mainstays.

But now that druggist is besieged by forces that resonate from the distant maneuverings of mega-pharmaceutical, insurance, and retail corporations. "It's the end, or the coming-to-the-end, of a way of life and a way of doing business in this country," said Merrill Lynch's Gary Vineberg in a discussion of the threats to mom-and-pop pharmacies on National Public Radio on May 7, 1996. "It's being made obsolete by chain-retailing and more efficient forms of distribution. And all of that puts a tremendous pressure on the person who's at the bottom of the food chain . . . and that's the independent retail pharmacist."[12] Indeed, the independent druggist is becoming an endangered species.

Threats to the survival of the independent drugstore are not new, but the depth and extent of the threats are the most serious in the history of pharmacies. The independent druggist is competing not only with Deep Discounters but also with a new system of pricing and distribution geared to those in the loop of the insurance companies, health maintenance organizations, drug companies, and big stores. HMOs, newly in the loop, call many shots that affect the welfare of the independent druggist. Many HMOs have their own pharmacies supplied with drugs from pharmaceutical companies at 25 to 30 percent discounts, compared to only 5 percent discounts to Deep Discounters, and no discount at all to the independents. If the HMOs do not have pharmacies, they can require patients to purchase prescriptions at only certain stores, or "sole providers," or allow a flat rate at any drugstore of the patient's choice. Patients are often forced to buy "maintenance" drugs from mail-order houses. This is the same pattern for patients using their own doctors under certain insurance plans. The pricing is not necessarily related to volume but to the connections of the provider to the insurance company. Such discriminatory pricing sounds the death knell of the independent.

The future looks rosy for the major pharmacies that are in the loop. Between 1948 and 1997 the number of employees in drugstores has more than doubled, even though the number of drugstores increased only slightly. The biggest change occurred in the large stores with more than fifty employees; in 1948 there were 381 such stores, and by 1997 there were 2,291. In 1992, the 20 largest drugstores made almost 60 percent of the country's total drug sales (compared to the 20 large home furnishings stores, which made about 20 percent of the total home furnishings sales). By 1995, 7 of the chain drugstores had more than 1,000 stores; Rite-Aid led the pack with 2,605 stores, followed closely by Revco with 2,082.[13] As the big operators consolidated and acquired smaller stores, the top two drug chains ballooned: by 1999, CVS had 4,095 stores with $17.2 billion business, and Rite-Aid, with 3,850 stores, had a $15 billion business.[14] These chains are also taking on the managed care industry by buying health systems, as when Rite-Aid purchased Eli Lilly's PCS Health System, while others, like CVS, signed contracts with the federal government and other groups.

At the same time, some newcomers, like one-stop supermarkets, mass marketers, and new e-drugstores, are moving aggressively into the pharmacy world. Aside from their scale of operation and ubiquity, many of these newcomers have hookups with insurance companies and HMOs. Among supermarkets, Kroger, Albertson's, Safeway, and Pathmark have the most profitable pharmacy operations, while mass marketers like Wal-Mart, Kmart, Shopko, and Costco are catching up. Wal-Mart, always the jumbo, was number one in pharmacy sales in 1999 among the mass marketers and number three of all types of drugstores in dispensing prescriptions; it beat out CVS and Rite-Aid in the number of prescriptions.[15] The next wave of newcomers is online drugstores; some are still loners, like PlanetRx, but many others are being absorbed by the major chains, like Rite-Aid. Like all e-commerce, these online newcomers have sparked interest in Wall Street, the press, and some of the public, but so far they have captured only a fraction of the market. As these newcomers move in aggressively and the chains expand their empires, the independent drugstores are left behind.

The 117-year-old Bower's Pharmacy in the New York suburb of Tenafly, New Jersey, closed in December 1999, as it could not continue to make it in the new era of managed care–insurance companies, even though the drugstore, with competition from nearby chains, had the same number of customers and dollar volume of business as ever. This pharmacy, with three druggists, was housed in a well-maintained, bronze-trimmed building with handsome interior wood paneling and cabinets. It smacked of a traditional, reliable, and substantial operation. For an independent operation like Bower's, 80 percent of its business has been prescriptions, so when managed care–insurance companies reimbursed 65 to 75 percent below cost, it was a losing battle, according to James Virgoina, one of the owners who replaced the last Bower in 1983. "I'd have to work twice as hard to make half as much," Virgoina explained.[16] As drug prices soar, the chains, with big-volume business, can negotiate prices with drug companies, which smaller-volume independents cannot. Then insurance companies have to approve the types and amounts of drugs a doctor prescribes. If these are not acceptable, the pharmacist has to deal with the doctor and insurers for an "override," or an exception to the rules. Virgoina ventures that drugstores may be owned in the future by drug companies, just like gas stations. The services provided by an independent drugstore like Bower's do not count in a system stacked against it. Selling nondrug items, such as English soap, lavender powder, upscale cosmetics, umbrellas, and greeting cards, does not offset the losses. The net result is that customers have lost a dependable service store and Tenafly's Washington Street has lost its only longstanding anchor.

In my Washington, D.C., neighborhood of Georgetown, the four independent pharmacies and one chain, CVS, have dwindled to two independents and one chain. Both independents have loyal clienteles. One of them, Dumbarton Pharmacy, with a major carriage trade business, is a respected institution in the community (fig. 30). The Dumbarton pharmacists know most of their customers, their drugs, ailments, doctors, community activities, and patterns of living.

30. Dumbarton Pharmacy in Georgetown, Washington, D.C., 2000

They deliver, which is desperately needed by those who are elderly, housebound, or ill, but the car and the delivery costs add up to $50,000 per year for Dumbarton. A customer knows that she can count on the delivery to come on time, and if you are bedridden and need something from the hardware store or grocery store, they will pick it up for you—picture hooks at the hardware store, food at the grocery store. The driver gives a friendly honk at Dumbarton's customers if he sees them walking the streets when he drives by. When the driver was ill the owners did not hire a replacement, so that he could return to his job when he recovered. The drugstore pays for its employees' worker's compensation and life and health insurance, including insurance for the driver's wife, who is seriously ill.

A fraternity existed among Georgetown druggists, allowing them to borrow from one another if a certain item ran low. However, after CVS took over the old chain drugstore, People's Drug, that practice of "obliging" was prohibited, fracturing the network of druggists. And as that network frayed, so have the community's close relationships with their druggists.

This community, like many others, will no doubt lose its independent pharmacies if policies proceed as they have in the recent past. "We cannot survive," stated Harold Sugar, an owner of Dumbarton's. This establishment, like Bower's Pharmacy, with up-to-date equipment and computers, with well-trained and appreciated staff, and with a loyal carriage trade, has not previously been fragile.[17]

The small, independent pharmacy has remained a holdout on many a town's Main Street, but not all have been lucky enough to be located in an upscale neighborhood like Georgetown. More often the demise of the drugstore has been part of the commercial abandonment of a city neighborhood or rural town, like the closing in 1994 of the small-town drugstore in Rural Retreat, nestled in the Blue Ridge Mountains of Virginia. This pharmacy was opened after the Civil War by a Confederate surgeon, Dr. Charles Pepper, who allegedly mixed a fizzy drink from roots, herbs, and seltzer. The drink was later mass-produced in Texas by an assistant as one of this country's most popular soft drinks—none of whose riches appeared to reach Rural Retreat. The drugstore survived for more than one hundred years, often dispensing prescriptions on credit until the next Social Security check arrived but filling only fifty-five a day, far fewer than the eighty needed to keep the store alive. Now customers get their prescriptions filled by Counts Drugstore in Wytheville, eleven miles away, and delivered every day to Rural Retreat Florist. But elderly Nettie Sage misses the personal service she had received; because she is unable to differentiate her prescriptions, the drugstore had color-coded them for her. When one ran out, she would say she needed the pills in the red bottle.[18]

The convenience, services, and comfort of the local pharmacy are almost gone. Drugs and the necessities that the drugstore offered can now be obtained by telephone, fax, e-mail, or a trip to a larger town—all remote from this small place. You do not stay in business when it becomes a losing venture, and that is the story for the independent druggists whose small stores (with fewer than ten employees) shrank from 84 percent to 50 percent of the total number of drugstores between 1948 and 1997.[19] This fatalism predominates, despite the efforts of the trade association for independent pharmacies, the National Community Pharmacists Association, to fight the discrimination in pricing by seeking equal access to prices and freedom of choice, two basic American ideas.

In no other retail activity is the consumer told where he has to shop. This exacerbates the plight of the independent pharmacist, who faces, like every other retailer, all the changing market forces and consumer desires. No matter how respected the independent pharmacy, how solid its business has been, how much customer—and community—loyalty have been built up over the years, the odds are stacked against these small businesspeople. Their days are numbered. Only the heavyweight drugstore chains with volume business can negotiate prices with the drug companies and acceptable terms with HMOs and insurance companies.

Chain drugstores have their problems, too. "Cannibalization," or just trying to kill your competitor, is rampant in the chain drugstore world, especially where these chains are trying to "penetrate" areas previously dominated by independent pharmacies. In city neighborhoods, like Manhattan's Upper West Side, major chains like CVS and neighborhood newcomer Duane Reade are locating opposite each other on the same corner, which one might think would be overkill. But for Duane Reade's chairman and CEO Anthony Cuti, it's part of "planned cannibalization" strategy. Of course, not all of these new chain drug–convenience stores will survive, but that is just retail Darwinism at work.

If the drugstore chains are cannibalizing themselves and the independent drugstores are disappearing, then the future of all those small, independent stores that used to line the Main Streets of towns and cities is indeed bleak. Copies of these stores can be found on Disney World's Main Street, in the festival marketplaces, in the villagey town centers designed by the New Urbanists, and on the commercial streets of upscale historic districts. But they are most likely part of a large national and sometimes international chain. Crabtree and Evelyn, Laura Ashley, and the Nature Company stores all look like small-town shops of the past, but their management, public relations, advertising, and marketing are as sophisticated as the modern corporations that run them. These franchised shops, selling nonessentials and projecting the image of the small store, contrast with the mainstream stores selling essential items—supermarkets, hardware stores, department stores, or clothing stores, which have long since lost their Main Street image—and often locations. Now efficiency, large-scale volume buying, and impersonality rule. Their small-scale ancestors seem like museum relics today.

In the Georgetown neighborhood of Washington, D.C., one by one the small shops and larger local chain grocery stores that served the community with useful items and products have vanished. The twenty-eight grocery stores in the neighborhood in 1914 had shrunk to seven by the 1960s. Woolworth's was the bellweather of change. When, in January 1980, it left its prime location near the neighborhood's major intersection, it signaled the change to a new tourist-oriented shopping focus, found now in many "in" neighborhoods, such as Columbus Avenue in New York, Brattle Street in Cambridge, Massachusetts, or King Street in Charleston, South Carolina. In Georgetown, the hardware stores outlasted Woolworth's, but first Meenahan's Hardware, with its rakes stacked on the sidewalk beside flowerpots and hoses and its inside packed with every conceivable object needed for home repair, vanished. Then the tonier Weaver's, catering to the builder and to the interior decorator, sold its first floor to the clothing store Structure and now continues a reduced and expensive line of fancy fixtures on the second floor. The chain drugstore now sells everything from drugs to nails and soap with little variety and no friendly or even grumpy shopkeepers to advise on the differences between sizes and ingredients.

The small, individually owned and operated stores with unique items, which along with grocery stores, hardware stores, dress shops, pottery

31. French Market in Georgetown, Washington, D.C., 1996

shops, Irish shops, and bakeries once lined the streets, have been replaced by the ubiquitous franchised Gaps, Benettons, Laura Ashleys, and a medley of stores that can pay Georgetown's inflated rents, such as countless stores selling men's clothing, often with a continental look and always at "reduced" prices, primarily to young black men.

One of the last holdouts, The French Market, which was started in 1958 by three French brothers, Georges, Robert, and Jean Jacob, was forced to close in July 1995 (fig. 31). The shop, stocked with every sort of French food, from all kinds of paté to pieces of meat stuffed and shaped to look like ducks, seemed like a timeless institution. The French Embassy relied on it for many items; grand dinner parties were successes because of its specialties. And plain folk came for brioches or fancy cheese. As customers and wholesaling procedures changed, the Market tried to flex. A delicatessen for salads, soups, and sandwiches was introduced, then some dining tables inside and on the back porch. Parking was made more accessible. But that was not enough to counter the changing tide. The Embassy could now buy directly from meat packing plants, like Armour and Swift, which could cut and slice and thereby eliminate the wholesalers. Thus the big customers who had provided steady business left the French Market. Individual customers, who had jobs but not servants, used caterers for dinner parties instead of the French Market. Others are going to new and trendier stores—Dean and Deluca or Sutton Place Gourmet, where they can buy French groceries, along with Greek, Italian, Japanese, and English specialties. The trade for the French

Market dwindled to occasional loyal customers, who never thought such a venerable institution might die. But it did—even though the brothers owned the building.[20] "George, Robert, and Jean were a big part of the neighborhood. Everybody knew them, and they knew everybody. It just won't seem the same without them," reported the *Georgetowner*.[21]

These streets, lined with small shops in three- or four-story buildings that have served the immediate neighborhood and other nearby neighborhoods, have become a stage set for stores appealing to tourists from the Washington suburbs and from foreign countries, who visit by the busload. While neighborhood people have to cross state lines to find hardware stores, out-of-towners visit the ubiquitous tourist stores. What they see is a shell of the old commercial life. The architecture of the buildings differs from that in Chicago, Portland, New Orleans, or Dallas, but the stores are the same. At least the streets are not dead, as they are in many downtown areas.

Despite the massive changes in retailing, the fact remains that stores were focal points for the community. For many, that is where you saw friends, heard gossip, exchanged information, and connected with the outside world. In Keene, New Hampshire, when the IGA store left its downtown location for an out-of-town shopping center, a local restaurateur felt that the "social circle . . . had been removed." In describing the social impact of the IGA's move, the restaurant owner told the local newspaper the IGA "was a common place for people in town to see each other. It brought the town together. You could count on seeing the same people at certain times of the day." The reach of the new IGA is regional, so the customer does not see the old townspeople. "It used to be I would know everyone in there and say hello to them," but now the store clerks do not even know their customers. It is "'Excuse me, sir, what's your number?' It used to be 'Hey, Bill, how's it going,'" according to another Keene native.[22]

City Neighborhoods

The small stores in city neighborhoods, the urban equivalent of small-town Main Street, have been tossed around by the volatility of retailing and by massive demographic, economic, and social changes. Yet one of the most dramatic jolts to the small inner-city neighborhood store came in the 1950s and 1960s from the federal urban renewal program. Its radical approach to slum clearance aroused a national controversy over the social benefits of life in urban neighborhoods, including the role of stores. Urban renewal threatened to bulldoze mom-and-pop stores because they were located in aging inner-city buildings deemed so blighted and unhealthful that they needed to be replaced. Propelled by often sincere sanitizing and beautifying motives, urban renewal proponents categorized these small businesses as marginal operations in rundown buildings that failed to contribute adequately to the city's coffers and to the image of an upbeat city. Articulate neighborhood residents and forceful research and writing by sociologist Herbert Gans and former *Fortune* writer Jane Jacobs reminded the public of the vitality of these crowded and busy inner cities; Gans's subject was the West End of Boston, and Jacobs's was New York's Greenwich Village, where she lived.

In the West End of Boston, Gans found that stores, restaurants, and taverns "served as ganglia in the area's extensive communication network."[23] The stores and luncheonettes took messages and passed them along. Often these stores had the only telephone in the neighborhood. Catherine Otten remembers delivering messages, fetching people, and even calling the doctor for people "all around the block," as her father's Milwaukee corner store had the only telephone in the neighborhood.[24] As communication centers, they were woven into community life because their staff usually lived in the neighborhood and knew the customers. Oldsters, teenagers, housewives, husbands, and workers all frequented the local stores, restaurants, variety stores, and lunch counters for goods and services. These establishments met everyday needs; they had pay telephones for those who had no phone at home; they cashed checks when the bank was closed; they offered credit until the paycheck or Social Security check arrived. And they provided a place for the important public discussion of ideas, as Judge Garibaldi confirmed in his dissent in the 1994 New Jersey case on the freedom of speech in malls: "The small stores, such as the corner grocer . . . used to serve as the forum for the exchange of ideas."[25]

In Greenwich Village, Jane Jacobs saw urban renewal replacing the neighborhood stores she frequented with "monopolistic shopping centers and monumental cultural centers," which "cloak, under public relations hoohaw, the abstraction of commerce, and of culture too, from the intimate and casual life of cities." For her, the small stores, where daily casual meetings with friends took place, were essential to the life of neighborhoods. And, as with the rural country store, a certain tolerance and a semblance of integration existed in these shopping encounters. Men and women, rich and poor, shy and gregarious blended together. Unlike the bars and taverns of the city, which were male haunts, shops were places where women could meet freely. Mrs. Kostritsky, who moved to a city neighborhood without the usual neighborhood stores, found that socializing in her new neighborhood occurred in people's houses rather than at the grocery store or luncheonette, as had been the case in her old neighborhood.[26]

Neighborhood surveillance was another benefit of these small stores, according to Jacobs. The shopkeepers were "great street watchers," keeping an eye on the comings and goings on the street.[27] The shopkeeper's customers walking the sidewalks to and from the shops also provided a continuous sidewalk safety service, as shopkeepers could sense when something suspicious was happening. This street intelligence was confirmed by a Lower East Side settlement house director, who could learn about dope pushers and the timing of rumbles from local shopkeepers.

These shopkeepers often lived in the community, if not above the store. Mario Cuomo and Margaret Thatcher both grew up living over the stores their fathers ran, and although they are political leaders of contrasting views, they always identified with their hardworking parents and the community in which they were raised. Sam Levy was another who lived over the store his father ran in Washington, D.C., and he operated the store himself after his father died. He eventually sold the business and became a major landlord of commercial property in his neighborhood, Georgetown. Such stores have provided important ways for many working-class and immigrant "city dwellers to climb the ladder to social and economic respectability," as Alexander von Hoffman reported in his thoughtful study of Boston's Jamaica Plain, where Irish, German, and other "ethnic entrepreneurs followed the example of Yankee storekeepers and exploited the economic opportunities offered by the growing neighborhood."[28]

In city and suburban neighborhoods and small towns, the innumerable personal services provided by these local stores strengthen customers' bonds to the community, as well as help the local economy. Cashing checks, offering credit, buying special products, taking messages, accepting UPS packages, and placing special orders are all part of the services that a small local business can provide. In providing such services, neighborhood stores, as Von Hoffman found in Jamaica Plain, "did more than dispense goods to the community: they linked customers to the urban place in which they lived."[29] Writer and social commentator Doris Kearns Goodwin recalls that neighborhood life in Rockville Centre, Long Island, where she grew up, "converged on a cluster of stores at the corner of our residential area." Here a deli, butcher, drugstore, soda shop, and barber shop–beauty parlor "provided all the goods they needed in the course of an ordinary day." The storekeepers, who "were as much a part of her daily life as the families who lived on the street," owned their stores, so "their work was more than a job; it was a way of life." And all the "personal services they provided were not motivated merely by the desire for good 'customer relations,' but by their felt relationship to the larger community which they served and looked upon as neighbors."[30]

Corner and neighborhood stores persist in some urban neighborhoods, though the former proprietor, often Jewish, has in many cases been replaced by a recent immigrant, who will experience some of the same problems his predecessors faced, such as credit and shoplifting.[31] Yet these stores still provide a meeting ground for neighbors and a social leveling for local workers, schoolchildren, and neighbors, whose paths might not otherwise cross (fig. 32). In the convenience stores in city neighborhoods as well as in

32. Corner store on Beacon Hill, Boston, 1999

suburbs and rural areas, people still see friends, but there is no lingering, even by the coffeepot: company policy does not encourage that. Nor does company policy allow credit.

The Country Store

Perhaps an even stronger type of community-related store has been the country store. Customers are still greeted by name in the remaining country stores, but most of the proverbial general stores, where local folk clustered over a pot-bellied stove in the winter or sat on the porch sharing news and gossip, have vanished (fig. 33). People came to buy or trade provisions, see their friends, pass the time, and pick up their mail, as many such stores also were the local post offices: in Montgomery County, Maryland, in 1878, one-third of its approximate 140 general stores housed post offices.[32] In 1822, when the population peaked at 2,754 in Hebron, New York, an agricultural town northeast of Albany, there were twenty-two stores serving a variety of shopping, trading (one store took "in trade" 1,200 dozen eggs in one week in 1906), and social as well as community functions for the scattered farm families. Many such stores continued for well over a century. Elections, dances, and Grange meetings took place in the hall above the store in East Hebron. The People's Exchange, now called Bedlam Corners General Store, one of the three stores still operating in Hebron, remains "an important social and community center for the surrounding community," according to a recent history of Hebron (fig. 34).[33]

In the South, the country store was a particularly strong establishment. "From 1865 to 1930 no institution influenced the South's economic, politics, and daily life of its people more than the crossroads store," according to the

33. *Country crossroads store in Arkansas, 1930 or 1931 (Library of Congress, Prints and Photographs Division, Washington, D.C.)*

34. *Bedlam Corners General Store, a country store in Hebron, New York, 2000*

Encyclopedia of Southern Culture. These stores became critical social organizers and builders after the Civil War; so much so that towns were named after storekeepers, Edgar T. Thompson reported.[34] The isolation of the rural South and its lack of settled towns were factors that contributed to making these stores such significant institutions. There were thousands of them scattered throughout the South; they provided phenomenally popular meeting places for planters and farmhands, rich and poor, black and white.

The social life of the country store broke through many of the South's binding prejudices, most notably segregation. Like the department store in the city, the rural crossroads store was uniquely democratic. Open seven days a week and jam packed with goods, they were places where all people were treated about the same because they were all seen as potential customers. Jim Crow did not apply in the store as it did in schools, buses, and churches. Some distinctions between black and white customers did exist, however, as Ted Ownby points out in his fascinating book on Mississippi consumer culture from 1830 to 1998, with many stores identifying black customers with "col" in the store ledgers. However, Ownby did not find that blacks "faced different prices or interest rates than whites."[35] In fact, Edgar Thompson, in the *Encyclopedia of Southern Culture*, wrote that "blacks and whites in the postbellum South more nearly approached equality in the store than anywhere else. . . . There was an air of familiarity and tolerance at the store rarely matched elsewhere."[36]

These stores flourished in the hard times after the Civil War, exchanging goods and services with a minimum of cash for both poor whites and freed slaves, who previously had not needed stores, as they had depended on the plantation owners for their needs. Bartering merchandise for crops was the way business was conducted in many of these country stores. In the devastating economic times of the postbellum period, the stores also acted as banks and lending institutions, which could be lucrative business (their interest was often incredibly high) but also risky because their customers were dependent on crops and the vagaries of the weather.

The owners of these country stores were important people in their regions. Aside from tending their stores and evolving into regional bankers, they often took up other trades, like processing crops and starting gristmills or sawmills. In a city there would be other options available for food and banking, but rural areas offered few alternatives to the country store, which helps to explain how the stores became so significant in rural living. Stores provided economic and political opportunities for the ambitious and energetic. That was the case with William Cooper, father of James Fenimore Cooper and successful land speculator and politician after the Revolution in upstate New York, where he founded Cooperstown. Eager for riches and prominence, Cooper opted to run a store rather than farm the land his father-in-law had given to him and his wife. But that store was only a stepping-stone in his career, for he next developed a "small commercial hamlet," his first real estate speculation, and then moved to Burlington, New Jersey, a trading center and the state's largest urban center, where he ran yet another store.[37] Cooper's selection of storekeeping as a launching pad for his speculative career on the frontier indicates the entrepreneurial nature of stores as well as their crucial role in the commercial and social life of early American towns.

The store has been a gathering place mostly for men, who would pass

The New Yorker June 9, 1997

35. New Yorker cartoon, 1997

the time talking, playing checkers, whittling, or discussing politics and practicing "cracker-barrel philosophy" indoors by the stove in winter and outside on the porch in summer. A gas pump was often located under a porte-cochere, as was a metal box with ice and soft drinks where many, teenagers especially, would hang out smoking and drinking sodas in the shade. For a long time the store had the only telephone around for calls to doctors, mail-order houses, and faraway friends. Some of these functions are still carried out at the country stores that have survived in the South. Today the merchandise may be more like a 7 Eleven's, and the gas pump might be gone, along with the porte-cochere, but you still would not have to pay first for your sodas (fig. 35).

All stores, but especially the southern rural crossroads stores and city neighborhood shops like the corner cigar store, were affected by larger societal changes—industrialized agriculture, loss of the family farm, drained rural villages—that altered the pace and style of rural living. In the cities, larger-scale operations, like chains and supermarkets, posed similar threats to the survival of small, independent shops and commercial establishments. In the laissez-faire world of retailing, such changes were accepted as part of the trade. Whether the advent of chain stores, which appeared in the 1850s, or of self-service stores, which came later, these changes provided a greater variety of products, cheaper prices, standardized goods, and simplified shopping for the shopper—and increased profits for the operators. Sporadic efforts to intervene in this capitalistic process have been made in times of heightened social conscience. Many inner-city neighborhoods have seen their neighborhood supermarkets disappear as the chains opted for areas with more affluent customers, taking jobs and convenient shopping from the neighborhood, as well as revenue from the city. Yet studies as well as actual store operations have proved that inner-city supermarkets can succeed, as Safeway, Pathmark, and Kroger have demonstrated. In recognizing these stores as both an economic and social service activity, public efforts, both citizen and government, can help induce supermarkets to locate in inner-city neighborhoods where millions of residents can procure provisions conveniently and where they can also see friends and familiar clerks. Such stores can also bolster neighborhood stability.

While the crossroads store, inner-city neighborhood luncheonette, and Main Street drugstore may seem romantic and anachronistic in today's global economy and remote living, the casual sociability and communitiveness of such small-scale stores remain important to human and community survival. We need that type of sociability today as much as Charlemagne's serfs needed it in the eighth and ninth centuries.

Downtowns

A sign in the central square in the heart of downtown Carlisle, Pennsylvania, states that the "public square since Carlisle's beginning has been the center of the town's civic and judicial life. Every problem relating to national or social betterment has within its confines enjoyed free and unhampered discussion."[38] And that has been the case in most cities. Downtowns have been the centripetal focus of public and private life in cities throughout the world. The courts and public agencies have been there, along with offices for doctors, lawyers, accountants, and service professionals, schools and colleges, like Dickinson College in Carlisle, as well as shops and stores patronized by residents of nearby neighborhoods and outlying areas. In the Middle Border towns described by Lewis Atherton, "stores clustered on the four sides of the square" and then spilled over to side streets as the town's commerce prospered. This is where the farm folk came for that Saturday shopping trip, a highly anticipated weekly event. Hamlin Garland described the excitement of his family's shopping trips in Osage, Iowa, for school purchases. Clothes, schoolbooks, and even slates were bought under the careful eye of his father, who carried the pocketbook and made the final decisions.[39] As towns like Carlisle, Pennsylvania, Davenport, Iowa, and Schenectady, New York, prospered and grew into larger and more important cities, so did their retailing.

The downtown department store probably represents the climax of downtown retailing. Aside from providing opportunities for people to purchase a wide range of goods, these stores also, with a touch of theater provided by displays and window decorations, imbued shopping with drama and romance and offered people a chance to escape the mundane world and to dream—and have fun. The downtown department store embodied urban excitement. Its well-trained, courteous staff, its many amenities—from doorman to luxurious bathrooms—and its pleasant tearooms and restaurants made the shopping experience not only exciting but pleasant and enticing. As the customers were coddled with service, clerks and staff were made to feel part of a big and happy family.

Being a leader in the world of commerce carried with it the responsibility of being a civic leader. The department store owner headed Community Chest drives, hosted Red Cross blood collections, and chaired charitable and social service activities. During World War II, Filene's in Boston sold more than $51 million worth of war bonds, with one section manager selling more bonds than any other American. In Atlanta, Rich's Department Stores, like many downtown department stores, came to the rescue of its city in crises: to its neighbors, who were burnt out by a seventy-three-block fire in 1917; to the city's schoolteachers, for whom it cashed the city-issued scrip in the depth of the Depression, with no provisions that it had to be spent at Rich's; and to soldiers discharged from the Army at the end of the war in 1945 on Labor Day weekend, to whom the store offered cash advances because banks were closed. "In each instance, Rich's took its stand for Atlanta," states *The New Georgia Guide*.[40] It should be noted that southern department stores followed the prevailing attitudes toward race by maintaining separate and not always equal treatment for African Americans. For example, restaurants and restrooms for employees and customers were segregated. African Americans could not use the dressing rooms in stores, including Rich's, so they had to take clothes home and return them if they were not right. Not until 1962 were southern department stores like Rich's fully integrated.

In 1880 two Bostonians, Samuel Walter Woodward and Alvin Mason Lothrop, came to Washington, D.C., and founded the Boston Dry Goods Company in a three-story building. They employed a staff of thirty-five serving seventy-five to a hundred persons per day. That store, later known as Woodward & Lothrop, or Woodie's, grew into a corporation. It took in more than $330 million in sales in 1981 at its massive downtown flagship store and nineteen branches, including the only department store in the Pentagon and two stores outside the Washington metropolitan area, one in Annapolis and another north of Baltimore.[41] As the city's major downtown department store, it was closely identified with the city. Woodward & Lothrop was "a name which has become synonymous with Washington. . . . For the development of Woodward & Lothrop is intrinsically linked with the development of Washington. . . . It is one of the few department stores to develop alongside a town blossoming into a city."[42]

With departments to meet every household need, Woodward & Lothrop provided a vast array of services, from birth announcements to a post office. You could buy your clothes, your electrical appliances, have your hair done and your silver repaired and your pillows re-covered, watch fashion

36. Earle Forrester, the doorman at Woodward & Lothrop's Washington, D.C., store in the 1930s, an era of gracious shopping (collection of the Historical Society of Washington, D.C.)

shows, eat in one of the restaurants, meet your friends, and just spend the day—all in a gracious, friendly atmosphere, from the moment the doorman greeted you until he said good-bye when you left (fig. 36). All that graciousness was what people reminisced about when it was announced in 1995 that Woodie's was going out of business. The letters to the editor column and human interest features sections of the Washington newspapers, as well as local television news reports, were filled with stories of the kinder, gentler days of shopping. "Woodward & Lothrop is gone, and we have lost not just a store, but a friend, a tradition, a landmark, and Washington won't be the same again," Doris Bruffey wrote from Gaithersburg, Maryland. She recalled that her first "hard-soled shoes" came from Woodie's, as did her engagement ring and her first credit card. Her brother's first haircut was at Woodie's, and her daughter modeled clothes there.[43] Looking at Woodie's Christmas windows was an annual excursion for many families. "Every Christmas," Rebecca Johnston wrote, "we would make an evening out of going down to see the national Christmas tree and then to see the windows at Woodie's."[44] But for Bruffey, Woodie's also meant a visit to Santa Claus. "At Christmas when I asked Mother how Santa Claus could visit so many stores so fast, she explained that the real Santa Claus was at Woodward & Lothrop . . . and the other stores had his helpers," she recalled. Trish Thomas remembered the "organ playing from the balcony," which, as she said in her letter to the *Washington Post*, she missed along with "the graciousness, the gentility of it all. Price isn't everything."[45] For many loyal customers, this outpouring of reminiscences was part of the grieving process for a lost friend. Woodward & Lothrop closed its doors in the fall of 1995.

With the store's closing, Washington also lost a major civic leader. Throughout its 115-year history, Woodward & Lothrop was involved in community affairs. Its president, Andrew Parker, grandson of one of the store's founders, was chairman of the Redevelopment Land Authority, director of Riggs Bank and the Better Business Bureau, member of the National Capital Housing Authority and Salvation Army Advisory Board, and trustee of the Boys Club of Washington. In its heyday of the early 1950s, before suburbanization had taken its toll on downtown stores, Woodward & Lothrop saw public relations benefits in a "long range integration of thousands of services which have multiple benefits for the community and which leave a stamp of continuing good in the memories and activities of the community's citizens."[46] The store publicized community charities and civic accomplishments; it donated tens of thousands of dollars to civic, church, and school organizations—$30,000 in 1951–52; it featured school, church, and local choirs and choruses; it sponsored all sorts of contests, like the Homemade Pickle Contest and Apple Pie Contest (winners' pies were Desserts of the Month for March in several of the store's restaurants); and it held conferences on careers for high school students and finance for their parents, as well as flower shows and events tuned in to community projects and seasonal interests.

Its Chevy Chase, Maryland, store, which opened in 1950, offered free use of a 300-seat auditorium on the second floor for civic, club, government, and school organizations. In advertising the 1956 opening of its "newest and largest store," at Seven Corners in suburban Virginia, Woodward & Lothrop touted its new 300-seat Fort Buffalo Community Auditorium, where "you'll see your friends at flower shows, art and historical exhibits, benefit card parties and other worthwhile activities . . . because we believe in being part of the community" (fig. 37). After a thorough inventory of community organizations, representatives from sixty-six civic associations were invited to the Seven Corners store opening. Many of those associations later would take advantage of the free auditorium. Eight years later Woodward & Lothrop developed a store in Annapolis, Maryland, also with a civic auditorium, which featured a kitchen for serving "light refreshments," a projector and a screen, making it an "ideal meeting place for lectures, films or slide showing, business meeting, flower shows or teas."[47]

Woodward & Lothrop was as allied to the city and its suburbs as local churches were. For its fiftieth anniversary in 1930, the store published a booklet, "Washington of the Future," with sketches of the White House, Capitol, Pennsylvania Avenue of the Future, the new Supreme Court Building, a Municipal Group, new House Office Building, and Great Falls Bridge, each with almost promotional captions describing the building and improvement plans. This booklet, with contributions from federal and local planning agencies, predicted that the "ambitious Federal Building Program . . . will, it is believed, realize the master conceptions of L'Enfant, Washington and Jefferson . . . and with far-sighted understanding . . . produce a national capital expressing to the world America's highest aspirations." Woodward & Lothrop's final words in this anniversary booklet sum up its pride in its associations: "To be worthy of the Nation's Capital, is no small accomplishment—to be worthy of the Nation's Capital of the Future—the Washington partially pictured in this booklet—is a high ideal. Woodward & Lothrop— abreast of Washington for fifty years—is ready for the future and is proud to take its place in a civic as well as community way with every advancement of Washington" (fig. 38).[48]

But the future was not as bright as pictured in that 1930 anniversary booklet. The department store, as a retail giant, remained undaunted by the whims of time until after World War II, when the suburban explosion forced changes. Some opened branch stores, at first "lone wolves" independently located but eventually part of small shopping centers and finally incorporated as anchors in large suburban shopping centers and eventually malls. Yet even then the full impact of suburbanization was not envisioned: "Opening of outlying stores by established downtown stores . . . does not result in any diminution of downtown business," according to a *Washington Post* editorial in September 1956.[49] In fact, the writer continued, "it is to the credit of Washington businessmen that they have adapted their operations to the growth and the living patterns of the community." The county seat, central business district of cities, and the market town remained the center for civic life, culture, major shopping, medicine, law, and all the key services one would require until well after World War II. In the 1940s and 1950s the suburbs were still bedroom communities to the big cities. However, the centripetal nature of metropolitan areas weakened as the suburbs spread ever farther and as suburban life was becoming more decentralized, automobile-determined, segregated, and self-sufficient.

The shift to suburban shopping reflected this diminution of centripetalism. Initially, just marketing for groceries or shopping for immediate needs was done in the local suburban stores. The new suburbs did not offer the range of stores available downtown, and it took time for stores to emerge, for markets to be built up, and for new patterns of suburban living to be accepted—and old patterns and habits of urban living to be broken. Many of these new suburbanites were city bred, so their friends, jobs, churches, and stores were still in the city. A 1955 Ohio State University study of Seattle,

37. *Woodward & Lothrop advertising its new Seven Corners store in suburban Falls Church, Virginia, in 1956 as a place "where friends and neighbors meet." A community flower show is featured in this advertisement (collection of the Historical Society of Washington, D.C.)*

38. *Woodward & Lothrop's flagship store in downtown Washington, D.C., 1930s (collection of the Historical Society of Washington, D.C.)*

Houston, and Columbus, Ohio, found the shift to suburban shopping started with groceries, then movies, medical care, furniture, and, last, clothing. Of the study's respondents, 73 percent from Columbus, 71 percent from Seattle, and 60 percent from Dallas still shopped downtown for clothing. The advantages of downtown stores were the variety in styles of clothing, as well as in size and price, and their sales; finally, downtown was considered the "best place to meet friends from other parts of the city for a shopping trip together."[50]

These same respondents in the Ohio State survey found that the suburban shopping center had three advantages: proximity to home, easy parking, and "more convenient hours" than those of the downtown store. "Neighborhood loyalty or sentiment," according to the study, "in no way influences shopping orientation," and "retail stores unfettered by sentimental, personal, or kinship considerations may locate wherever various factors combine to produce the maximum profit." Although the 1955 study considered suburban shopping centers incapable of competing with the downtown store's selection of goods, it recognized that parking was the biggest problem for the downtown department store. The study concluded that "the advantages now enjoyed by the CBD (Central Business District) are not easily alterable, for they are rooted in the ecological structure of American cities and in their cultural and social system, but rapid social changes so characteristic of our dynamic urban society blur the outlines of the patterns of tomorrow."[51]

Those outlines were not blurred in urban renewal's attacks on the slipping cities. In the mid-1950s it was thought that cities could regain their former glory with more parking, radical surgery to festering slums, and infusions of up-to-date glass-walled buildings and civic centers—and with help from the federal urban renewal program. While many cities tried to convince themselves that they could be resuscitated by such efforts, the hard facts were that the middle class was leaving the cities, taking with it its taxes, its discretionary money, and its social commitments. Following not far behind were the cities' stores, which were seeking the growing suburban honey pot of middle-class consumers. The progressive and aggressive mayor of New Haven, Connecticut, Richard C. Lee (1954–1970), was able to get more federal dollars per citizen for his city than any other mayor, and with that money he hired some of the sharpest redevelopers in the country, like Edward J. Logue, later head of the Boston Redevelopment Authority and New York State's Urban Development Corporation. But these experts were unable to stem the suburban tide. Flanking New Haven's central Green was an area that the city hoped to redevelop into first-class shopping with New York department stores, and in the process replace the local department store, Malley's. For the redevelopers, Malley's represented the forlorn state of New Haven's downtown. But after snubbing Malley's and failing to lure a New York store to New Haven's Green, the city had to turn around and invite Malley's into the prize location. The fizzle of that redevelopment effort was compounded by the slow reconstruction of the rest of the heart of New Haven, which looked for many years like a blitzed city after World War II.

Meanwhile, center cities, incapable of competing with the pull of the suburbs, became ever more remote from the burgeoning suburban areas. Bulldozed central business districts remained vacant for years, and what remained of downtown shopping were straggling shops selling wigs and records to a growing inner-city minority population, plus a few stalwart downtown flagship department stores. Shopping malls, which had numbered only a few hundred at the end of the war, grew to 22,000 by 1980; 200 were regional malls serving a gigantic geographic area.[52] By 1954 suburban shopping sales had outstripped retail sales of all metropolitan centers of more than 1 million population, according to Homer Hoyt.[53] That pattern continued as sales declined from 1972 to 1977 in the northern cities while their suburbs experienced a growing increase in sales.[54] No wonder S. O. Kaylin, editor of *Chain Store Age*, observed that "there is no logical place to locate stores but in the suburbs."[55]

Aside from the powerful pull of the suburbs and their shopping malls, the locally and family-owned department stores faced a new era of industrialization in retailing. High-powered management increased concentration of ownership, centralized financial control, and formed a new corporate pyramid with unskilled, often part-time labor on the wide foot of the pyramid and a small, highly paid managerial group at the apex. Advertising and computers were used to replace full-time, knowledgeable clerks in the glove department. Retailing was starting to be considered a major economic activity—like manufacturing—and was being managed like a big corporation. A new bottom line resulting from new economies of scale was emerging—as was a new and difficult era for the family-owned department stores, especially the downtown flagships.

This was a time from the 1970s into the 1990s when old and respected stores, like Best's and Bonwit Teller in New York, and Woodward & Lothrop and Garfinckel's in Washington, disappeared. Others left to become anchors in malls, and many were absorbed in hard-fought takeovers by a handful of national holding companies, such as Federated, Allied, and Dayton Hudson. In city after city family-owned stores succumbed to the pressure of these retailing giants. Merchandise was upgraded—that is, higher-priced fashion items were featured and low-profit notions were eliminated. The individuality of these family-owned department stores, their loyalty to their communities, and their level of service to customers were not part of the new formulas for efficient and lucrative retail management. Television advertising of brand names was expected to sell products, not a skilled clerk. Selfridge's philosophy that happy clerks and contented customers made for good business was replaced by hard-line MBA policies aimed at replacing that fuzzy approach with computers for the stores' operations and advertising of name products for selling merchandise. Low-paid, high-turnover, part-time unskilled clerks with no benefits and no commissions could operate the cash registers and process the credit-card purchases—such workers are called "deskilled" labor by the trade. Seventy-five percent of department store workers in 1981 were part-time, and almost 80 percent had worked in the stores for only three years or less.[56]

Department stores found merging theater and retail an answer to their problems, as did Zola's Aristotle Boucicaut and the early department store entrepreneurs. To lure customers, jazzy displays, festivals, themed areas, and new store images were programmed. In clerkless spaces filled with racks of designer clothes in no clearly designated departments ("flexible interior envelope and open architecture"), customers were meant to roam, making unexpected and spontaneous purchases. The time expended in roaming and often in disorienting shopping in department stores frustrated some, who turned to new, cheaper, and easier ways to shop: by catalogue or at the new discounters.

In contrast to the excitement that a store like Bloomingdale's introduced, bare-boned discount and warehouse shopping became increasingly important in retailing. Bargains could be found at periodic holiday, pre-school, and white sales at department stores, at bargain basements like Filene's, or at a handful of low-price stores, like New York's famous Klein's at Union Square. But it was not until the 1960s and 1970s that the number of discount stores mushroomed. From 1966 to 1977 the number of stores more than doubled—from 3,503 to 7,363—as did sales. Yet in that period the number of firms shrank from almost nine hundred to just over six hundred. But the most dramatic change in those years was the rise of the big firms (those with more than fifty stores). In 1966, there were eight of these large firms, which had a total of 3,503 stores, with sales of $15 billion. By 1977 these large firms had grown to thirty-one, with almost 4,500 stores with sales of $39 billion. The pattern of the big getting bigger is clear from the statistics of this important growth period for discount chains. And that pattern has continued. In the latest Census of Retail Trade in 1997, the number of large firms with more than fifty stores was thinned to thirteen, but the total number of stores increased to 6,259 and sales ballooned to over $122 billion, a more than 800 percent increase in thirty years.[57]

The discount stores were fast-paced, automated, and competitive operations whose livelihood hinged on small profits from multiple sales. Their stores resembled warehouses, not the marble palaces of the department stores, and their ambience was that of a bargain basement. Gone were the gentility, grace, and style of the old department stores and their downtown retail neighbors. Located in low-rent areas, often fringe warehouse-industrial sections of cities, or in commercial strips ribboning out from the city into suburbia, these discount and bargain stores were not a part of any community. The manager of T. J. Maxx or Loehmann's was not heading the local Community Chest drive, offering meeting rooms for local groups, or identifying with the future of his store's neighbors.

Meanwhile, the inner cities, still struggling with the tarnished images of a deteriorating tax base, increasing minority populations, and lifeless downtowns, were getting a much-needed boost from gentrification, both in housing and shopping. The character of the city, its old architecture, its diversity of peoples and activities, its cultural institutions, its markets and waterfronts offered an inviting contrast to the homogeneity of suburban life. Old sections of inner cities were attracting new, often educated middle-class residents, who were fixing up houses and bringing neighborhoods back to life. Cobble Hill and Park Slope in Brooklyn, Bolton and Federal Hills in Baltimore, Adams Morgan in Washington, the North Side of Chicago, the Upper West Side in Manhattan, and waterfronts like those in Portland, Maine, and Baltimore were being rediscovered. With this residential gentrification came retail gentrification. Old hardware stores were being replaced with wine and cheese shops, clothing boutiques, and franchised stores.

Perhaps the most publicized inner-city retail resuscitator was James Rouse, whose festival marketplaces, like South Street Seaport in New York, were sought by dozens of cities, including Atlanta, Boston, and Chicago. "Cities are where the action is," Rouse was quoted as saying in *Time* magazine's August 24, 1981, issue, which featured him on the cover. Rouse, benefiting from his experience as a developer of suburban shopping centers, was able to garner public suport and hefty public funds to create touristy shopping centers, often in historic buildings in key downtown sites. The suburban shopping mall, a catalyst in the death of the old downtowns in the 1950s and 1960s, returned in a new guise to be a catalyst in cities' rebirth.

While the urban renewal of the 1960s bulldozed people and activities out of cities, this new gentrification priced people and activities out of the cities. New blood was seen as needed to replace the older, marginal urban world, which was felt to lack the excitement sought in the new entertainment retailing of urban festivals. These popular festivals were a safe, clean, and fun answer, with their many restaurants, small-scale boutiques, and colorful mimes, clowns, and performers. The smell of fudge and the sight of outdoor cafes, funky pushcarts, and milling crowds helped to make these festivals seem lively and welcome oases in otherwise bleak cities. They were a manifestation of the new entertainment retailing and almost a theater of consumption. As a young Boston banker sipping wine at the Bunch of Grapes Bar in Faneuil Hall Marketplace remarked, the festival marketplaces have become "adult playgrounds" in the middle of the city.[58] Such theme-park marketplaces have helped to energize tired cities while they simultaneously have eliminated much of the cities' former life, people, and activities. With buildings recycled for more profitable and chic uses, the small, diverse, random, and often marginal businesses, which once provided much of the color and character of a place, have been priced out. The watchmaker, Hungarian restaurant, invisible weaver, and the five-and-ten cannot afford the increased

rents; besides, they do not fit the image of the new downtown with its entertainment retailing.

The coexistence of longtime commercial activities near some of the
Rouse marketplaces—New York City's Fulton Fish Market adjacent to the
South Street Seaport and the open food markets in and abutting Boston's
Faneuil Hall Marketplace—has not been easy. They have been seen by the
Rouse marketplaces and other downtown redevelopers as difficult neighbors.
The smells, clutter, and confusion of these traditional uses do not fit in with
the clean and controlled retail entertainment meccas. Yet these centuries-old
markets have had their defenders. When Faneuil Hall's market was threat-
ened in the late 1950s, Francis W. Hatch, a prominent Boston advertising
executive and versifier, came to its defense with a poem, "In the Name of
Peter Faneuil Beef Before Baubles," appearing in the *Boston Globe*.

> What's this I hear
> A plan's on foot
> To raze each whitewashed stall
> And proffer tourist souvenirs
> Henceforth in Faneuil Hall.
>
> S'elevez!
> Peter Faneuil
> Old Frenchman in your grave
> 'Twas not for tourist folderol
> Your deed of trust you gave.
>
> You planned and gave
> A Market Hall
> Designed for Honest Trade
> With quarters up above, where men
> Could call a spade a spade.
>
> Here orators
> In ages past
> Have mounted their attack
> Undaunted by proximity
> Of sausage on the rack.
>
> •　•　•　•　•
>
> Let tourists come
> Let tourists go
> And carry home belief
> That Boston patriots are backed
> By honest Yankee Beef![59]

As shopping centers recognized the role of entertainment to keep the crowds happy, so have cities. To counter the image of themselves as crime ridden and gloomy, cities have become stage sets for tourists, whether from distant lands or nearby suburbs. Mimes, clowns, and entertainers wander among the crowds in these new marketplaces, whose innards are filled with the same nationally franchised stores that are in most malls, but with a few pushcarts to enliven the corridors. Beside them are new, city-funded convention centers, aquaria, and sports arenas, which bring in even more tourists—and suburbanites. This is part of the service economy, built on shopping and eating, called eatertainment by some. Yuppies, having children later and earning double incomes, enjoy eating out and shopping. People swarm to the popular inner-city neighborhood's shopping streets, where it is hard to get your shoes repaired but easy to buy expensive shoes or men's suits and eat ethnic food. Here the streets are lined with shopping center stores targeted to those with disposable income for disposable food and goods. Only the stage-set backdrop differs from city to city. Although much of the character and authenticity associated with the old city have been lost, the new shopping—whether Rouse festival marketplaces or shopping streets in Charleston, South Carolina, or Georgetown in Washington, D.C.—is safe, clean, and reliable, like the food in the old Howard Johnson's on the highway strip.

Even one of the world's most renowned urban and urbane shopping streets, Fifth Avenue in New York, has been invaded by the mass retailers from suburban malls and highways. Once known for its premier department stores—Bonwit Teller, Saks Fifth Avenue, Best's, Bergdorf Goodman, B. Altman's, Arnold Constable, and Lord and Taylor, along with Tiffany and Cartier—only a few are left on the Avenue. Some fancy shops remain, but they have new neighbors, like Nike, Tower Records, Levi's, Disney, Staples, and Warner Brothers' Studio Store. Many see a class versus mass conflict and a general dumbing down of this fashionable street, where people come to show off their finery on Easter Sunday. After a period during which airline ticket offices and banks filled in gaps along Fifth Avenue, these mall-type stores seemed to help the avenue rebound from the difficult times, according to Tom Cusick, president of the Fifth Avenue Association, the merchants' group. While the debate persists on if and how the different classes of stores can coexist on Fifth Avenue, hard economic reality may decide that debate, because the avenue's rents are among the highest in the world. Georgetown, New Orleans' French Quarter, and Charleston all found their small stores routed by the mass retailers or stores selling fast-turnover, touristy items like T-shirts and a similar fate may await Fifth Avenue. But the change in the avenue is yet another indicator that suburban-style mall shopping has become the norm. Those who could only window shop the pricey items of the elegant stores of Fifth Avenue can now buy a pricey but affordable Coke and a CD.

Another bit of suburbanization is the arrival of the Big Boxes in the city. Some may squeeze into high-rent areas or choose not-such-high-rent areas, but most are well suited to the many large, vacant spaces and vast, empty buildings in many North American cities. Costco, formerly Price Costco, one of the earliest Big Boxes and in 1999 the sixth largest retailer with almost 300 warehouse "clubs," has pioneered with city locations. In late 1993, Costco retrofitted a large masonry industrial building on a five-acre site at 10th and Harrison streets in San Francisco into one of its first in-town stores. Instead of its usual requirement of thirteen to fourteen acres, Costco fit itself into a city-block-sized building and used the roof for parking. Costco provided some visual amenities by adding a variety of blocks to the vast, dull masonry walls and erected trellises to hide the sea of parked cars on the roof—also offsetting the dreary warehouse image.[60] Not only does Costco see a growing market in cities, but it anticipates reducing air pollution as its urban stores cut down car trips. Within sight of the Pentagon in Washington and at the Pentagon City subway stop, another urban Costco has opened in a one-story warehouse with front-yard parking.

In cities like New York, whose residents have had to drive to the suburbs for Big Box and mall shopping, officials have recognized that Big Boxes and malls are a necessary part of contemporary retailing and should be allowed in their cities. The consumer demand seems to be there, and these large stores have adapted to tight urban sites. The Queens Center Mall, an older mall in Elmhurst, New York, jam-packed with customers from every corner of the globe, rang up $760 in sales per square foot in 1999, twice the national average. In Brooklyn's Sunset Park, a new Costco superstore attracted more than 12,000 people on its opening day in November 1996. In Queens, Bronx, and Brooklyn, other imaginative projects have been devised to incorporate certain types of discount shopping into sites right in the heart of their boroughs, near libraries, subways, office buildings, other retail outlets, and plenty of parking.

However, Mayor Rudolph Giuliani's proposal in the fall of 1996 to allow megastores in underused industrial areas—maybe as many as fifty-seven megastores—provoked a controversy tinged with political overtones due to an upcoming mayoral election. Interest in the city's poor and minority residents having opportunities to shop at discount superstores was countered by concerns that such megastores would dry up neighborhood stores, alter the quality of life in city neighborhoods, push out what industry has remained, and benefit the big developers. Beyond these concerns lay a very basic problem as Giuliani's proposal skirted community—and City Council—review of the siting of such megastores. One lesson from this experience is that any proposition for a major retailing innovation that can produce drastic changes, whether real or perceived, ought to require open, conscientious community review and input, such as the environmental impact review process.

Flexibility and creativity are needed if a retailer wants to build and operate an inner-city superstore, according to Pathmark spokesman Harvey Gutman. And he was correct. The siting, planning, and development of such stores in cities is much more complicated than locating on vacant land on a thoroughfare in the outer reaches of suburbia. In built-up neighborhoods the noise, congestion, pollution, and traffic have immediate impacts on the livability of those neighborhoods. A way of life has been built up, vested interests have arisen, vocal civic organizations exist, and retailing patterns have been established in such city neighborhoods, all of which are threatened by superstores of any kind. While people often object to the appearance and scale of these stores, far more than architecture is at stake. It is easier to grasp what different buildings look like than it is to understand the transportation and other nuisances affecting adjacent neighborhoods, as well as the profound social and economic impacts that such retailing has on cities. These new types of mass retailing—whether mall-type stores, Big Boxes, Category Killers, or the mall management guiding the festival marketplace—once thought to be primarily a suburban phenomenon, are now part of the urban landscape.

Bookstores, hardware stores, and department stores, traditionally locally owned and managed, were at first taken over by national companies but still run by local people, then they became franchises or "wards" of larger companies, and then they were finally replaced by mass retailers. The family-owned hardware store became part of True Value only to be replaced by Home Depot. The loss of local management meant the disappearance of traditional ties to local people, activities, and customs. The new mass retailer may contribute to United Way and provide support for some local good works, but that participation is part of a prescribed public relations effort dictated by the home office many states away. One store in a chain looks like another. Ikea in Berlin, Germany, is just like Ikea in Elizabeth, New Jersey. Meanwhile, a basic sense of loyalty and pride, on the part of the employees and customers, has disappeared. These mega-corporation stores may be efficient and may sell affordable items, but they are run by remote institutions beyond the grasp of the locals. And that distant corporate control reinforces a sense of powerlessness pervading the country and the world. Such powerlessness is part of the new age of mega-corporations, global economies, and information highways—all reaching into your lives but all run remotely.

Suburbs

Ever since people could take trains or streetcars, or drive, the ideal of suburban living with a detached single-family house on a plot of land away from the grit and congestion of the "dismal city" has appealed to an upwardly mobile segment of the population. Those who could make it to the suburbs, initially mostly renters, became homeowners as their quest for independence

WORLD WAR II
and the
AMERICAN DREAM
How Wartime Building Changed a Nation

39. Dreaming of a new home (National Building Museum)

and dignity was backed up with federally insured mortgages (FHA), which not only helped many to buy homes, but also helped to stimulate home construction. Home ownership increased from 45 percent in 1940 to 60 percent in 1960.[61] This post–World War II suburban sprawl of single-family houses rolling over hill and dale, some in planned developments and most in scattered, leapfrogging clumps, created a new style of living for American families, who were catching up on lost time from both the war and the Great Depression and enjoying VA mortgages, new jobs, and disposable income. Along with this new style of living came explosive changes in retailing—probably similar to the changes in the eighteenth century and the end of the nineteenth century (fig. 39).

World War II brought about a new speed and scale of development. The 4-million-square-foot Pentagon, then the world's largest office building, was ready for its 40,000 defense workers sixteen months after construction started in 1941, and massive housing projects for defense workers were constructed all over the country—many with designs by some of America's leading architects, such as Walter Gropius, Richard Neutra, and Frank Lloyd Wright. Some of these housing developments were near factories and shipyards, like Henry Kaiser's Vanport, with 42,000 people in Portland, Oregon.

Others, like Linda Vista, California, where 3,000 houses were built in thirty days, were far from existing cities and towns. In isolated locations, such as Linda Vista, community facilities, including four shopping centers, had to be built to serve this new population. Using industrial mass-production skills, developers were able to build on a hitherto unknown scale and at an astonishing speed. And those same mass-production techniques were used to help meet the swelling postwar demand for housing from returning veterans and civilians, who were unable to find housing in the Depression and then the war years. Westside Village in Los Angeles was the first community-housing development using "principles of mass building, organizing the site into a continuous production process," ten years before Levittown.[62] One of the country's best-known developers of large-scale postwar housing, William J. Levitt of Levitt and Sons, honed his skills in constructing wartime defense housing in Norfolk, Virginia, with a method called "reverse automobile assembly line production" by Long Island planner Lee Koppelman.

With help from the government and banks, Levitt was able to build houses that young veterans and their families could afford in his Levittowns, one on Long Island and another in Pennsylvania. In Levitt's Long Island development, the first houses he built, in 1947, were 2,000 Cape Cods, which rented for $60 a month. They were snapped up before they were even constructed; 650 went in five hours, according to *Newsday*.[63] This enthusiastic response to his early development spurred Levitt to greater production. Another 1,000 houses were added in five months, then another 1,000, so that by the end of 1948, 6,000 houses had been built. From 1949 to 1951, Levitt built and sold ranch-style rather than Cape Cod houses, and by the end of 1951 Levittown had 17,500 houses.

A house could be bought in this "instant community" by people with an income of just a little over $3,000. These basic four-room houses initially sold for $7,500, reducing "the American dream to a practical and affordable reality," observed Barbara M. Kelly in her excellent book on the Long Island Levittown, *Expanding the American Dream*.[64] Aerial photographs of the 17,500 Levitt houses, covering acres of flat potato fields, created a "low-grade uniform environment," as Lewis Mumford described it—with what seemed like tacky houses to some. But for the young couple living in a cramped city apartment or sharing a house with in-laws, the new house seemed like paradise. The dream of owning one's own home with a yard and nearby good schools and shops made the Levitt houses seem the "houses fit for heroes" they were advertised to be. "It's just heaven," declared an early Levittown pioneer, Mrs. George Dittus, as she moved into her bungalow in October 1947.[65]

A single-family house and a car had become essential to the American dream. In fact, the home became increasingly important in the life of the family. In the city, activities like church, clubs, movies, and organizations took the family outside the home. In the suburbs, those activities were not

nearby and, besides, the home was equipped with telephones, washing machines, radios, and televisions, bringing the world right into the family room. There was little need to go to the laundromat or bar to find out what was going on in the world. "As the home itself, rather than the neighborhood, becomes the chief gathering place for the family," according to David Riesman, in his 1964 discussion of suburban living, "either in the 'family room,' with its games, television, its informality or outdoors around the barbecue," the focus of activity moved away from public places, such as parks, stores, and recreation centers.[66] With suburbanization spreading farther from the old city, the home became more central in the lives of suburbanites. Eventually even their strongest ties to the city—like jobs, church, and stores—followed and sometimes even preceded them to the suburbs.

Few established town centers existed in the open lands that many of these developments were now occupying, whether in Rockland County, New York, or Orange County, California, where the population increased from 130,760 in 1940 to 1,420,386 in 1969. The infrastructure of roads, water and sewer systems, and all the institutions and establishments (churches, schools, police departments, fire stations, parks, stores, and municipal buildings) that were taken for granted in cities had to be created in these suburbs. Indeed, "a house is not enough," as William Levitt reminisced in 1964.[67]

Despite the portrayal of Long Island Levittown as rows of identical bare-bones houses with few amenities, Levitt provided the basics for a large new community, including the infrastructure of streets, water mains, and distributing wells—and land for parks, schools, and churches. Village greens were established in central locations in different sections of Levittown on land Levitt gave to the park district, along with swimming pools he constructed, as well as land he donated for churches, bowling alleys, and commercial buildings for retail use. These village greens were designed to meet the community's everyday needs, including shopping. Here were located small-scale mom-and-pop operations resembling the old Main Street stores: often a single jeweler, a family-run delicatessen, a hardware store, a bakery, a barber, a cleaner, a drugstore, and a small chain supermarket, like a six-to-eight-aisle Bohack's.

The first village green, referred to as Neighborhood Center #1 and designed to serve the first 2,000 families, had a swimming pool, church, playground, and bowling alley; it also had four one-story commercial buildings with storefronts and parking on both sides. It met the standards for neighborhood centers, one for 2,500 houses, established by the Urban Land Institute in its "Community Builders Handbook." Although within walking distance of many families, the street pattern of long blocks, combined with the availability of parking, encouraged shoppers to drive to these village greens (fig. 40).

Although William Levitt saw the need to incorporate these neigh-

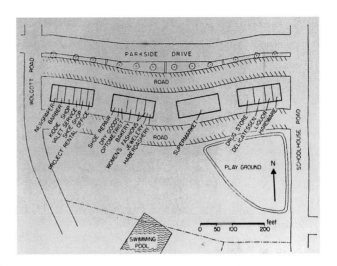

40. All the stores to serve the neighborhood—drugstore, supermarket, delicatessen, and shops for clothes, liquor, and shoe repair—at Levittown's Neighborhood 1 shopping center, as printed in Architectural Forum, *March 1948*

borhood centers into his sprawling community, most developers were concentrating solely on building houses, leaving amenities and often necessities, such as the siting of stores, to the marketplace. In this postwar period, stores and shopping centers were locating not in older centers but along arterials and highways, where they could reach beyond local markets and where there was ample parking. Hempstead Pike, a six-lane arterial dividing Levittown, has followed the pattern of many commercial strips on the outskirts of development, not necessarily part of any community nor connected with any town. Such strip commercial operations metastasized from stores serving daily needs into shopping centers, then into larger stores serving larger markets, then into bigger shopping centers under single management, and some into full-blown malls or Big Boxes of all sorts, along with many stragglers from earlier times.

And as car ownership increased along with this familiar proliferation of stores along the shopping arterials, the downtowns—and even the interior community centers of Levittown—dried up. But the death of the smaller stores in Levittown's village greens can be attributed to a mix of causes emerging over time. Daily shopping in the six-to-eight-aisle supermarket was being replaced by a new "mall mentality—the bigger-is-better, shop-in-one place-attitude," as Levittown scholar Barbara Kelly stated.[68] And the big stores, whether a Category Killer like Long Island's hardware/lumber Pergament, later eclipsed by Home Depot, with its "bulk buying, large inventory, and low prices," or one of the fifteen-aisle mega-supermarkets with vast selection and long hours, provided opportunities to satisfy the shopper with the new mall mentality.

The Levittown village greens' mom-and-pop stores' service could never compete in the mall culture, with the sophisticated retailing of the Big Boxes, Category Killers, or even franchised convenience stores like 7 Eleven. "The supermarkets and hardware stores," Kelly writes, "would have been the two 'anchors' at the greens. The supermarket would draw the women; the hardware stores, the men. Once the supermarket went out of business, the women moved their shopping elsewhere, thereby drawing off the clientele for the other village green shops. In turn, the man could now stop at Pergament on the way home from work or go there on a Saturday, bypassing the greens."[69]

Levittown's interior village greens now have blocks of vacant buildings, and others with doctors' offices and stray incubator businesses, while the community centers abutting main roads still have fast food, carry-out businesses, and convenience stores. The story of Levitt's village greens parallels that of many towns and cities whose traditional shopping hubs were dying, as the last stalwarts—pharmacies, liquor stores, and delicatessens—were unable to survive in the new retail world of stores run by distant megacorporations that provided overwhelming inventory, sometimes low prices, and usually long shopping hours seven days a week.

A casualty of this new scale and pace of shopping has been its sociability. Shopping became a physically remote activity as it moved ever farther from residential neighborhoods, which were not to be tainted with commerce. Whether from a desire to return to some sort of mythic American small town, or to create a place that did not mix people and activities, the prevailing ideal was segregated single-use areas. Residential areas were for houses, commercial areas for stores, and industrial areas for factories. Planning was the way these ideas were expressed, and zoning provided the tools to carry out the ideas. Purity of the residential areas was to be safeguarded, and all-important property values would be sustained by this monogamous thinking. But this same thinking helped usher in an impersonal shopping era. Now one drove to the shopping center on the highway, parked in a vast lot, purchased a week's supply of food for the freezer, and maybe ran into a friend or two pushing a cart down the wide aisles of the store. Yet the irony is that as the shopping experience was becoming more impersonal in large and distant shopping emporia, and even more remote with mail-order, television, and online shopping, the influence of retailing on the lives of everyday people has increased dramatically.

For the individual, shopping was being converted into a recreational activity, as evidenced by "I Love to Shop" and "When the Going Gets Rough, the Tough Go Shopping" bumper stickers. Excessive compulsive shopping has been diagnosed as a psychiatric disorder. In the new dimension of the industrial revolution, advertising and public relations infiltrated the minds of

Americans of all ages and inculcated a psychological need for more products—and for shopping and spending to become a recreational outlet. In fact, shopping has been found to be the most popular "out-of-home entertainment."

In planning, new suburban shopping centers were even stimulating residential development. Instead of retail stores growing incrementally in the centers of towns and cities to meet the needs of new populations, shopping centers were starting to precede residential development. "Retail trade is decentralizing independent of population and . . . people are following retail trade to the suburbs," the Urban Land Institute stated in a report on shopping centers in the 1970s.[70] This pattern of shops preceding development, rather than shops following residential development, has been distinctly American. Although the United States, with its automobile and consumer society, has led the world with low-slung development and out-of-town shopping, other countries seem to be following that lead. "Retailing and shopping center development seem likely to become more, not less, of a force in determining the physical and economic landscape," according to Elizabeth Howard and Ross Davies of the Oxford Institute of Retail Management.[71]

Tysons Corner, less than ten miles from Washington, D.C., in Fairfax County, Virginia, is an example of such retail determinism. From humble beginnings as a rural crossroads with a general store and gas station as late as the early 1960s, Tysons Corner has evolved into "one of the most successful business centers in the United States," according to Fairfax County's Tysons Corner Plan (figs. 41 and 42).[72] Now a true Edge City adjacent to the region's Beltway, it boasts 35 million square feet of development, 70,000 employees with mostly white-collar jobs, two regional super-malls with 3.5 million square feet of retail space, six hotels, eighty-five acres of automobile sales and service establishments, and some housing, mostly apartments, on 18 percent of the land.

Tysons Corner has become Fairfax County's "downtown," as the planning report states, with 30 percent of the county's total office space, six of the county's ten hotels, the malls, and many smaller shopping centers, free-standing Category Killers, restaurants, and sundry retail and office activities. High-rise buildings, some with company logos, punctuate the skyline, and the ground is covered with vast expanses of asphalt parking lots and one-story buildings. This "dispersion of uses," according to the county's planning study, with "a restaurant here, an office building a fair distance away" forces people "to get into cars to even travel short distances," especially when the destinations are separated by six-lane roads. The county, in its own report, decries the lack of a sense of place, for "there are few landmarks to give definition to its interacting uses."[73] But this lack is more than a visual matter. The new suburban downtown, or the county's Urban Center, as the county itself refers to it, has no social, physical, economic, or civic hub. While its

41. *Tysons Corner, Virginia, in 1956, when it was still a rural crossroads (collection of the Fairfax County Public Library Photographic Archives)*

42. *Tysons Corner, Virginia, as an emerging Edge City in the 1980s (collection of Fairfax County Office of Comprehensive Planning)*

commercial space is second only to Washington's Central Business District, its sprawled activities have some of the same uses you find in the old downtowns, but after forty years the communal synergy has not yet evolved.

The increasing size of stores is an indicator of the growing impersonality of stores. And the trend of these big stores getting bigger is evident in Census figures. By the mid-1990s, 4 percent of the general merchandise stores had more than a hundred employees compared to only 0.2 percent fifty years ago (669 stores compared with 54 stores). Two new categories—500 to 999 employees and over 1,000 employees—had to be added to the Census's County Business Patterns to accommodate today's larger stores.[74] Home Depot alone had more than 60,000 employees in its 512 stores in 1996.[75] In store after store the same pattern exists. In 1948, 82 percent of the country's drugstores had fewer than seven employees; now 53 percent have fewer than seven.[76] Of the country's family clothing stores, 91 percent were staffed in 1948 by fewer than twenty employees; by 1997 that figure was 77 percent.[77]

These figures confirm what one sees everyday. Bigger stores, fewer employees, and less service—and more impersonality. Malls illustrate that story with their phenomenal expansion in numbers, size, and dollar volume of business. In the 1960s, malls became enclosed and larger; in the 1970s, they added multiple levels; in the 1980s, they were so successful they became targets for corporate takeovers, and by 1999, shopping centers numbered 44,426 with 5.5 billion feet of retail space—remember that a large mall may have up to 1 million square feet.[78] But by the late 1980s and early 1990s, this upward spiral was slowed by overexpansion, by changing lifestyles, and by a new set of competitors in a wide range of discount stores and nonstore alternatives.

This bleak news did not deter the development of a megamall; in fact, America's largest enclosed mall, the Mall of America, was built in 1992 on the outskirts of Minneapolis in the Edge City of Bloomington by the Canadian Ghermizians' Triple Five Group, which already had developed the world's largest mall, in West Edmonton, Alberta, with 5.2 million square feet, 800 stores, 11 department stores, 5 amusement parks, 110 eating places, and entertainments for all. The Mall of America is just slightly smaller, although management boasts that it is big enough to hold thirty-two Boeing 747s. It has more than 4 million square feet, of which more than half is in retail use, 15,000 parking spaces, and 12,000 employees. This whopper boasts not only four anchor department stores (Macy's, Sears, Nordstrom, and Bloomingdale's), 400 specialty shops, and hundreds of kiosks, but seven "junior" department stores with upscale, discount, and specialty stores—all mixed together. Besides stores, the mall also features, in its center, a seven-acre amusement park, Knott's Camp Snoopy, with a roller coaster and all the rides and activities of a county fair midway, and Golf Mountain, an eighteen-hole miniature golf course (fig. 43). If that were not enough, there are also nightclubs, movies, bars, and twenty-five "sit down" and twenty-seven fast food restaurants, a LEGO Imagination Center, and a 1.2 million–gallon walk-through midwestern lake ecology aquarium, UnderWater World, to provide a taste of education.

In its first six months there were 16 million visitors to the mall, and in its first year the number of visits rose to 35 to 40 million, compared to Disney World's 29 million annual visitors. From its 1992 opening until 1996, 100 million visits have been made to this mall, jointly owned by Triple Five Corporation, Melvin Simon & Associates, and the Teachers Insurance and Annuity Association. These gross figures do not convey a picture of the diversity of people attracted to this Moby Dick of shopping malls. International airlines like KLM and domestic

43. Snoopy dominating Camp Snoopy at the Mall of America near Minneapolis, 1996

airlines like Northwest have offered "Shop 'til You Drop" packages, and more than 30,000 organized tour groups, including 800 Japanese groups, have blended millions of foreigners and out-of-staters with the local and regional shoppers. Teenagers frequent the arcades, bars, and nightspots—mostly tucked away on the top floor. But their revelries have caused so many problems that a curfew on Fridays and Saturdays for those under sixteen unaccompanied by an adult (someone over twenty-one) was established in September 1996. During the weekdays when I visited the mall, the thin crowds seemed to have a disproportionate number of seniors wheeling around in rented electric carts. The mall has been the site of an astounding number of weddings—more than 2,647 by the year 2000, some in mass weddings and most in the Chapel of Love, "the nation's first wedding chapel/retail store," according to the mall's public relations. The seventy-five-seat all-white chapel, just behind the store selling wedding items like satin pillows for the ring bearer, is available for candlelit services for those with wedding licenses and no interest or time for planning elaborate weddings. Three ministers are on call for the Chapel of Love; not only local and regional couples, but couples from throughout the country and the world have availed themselves of the mall's wedding services (fig. 44).

This mammoth entertainment and shopping complex understandably provoked consternation in the retail world around Minneapolis—and

44. *Chapel of Love, Mall of America near Minneapolis, 1996*

stirred renovations in the older, smaller malls, like Southdale in Edina (the first enclosed mall in this country), as well as in downtown Minneapolis' Nicollet Mall. St. Paul, on the other hand, chose to publicize its cultural attractions, including the Science Museum of Minnesota and the Children's Museum, rather than bolster its retailing.

Architecture critic Witold Rybczynski thought the Mall of America could be "poised to become a real urban place" with the addition of housing.[79] But for well-known local architect and planner Weiming Lu of St. Paul's Lowertown Redevelopment Corporation, the mall's restrictions and controls on both visitors and tenants prevent it from becoming a truly urban place. It is not even suitable for every shopper, as Suzanne S. Rhees noted in her article in *Planning* magazine: "The mall's size and noise may overwhelm would-be shoppers and send local patrons elsewhere for their quick shopping trips."[80] Despite attempts to differentiate sections of the mall by themes, the vastness of the place, the staggering number of stores, and its overall sameness can be extremely disorienting, even with constant references to the mall map. It seems unlikely that the mall will become the urban place of tomorrow, given its overpowering commercial nature and corporate control, where sophisticated marketing strategies guide one's every footstep and thought. Moreover, the absence of urban grittiness and diverse city functions, from housing to public libraries to serendipitous activities, such as artists' co-ops, argue against this ever becoming a truly urban place.

In spite of the number of stores, even its shopping is limited. The drugstore is more a souvenir shop than a useful pharmacy. A needle and thread could not be purchased anywhere. The only public services consist of a counter, office, and conference room run by AARP near an underused entrance on the third floor, and a small post office window in the back of a commercial store called PostMark. Although the mall's commercialism still attracts tourists from all over the world, the nagging question today is what is the future of this type of massive entertainment retailing. Not only is the future of enclosed malls uncertain, but the Mall of America, like most malls, is not part of any community. In fact, this amusement park–entertainment–shopping mall seems as isolated as an island and as independent as a landfill from traditional community life.

Another type of retailing that has surged, as the popularity of many malls has been flagging, is discount shopping. The interest in such shopping is easy to understand, as the cost of most commodities has risen so dramatically and shopping at traditional malls and department stores has become disorienting and time-consuming. The Greater Washington Research Center found in a 1994 study that 33 percent of the area's residents shop once or more a month at outlet malls, 29 percent shop once a year at these outlets, and 16 percent between once a month and once a year. Only 21 percent reported that they did not shop at these outlets. And these discounters are swelling in number. One chain, Phillips–Van Heusen Corp., the women's and men's clothing manufacturer of Van Heusen, Bass, and Geoffrey Beene lines, had 500 outlets in 1990, and five years later it had 800.[81]

Discount stores come in many different shapes. Discontinued and overrun merchandise is sold in straight discount stores, such as T. J. Maxx and Marshalls. Then there are outlet stores for such manufacturers as Coach, Maidenform, and Anne Klein, and for single stores, like Brooks Brothers. Although often called factory outlets, they are more likely to be in stand-alone locations or in outlet shopping centers, but rarely near factories. Two relatively new types of discounters are Big Boxes and Category Killers. Big Boxes are superstores, such as Wal-Mart and Kmart, housed in low-slung buildings initially in isolated locations; they are sometimes the "lone wolves" that precede other retail development. Some of these Big Boxes also run warehouse clubs for volume purchasing. Category Killers are large stores, such as Home Depot and Toys "R" Us, which concentrate in a particular line of products and often kill competition in that line of trade.

Many discount stores are in stand-alone locations surrounded by parking lots, but others have clustered in the new shopping centers of the 1990s — Power Centers for Category Killers and Big Boxes, and Outlet Centers for discount and outlet stores, some now in villagey centers. The discounters are usually located near major highways but away from traditional community centers. As you spill off the San Francisco-Oakland Bay Bridge, for example, you are right at Emeryville, California's Powell Street Plaza Power Center, where you'll find Circuit City, Tower Records, Headlines, and Copeland's Sporting Goods. Nearby is another Power Center, with Home Depot, Kmart, and Pak'n Save, and a few miles down Interstate 880 in San Leandro is Marian Square Outlet Center, with Eddie Bauer, Nordstrom Rack, Gap, Talbot's, and a twenty-four-hour Kinko's.

Every major urban area finds discount stores cropping up on its outskirts. Like the malls, these stores have often moved to where land is available, cheap, and often unzoned. Within an hour or more from downtown Washington are four Outlet Centers, the largest, with its own access ramp off I-95, is Potomac Mills in Prince William County, Virginia, touted by the Mills Corporation, its management company, as the state's number one tourist attraction, with 14 million visitors a year. This ten-year-old, 1.6-million-square-foot outlet megamall, with five anchors and more than two hundred "value-oriented" stores, and fifty-two acres of asphalt with 9,000 parking spaces, has been a magnet for other low-cost stores and restaurants, which have located nearby. This former backwoods exurbia boasts three strip malls, a Wal-Mart, a Sam's Club, banks, gas stations, and a clutter of fast-food restaurants. That pattern is repeated throughout the country. Mills alone runs ten other "value-oriented" megamalls, each located on major highways fifteen to thirty miles from large cities, including Philadelphia, Houston, Fort Lauderdale, and, most recently, Baltimore. Each mall is designed to serve 12 million to 20 million people a year.[82]

Whether Outlet Centers, Power Centers, malls, shopping centers, or shopping strips, these stores are a mixed blessing for the areas in which they are located. They provide jobs and taxes — $20 million for the Commonwealth of Virginia and Prince William County per year from Potomac Mills — but require heavy public investment and services. Prince William County built a six-lane highway, and the state and federal governments paid for access to I-95 for Potomac Mills. Traffic congestion around these malls forces local residents to avoid the area at peak times and to live with a myriad of facilities, like motels serving outsiders.[83]

These islands of retailing, surrounded by moats of parking, are not physically, culturally, or socially part of the communities in which they are located, nor are they friendly or sightly neighbors. Physically, their backs are turned to the outside world as their life is internalized. Seas of parked cars buffer these big centers from their neighbors. In sprawling one-story buildings, these retail operations have the universal walled exterior of fortresses, their only apertures the doors for customers' entrances and exits and the service ramps. Although the loss of ties and loyalty to community and employees has been gradual ever since local stores were first overtaken by chains, their community involvement becomes less important and their price competition more significant as retailing corporations become larger, more polyglot, and more distant. Girl Scout troops and volunteer fire departments suffer. These large-scaled retail fortresses are remote neighbors.

The proliferation of large shopping centers, whatever their nature and whatever their individual retail operations, has presaged a steady movement out of the old center cities and the never-ending parade of change in the retail world. While discounting is popular, rumblings of discontent about the time required for this kind of shopping, and about the quality and integrity of such bargains, are being heard. "I want a J. C. Penney's regular store, a Hecht's or a Woodies's," stated Lisa Shacklette, a forty-two-year-old librarian at the Gar-Field High School almost across from Potomac Mills. "I am tired of seconds and irregulars."[84] But the industry is pressing on with newer and larger outlet centers and newer and larger megamalls, like the massive Cottonwood Mall in Albuquerque, New Mexico, opened in 1996 by Simon DeBartolo, the country's largest shopping mall owner and manager. Once some of these are up and going, it may be time for yet another generation of retailing.

Attempts at Communal Retail

Mainstream community and retail development is capitalism at work. Propelled by private entrepreneurs with their eyes on profit making, these developers take the initiative and the risks in forging new frontiers. Some have been imaginative and others not. Among the most outstanding examples of innovative developers who have striven to produce livable environments are those who have been planning and creating new communities and towns. Concern for the quality of life in these communities has included attention to the role of shopping.

J. C. Nichols's Country Club development in Kansas City, begun around 1907, is an early and lasting example of shopping blended into community plans. Other examples are the community commercial building of Riverside, Illinois, the Roland Park shopping center in Baltimore, the many garden apartment developments built during World War II—like Gustav Ring's Arlington Village in Arlington, Virginia, where a small shopping center was located at the edge of the development on Columbia Pike—and, of course, Greenbelt, Maryland, where shops were designed as part of the community's civic center. These projects broke the cardinal rule of suburban living: that the car, not your feet, took you to the shops. And it challenged the accepted notion that shopping and housing should not mix—indeed, should be separated. In these projects the developers and involved public agencies recognized the public and social functions of shopping.

In the 1960s, two new towns outside Washington, D.C.—Columbia, developed by the Rouse Company, and Reston, developed by Robert E. Simon—show how contemporary retailing can enhance the everyday civic life of communities. In both these towns the stores and community facilities have been planned in village centers, meant to be the heart of community and civic life for each development within these towns. "As far back as the community well and pump, these have been social centers," Simon observed, in recognizing the historic civic and social function of community centers.[85]

The village centers that serve the neighborhoods in Columbia and Reston feature supermarkets, drugstores, cleaners, florists, video rental shops, galleries, restaurants, and other sundry stores, as well as community buildings for associations, senior centers, child care facilities, gyms, libraries, and churches. While the configuration of these centers and the size and types of stores have changed over the years, the function of the village center has remained the same: to provide community services to meet everyday needs. The smaller and more intimate earlier villages with limited parking focused on interior open spaces designed for socializing, while the more recent centers, geared to the time-pressed young couple eager to get in and out quickly, look more like a garden-variety shopping center, with generous parking but nearby community facilities.

Besides the neighborhood-oriented shopping centers, major town centers have been developed in both new towns as their central hubs. Reston's Town Center's neotraditional Main Street is lined with a high-rise hotel, local and franchised mall-style stores, an old-time movie theater, high-rise office buildings, and a central open square for skating in the winter and for an outdoor cafe and community events in the summer. Nearby are Big Boxes and major public facilities, like the Government Center, police headquarters, library, and hospital. Columbia's Town Center is a suburban-scaled development with a large mall with department stores, two hundred smaller stores, the ubiquitous food court, office space, restaurants, and community buildings, like the library and the community college. A long stretch of Power Centers, Snowden Square and Columbia Crossing, are far from the the villages and town center near I-95.

Although both towns' shopping areas remain retail and civic centers, their planning and management have differed considerably. Reston's corporate management never paid as close attention to retailing as the Rouse Company did in Columbia, and then its owners changed several times over its history, with Mobil, one of the owners, backing out of its overall managerial role in 1996 and spinning off parts of Reston, including its village centers, the Town Center, and the Power Center. Columbia, on the other hand, has benefited from James Rouse's background in shopping center development and management and the continuous management of a single company, the Rouse Company, and its subsidiaries, such as Columbia Management, Inc., which manages the village centers, and Columbia Mall, Inc.

Shopping in both Columbia and Reston, planned and developed with the idea of creating a communal synergy, contrasts dramatically with shopping in most American retail areas and malls. The village centers of both towns have not been not merely retail projects but an "aggregation of community activities . . . as a service to the community," according to Alton J. Scavo, senior vice president and director of community development for the Rouse Company. That philosophy is what makes these shopping areas in these new towns so remarkable.

Some of the early developers, planners, and architects of malls also hoped that shopping centers would become honest community centers. Victor Gruen, a Viennese architect, Nazi evacuee, and one of America's most articulate and imaginative shopping center planners, saw the promise of these centers as not merely commercial places, but as centers for community and cultural activities. Throughout his work, beginning with the 1947 shopping center in Westchester near the Los Angeles airport, Gruen hoped that shopping centers could become a focal point for suburban community life modeled on town squares in European cities, the medieval marketplace, the Greek agora, the New England town green, and Nichols's Country Club Center. The centers would vibrate with the verve of the crowded city street without all the noise and danger of cars, as Gruen had already experimented with separating car and people in pedestrianized commercial streets.

For Gruen, shopping centers could incorporate the best of the old city and the new suburbia, public and private life, shopping and culture, design control and individual expression. "The shopping center," he wrote, "became the place where friends met, where new friendships were started, where gatherings of all sorts were held, where ladies met for luncheons and families met for dinner. Inactive civic, cultural and art organizations became active, and many new ones were started because they finally had a place in which to meet." Gruen tried to include "manifold human activities" in his centers.[86] In 1954, the Northland shopping center in suburban Detroit, the largest in the country at that time, had the only Detroit-area theater mounting legitimate plays during the summer months; later the annual ball of the Minneapolis Symphony would take place in his Southdale center. Symphony orchestras played in other centers, and the public rooms and auditoria were used by camera clubs, civic clubs, flower clubs, and theatrical groups. Gruen believed that introducing "beauty and enjoyment" into the shopping environment would result in good business for the shopkeepers and provide a much-needed community focus to suburban life.

Gruen also saw malls as invigorating tired downtowns. His Midtown Plaza in the heart of Rochester, New York, was the country's first downtown shopping-business center. This center, built in 1962, with offices in the skyscraper above and parking underground, had an enclosed, air-conditioned mall with department and other stores on the ground floor. Its open space, featuring a large cuckoo-like clock and international programs, was planned for "intense pedestrian activity" and civic and private activities, from school

45. Dancing at Midtown Plaza in Rochester, New York, in the 1960s, when this downtown shopping center's main space was used for community events, as Victor Gruen envisioned (collection of Victor Gruen Associates)

46. All's quiet in Midtown Plaza in 1999

academic competitions to dinners for Xerox employees (fig. 45). But downtown Rochester and this mall suffered the same problems of most downtowns, and by 1999 the mall seemed comatose (fig. 46).

Gruen's ideas survive, however, as malls have been trying to meet more community-related needs. In 1993, Linda Crowley, President of Irvine, California, a new town on the vast Irvine Ranch, found that "customers want a feeling of a town center somewhere."[87] In fact, some malls are even calling themselves Town Centers, as they attract post offices, municipal offices, army recruiting offices, banks, and churches. Churches have been as favored by mall managers as community facilities, even though they may be in out-of-the-way, low-rent locations. In the 1960s, Bergen Mall in Paramus, New Jersey, had a Catholic chapel, and since then there have been a Presbyterian church, the Church on the Mall in Plymouth Meeting Mall outside of Philadelphia; a Franciscan chapel at the Northway Mall in Albany, New York; an interdenominational church at the mall in Voorhees, New Jersey; a synagogue in California Club Mall in Miami; and, of course, the Mall of America's Chapel of Love.

In the second generation of malls in the 1980s and '90s, traditional retailers are being joined by such commercial and professional tenants as real estate companies and financial advisers, making malls more like Main Street. The community-related facilities in these centers not only provide services, they bring in shoppers. In the Galleries in downtown Syracuse, New York, 29 percent of the visitors used the public library in the mall in 1990. A rent-free health library, set up in a Stanford, California, shopping center with a $200,000 grant from Stanford Hospital, had 11,350 visitors in its first twelve months.[88] Olympic spoiler Tonya Harding's ice-skating practice sessions brought 2,000 to 4,000 people to the Ice Chalet rink in the middle of the food court in a suburban Portland, Oregon, shopping center. Walking clubs are popular in malls, with an estimated 3 million people walking in 2,800 malls, according to the National Association of Mall Walkers.[89] Although doctor's orders often initially stimulated the interest in mall walking, mall walkers now include many who do it just for fun.

Two constant groups of mall shoppers have been the elderly and teenagers, since both have spare time and some have money. Senior citizens, referred to as "new age" older consumers by the major shopping center trade group, International Council of Shopping Centers, continue to be a growing segment of the population. Those over fifty-five already account for approximately 20 percent of the total U.S. population, and by 2010 the Census estimates that one out of four Americans will be over fifty-five.[90] And they like malls. The ICSC found that 58 percent of the seniors shopped in enclosed malls; those between age fifty and sixty-four were the big buyers, and 39 percent of their purchases were made in department stores, as this was a generation accustomed to the service of the old department store.[91] With leisure to browse and money to spend, the elderly are good "mall rats," even though they may not present an upbeat image for the malls.

For teenagers, especially suburban teenagers, malls have replaced the street corner and country store for hanging out. They want a place to gather where they can see others, ogle, and just shmooze. "To a lot of teens, the mall's function is for the social experience—to see and be seen," according to Ms. Berkey of Hahn Company, recognizing that the "old places to socialize are disappearing."[92] Seventy-one percent of teenagers shopped at malls—more than any other type of retail operation, according to an International Council of Shopping Centers report. In 1998, 63 percent of teenagers shopped at a mall at least once a week.[93] When asked by *Parade* magazine what she did at the mall, sixteen-year-old Beth Bushard said, "Most of the time we'll just walk around, or get some tapes. And then we'll walk down to the movie theater to see what's playing. And we'll go down to the food court and get something. They have a thing called Tilt, a big game room, and we'll go down there and play games. And then we'll go into the stores and try stuff on. We get lots of dirty looks. And it's true, a lot of time we don't have the money with us. But if we like something, we go home and get our money and come back." Beth complained mall managers think all teenagers are hoodlums because of their appearance. While they may be wearing ripped jeans from the thrift store, "we may have $50 in our pockets to spend."[94] In fact, the teenage generation is "the only generation who has money to spend just on themselves," according to Nina Gruen of the San Francisco demographic and research firm Gruen and Gruen.[95] And with dual-income families, teenagers have even more purchasing responsibilities than in the past.

While malls are meant to have the image of a community place, they are private spaces with their own rules—and their own security forces (fig. 47). They want to protect their property and not mar the safe, controlled feeling that they try to project. Maintaining the mall as a free world away from the

47. Everything is under control at Tysons Corner Mall, Fairfax County, Virginia, 1973 (Library of Congress, Prints and Photographs Division, Washington, D.C.)

48. The bookstore as an anchor on equal footing with Bloomingdale's and Lord & Taylor at White Flint Mall, North Bethesda, Maryland, 1994

grime, grit, and crime of the old downtown has been a major public relations goal of mall managers. Not only teenagers but also solicitors, politicians, and demonstrators of all kinds are seen by mall management as problems to avoid. When I started to photograph the exterior of White Flint Mall in Bethesda, Maryland, from its parking lot, a security guard appeared in a black station wagon to inform me that such photography was not allowed. I was granted permission by the management office to photograph after I stated that I was not interested in the mall's bland architecture but in fact wanted to photograph the Borders bookstore, which occupied the center of the mall, where I. Magnin had been the previous anchor (fig. 48).

If ordinary photography is not allowed on the grounds of a mall, one can imagine the horror with which many teenagers' gatherings are viewed by management. Some, like McKinley Mall in Hamburg, New York, banned teenagers on Friday and Saturday nights after a weekend clash of teen groups. Trumbull Shopping Center in Trumbull, Connecticut, tried to bar the Greater Bridgeport Transit District from stopping at the center on Friday and Saturday nights because of fighting between groups of Bridgeport teenagers at the mall bus stop.[96] Sunrise Mall in Corpus Christi, Texas, even barred teenagers from wearing baseball caps backward because its management company, Land Grant Development Company of Phoenix, Arizona, viewed the reversed baseball cap as a sign of gang life.[97]

The most serious public-private conflicts in shopping centers and malls have not been about teenagers hanging out or undesirables loitering, but about the right of free speech. Demonstrations have been barred in mall after mall, and these decisions have been upheld by the courts in several states. Typical are the rules of a Niles, Ohio, mall stating that you can't "picket, patrol, handbill, solicit or engage in any other similar activities" in that mall. The Ohio Supreme Court upheld an injunction prohibiting a picketer wearing a sandwich board inscribed "Eating at McDonald's may be hazardous to your health."[98] Even Salvation Army bell ringers at Christmas were barred from a Washington mall until First Lady Barbara Bush protested. The courts, including the Supreme Court in *Pruneyard Shopping Center v. Robins* in 1980, have considered malls private places, where regulations could be imposed to bar the distribution of political literature on the grounds that such activity could disrupt the commercial purpose of the private property. But the Supreme Court noted that a state's constitution "may furnish an independent basis that surpasses the guarantee of the federal constitution in protecting individual rights of free expressions and assembly."[99]

However, an important decision supporting free speech in malls has recognized malls as community centers. In December 1994, the Supreme Court of New Jersey decided that its state constitution protected the rights of free expression within private regional shopping centers when it ruled that regional shopping centers would have to permit the distribution of leaflets on public issues, subject to reasonable conditions. The critical finding of this case was the court's determination that suburban shopping centers have "substantially replaced downtown shopping districts as centers of commercial and social activity." This ruling by Chief Justice Wilentz pertained only to regional shopping centers defined as the "functional equivalent of [a] downtown business district"—not to highway strip malls, single suburban stores, or small-scale shopping centers—because of their limited implied invitation to the public.[100] The large regional shopping center was recognized, in this breakthrough case, as the new downtown for extensive suburban areas.

This case was brought to court by several dozen political and religious groups, including the New Jersey Council of Churches, New Jersey SANE/FREEZE, and Vietnam Veterans Against the War, which organized a leaflet distribution program opposing the 1990 Persian Gulf War in thirty locations, at train stations and other key public places in the state, on November 9, 1990, and then in ten major regional shopping centers on November 10. Four of the malls permitted the distribution of the leaflets. In one mall the plaintiff was not allowed to "approach passersby to offer literature," and in another proof of liability insurance for $1 million for bodily injury and $50,000 to $1 million for property damage was required. Of the six malls that refused permission, one did finally allow the leaflet distribution. These are large shopping centers, with up to 244 tenants on hundreds of acres and with 3,000 to 9,000 parking spaces. They contain every conceivable commercial establishment, from department stores, art galleries, banks, theaters, doctors' offices, automotive centers, brokerage firms, and insurance companies to U.S. post offices for holiday periods. One of the malls, Woodbridge Center, serves a population of almost 1.5 million people; almost 30,000 shoppers visit the mall on an average day.[101]

The finding that these shopping centers are today's equivalent of yesterday's downtown seems reasonable in light of the "all-embracing" nature of these centers. "Although the ultimate purpose of these shopping centers is commercial," Wilentz stated in the decision, "their normal use is all-embracing, almost without limit, projecting a community image, serving as their own communities, encompassing practically all aspects of a downtown business district, including expressive uses and community property."[102] This important decision clarifies the ambiguity of these large shopping centers, whose managers want them seen as all-encompassing shopping *and* community centers yet want to operate them as private places where activities can be controlled by mall management. Managers argue that a myriad of public activities are allowed in their malls. That is correct. The shopping center defendants' brief lists hundreds of them: bridal festivals, Toys for Tots, March of Dimes, Seeing Eye Dog Walk, Picasso of Pumpkins show, etc., but these are safe and noncontroversial programs designed to attract people to the malls. Distributing leaflets on societal issues is a different matter.

Free speech is allowed on the streets of a downtown shopping district, but in shopping centers this constitutionally protected right is limited. Recognizing the legitimacy of the mall managements' concern about unruly activity, the court prohibited megaphones, soapboxes, speeches, demonstrations, pursuit, and harassment. But the basic finding was that these large regional malls *are* the public places where the constitutional right of free expression should be protected, even though limited in this case (fig. 49). Wilentz's decision makes this clear in stating that mall managers "recognize the legitimacy of the constitutional concern that in the process of creating new downtown business districts, they will have seriously diminished the value of free speech if it can be shut off at their centers."[103]

Six years later, in 2000, another New Jersey Supreme Court decision affirmed and expanded Wilentz's findings.[104] In 1996, James Mohn applied to The Mall at Mill Creek in Secaucus to set up a table to distribute leaflets and gather signatures for the Green Party's presidential candidate, Ralph Nader. The mall's restrictive regulations virtually prevented Mohn's political activities. An exorbitant $1 million insurance policy was required, as well as an indemnity agreement for claims and losses—and then Mohn could leaflet only one day between January 1 and October 31. The court found that these regulations "would prevent the exercise of expressive activities" and that "leafletting in heavily visited shopping areas has a very high value in our system of political discourse. Putting too high a price on the exercise of freedom may destroy it."[105] The court "hoped that mall owners would sense the connection between the colonial pamphleteers who secured our liberties and the pamphleteers who today seek access to the new forums of commerce," recognizing that "throughout much of New Jersey today there is no place to go, other than shopping centers and regional malls, if one is to have an opportunity to meet face-to-face with large groups of people" for leafletting.[106]

49. *Political campaigning at the farmers' market in Arlington County, Virginia, 2000*

In less than a century, storekeepers' attitudes toward their communities have radically changed. In 1909, Selfridge boasted that his store was a "community centre," and in 1994 and 2000, New Jersey Supreme Court justices forced reluctant mall owners to accept their role as managers of "all-encompassing" shopping and community centers, the country's "new downtown business districts," similar to "centers of commerce" that historically "have been meeting places for those who wish to speak, write, or exchange ideas."[107] These New Jersey cases reveal not only changes in storekeepers' attitudes toward community, but dramatic changes in the functions and roles of shopping establishments, suburbs, and old city downtowns. The southern country crossroads store, the old downtown department store, and the small-town general merchandise store may still exist in some places, but mainstream social, economic, and cultural forces—and technology—have produced different types of retailing in the United States. And in that process the sense of community and the casual, intimate sociability of shopping have almost disappeared. "The mall," said Edward de Avila, former director of retailing at Reston's Town Center and now an executive at AMC Entertainment, Inc., "is not meeting the social needs of many communities as a popular central gathering place."[108] Nor do all the online communities allow for essential face-to-face encounters. Until the social functions of shopping are recognized as public concerns in making communities livable and humane, the private sector will continue to promote retailing that will bolster the corporation's bottom line without adequate consideration of the community's welfare.

CHAPTER THREE

Shoppers

Matching Dreams with Realities

Hopes and Dreams

In describing his cosmetic company's manufacturing and selling, Revlon's former chairman and CEO Charles Revson is often quoted as saying, "In the factory we make cosmetics, in the store we sell hope." And indeed, hope dwells in the hearts of most shoppers and clearly is one of the driving motivations for shopping. Yet decisions about what to buy and what not to buy are motivated not only by hope but by a mix of psychological, ethical, political, and moral factors, which all help determine what we believe and value. From the time of William Cobbett's peasant family, who saw no need to buy anything beyond the necessities, massive changes in society have influenced decisions concerning how we want to live. Shopping for not only essentials but also for luxuries has become a recreational outlet as well as a way for many to fulfill themselves by attaining a sense of identity along with power, freedom, and upward mobility. Boopsie, in Garry Trudeau's *Doonesbury* comic strip, surprised her husband, B. D., by declaring that during her sixty-three days of O. J. Simpson sequestered jury duty, shopping was what she missed most. "It's like sensory deprivation! I feel completely cut off from

ON NOVEMBER 8,
FOREST CITY RATNER
RETURNS THE
NATIONAL PASTIME
TO BROOKLYN:

SHOPPING.

50. *A shopping center and the new national pastime of shopping are replacing the Dodgers and their proposed new Ebbetts Field in Brooklyn, according to this 1996 advertisement by the developer, Forest City Ratner Companies*

everything that defines me as a person." Then she told B. D., "You're not a woman, B. D. You couldn't possibly understand."[1] While shopping has been primarily a woman's activity—from the traditional housewife shopping for groceries to the contemporary woman cruising boutiques—increasing numbers of teenagers, elderly people, and men are also seeking the latest styles and satisfactions that shopping offers.

Shopping has become a national pastime for Americans at large, as Juliet Schor notes in *The Overworked American*—and as the advertisement for the shopping center at the former site of Brooklyn's Ebbetts Field confirms (fig. 50).[2] According to Schor, it is the most popular "out of home entertainment" in the United States. From 1984 to 1988, Americans spent 20 percent of their household income on clothing, household furnishings and equipment, and personal care items (excluding food).[3] The commodity expectations for consumer products or material possessions of the American middle class have soared. From 1960 to 1980 personal commodity expenditures more than quadrupled.[4] More and more people own their houses and apartments, which have increased dramatically in size and are packed with the latest appliances. Some families also have vacation homes and condos. In 1997, 99 percent of all American households had at least one color television set, 87 percent a frost-free refrigerator, 71 percent a clothes dryer, 61 percent cordless phones, 47 percent central air conditioning, and 35 percent a computer, according to the Department of Commerce.[5] Money, instead of being stashed in savings accounts, is being used to pay off shopping purchases charged to credit cards. Today's shopper is bolstered by the "you can't take it with you" attitude (fig. 51). "Enjoy your money. That's what it is for," says Judy Bonderman, a well-educated fifty-year-old Washington, D.C., divorced lawyer with two children.[6] Born well after the Depression and enjoying a carpe diem approach to life, she has little fear of the future, like many in her generation. So she is a good shopper.

Opportunities abound for all kinds of shopping. Malls are in the suburbs, in downtown office buildings, and in large airports, or disguised in gentrified mills, waterfronts, and factories. And then there are all sorts of strip shopping centers, Deep Discounters, and boutique museum shops—all within reach of most urban and suburban dwellers, as well as of many rural residents. And now you do not have to budge from the telephone or the computer to indulge in shopping (fig. 52). Many in the middle class find themselves caught in an exhausting work/spend cycle as they drudge away at jobs to bring in income to pay off their shopping debts. Others are left out of this cycle for lack of money, not necessarily lack of interest.

And for some, shopping is an absorbing pleasure. Playwright Wendy Wasserstein wrote in the New York Times that she is a shopper. "There is no department store, specialty shop or even supermarket that doesn't whisper to me 'We're open. Please come in.'"[7] Gerry Medley, a svelte black ex-model living in suburban Washington, D.C., and now engrossed in family and community activities, gets a "rush" just thinking about shopping. Knowledgeable about quality clothes, materials, and designers from her modelling days, Medley carefully considers her purchases, for she likes "beautiful things" and has a "good eye" for discounted "quality merchandise," high-end designer goods, here and abroad. Shopping is not a compulsion for Medley but rather a "creative" break from her work, recently organizing a blues festival in northern Virginia.[8]

For many, shopping is a competitive sport—a hunt. The game of looking for bargains, haggling over prices, waiting until the prices drop, and sifting through racks or mounds of reject merchandise until the prize is found is zestful entertainment. Finding the prize is like eating a delicious candy. For the aggressive bargain shoppers, called "guerilla shoppers" by some, the hunt can be serious business. With the interest in designer and name-brand merchandise has come an increase in guerilla—and just bargain—shoppers. That is not surprising, as designer goods command inconceivably high prices. High-fashion shoes can cost hundreds of dollars, and coats and dresses thousands. A Jil Sander black silk tunic with leather-covered buttons is listed in the New York Times at Loehmann's as reduced to $1,500 from $5,460, a full year's salary for some.[9] When Loehmann's, the matriarch of high-end discount stores, opened a new store—its first in Manhattan—in October 1996,

51. Self-fulfilling shopping (photograph by Barbara Kruger, published by Fotofolio, New York)

52. The online shopper does not have to budge (advertisement for Bluefly, Inc., published in Wired magazine)

crowds swarmed through its doors. Its Back Room, with the higher-priced designer goods, was swamped with bargain hunters seeking that La Croix jacket or Isaac Mizrahi dress at just the right price. The excitement of the hunt stimulates the true bargain shopper and creates a contagious frenzy in a store, with people scrambling and almost fighting for the elusive gems tucked into the pile of sweaters or lost in the racks of polyester suits.

This sport of bargain shopping is ages old. The bazaar and hawkers of the Middle East, the street peddlers in cities, and even the proverbial Yankee peddler operated on the timeless principle of haggling. For the refined

Anglo-Saxon, bargaining is often distasteful, but getting bargains is welcome even to the familiar bluestocking New Englander, who might shy away from haggling. For others familiar with the rough-and-tumble world of haggling, bargaining is a pleasurable experience. Ninety-seven-year-old Clara Lamb, nurtured in Brooklyn, where bargaining was part of everyday life, lit up when she thought of the fun of haggling to get a good buy. Maybe bargain shoppers are more aggressive in Gotham, but the hunt for good deals and the willingness to go to combat for them are universal. And that hunt has leapt beyond the bounds of real stores and flea markets into the world of cyberspace, where sites like eBay have captured the time, attention, and money of millions. More than 2 million "visitors" haggled over hundreds of thousands of items on an average day in September 2000 at eBay, the most popular website, with 19 million users.[10]

For most people, however, shopping is an activity that is necessary to meet real and aspired needs. It can also provide a variety of pleasures and frustrations. Although shopping is spurred by a wide range of conscious and unconscious urges, fantasy is one of the more constant and persuasive shopping fuels. The shopping experience itself is enveloped with mostly pleasurable fantasies: from the anticipation of the purchase to the actual purchasing, and finally to using the purchase. Even in eighteenth-century America, shopping could transform the purchaser into idealized gentility as the shopkeeper treated customers with a dignity rarely offered to those struggling to ascend the social ladder. "For those few moments in the shopkeeper's presence, the customer became genteel." Indeed, as Richard Bushman, a scholar of eighteenth-century consumption, writes, "Shopping gave them a delicious taste of a superior culture."[11] The underlying fantasy is that the purchased item will improve and transform the person or the function for which it was purchased. The new dress will make the shopper look like Greta Garbo, or the groceries will soon be a Julia Child meal. Just the unwrapping of the package can spark excitement in a person of any age, as that purchase is hoped to endow the purchaser with imagined qualities. Les Wexner, head of The Limited clothing conglomerate, said, "There's nothing in the store you need. There are only things you want."[12] And those things you want have many different possibilities. "Mundane and everyday consumer goods become associated with luxury, exotica, beauty, and romance with their original or functional 'use' increasingly difficult to decipher," according to Mike Featherstone's *Consumer Culture and Post Modernism*.[13] The new dress will make the homely girl look like a princess and attract Mr. Right, so she can live happily ever after. New curtains will make the cramped ranch house look like a mansion on the hill. The new suit will make the boss look more favorably on the new employee. The souped-up car of the teenager becomes a way of expressing his fantasy for public display. Martha Stewart's household items, sold at Kmart, can lend some class and respectability to any house. Thus, objects can become both means of self-enhancement and important tools for communication.

Yet the shopper's instinctive hopes and fantasies, though manipulated by overt advertising and covert persuading, are rarely realized. In fact, it is that gap between the hope and reality that continues to drive modern consumerism. The shopper is ever hoping that his fantasies will be met in real life, but reality is never quite as glorious as the dream. As the dressmaker was putting the final touches on her new dress, Virginia Woolf imagined herself a new person. "She looked at herself with the dress on, finished, an extraordinary bliss shot through her heart. . . . Rid of cares and wrinkles, what she had dreamed of herself was there—a beautiful woman." In fact, she saw "a grey-white, mysteriously smiling, charming girl, the core of herself, the soul of herself; and it was not vanity only, not only self-love that made her think it good, tender, and true."[14] But when she goes to the party, the magical qualities of the dress seem to disappear; she is not that beautiful woman but her same old self. Despite disappointments, the dream persists of a material object like a dress endowing a wearer with fanciful qualities and exposing her true soul, otherwise smothered by self-doubt and self-consciousness. And it is this dream that drives the shopper to seek ever more consumer products, hoping that someday the fantasy will come true. Retailers know how to capitalize on those fantasies down to changing the standard sizes for women's clothes, allowing the woman who used to wear a size twelve to fit into a svelte size six and think of herself as trim as a Vogue model. But the reality usually produces a general "unfocussed dissatisfaction," as described by Colin Campbell, which in turn helps to keep the engine of consumerism going.[15] And so the retail world continues to intensify shoppers' desires and fantasies.

Along with all these desires are other critical shopping motivators like image and emulation, especially important in fashion. During the eighteenth century, emulating the upper classes in Europe became part of the life of the recently moneyed middle classes, as new objects became symbols of material success connoting an ability to live like royalty. Fashion became a new means of communication. When George Washington complained that his orders for furniture and clothes from London produced shoddy goods "that could only have been used by our Forefathers in the days of Yore," he exposed his interest in keeping abreast of fashion and confirming his place in society as a gentleman. In fact, "his London orders were a crucial element in Washington's most fundamental social identity," Richard Bushman writes.[16] As Thorstein Veblen noted, "Our apparel is always in evidence and affords an indication of our pecuniary standing to all observers at the first glance."[17] Previously, the older the furniture, buildings, and objects, the better, because with this age they evoked a feeling of an inherited wealth and hence visibly differentiated the upper from the lower classes.

The symbolism of old consumer products, called the "patina" system of consumption by Grant McCracken, declined as new products were being produced at an increasing rate and as more new money was around.[18] Fashion and a new type of emulation became popular. New was replacing the old. Being a style setter at the forefront of new styles and tastes in a changing world became the goal. This did not mean looking back in time or up to aristocracy; it was a way of expressing the desire to belong to the future and to take on the undiscovered. An implied condescension was at its core. Inherent was a trickle-down and put-down process, in which those in the forefront led the way. But by the time the slowest caught on, another fashion was often in vogue. And so this squirrel cage kept the producers producing goods, and buyers buying them.

Whether one wants to be in the vanguard of fashion, an interest in belonging has been another drive in consumerism. "Keeping up with the Joneses" takes many different forms, but it is usually a quest to acquire visible objects or services, preferably luxuries, to indicate material achievements to the outside world. One does not want to feel behind or out of the mainstream. Household appliances, for example, have futuristic design elements, giving the impression of progress and modernity. The industrial designer Henry Dreyfuss found that both the car and the airplane influenced kitchen design, as they were "symbols of the nation's scientific imagination and a vital part of its psychology, establishing trends and influencing people in everything they buy." More recently, the architect Michael Graves's handsomely designed household objects, sold at Target superstores and advertised in the *New Yorker* and elsewhere, add class to Target—and the latest design to any kitchen. New designs had to look different from old models to stress their modernity. Science with its latest inventions was seen as solving domestic work problems by saving time and freeing the modern woman from the labor and drudgery of housework. So the house, like clothing, is "both a factory of private illusions and a catalogue of ready-made tastes, values, and ideas," as Adrian Forty describes so well in his book *Objects of Desire*.[19]

Consumer goods, whether household appliances or clothing, reveal many shoppers' hopes and desires, as well as the broader conditions of society. They have also become an economic yardstick of success or failure in the material world. And for many whose work does not provide emotional satisfaction, the accumulation and use of material objects may provide a substitute satisfaction. The new boat or truck indicates status as well as fulfillment for many in all classes, from the blue-collar factory worker to the high-salaried corporate executive. One's self-esteem in a sense becomes society's esteem.

Fashion permeates almost every commodity today. Necessities are transformed into luxuries thanks to fashion, hungry manufacturers, and sophisticated advertisers. Eyeglasses, once functional and made of sound and inexpensive products, are now expensive designer objects with titanium frames in a wide range of styles, which change with the frequency of high-style clothes. Working clothes like blue jeans, originally called dungarees and purchased at country general stores, have become front-runner designer products commanding designer prices. Names of manufacturers and designers are affixed to the outside of clothes and commodities to indicate their fashion value—and their cost. This designer/manufacturer labeling occurs especially on sports items, so the average consumer cannot buy a sports shirt without an alligator or polo pony emblem or a name like Head or Nike. Sneakers, once prosaic rubber-soled canvas shoes, have become not merely high-priced sport shoes with all kinds of elaborate pump mechanisms, but manufacturer-labeled shoes advertised on television and in sports magazines by national sports heroes. The advertising success in making these labeled shoes so popular is proved by the deaths of urban teenagers, beset with envy, who kill one another to obtain such shoes. Advertising designer products has even penetrated the infant's bassinet: babies are attired in Gap and Oshkosh labeled costumes. Until the 1950s children's clothes were not a matter of public display, but now fashion labeling causes such disruptive rivalries that public schools in many cities are experimenting with uniforms, which are proving popular with students and parents alike. Although fashion has always been a code or communication tool, it never permeated as many levels of consumer purchasing as it does today. The prevalence of designer and brand-name labeling, together with the advertising saturation of those products on television and in newspapers and magazines, show the progressive democratization of what was once called fashion. The exclusivity of designer consumer products is diminished by the mass consumption of "designer" items.

Luxury has been intertwined with fashion throughout the history of civilization. When production and money increased, so did choices. With choices came opportunities for new consumer products, introducing yet a new level of luxuries, which Webster defines as a "mode of life characterized by material abundance; anything that pleases the senses, and is also costly, or difficult to obtain; an expensive rarity." But the luxuries would be static if it were not for fashion, the engine that drives changes in tastes. The existence of luxuries and fashion depends on an advanced society in which basic needs are met and in which excess production of nonessentials is possible, and in which buyers who want and can afford the nonessentials are plentiful. As Veblen pointed out at the end of the nineteenth century, fashion was more an urban than rural phenomenon that dominated "large modern civilised cities, whose relatively mobile, wealthy population to-day sets the pace in matters of fashion." "Consumption," Veblen continues," becomes a larger element in the standard of living in the city than in the country."[20] In Theodore Dreiser's *Sister Carrie*, the heroine realized—shortly after arriving in Chicago from the country to make a new life for herself—"how much the city held—wealth, fashion, ease—every adornment for women, and she longed for dress and beauty with a whole heart." Later, when she went to a department store, "She paused at each individual bit of finery. . . . Her woman's heart was warm with desire for them. How would she look in this, how charming that would make her! . . . She lingered in the jewelry department. She saw the earrings, the bracelets, the pins, the chains. What would she not have given if she could have had them all! She would look fine too, if only she had some of these things."[21] Like Zola's Denise, another country expatriate in the city, worldly goods represented the wonders, glitter, and excitement of the city—all within reach if you only had the money. If you worked hard, and had some luck, these prizes could be yours.

If fashion is to flourish, materialism has to be incorporated into the social values and attitudes of the times. "Once a society places values on material gratification, both luxury and fashion are the immediate and inescapable consequences," according to Dwight E. Robinson, in his discussion of the importance of fashion to business history.[22] Underpinning the notion of fashion is social mobility, usually associated with the middle class and its efforts to improve itself, be in the swim, and to impress those above them and put down those below them. Usually wherever mobility is possible, the middle class can be seen as a critical agent in stimulating fashion. Power is another corollary in the luxury/fashion equation, as well as another indicator of a mobile society in which power has not been out of reach for the aspiring. Fashion cycles, according to the urban historian Gunther Barth, "increased membership in the society of consumers and stimulated identification across social classes."[23]

Interest in fashion historically has usually signified a breakdown in customs as well as an era of prosperity, when wealth could be exhibited. While all the ingredients for a swelling interest in fashion coalesced at the time of the Industrial Revolution (mid-eighteenth to mid-nineteenth century), signs of breakdowns in customs and prosperity appeared at different times. In the sixteenth century, for example, a new, scornful attitude toward old-fashioned clothes and designs appeared. The dramatic demolition by Francis I in 1527 of the medieval castle of the Louvre—the residence of St. Louis and the revered headquarters of the French monarchy—to make way for an Italianate palace, indicates this new attitude toward things of the past. Old styles were not as inviolate as they had been.

The mass production of the nineteenth and twentieth centuries did not kill high fashion, as some thought it might, but it introduced a democratization of luxury generating more consumers, which provided yet another incentive to industry. With the invention in the mid-eighteenth century of the sewing machine and dress patterns, it became possible to mass produce haute couture. And France, the world's leader in women's fashions for centuries, enjoyed a long-standing, cozy relationship between its textile industry, couturiers, and government, which had been able to pump up demands for clothing and fabrics. Dior, for example, was a product of the Cotton Industry Board, which financed him and virtually launched him. For years Dior, Cardin, Givenchy, and other French designers determined the international fashion styles, served a limited luxury market for the likes of the Vanderbilts, and set in motion styles that trickled down to everyday citizens. Today we do not have to wait for that trickle-down because Dior and his confreres, along with a myriad of new designers, from Liz Claiborne to Ralph Lauren, have all sorts of clothes and products for sale in stores all over the world. Pierre Cardin, for example, has licensed his logo to more than 800 products. Department stores of every stripe have such goods displayed not by category but by designer. Designer labels are a code that the product is upscale. This brand identification and advertising further democratized fashion, so now it is "polymorphous and pluralistic," as Fred Davis wrote.[24]

For social and economic critics like Thorstein Veblen, fashion and luxury seem to smack of self-gratification, social climbing, and a lack of identity and character. Nonetheless, interest in fashion and luxury is an inescapable aspect of human nature. That is what Veblen missed in his astute observations of conspicuous consumption, for such frivolous conduct was quite alien to Veblen's Scandinavian background. Yet human beings are not only economic animals; as the business cycles turn on the vagaries of human emotions, so do styles and tastes. After its revolution, Russia deemphasized fashion for a simple, utilitarian dress, which its people eventually found so dull that the country was forced to import as well as produce diverse clothes. And as the doors to the outside world have been opening in China, the drab gray costumes worn by men and women are being replaced with clothing in colors and patterns. Consumers thrive on change and variety.

As new, trendy clothes give the shopper a feeling of being au courant and escaping the dreariness of yesterday, so shopping provides all sorts of escapes from drudgery, boredom, and depression. Early on, department stores recognized the opportunity of offering the housebound woman an escape into a world of fantasy and luxury. Whether Selfridge, Stewart, Wanamaker, or Boucicaut, all the department store pioneers created a "phantasmagoria" for their customers, as Kristin Ross described it, with "orchestrated spectaculars of other worlds."[25] Their intent was to mesmerize the customer and send her into a world of fantasy shopping far removed from her dreary domesticity.

Whether Stewart's marble palace, Bon Marché's fantasy, or Selfridge's "new and wonderful shopping centre," the store became urban theater for the shopper. Theater, of course, was not new to retailing, as entertainment, plays, and feasts had been part of the large regional fairs on the Continent in the late Middle Ages. Such theater became even more interactive at international expositions around the turn of the twentieth century. The 1901 Pan American Exposition's *Short Sermon to Sightseers* advised visitors, "Please remember when you get inside the gates you are part of the show." But it was department stores, the "palaces of consumption," that dramatically exploited the theatrical aspect of retailing.[26] Ordinary store commodities took on a new aura as window displays, store counters, and the whole interior of the store made them seem almost exotic, just as Zola's Denise Baudu felt when she first gazed into the windows of Bon Marché. No longer were these objects seen just for their functions, but as luxuries that could remake a world. The shopper became part of that world when she entered the department store, often publicized as palaces, like A. T. Stewart's marble palace in New York City (fig. 53). As the doorman whisked the snow from her coat and then the cloakroom attendant checked it, she was far removed from her household chores and burdens. The shopper was swept into a sumptuous realm of glamour, with chandeliers, Greek columns, flowers, marble floors, wide stairwells, and high ceilings. In case she never got to Paris, Wanamaker had a life-sized replica of Rue de la Paix. She was a player in the theater of consumption. As Gordon Selfridge said, people came to his store because "it's much brighter than their own homes"; that was how he planned his store with its tearooms, attended marble bathrooms, silence rooms, and attentive clerks. His London store—designed, according to Selfridge, to project "the subdued and disciplined atmosphere of a gentleman's mansion"—reflected the values and attitudes of the time and place and, importantly, responded to the hopes and fantasies of its customers.[27] "It constantly assessed people's hopes for a better life," Gunther Barth states, "and responded to their dreams."[28]

Aside from an escape from reality, department stores offered novelty and change, qualities increasingly in demand as the pace of life quickened and stimuli multiplied. At the dawn of the twentieth-first century, gentility and refinement, the goals of department stores and the driving cultural tenets of the previous century, became passé. In fact, respectability, the emblem of the middle class of the past, now seems almost dowdy and out-of-touch. When the announcement that Washington, D.C.'s, 115-year-old department store, Woodward & Lothrop, was being taken over by Federated Stores, which intended to close its downtown flagship store, the *Washington Post* was flooded with letters, op-ed pieces, and articles lamenting the passing of "the graciousness, the gentility of it all," as Trish Thomas wrote.[29] "Farewell to the days of the downtown department store," Roxanne Roberts wrote in the *Washington Post*, "where ladies put on hats and gloves to shop for sheets."[30]

Wearing hats and gloves to shop and eating sandwiches in the tearoom while models paraded by, and requesting certain tunes to be played on the store organ, are as foreign to a young shopper at Wal-Mart as living in a Venetian palace. Trish Thomas, who is clearly old enough to speak of enjoying a water aerobics class for her creaky limbs, observed: "It's not that everything was good about those times. Women didn't have the control of their own money as they do now, and the only black people in sight were the elevator operators and janitors. But I do miss . . . it all. Price isn't everything.

53. As grand as any Parisian store—the interior of A. T. Stewart's Astor Place store, 1869–70 (collection of the New-York Historical Society)

Bring back manners and serenity, and this shopper will come."[31] And Roberts expressed a more mainstream feeling about the demise of this Washington retailing institution in her farewell "to you fusty, dowdy friend." A friend younger generations did not know nor want to know.[32]

Throughout history, loyalty has been a basic ingredient for successful marketers, whether at the bazaar, corner store, downtown department store, or at cyberspace's dot.com stores. The new online store hopes that an accessible website, popular brand items, and an effective delivery process will inculcate a sense of familiarity and build early customer loyalty calculated to beat the emerging competitors. This loyalty, instead of relying on an old or traditional relationship, stems from brand recognition of specific products and sites, which can change with the speed of fads. Familiarity with and ease of coping with the mechanics of Internet ordering may well produce today's equivalent of knowing what clerk in what department was most help-ful in yesteryear's department store. As Internet shopping loyalty depends on short-term identifications, it seems to be far more mercurial than the senti-mental loyalty to stores in the past. London writer Ann Colcord, in looking back at her childhood trips with her mother in the 1940s to San Francisco department stores like the White House, the City of Paris, and I. Magnin, recalls how each inspired a different sort of loyalty. Much of that loyalty was created by the sense of stability, order, and tradition that the stores symbol-ized. They became reliable friends. You knew each store's features, its layout, departments, its display counters, lighting, elevators and operators, and com-petent clerks, all conservatively dressed in navy dresses or dark skirts and white blouses. "There was something very stable about the stores—and stabilizing about using them," Colcord says.[33]

No longer is shopping a day-long activity with time for pleasant lunches with old friends. There is neither the time nor the inclination for that type of leisurely shopping. Two-thirds of adult women have jobs, and the many demands on their time do not allow them to amble down store aisles checking out rack after rack of clothes, and maybe buying impulsively. For those who have not been exposed to gracious living, the refinement of yes-terday's stores makes them feel uncomfortable, as they sense that the stores are unwelcoming and their clerks condescending. They do not aspire to that kind of gentility, and they fear that all the extras mean higher prices. Also, because they are used to making their own decisions in the supermarket, they do not necessarily want help—or interference—from clerks in other stores, especially clothing stores. Supermarket-style shopping is fast in and out; you see whether what you want is there, and then you leave—without talking to anyone, except maybe exchanging a few pleasantries with the checkout clerk. Then you move on to another store to see whether you can find what you need at the right price.

A restlessness typifies this type of shopping—indeed, it pervades our culture, with fast-changing fads beamed all over the world by television, Inter-net, and faxes, with people winging from one continent to another in a matter of hours, e-mailing everywhere rather than sending letters, skiing the highest peaks, sailing the roughest waters, climbing rugged rocks, microwaving instant meals, and eating fast food faster and faster. The restless pace of shopping is an inherent part of the world of retailing, as new purchases keep the wheels of commerce going. In 1892, Simon Patten noted in *The Consumption of Wealth* that the "standard of life is determined, not so much by what a man has to enjoy, as by the rapidity with which he tires of pleasure, to have a high standard means to enjoy a pleasure intensely and to tire of it quickly."[34]

Although retailing has a kinetic nature as it tries to stimulate the shop-per to buy more and more, stores also offer some durable and lasting social amenities and egalitarian benefits, which can indirectly stimulate continued shopping. In providing a place away from home and work where people feel welcome and where they can meet friends, neighbors, and strangers, stores have continued a timeless social and often egalitarian function. The picture of the proverbial country store with people chatting around the pot-bellied stove may romanticize the past, but it does not portray the full dimensions of the store's social functions. Whether at country general stores or at the fairs and expositions in the Middle Ages, at the city department store or at today's e-commerce sites, the rich, poor, black, white, foreign, or native have all been seen as potential customers. This egalitarianism is a constant factor in retailing in all but a handful of exclusive shops and salons—and that important feature of shopping is often overlooked. Indeed, shopping can be seen as a social leveler. As Daniel Boorstin, paraphrasing Emile Zola, said, "The department store democratized luxury."[35] But the only fact that distorts that democratization is the economic reality that money is needed to pay for the purchases.[36]

Primarily and historically a woman's activity, shopping mirrors a woman's attitude toward herself, her relationship with men, men's attitudes toward her, and her status in the world. Over time we see how women's roles and attitudes have changed—and also how so many have remained the same. Woman has been a commodity for man—"man's chattel," as Veblen bluntly put it.[37] And yet men have also been seductive targets for women. Despite the emancipation of women and the recent feminism, the captor-captive, possessor-possessed, and seducer-seduced roles continue in a variety of forms: clothes, commodities, perfume, jewels, luxuries—and shopping—are entangled in the male-female relationships. As the reins of Puritanism loosened during the Industrial Revolution and commodities were produced in greater volume, money seeped into the middle classes, encouraging social and economic mobility. Shopping emerged as a new recreation for women. Items once considered luxuries, like clothes, lace, and handsome furniture, became necessities—and were available at shops, stores, expositions, and markets, which mushroomed in all the large cities and many smaller ones. Shopping became an enjoyable and time-consuming activity for those with money and inclination to spend. It became a bourgeois pastime. Consumer goods became the objects as well as the tools of desire (fig. 54).

Romance, smothered by rigid religions and corresponding mores, emerged along with sentiment in this period as a corollary of taste, aesthetics, and civilized society. In the era of Jane Austen, sentiment both of thought and feeling was accepted. In fact, romance was part of a large amorphous ideal of beauty, although it was restrained and ordered, as in the aristocratic ethic. By the late eighteenth and early nineteenth century, the romantic ideal blossomed. Where it was once banned, it was then considered acceptable in a constrained fashion, and the romantic ethic translated into beauty and became an inspirational factor in one's life. Art and taste were seen as a "sign of moral and spiritual worth," according to Campbell.[38]

54. Window Shopping, *painting by Everett Shinn, 1903 (collection of Arthur and Holly Magill)*

This was an important step for consumerism, because pleasure was recognized as an aspect of human dignity and the search for pleasure was good in itself. This laid the groundwork for a philosophy of self-realization and self-expression that legitimized emotional pleasure. Buying beautiful china was acceptable in this strain of sentiment. The commercial world, still charged by the utilitarian philosophy stemming from the rationalism and harshness of the Puritans, was tied to the romantic through an acceptance of individualistic ethics. But the bourgeoisie of the eighteenth century was able to blend both the utilitarian and sentimental into its pursuit of upward mobility. Both men and women were intertwined in this emerging thinking, as were money, social climbing, consumption of goods, and self-esteem. Consumer goods were magnets for pleasure, and women were often seen as commodities of pleasure. Womanly attractions might be featured, and these could appeal to women's instincts for attractiveness and their interest in being seductive to men, or, in an extreme, their being narcissistic. For Freud, such narcissism was seen in the late eighteenth and the nineteenth centuries in bourgeois, domestically involved women who were "absorbed in themselves, their beauty, their desirability as potential objects of male love," as Rachel Bowlby observed.[39]

Women were often pawns in this world of pleasurable shopping. They were viewed frequently as status symbols used to show off the husband's material success and his hard work to achieve that success. Not only did this type of shopper help to propel a family up the social ladder, but she let the world know that her husband had money to burn. The woman could wear the finery, furnish the house, and be the agent of ostensible wealth. "Women were still in the full sense the property of the men," Veblen states. "The performance of conspicuous leisure and consumption came to be part of the services required of them. . . . In the modern civilised scheme of life the woman is still, in theory, the economic dependent of the man,—that, perhaps in a highly idealised sense, she is still the man's chattel."[40] She could spend her time shopping, and indeed thinking about fulfilling her pleasures, but these pleasures also had to reflect the husband's desires and needs. Eighteenth-century shopping opened the door to a new cult of women: a world of pleasure, beauty, body, fashion, and flirtation. A new excitement was brewing, as was a passion for possessions, but they all required the husband's money and approval. Women were the "willing consumers" but also the "yielding objects to the powerful male subject forming, and informing them of their desires," according to Rachel Bowlby. "The success of the capitalist sales project rested on the passive acceptance or complicity of its would-be buyers," she observes, "and neither side of the developing relationship can be thought independently of the other."[41]

Although women were pawns in the world of galloping consumerism, shopping did enable them to get out into the world (fig. 55). The nineteenth-century department store, for example, "became permissible public space for women's social interchange, replacing in a sense both church and salon,"

55. *Women shoppers stepping out on Tremont Street in Boston, 1891 (Library of Congress, Prints and Photographs Division, Washington, D.C.)*

according to Kristin Ross.[42] This was a step in the emancipation of women. The early department stores served an important role in transforming the role of women—bolstering women's sense of independence and helping them enter the public sphere on their own, as contemporary scholars like Erika Rappaport and Lynne Walker have discussed in their work on Victorian women shoppers. For Selfridge, as Rappaport mentioned in her book on women in London's West End, *Shopping for Pleasure*, "shopping was pleasurable because of its public setting. He idealized this public sphere as a site for personal exploration, self-fulfillment, and independence." Not only did his store provide respectability as well as sensual pleasure, but "access to social metropolitan culture." Thus, these Victorian safe havens catering to women's wants ironically opened doors so women felt empowered to publicly participate in the outside world. "I helped emancipate women," Selfridge stated. "I came along just at the time when they wanted to step out on their own."[43] And he was correct, as he and other early department store entrepreneurs did help in the emancipation of women.

These women shoppers were partial decision-makers in consumer shopping. And that buying was power. The suffragist Elizabeth Cady Stanton advised the congressman's wife, who consulted her husband on every purchase, to go buy a new stove because her poorly equipped kitchen prevented her from producing the quality meals that her husband expected. Yet the congressman's wife hesitated, as she had "never purchased a darning needle without consulting" her husband and "he does not think a new stove is needed." To which Stanton responded, "Buy a new one this very day! . . . Now when your husband explodes . . . sit and gaze out of the window with that sad far-away look women know so well how to affect. If you can summon tears at pleasure, a few would not be amiss. . . . Men cannot resist beauty and tears."[44] This early feminist's advice blended a new empowerment with ageless feminine wiles. And mixing the new freedom of shopping on one's own with the old role of the woman subordinate to her provider husband continued for generations. Buying the kitchen stove was not like buying a frivolous dress that was meant to seduce, but it was a means of pleasing her husband. Still, this generation of female consumers moved women one step up the ladder toward emancipation. And women were gaining more rights in the late nineteenth century as they sought higher education, divorce, and more legal rights to own property and eventually to vote. Even in the early twenty-first century, shopping provides some similar yet elementary emancipation opportunities for women bound by religious restrictions in countries like Saudi Arabia. In Riyadh, the capital of Saudi Arabia, women shrouded in black from head to foot feel that they can escape some of those binding restrictions as they drop their veils and show their hair in new westernized shopping malls. These contemporary emporia are public spaces where, escaping the watchful eyes of the religious police, women and men mall-crawl together and women enjoy some wafts of freedom.

The woman's subordinate role, either in the house, with her husband, or in society in general, often stemmed from her low opinion of herself. For women, shopping has been intricately involved with self-esteem—and low self-esteem is the weakness that the retailing world has always tried to manipulate. All the fantasies of being transformed by the new dress imply that the old dress—the old self—is not glamorous enough. The self-confident dowager does not need to swing with the latest fashion, for her self-respect requires no artificial bolstering. That dowager can wear her age-old tweed suits and not care what people think of her. Most people need a boost now and then to help "define themselves," like Doonesbury's Boopsie, but for some people the self-esteem problems are so severe that they can become addicted to shopping.

For some shoppers, "buying can become an all-encompassing central part of their existence," according to Ronald Faber. "They experience uncontrollable urges to shop or buy," whether or not things are needed for themselves or others.[45] Their disease, called oniomania, results from low self-esteem and a feeling of inadequacy, according to some experts. Even though self-help groups exist, like Shopaholics, Ltd., the problem is compounded, Faber speculates, because it is not taken seriously by the general public, so shopping addicts have trouble finding people willing to listen to their troubles, which only makes them feel worse about themselves. London scholar Ann Colcord's studies of people who, like Imelda Marcos, buy far more shoes than they need, reveal that shoppers are driven by a mix of motives, from ambition, restlessness, and vengeance to the need for treats, second chances, and the illicit.[46]

Shopping provides many with psychic satisfactions, called retail therapy by researchers. For a busy person like Candice Carpenter, CEO of iVillage.com, "the Women's Network," a shopping trip "to buy a few Versace gowns was really therapeutic," she reported.[47] For lonely individuals, it is a pleasure just to see other people in a store and to participate in the outside world. For those who feel they accomplish little, the completion of a sales transaction in the store provides that needed sense of accomplishment as well as a product to use or wear. For those who feel low, the prospect of a new piece of clothing or appliance can pick them up. "Had the blues. I bought me a dress," wrote Maria Dyer, a young woman from a relatively substantial cotton farming family near Macon, Mississippi, in her diary in June 1852.[48] "Shopping should be fun," according to an article, "Your Smile Means a Lot to Your Customer" in Baltimore's Hutzler's department store's employee magazine, *Tips and Taps*, "because deep-seated personal and social needs can be satisfied—if shopping is a pleasure. Self-gratification—relief from boredom—contacts for the lonely—opportunities to command attention, and respect—the pleasure of acquiring lovely things—all are important psychological needs. . . . And all can be satisfied through shopping."[49] But on a different note, Eugene Linden in his book *Affluence and Discontent* concluded that "a consumer society harnesses the energy of the discontents."[50]

Those psychic needs have always been played on by the Willy Lomans of the world. Some of their sales pitches have been merely rational—describing a product's price, attributes, warranties, and maintenance, but they have also entailed manipulating the irrational and emotional side of the buyer. While the essence of selling may be timeless and universal, the process of selling has grown unbelievably complicated and sophisticated. Selling a product was initially the job of the individual seller, peddler, hawker, or shopkeeper. Then, manufacturers themselves got into selling, and later the influential and growing industry of advertising and public relations emerged to assist manufacturers in the selling process. "New techniques for national marketing emerged in tandem with the mass-produced products they promoted," as Susan Strasser discusses in *Satisfaction Guaranteed*. "A population accustomed to homemade products and unbranded merchandise had to be converted into a national market for standardized, advertised, brand-named goods in general."[51] The possibilities of advertising products in newspapers were demonstrated by the success of the first full-page advertisement placed by John Wanamaker in 1879, not for a consumer product, but to celebrate General Grant's return from his trip around the world. That advertisement opened a Pandora's box of possibilities for advertising brand items. By the end of the nineteenth century, advertising was seen by Jacques Offenbach, a foreign traveler in the United States, as "playing upon the brain of men like a musician does upon a piano."[52] Advertising was soon infiltrating every crevice of our lives, from the products we want, the newspapers and magazines we read, the television, movies, videos, and computer screens we watch, the clothes we wear, to the buses, subways, and cars we ride. Some of this advertising has been overt and some much less so.

The growth of advertising parallels the development of the behavioral sciences, which have provided the intellectual fuel for this engine in the capitalistic consumer world. The manipulation of the buyer hinges on how that buyer is conceived as functioning—psychologically, morally, and ethically—and how those functions can be reached. The success of advertising, public relations, and all marketing depends on perceptions of cultural changes as well as methods of trying to change them. As capitalism and the enjoyment of the fruits of industry required a revamping of moral and ethical sanctions, so did advertising need new values, attitudes, and basic interpretations of human functions and inclinations. Merle Curti suggested that changing concepts of human nature were at the crux of the innovations in the relatively brief history of advertising. From 1890 to 1910, Curti saw the dominant rationalistic image challenged in the struggle of "reason and will over feeling." From 1910 to 1930, the irrational concept of human nature was explored and the nonrational impulses were viewed as critical factors in the chemistry of human decisions. Men and women were considered malleable, and their purchasing habits, therefore, were influenced by "inspirational hunches." This opened the door for advertising and public relations to use the new behavioral sciences to change people's habits—and their thinking. By the 1940s, according to Curti's interpretation of the evolution of advertising, the shift to "high powered" behavioral sciences was fully accepted, with Freud's emphasis on the unconscious inspiring a new and significant direction in advertising.[53] This motivational research provided powerful tools in the manipulation of the advertising target, most often the consumer.

A more covert manipulation of the consumer, or

56. Ziegfeld girls stay slender by avoiding sweets and reaching for Lucky Strikes, the "healthy cigarette" (advertisment published in Hearst's International Cosmopolitan, March 1929)

"persuasion"—using both motivational research and plain common sense—was introduced in the emerging profession of public relations led by Edward L. Bernays, whom former city editor of the New York Herald Tribune Stanley Walker said had "taken the side-show barker and given him a philosophy and a new and awesome language."[54] Bernays, who insisted on calling himself a public relations counsel, saw his field as "cooperative relationship with the public," interpreting "the client to the public and the public to the client,"[55] and that included "persuasion to modify attitudes and actions and integrating attitudes and actions of institutions with its public and vice versa."[56] This covert type of marketing was subtle and pervasive.

In his aggressive work for the American Tobacco Company's Lucky Strike cigarettes, Bernays introduced a "new competition" between cigarettes and sweets (fig. 56).[57] "Reach for a Lucky instead of a sweet" was the slogan of a campaign involving surveys by third-party institutions, often under the guise of obtaining information.[58] Doctors, medical groups, diabetics' organizations, and home economics specialists offered statements about excessive consumption of cane sugar, military men offered testimonials—some in articles prepared for newspapers, others in letters written to important people—to substantiate Bernays's claims. Women were a part of this "propaganda" campaign, as Bernays described his efforts to George W. Hill of the American Tobacco Company.[59] With the "slender Modish" woman as the model for the new female smoker, one of Bernays's many efforts to encourage women to smoke involved infiltrating a Galveston, Texas, beauty contest in 1929. First, it was necessary to determine what the Chamber of Commerce felt about women smoking, and then to "penetrate with our idea of Lucky Strikes for women. It might be possible to get them to smoke in the parade or to have Lucky Strikes at the banquet given to the beautiful girls."[60] Bernays also tried to interest Cartier and Dunhill in featuring accessories for women smokers, like cigarette holders, cases, and vanities, to encourage smoking as "reflected by the use of smart smoking accessories."[61] He wrote to Dunhill, "It's a wise girl who knows when to exchange a toasted marshmallow for a toasted cigarette."[62] Fashion editors of magazines would receive stories on the "importance of cigarette cases and holders to smartly dressed women."[63]

To the Seven Sisters women's colleges, a questionnaire was sent inquiring about their rules and regulations for smoking; Smith College would not reply until it understood how the requested information would be used.[64] Smith was not the only uncooperative institution leery of surveys, articles, and press releases from often unknown organizations. The editor of the *Ludington (Michigan) Daily News* found the articles sent to him "cleverly camouflaged, but they go to the waste paper basket without a detour."[65] The Stevens Point, Wisconsin, newspaper had a printed postcard, "It is contrary to our policy to publish advertising material in the guise of news. We will appreciate it if you will discontinue sending press agent copy on _____." "Tobacco" was filled in the blank.[66]

The successful propaganda campaigns of the two world wars, which discredited the enemy while building patriotism, proved the possibilities of "engineering public opinion," Bernays stated. Propaganda was no longer an esoteric term but a field with vast opportunities to change how people thought and behaved. The federal propaganda, with all its posters, radio spots, and slogans, was dramatized by President Wilson during the First World War and later by President Roosevelt's radio chats, and more slogans, posters, and radio spots, and also by such national organizations as the American Red Cross. This recognition of the power of propaganda coincided with the development of large-scale industrial publicity and the role of public relations in its two-way operation of persuading and informing for the "mutual understanding of institutions and the public," as Bernays explained it. During the Depression, American industry learned how to sell products in tough times, realizing that "good will" had to be part of the selling equation, which was a big advance from the days of William Vanderbilt's "the public be damned." As Theodore Vail, president of AT&T, said earlier, "We have found . . . that our interests were best served when the public interests were best served," and that required some understanding of the public and its interests.[67]

Motivational research, or consumer behavior theory, provided some of the clues to the workings of the consumer. Because of the push for war materiel during World War II, mass-production techniques were refined, so after the war, peacetime consumer products could be mass produced faster than the old ones wore out. The general public, with pent-up needs from both the war years and the Depression, along with the veterans setting up new homes, provided a large supply of ready-made consumers. But, as the supply of goods was greater than the demand of consumers, advertisers still needed to invent ways to stimulate even more consumer demand. The challenge for the advertiser was "convincing the consumer that he needs a new product before the old one is worn out," said Gordon Lippincott, an industrial designer, in 1947.[68] The problem was not with the real need or the basics, but with items known as perceived or learned needs by advertising and motivational researchers. "One of the outgrowths of mass production and the tremendous advertising indulged in to have people consume the products of mass production," reads a 1929 letter from the Toledo Owens Bottle Company in response to a Bernays letter from Lewis Haney of New York University's Bureau of Business Research, "will be the creating of new and larger desires on the part of the people which, eventually, will raise them to higher cultural levels provided they are kept in position of employment and in a condition of employment that enables them to satisfy the wants that are created."[69]

These learned desires are not inherent but are the products of careful manipulation. At first, advertising concentrated on preventing social threats, like body odor, and health threats, like disease. Johnson and Johnson's early advertisements, for example, focused on the mother's interest in her baby, not the products; and in a sense the advertising company was playing the role of mediator. But that role became more explicit as the advertiser became the interactor, trying to enhance social interactions with products like cosmetics—for instance, Pond's skin creams could make your face so smooth and alluring that no Mr. Right could resist you.

Advertising in women's magazines illustrates the nature of today's motivational advertising and its role in the business and consumer worlds. In analyzing advertisements in women's magazines, Ellen McCracken describes the role of advertising on both the magazine and the reader. With women recognized as primary purchasers of goods and services, women's magazines are targets of massive advertising; in fact, 95 percent of the space in some women's magazines is devoted to advertising, a good portion of which is selling food and cosmetics. And this advertising starts bombarding women at an early age. In *Seventeen* magazine, the teenage reader is marked as "born to shop," so advertising begins to shape the teenagers' desires and fantasies in puberty, when peer pressure and interest in sex mount. Seen as "windows of her future self," magazines like *Mademoiselle, Glamour, Self, Seventeen, Teen,* and *Young Miss* can teach lifelong habits of consumption. Indeed, these magazines wallow in the commodity-based culture and even have difficulty separating advertising and editorial content. As McCracken explains, advertising and editorial content form a continuum; publishers use advertising on the basis of "editorial suitability" and then "showcase" products in an "appropriate background." Brands are explicitly mentioned in articles, a practice called brand reciprocity. In *Teen's* June 1982 issue, two Schering-Plough products, Dr. Scholl's Athletic Foot Gel and Coppertone's For Faces Only, are recommended in its "Dear Beauty Editor" section and are also "subtly connected" to nine purchased advertisements and three covert advertisements for Schering-Plough products, McCracken found. Covert advertisements, as defined by McCracken, are "promotions disguised as editorial material or hidden in some other form so that they appear to be non-advertising."[70]

By the year 2000, the line between advertising and editorial content had disappeared with Condé Nast's new magazine *Lucky,* "a magazine about shopping . . . created for—and, of course, by—enthusiastic, even obsessive, shoppers," writes Kim France, *Lucky's* editor-in-chief.[71] What would have been advertising items in older magazines, maybe with some mentions in editorial pages, have been transformed into overt editorial material in *Lucky.* The magazine's feature on shoes, fifty-five of them on eleven pages, lists style numbers, manufacturers' or designers' names, prices, and telephone numbers, just as they would be in a catalogue. And *Lucky* even provides the reader with detachable adhesive labels to "flag your favorites." When crossing the line by transforming advertising into editorial material, a magazine, not usually considered a selling device, carries more authority than a commercial company's catalogue and, one would think, more ethical responsibility.

Blending advertising and editorial material in these women's magazines not only feeds female fantasies but projects a glamorized, commodity-driven world to potential shoppers, from teenagers trying to be adults to seniors hoping to cling to their youth. And although women have been seen as primary purchasers of goods and services, men are increasingly the targets of national advertising. The men's fashion section of the *New York Times* has become as thick as its women's fashion section. In the February 20–27, 1995, issue of the *New Yorker,* 24 percent of the advertisements was directly targeted to men and 21 percent to women, with 65 percent geared to both sexes—including car advertisements once thought mainly of interest to men but now of interest to both sexes thanks to increased unisex purchasing, single households, and women's influence in major decision-making.

Men, teenagers, children, and seniors, as well as women, are treated as potential consumers by manufacturers and advertisers. Commercially driven media reach all ages. Children are bombarded with advertisements—some estimate 20,000 per year—and perhaps most troubling are the television ads, which are blended in children's television programs. Children watch Power Rangers, who also appear in advertisements for the program. Some very young children may well find it difficult to differentiate advertisements from the substance of the programs. But evidently that differentiation occurs fairly early, as proved by children's high brand recognition and their appetite for nationally advertised goods. Education of the young about brand products results from advertising saturation, even with what have been considered innocent and safe children's activities, like viewing Disney movies. A Disney movie such as *Pocahontas* is not an event by itself but part of a larger effort to sell dolls, T-shirts, games, videos, and other paraphernalia. While national attention was focused on violence and crime in films, on the Internet, and in other media, the alarming commercial pressure put on this young and vulnerable market has not been adequately addressed.

Yet when advertising is criticized, a defense of jobs and employment is proposed: "Advertising has stimulated work," the Ayer Advertising Agency states.[72] Advertising creates consumer interest, which stirs the consumer to work hard to buy consumer goods, which in turn keeps the production line whirring. That same justification was used by Samuel Johnson several centuries ago for capitalism's want/get–make/advertise mentality. The wheels of capitalism run on the growth of new and more consumers—which involves ever "improving" production technologies, advertising, and marketing skills. And advertising and its motivational research have helped find consumers for the products of capitalism's industries to the point where "contemporary man has an unlimited hunger for more and more goods," according to Erich Fromm.[73]

The success of consumerism, as promoted by the economic pacemakers and their team in making an individual's self-fulfillment dependent upon possession of material goods, hinges on combining many social, economic, ethical, and moral factors. One new factor, which has made consumer purchasing available on a scale never previously contemplated, is the mass availability of credit. There is no need to defer any gratification when one holds a plastic credit card. For generations, purchases were made only when there was money in the bank to pay for them. Now, for the e-shopper, the credit card is the only way to pay for purchases. All you need is a small monthly payment—with whopping interest to the bank, retailer, or whoever issued the credit card. Consumer credit card balances experienced a tenfold growth from just 1980 to 1997.[74] Retail installment credit went from $13.9 billion in 1970 to $39.2 billion in 1985.[75] It was not only the large number of credit card holders—100 million people owned bank credit cards like Visa and Mastercard—spending $678 billion in 1997 that was remarkable, but the growing shopping debt incurred by those card holders. Fifty-nine percent of the 1997 bank credit card spending involved debt, which amounted to almost

$63 billion in interest for a year. For retail store credit, 108 million card holders with 614 million cards spent $121 billion with 73 percent of the spending involving debt.[76] These are heavy debt burdens for the consumer—and major sources of income for banks and other credit card issuers like retail stores. As Galbraith pointed out in *The Affluent Society*, the acceptance of credit as part of everyday consuming was a triumph of modern merchandising over one of the lingering basic Puritan values, living free of debt. No longer need one be haunted by debt, like Benjamin Franklin, who said that he would "Rather go to Bed Supperless than rise in Debt."[77] Now along with production and marketing, there is a new member of the team, credit.

The consumer is caught in a squirrel cage—new products and styles are continuously being introduced, generating even greater consumer demand. It is hard to determine whether rising aspirations or the economy's need to sell more goods came first, but they have been intricately connected. With the economic machinery producing ever more products, advertising pushing more goods on the consumer, more workers earning higher salaries, and fewer moral restrictions on enjoying material and luxury goods, it is no wonder that consumers have found themselves in a work/spend cycle.

A critical factor, of course, in these consumer shifts has been the changing role of women. Time-saving products of the industrial system and manipulation by the wily advertisers of that system and the values it was promoting have affected women's buying habits. Women, once so occupied with "household industries," as the economist Paul Nystrom called them, that they had little time for shopping, became the major family shoppers by the 1920s. As advertising geared to women increased in the early 1920s, women became the major shoppers by the late 1920s: 85 percent of goods were purchased by women at the end of that decade.[78] Also helping women to get out of the house were new labor-saving devices, such as washing machines, vacuum cleaners, and refrigerators, as well as ready-made food, like bread and cakes. Women in cities, noted Nystrom, "have nearly all forgotten how to make bread. The women in town and country now buy at least one half their bread."[79] This urban woman often required more consumer goods, both because she was not as self-sufficient as her country cousins and because her urban life called for more and better goods and clothes. While a farm family might spend 10 to 17 percent of its income for clothing, an industrial family would spend 13 to 18 percent and the clerical family 20 to 22 percent.

Today, with more women working than staying at home, a new dimension has been added to the role of woman as consumer. Two-thirds of women work, half of them are married, and of those married workers, 60 percent have children under six. Housework has been devalued to the point where "some working wives are motivated less by what they are going toward than what they are getting away from. Their reasons for working are to escape from the confining, narrow lives available to them as full-time homemakers." Work is a "passport that will take them out of the kitchen."[80] And the outside world of business and production provides many satisfactions formerly found in homemaking, a radical change in women's perception of themselves. They no longer need to depend on their spouses for a "derived status." Women, not just a handful of "career women," but a majority of working women, can create their own status. At the cocktail party in the 1990s a woman was embarrassed to admit she was just a housewife. Unless she had a worthwhile or seemingly successful job, the college alumna is hesitant to appear at college reunions or write to college alumnae bulletins. The housewife is passé in the era of attaché-carrying, pinstripe-suited professional women, and so is the inveterate shopper of the housewife era.

Along with the changing roles of women, increasing democratization has appeared on the retailing scene. No longer do styles necessarily trickle down from the world of haute couture, but in many cases they percolate up from working-class clothes. Instead of fashion styles being broadcast from the latest worn at Newport, New York City's Eighth Avenue Subway A train riders often set the new styles. Blue jeans, once associated with blue-collar workers, became a universal uniform. Youths seeking more and different styles worked in tandem with the producers whose world requires perpetual changes and creates the wants they seek to satisfy. But societal waves come and go. Whereas the suburbs were the goal of most middle-class families from the 1940s to the 1960s, the younger generations growing up in those postwar suburbs revolted against the dull, confining, and conforming life molded by mass production, advertising, and straight values. A rejection of the "conformist quietude of cold war suburbia" was diagnosed by the Ewens, who elaborated by describing the suburban way of life as "one in which consumption was patriotic duty."[81] Although postwar suburban life was consumption-bound, the reaction to it was not necessarily anti-consumption, but that of a different kind of consumption. The mood of the late 1960s and the 1970s, bucking the blandness of mass-controlled suburban life, set in motion a new trend: the casual, anti-mainstream, nonconformist style. The angry young knocked the gray-suited suburbanite off his pedestal only to have him replaced by a Ralph Lauren–bedecked yuppie. Even Wall Street lawyers have exchanged pinstriped suits for carefully considered "casual" dress. And a new line of self-consciously nonconformist clothing became the fashion—blue jeans, pants, and casual dress for everyone.

Today a cacophony of styles prevails with less rigidity than in the past, but with this greater range of permissible styles comes a greater range of retailing possibilities. Even those who fought the country's involvement in the Vietnam War and sought alternative ways of life—whether in communes or on Vermont farms—have provided a stimulus for new consumer styles. Long hair, loose clothing, natural fabrics, rugged work clothes, sturdy boots, native goods, and recyclable products had made their way into the retailing main-stream by the late 1980s. The consumer, now swamped with catalogues for outdoor clothing, finds chunky shoes, work boots, and natural fabrics in style, despite all the advances made in drip-dry, no-care materials. Thus, the counterculture can become part of the mainstream as retailing responds to the changing tastes, desires, and, of course, hopes of potential shoppers.

Another consumer is the boutique shopper—a recreational shopper for nonessentials—the opposite of the counterculture shopper, for whom authenticity has been a priority. The boutique shopper is looking for treats, not gritty, authentic experiences. Boutique shopping has become a major attraction in urban shopping for new urbanites, for suburbanites who fled the crime-scarred cities, and for tourists looking for safe entertainment. The festival marketplaces led the way in this type of shopping, which features cutely named boutiques and eateries with a veneer of old-fashioned places. Instead of meeting a friend for lunch at the downtown department store, the shopper—or office worker—meets her friend at the usually franchised restaurant in the gentrified waterfront bontopia, such as South Street Seaport. Like the patrons of Howard Johnson's of the past, these boutique shoppers have been seeking safe and reliable retail havens. The popularity of this type of shopping has spread to downtown streets, interiors of buildings, and even airports.

Shopping provides the illusion of freedom. New items, new stores, new choices, new advertising seem to offer endless opportunities to possess countless items—both seemingly essential, like microwave ovens, to frivolous luxuries, like furs. Consumer luxuries like yachts, formerly associated with the Vanderbilts and New York Yacht Club members, can theoretically be owned by any upper-middle-class person interested in plying the crowded waters of Long Island Sound or Chesapeake Bay. This freedom of choice, heralded by the capitalist machinery of production and advertising, while apparently democratic, is quite the opposite, because consumption depends on the ability to pay for the goods. Many Americans with limited funds are either priced out of the game of consumerism or, if they try to play, are sunk in overwhelming debt. Underlying much of consumerism is an assumption of exclusivity—of having something that others do not have, of seeming to be a favored person by virtue of owning something expensive and therefore special. As soon as others acquire that item, that exclusivity disappears, and it is time to get something new. So the cycle continues; the consumer always wants more, thereby perpetuating the want/get gap and the drama/reality mirage. But this constant drama has many subplots. Many play this want/get/impress/put-down game, but many others are left out because they cannot afford to get into the theater. Those who are disenfranchised suffer from the stigma of not being in the mainstream and not having those consumer goods, as well as from simply coveting those consumer goods, symbols of success and well-being. Some argue that the system is democratic, as all you need to enter is money, and everyone has the ability to earn money. But history shows that in fact all do not have equal opportunity of earning due to educational, psychological, and environmental deficiencies.

The consumer is both a willing and captive player in the game of consumerism. For the most part enjoying a culture defined by consumer products, the consumer is also a captive to a system with sophisticated communication techniques subtly manipulating his or her desires and wants. This system, run by fewer and larger corporations, determines what can be chosen by the consumer. Whether because of the power and skills of the corporate world or a lack of interest or understanding on the part of the consumer, efforts at consumer reform and empowerment have difficulty succeeding in the United States. Some safety and health issues of consumer products are now under government scrutiny—usually after egregious problems. But cooperatives and community-owned stores have been a rarity. Even the Co-op store in Berkeley, California, failed. Instead, a retail Darwinism, propelled by the free enterprise system, has produced the dominant pattern of the small, independent, and often convenient grocery stores being swept aside by larger chain stores, which become larger and larger one-stop shopping centers, farther and farther removed from many of their less mobile and less affluent consumers.

The consumer has an extraordinary willingness to participate in a culture continuously defined by consumer products. These goods have captured a place in the upwardly rising society that none of our ancestors would have envisioned. The endless quest for more, newer, bigger, and better products to bolster one's ego, prop up one's image, or just provide pleasure and entertainment reflects an expanding cultural gap in our society. "Things fill up the empty spaces in our lives," according to Juliet Schor.[82] Emptiness and boredom, along with all the related problems of loneliness, drug and alcohol addiction, and depression, seem to smolder in our lives, and for many Americans, consumer products are bought in the hope that they will squelch that smoldering. Some observers of the socioeconomic scene see this endless quest for material objects as an indictment of our educational system and cultural values. Compared to people in other countries, American shoppers seem to buy more quickly with less attention to quality and product value.[83] But then the American standard of living is higher, the income level is higher, and rising aspirations more frequent, as are the producers of consumer products and their advertisers.

Homes have been transformed into electronic pleasure domes, with television sets, computers, video players, CD players, Jacuzzis, pools, and microwave ovens to provide instant treats to all those for whom life requires constant pick-me-ups. And the inhabitants of these pleasure domes seem to have little time for such traditional home activities as baking cakes, making Halloween costumes, or collecting stamps. Instead of taking pride in the homemade birthday cake, the working mother picks up one at the bakery section of the grocery store. The Halloween costume is now purchased ready-made at any price, depending on taste and income. The father and son play computer games instead of pasting foreign stamps into the stamp album. A lack of creativity and self-confidence seems to prevail. Others are relied on for advice on the simplest of daily decisions—on what to wear, how to decorate the house, how to exercise, and what to eat. The time and effort spent in sewing doll's clothes or collecting stamps are not part of the age of quick bytes, Barbie dolls, and Power Rangers. And this means less involvement in the step-by-step creativity of everyday activities and fewer opportunities to develop skills that can bolster a sense of accomplishment and pride in oneself.

The habitual and almost addictive quest for consumer products can be an empty activity for the individual and culturally draining for society. While some "things" are needed, many provide only short-term pleasure— and then they often require replacement. Few add to the richness and depth of the culture. Indeed, Americans have the shrunken inside lives that D. H. Lawrence observed in the 1920s.[84] On the other hand, America's outside lives are well supported by consumer products—and that certainly helps to recharge the engine of production. And this engine—along with the powerful assistance of overt advertising and covert public relations—continues to stimulate new desires and hopes in susceptible consumers.

Societal Pressures

When Boopsie joined the ranks of the "I shop, therefore I am" crowd, she was propelled by more than a quest for individual satisfactions. Major social, economic, and moral shifts were changing the way she—and everyone—lived and shopped. As the strictures of Protestantism loosened in the eighteenth and nineteenth centuries, making it possible for the products of the Industrial Revolution to be bought and enjoyed, so have more recent societal shifts changed attitudes about shopping so that it has become a national passion. But there are hints of cracks in that consuming passion.

Many forces have been at work. Americans' most basic fears and hopes have been reshaped by tumultuous events, like advent of the atomic bomb, the Vietnam War, automation, and a global economy, all of which defy our control and threaten our sense of individual power and freedom. Automation is having as profound an impact as the Industrial Revolution on how, why, and where we live, work, and shop. The security and conformity of the corporate organization man of the 1950s seem as remote as the horse-drawn buggy, for in fifty years corporate culture has changed almost as radically as the technologies spawned by automation. Today's corporate world bursts with newly created Silicon Valley–type companies in which brain power matters, not loyalty, and the country's old blue-chip companies, sleek with pared-down staffs and boosted profits, suffer few conscience pangs as they fire thousands of workers yet reward their CEOs with salaries, stock options, and bonuses totaling millions of dollars. Individual entrepreneurs like Donald Trump enjoy their "ego deals," which Trump found a "great way to do business" as he lets his "ego rule his instincts."[85] In retailing, today's Category Killers, Big Boxes, and dot.coms, products of modern technology, have not a trace of yesteryear's corporate loyalty to workers or community. Instead, a new individualism and a new corporate ethic, symptoms of profound changes in values and attitudes, expectations and fears, have helped to create a mainstream style of living that has been lengthening our lives while changing our attitudes about credit and debt, and time and distance—and, most important for shopping, the role of women.

Paradoxically, in this period when our lives and activities have been stretched, a shrinkage has started to appear in our cocoon living and in some of the values of the new individualism. Despite this stretching and shrinking, a striking common trend appears: a growing remoteness in our daily lives. And for shopping, this increasing remoteness has important physical, economic, political, and social implications for individuals and communities. Mega-corporations with distant headquarters own networks of vast and impersonal stores staffed by "deskilled," usually part-time workers, who receive few if any benefits. The local store run by a townsperson, often the grandson of the founder, is disappearing, along with personal service and a low-key atmosphere, which provided time and opportunities for socializing. As automation enables stores to be run remotely and the Internet allows us to shop remotely, the face-to-face sociability associated with shopping is reduced—and yet, the need for it persists.

Stretched Living

As incomes, expenditures for consumer goods, and the taste for more and better things have increased, a stretching has occurred in family budgets, in daily schedules, in responsibilities as parents and children, in loyalties, and even in the suburban style of living. Money, time, life, and distance have been extended in ways that people would never have imagined fifty years ago, and this stretched living will have powerful influences on how people live and shop.

Suburban Living

Among the factors influencing shopping, such as the role and attitudes of women, economic and corporate changes, and attitudes toward community, government, and the private sector, one of the most significant has been suburbanization and the fundamental divide created between downtowns and the suburbs—between rich and poor, black and white, middle class and indigent, and growth and decay. Race, along with the growing numbers of people unable to attain America's mainstream middle-class suburban way of life, has created problems that affect every aspect of urban and suburban living—and, of course, shopping.

This volcanic shift in the roles of the cities and their suburbs started slowly. Until the 1950s, downtowns were still the hub, and suburbia was considered an extension of the city. In describing the early suburb Riverside, west of Chicago, designed by Frederick Law Olmsted and Calvert Vaux in 1871, the Riverside Improvement Company assured prospective residents that a "life at Riverside involves no banishment from all that is good in city life."[86] People lived, worked, and shopped in the center city; that was where the offices, restaurants, stores, movies, theaters, symphonies, clubs, main library, doctors, and hospitals were. Until the late 1960s and early 1970s, the suburbs had shops, doctors, and services for everyday needs, but if you wanted a good medical specialist, quality clothes, specialty food, and culture, you went downtown. If you wanted to see big parades or the Christmas window displays, you went to the downtown department stores. If you wanted to meet your friends for lunch, you would meet at a downtown restaurant. When a young woman left the farm or country to come to town, she would stay at the YWCA and get a job in an office. The train and bus stations were downtown.

That downtown hub pattern persisted, even as suburban development increased until well after the end of World War II. The Levittowners were oriented to New York City as much as the early suburbanites in Montclair, New Jersey, Chappaqua, New York, Englewood, New Jersey, and Greenwich, Connecticut. "Come out to Park Forest," read the advertisement for this new postwar community just south of Chicago, "where small town friendships grow—and you still live so close to a big city."[87] But when that critical mass of people, money, development, highways, and housing seemed to move toward the suburbs, the exodus from the cities quickened in this invasion/succession process. Then some of the most stalwart downtown players—the corporations and department stores—started to leave, so that by the 1990s many downtowns, including Baltimore and Richmond, had none of their former department stores and only a few corporate headquarters. In New York City alone, in the twenty-five years after 1965, 80 of the city's 128 Fortune 500 firms had left.[88] The major department stores, loyal members of downtown improvement and renewal committees, joined the bandwagon of suburban development, first with their independent branch stores, then as anchors in suburban shopping centers or malls. As these anchors catered increasingly to their middle-class clientele, they upgraded their suburban stores, leaving the downtown marble palaces to the shrinking lunchtime middle-class market and the growing minority inner-city population. Instead of women meeting their friends for lunch in the downtown department store restaurant, they now met at the Bird Cage restaurant in the suburban Lord and Taylor.

Shopping suburbanized as the country suburbanized; in fact, many shopping centers actually led the population and job decentralization. What had begun in the 1950s and 1960s was well entrenched by the 1970s. By 1980, suburban decentralization was the major pattern of living, with the number of city dwellers shrinking: from 1970 to 1980 thirty of the fifty largest cities in the United States lost population.[89] Necessity shopping had always occurred in the suburbs in one form or another. There were shopping villages in the old suburbs like Greenwich, Connecticut, Evanston and Oak Park, Illinois, Falls Church, Virginia, and Brookline, Massachusetts, and strip shopping centers on the arteries from downtown, but these places did not offer comprehensive shopping opportunities. Not until the additions of big shopping centers and malls in the 1960s did the suburbs become self-sufficient in shopping. After that the old downtowns might still have a few specialty shops that were not in the malls, but most everything a suburbanite needed was just a short drive away at the mall.

These malls had not only all you might ever want, but they were in a clean and safe environment far removed from the grime and crime of the city, just as the early twentieth-century suburbs were a sanctuary from the grit, noise, and crime of the industrial city. The once vibrant cities were left with glistening corporate towers with landscaped entry plazas, museums, spruced-up movie theaters, pedestrianized streets, maybe a department store, a scattering of wig shops, record stores with booming music, perhaps a festival marketplace, and a dwindling and changed population. However, countering the general exodus from the city from the 1950s on was a growing group of educated middle-class people interested in historic preservation, architectural quality, and urban living, who moved into some older inner-city neighborhoods, like Bolton Hill in Baltimore, Georgetown and Capitol Hill in Washington, D.C., Beacon Hill in Boston, College Hill in Providence. These inner-city pioneers found themselves going to suburban malls for clothes, to suburban discount stores for their appliances, and to suburban movie theaters for the latest flicks, while suburbanites and tourists came to the city for museums, concerts, ethnic restaurants, and uplift. Not until the 1980s did shopping reemerge in the old cities, and then it was in new novelty boutiques or franchised stores at gentrified waterfronts. Tourism and culture—and shopping—were becoming major industries in the cities, and the suburbs retained their hold on mainstream shopping.

Suburban life was a "family" life style, heavily dependent on consumption. In the city, you rented an apartment furnished with appliances that the owner's superintendent repaired. For the suburban house and grounds, one bought one's appliances, cut the lawn, and made house repairs, which all involved purchases. Some of these involved major investments, like the car required for the trips to work, to the mall, to the doctor's office, and to visit friends. Such purchases in the new suburbia were not made lightly, for your house, car, and possessions bespoke who you were—what you could afford, what taste you had, and what values you respected. In the old neighborhood you were known at the church, PTA, clubs, and the store; your family might well have been known for generations, so your identity was inherited. It would have been difficult to reinvent yourself. "I could never change my identity. I could never change my role," complained a woman discussing her youth in Cambridge, New York, a small town forty miles from the Albany-Troy area. But the young wife in a new subdivision in Rockland County, New York, could create a new persona and new environment, if she had the imagination and money. That need to find an identity and place in a new community, encouraged by advertising, was yet another stimulant to increased consumerism.

Women

Women were important participants in the changes in suburbia—and sub-urban shopping—in the past. They were housewives in the 1950s and the early 1960s, at home with the children, tending the house, chauffeuring, and shopping. Their goal was to marry right after college graduation, settle down, have a big family—four and five children were quite common—and enjoy domesticity. After the sacrifices of the Depression and the war, women were taking advantage of peace and security while men were catching up on their lost years in the war with accelerated college study and newfound corporate jobs. Patriotism loomed large for this suburban generation—the country had survived the Depression, won the war, and then, with the G.I. Bill and VA and FHA mortgages, brought new opportunities. Society—and govern-ment—had been good to them. In fact, these suburbanites and their new decentralized way of life were generously subsidized with federally backed mortgages, tax deductions, and essential infrastructure improvements, such as highways.

 This upwardly mobile, middle-class postwar generation was oriented to the group, as their experience in the war and the Depression proved that if you pulled together you could win. The individual, "by sublimating him-self to the group," according to William H. Whyte's *Organization Man*, "helps produce a whole that is greater than the sum of the parts." A greater whole could be found through group activity, along with a basic emotional security. "The feeling of security and certainty derives always from assured membership of a group," according to Elton Mayo, a Harvard Business School professor whose studies of anomie in industrial workers made him an expert on the role of a social system for workers.[90]

 Organization life steered many personal decisions. As families moved from one assignment to another in different cities with their chosen corpo-rations, the disruptions of those moves were offset by the assurance of the continuity of corporate community and the benefits of that paternalism. In a time of change, the corporation was a constant. Instead of your identity being inherited, it was bestowed on you by the corporation. Belonging was the goal of everyone—belonging to the corporation, the church, the community, the family. The rules of the group guided your life. New communities like the Levittowns and Park Forest, twenty miles south of the Loop in Chicago, were havens for young mobile couples where communality offered friendships and security. The proverbial kaffeeklatches were only part of belonging to the community; baby-sitting sharing, tool sharing, and church and school activities brought young couples together so their rootlessness could not fester, even though they knew they would soon be moving on. For many, these years in their first houses in these new communities are remembered as happy times with an intense social life, good friends, and community institutions like churches, schools, or just baby-sitting cooperatives. "We were all in the same boat," reminisced a Levittown pioneer. "We didn't have much money, but we worked together; everyone pitched in. We shared everything; we shared tools and cars, minded each other's kids. . . . It was—at least to us—a Paradise."[91] And this communal world of clustered houses and shared experiences also widened the vistas of the individual suburbanites. In looking back at her childhood in Rockville Centre, Long Island, the writer and historian Doris Kearns Goodwin realized that "there was a special benefit in the clustered structure of our block. For the lives within these homes, the stories of each family, formed a common lore through which I could expand the compass and vividness of my own life."[92]

Women were responsible for much of this paradise. The house, home, and community were essentially matriarchal, middle-class havens because women were there all day long. For the men the homes were dormitories, but for the women they were centers for the family. After the men left for work, "our neighborhood, like some newly acquired province, belonged to the women and children," Goodwin remembered.[93] Emphasis on the group influenced the style of living in these suburbs, the appearance of the house, the children, and the parents themselves. As the gray suit was seen as the dress code for the organization man, so the wives and children were bound by similar conventions. They straddled a narrow line on conspicuous consumption, for although they did object to conspicuous consumption on principle, they did not want others to think they were "high hatting" it. As William Whyte observed, "When they see a neighbor vaunting worldly foods, they can see this as an offense—not to them individually . . . but to the community."[94] Luxury was determined by the group. A critical mass of purchases in the community could tip possessing a new object like a dishwasher into an acceptable social act.

The family became a "consumption unit," as John Seeley described in his study of suburban life in *Crestwood Heights*, published in 1956, the same year as the *Organization Man*. While Seeley studied a Canadian suburb, his observations of the culture of suburban life were essentially universal for North America. The matriarchal tendency was dominated in a child-oriented life, with the house a "vehicle for competitive display." Economic and social success were connected to the ownership of property, so eyes and hearts were on larger and better houses in more upscale neighborhoods. As the husband yearned to rise up the ladder in the organization, the wife had similar aspirations, but along domestic lines. In such a fluid society, one's prestige was no longer based on lineage and background, but on wealth, making the Crestwood Heights resident a "present day . . . pioneer," according to Seeley.[95] Upward mobility has been a longstanding ingredient in capitalistic democracies, and conspicuous consumption in its variety of forms emerges in all affluent societies.

After World War II, the scattering of young families into the suburbs and the wage earners into expanding paternalistic national corporations produced an environment in which the group and conformity dominated. But it could not last. The tight world of the corporation and its organization men—and families—was breaking down. The cracks in the picture window were appearing, and authority was being questioned. The teenager was an important agent in these changes. In the 1950s, teenagers, while wallowing in the conformity of the times, were seen as a special group with distinctive styles and cash to spend. Ponytails, bobby socks, and pedal pushers were their new uniforms, while Elvis Presley helped launch rock and roll music for this new market. Then bobby socks gave way to long hair and grungy clothes. Hippies, often the children of the organization men, represented the overthrow of their gray-suited parents, and the Vietnam War emerged as the ultimate perversion of authority. The individual, no longer a cog in the large machine, became a solo operator who could dance in the mud at Woodstock or raise goats in the hills of Vermont. Drugs often offered a way of escaping from the strictures of the past. While rebellious youth were seen by many as ragtag, drugged, and shiftless, they nevertheless raised questions about society that have had lasting and constructive effects. Public and private institutions have been forced to reexamine their ways of operating. City governments have become more decentralized and responsive to diverse voices. Everyone has become conscious of the need to protect the environment, recycle materials, and confront the problems of nuclear power and its waste. But it was not only the flower children who were questioning the role and responsibilities of authorities. Straight-arrow men and women were joining anti–Vietnam War marches and pro-choice rallies, wearing blue jeans, and leaving the Fortune 500 companies and plunging into new fields, like the exploding computer world.

As men were getting freed from the corporate bonds, so women were freeing themselves from the role of the subservient housewife. Women's liberation emerged as a major force in the middle-class world. When women shopped they did not take their husbands along, as in the case of Hamlin Garland's family, since women had their own checkbooks and their own credit cards. They were making their own decisions—and shopping became more and more important in their empowerment. Many were lonely, many had free time, many had more disposable money than ever before, and there were stores everywhere. In a mall you were anonymous and could shop without ever seeing someone you knew who might cast a negative eye on your extravagances. Shopping was no longer just a necessity for the middle class; it became an entertainment. As in the eighteenth century, when the middle class discovered the pleasures of shopping, so in the 1980s women rediscovered those pleasures, but with new freedom and drives. Empowered by the benefits of material comforts—houses, cars, barbecues, televisions, hi-fis, machines such as dishwashers, clothes washers and dryers, and time-savers like drip-dry clothes and linens—it is not surprising that women—and all the middle class—enjoyed this new materialism. There was more disposable time and income. Material success could be possible if you worked hard, had money and the drive to succeed—and the ability to take advantage of opportunities. You did not need the protection of the corporation, the union, the church, the community, or anything else; you could do it on you own.

Women were no longer judged by the quality of their housework. In fact, women could be judged on their own merits just as men were—and they could work just like men. Women who worked had been the exception. In the early 1900s, Jane Addams and Sophonisba Breckinridge were pioneering and independent career women, both reformers in social work and in the settlement house movement. In the 1920s prominent women were involved in publishing, advertising, and creative fields—Dorothy Parker, Dorothy Canfield Fisher, Clara Littledale, Frieda Kirchwey. Few were in business. By the mid-1950s only a handful of women had been admitted to major law schools. Middle-class women who chose to work were still the exception in the 1950s and 1960s, as careers and jobs were viewed as waystations until women got married. Marriage and family still defined women. Yet within thirty-five years, work has assumed a new role in the lives of women and, in turn, women have become a major part of the workforce. Census figures show that women's participation in the labor force increased in every age, race, and education category in the past few decades. The number of women in the labor force between twenty-five and forty-four years of age has increased by almost 22 million from 1970 to 1998—the most of any age group, according to the Census Bureau. In 1998, 64 percent of married women with children under age six were working, and 83 percent of all working women were college graduates. By 2006, the Census Bureau estimates that older working women (those over forty-five) will number 30 million, 12 million more than in 1970. But perhaps the most dramatic statistics about working women are the participation rates. In 1970, 50 percent of women between twenty-five and fifty-four years of age worked, and by 2005 that age group's participation is estimated by the Census Bureau to climb to almost 80 percent.[96]

Women were working in not just one job, but in several. And the number with more than one job increased nearly five times from 1970 to 1990, with widowed, divorced, or separated women most likely to hold more than one job. Most of these 3.1 million multiple job holders were between thirty-five and forty-four years of age, and the need to earn more money to pay regular household expenses or pay off debts was the major reason for their employment. And in 1991, far more women than men were working at several part-time jobs (36 percent vs. 14 percent).[97] By 1998, 3.7 million women were working at several jobs to help meet household expenses; half of these women had a full-time job along with a "secondary" job, while a third held two part-time jobs.[98]

Most dramatic is the increase in the number of working women who are married with children under age six. These were the homemakers tending the household chores, taking care of the children, doing the laundry, and drinking coffee in their neighbors' kitchens in the 1950s; their husbands were gray-suited corporation men. In 1960, only 19 percent of these young married homemakers were in the labor force; by 1970, 30 percent of them were working; by 1980, 45 percent; and by 1998, 64 percent.[99] Being the model housewife with the clean house, starched shirts, polished silver, and carefully chosen, home-cooked meals no longer satisfied the needs and aspirations of women. Now women could work just like men, dressing in gray flannel suits and carrying attaché cases, have their own credit cards, and spend their own money; but they lacked the leisure in which to spend it.

Shopping and all its fantasies for self-transformation and better days ahead continue in new forms. The "shop-till-I-drop" syndrome still drives many. Others see shopping as a perennial pleasure or as a time-consuming necessity, but the majority of women—and men—view it as a mixture of pleasure and duty, necessity and fun. Women will no doubt continue to blend homemaking with work outside the home. For some, full-time homemaking may return. But the challenges and satisfactions of involvement in activities outside the home, opportunities to contribute to the general welfare of the country, as well as the resultant sense of independence will continue to attract women to the working world. And women's mix of homemaking and working outside the home will have profound effects on how time and money will be spent on shopping.

Life

Life has been lengthened for many Americans, and with modern medicine and preventive approaches to health care it will probably continue to be lengthened. Casual glimpses at Willard Scott's birthday greetings on television's *Today Show* over the years indicate the stretching of the life span. Not long ago people in their early nineties were featured, then there were those in their late nineties, but now you have to be a centenarian to get a birthday greeting from Scott. This aging population, with time on its hands and often money in the bank, is a growing market for the retail world—and not just for Geritol.

The U.S. population over sixty-five is growing in sheer numbers, as well as in its ratio to the total population. In 1970 those over sixty-five made up 10 percent of the total population, in 1980 11 percent, and by 1998 13 percent. And of those oldsters, women over sixty-five held their own at about 60 percent of the population from 1980 to 1998. During that time they steadily increased in numbers: in 1970 they numbered 11.6 million, in 1980 15.2 million, and by 1998 20.2 million.[100] Interestingly, the Internal Revenue Service found that wealthy men and women lived longer than average Americans. And among these "top wealthholders," according to the Internal Revenue Service, the oldest women, those over eighty-five, outnumbered the men almost two to one and also had slightly more money.[101]

This population, often lonely and feeling out of touch, may try to compensate by buying. "It makes me feel part of the world when I go shopping and buy things just like everyone else," said ninety-year-old Janet Swart.[102] Whether walking the malls in the early mornings, wandering through the mall shops during open hours, or ordering by catalogue at home, elderly shoppers are on the increase. The closings of downtown department stores like Woodward & Lothrop have produced an outpouring of testimonials from older people, who feel as though they have lost an old friend. Lunching at the department store or old downtown restaurant was a highlight of the week, and there were always the familiar waitresses, also often older. For the elderly, the socialization of shopping is and will be increasingly important as their ties to and activities in the world at large diminish. Countries like England have national policies to assure that the elderly have continued access to shopping. But in the United States little public concern has emerged on ways to continue to integrate the elderly into society, much less to provide easy shopping.

Money

Attitudes toward money and its sanctioned uses provide a litmus test of a country's values. Radical materialism—and consumerism—flourished in the 1980s and 1990s with the panache of the 1920s and the ruthlessness of the 1890s robber barons. The swelling of the ranks of American millionaires, once considered an achievement possible only for the few, like John Jacob Astor or John D. Rockefeller, was just one indication of American materialism in the 1980s and 1990s. In 1976, the country had 180,000 millionaires, but by 1995 that number had increased to 1,572,000, with more than $4.6 trillion in net worth.[103] With the rising incomes, inflation, booming computer-age companies, and mounting stock prices of the 1990s, cyber moguls seemed to become instant multimillionaires. Young stockbrokers were getting million-dollar bonuses, and CEOs at blue-chip companies were receiving millions of dollars in stock benefits per year. Microsoft's Bill Gates, AOL's Steve Case, and GE's John Welch were no longer dealing with profits in the millions, but in the multiple millions—and sometimes billions.

The world increasingly was being seen as a casino, according to Paul Leinberger, who grew up in the postwar new community–organization man dormitory of Park Forest, Illinois, where his father was the nondenominational Protestant minister. No longer constricted by the "save for tomorrow" mentality of the 1930s and 1940s, these postwar consumers were buying bigger houses, more cars, appliances, clothes, and vacations as though there was no tomorrow. Instead of repairing the vacuum cleaner, you would buy a new one. Instead of bringing the small television set into the kitchen for the news, you'd buy another television. Telephones and television sets were no longer single luxury items in a house to be shared by all household members. Each member could have his or her own. And then there were new appliances— microwave ovens, VCRs, portable and cellular telephones, cable-ready television sets. While the plastic surgeon or the corporate lawyer might make more and costlier purchases, consumption was rampant at almost all income levels. Americans had more money and more products than ever before. From 1950 to 1993, disposable income increased 225 percent and personal consumption 262 percent—and that is measured in constant 1987 dollars.[104]

Debt

Debt, once considered the curse of poverty and a dreaded stigma, has become a part of middle-class living. Despite increased incomes, swelling consumer purchases, an overall trickling-down of former luxuries, and raised material standards of living, life is not all Caribbean vacations and gourmet meals at fancy restaurants. But as a new consumerism with a frantic work-and-spend cycle evolved, material aspirations have ballooned, along with debts. The pace of consumption has increased to the point that it is necessary for families to have two or more wage earners just to keep abreast of expenses and credit card bills. By 1997, more than half of all wage-earning families had two or more people in the workplace. "Meeting household expenses" and "paying off debt" were the major reasons given for all these people working multiple jobs, according to government statistics.[105]

Consumer credit for individuals in the 1980s swelled by $458 billion, and for automobiles alone consumer installment credit more than doubled, from $112 billion to $284.7 billion.[106] In 1997, 108 million people held credit cards from retail stores; they spent $121 billion and incurred a debt of $88 billion. It is estimated that by the year 2000 there will be 458 million bank credit cards held by 105 million people, who will spend $891 billion and incur a

$486 billion debt—or a 55 percent debt ratio.[107] By 1997, there were 4.5 credit cards per American family, according to Standard and Poor's, and the use of those cards accounted for a quarter of all retail transactions.[108] For many the cards were used for outright purchases, but for those struggling to hold their heads above water, they were often used to obtain money, sometimes to pay off other credit card debts.

Debt was no longer a humiliating matter for the individual. The days of cash-and-carry or paying on the spot reflected an earlier time, when there was uncertainty about the future, a lack of trust that others would pay later, and, most important, a strong moral feeling that you should live within your means and not take risks encouraging debt. For Benjamin Franklin, that early "philosopher of the common man," as described by Henry Steele Commager, debt was a moral sin in which "you give to another Power over your Liberty" and, "if you cannot pay on time," you will sink in to the quicksand of excuses and "by Degrees come to lose your Veracity." Relying on the bedrock moral tenets of his Presbyterianism in "The Way to Wealth," the preface to *Poor Richard Improved*, 1758, Franklin preached "Disdain the Chain, preserve your Freedom; and maintain your Independency: Be *industrious* and free; be *frugal* and *free*."[109] Debt could literally take away one's freedom, for debt was considered a crime, which could lead to debtors' prison. Charles Dickens's naval clerk father, for example, was imprisoned for debt, forcing twelve-year-old Charles to work in a blacking warehouse. For Dickens, these experiences no doubt influenced his outlook on life and his future writings. Until laws on debt changed in the late nineteenth century, debtors' prisons were overcrowded with people who couldn't meet their creditors' demands.

Consumer credit has been in use for centuries, but in limited situations. In colonial days in the United States, stores had open-book accounts that consumers like farmers would settle when their crops were harvested. Before the Civil War the small general stores had open-book accounts for planters, farmers, and wealthy city dwellers, and after the war this type of credit was open to average citizens. In 1850, the Singer Sewing Machine Company instituted an installment plan for its purchasers, but not until 1914 did a credit card appear as a means of paying for retail purchases. Consumer credit cards evolved from cards for individual stores to multistore cooperative cards to universal cards, which appeared in the early 1950s. The Diners Club card was founded by Frank McNamara after he could not pay for his dinner in a New York restaurant in 1949 because he forgot his wallet. By the end of 1950, 20,000 people carried Diners Club cards. The American Express card, introduced in 1958, was conceived as a supplement to traveler's checks, which were popular and easier to use than the traditional bank-to-bank letter of credit used in the United States and abroad. But a giant step was made when banks introduced credit cards in 1958–59 that allowed consumers to pay off balances on a revolving basis. In 1958, the year the Chase Manhattan Charge

Plan was initiated, it attracted 350,000 cardholders. BankAmericard was introduced on the West Coast the same year. By 1966 BankAmericard could be used all over the United States. Three years later Master Charge was taken over by Interbank Card Association, and eventually Master Charge became Mastercard and BankAmericard became Visa. For banks, the credit cards lived up to their expectations of "creating enormous profit."[110] The returns from credit cards beat out mortgages, consumer installment debt, and commercial and other loans for banks, especially in the 1980s, when the cards carried high annual fees.

For the consumer, the bank credit card, accepted at more than 2 million locations in the United States and at almost 6 million throughout the world, was a boon. Those same cards can be used to withdraw money from automatic teller machines. Some provide rebates (cards like Discover), and others can produce frequent flier miles. Several weeks after the O. J. Simpson trial, Simpson's seized property was returned to him, including fifteen credit and membership cards, among them Sears, AT&T, Blockbuster, Chevron, and American Airlines Advantage Gold. While Simpson is not a typical citizen, his large number of credit cards is not atypical for many middle-class Americans. For the retailer, the possibility of being paid by banks with minimal delay has always been an asset, so it is not surprising that the marketplace and the retailers have come to depend on the use of consumer credit cards. As the largest source of consumer goods, retailing has become one of the most important customers of credit card companies. Indeed, "consumer credit has accomplished the institutionalization of consumerism," as Lloyd Klein wrote in his thesis on consumer credit.[111] Individuals sleep at night with no twinges of guilt as their credit card debts—and national government's debts—mount.

The role of the credit card has been critical for the rise of consumerism, but it has been accompanied by stretched consumer expectations. Consumption is the major economic activity for the average family. During the high consumerism of the early 1990s, personal consumption rose to 93 percent of disposable income, measured in current dollars.[112] From 1980 to 1990, the increase in personal consumption of clothes, jewelry, watches, and new cars each almost doubled. Expenditures for radios, televisions, recorded music, and musical instruments tripled, and food for off-premise eating soared even more astronomically in the radically materialistic 1980s, when spending, credit, and debt may have been stretched to their limits.[113] Government statistics indicate that personal consumption slipped slightly from 1990 to 1997 despite a considerable rise in personal income.[114]

Time

The stretching (and shrinking) of time is another aspect of American life that affects so much of our daily living—and how, when, and where we shop. Modern technology and equipment can shorten tasks and save time, whether washing dishes in a machine, e-mailing by computer, or ordering food by fax. "Speed and efficiency" is the motto. Yet this fast-paced world of swift jet flights, instant microwaved food, and disposable products has not necessarily created more spare time. Even the seeming availability of leisure for the wealthy to enjoy travel to exotic islands and long weekends at trendy watering spots is often misleading. Most people are stretched out and short on time. What time is left over from work is spent on the most necessary activities—school PTAs, "quality time" with the family, and obligatory shopping.

As budgets and time for many people have been stretched, so has the physical spread of daily living, whether in the house, community, region, school, stores, or office. This new scale of suburban living, dependent on the automobile, has caused a profound decentralization that influences every aspect of personal and business activities, including how and where we shop. Travel time in automobiles, usually alone, has skyrocketed. Sixty percent of American workers commute from suburb to suburb, according to Benjamin Chinitz.[115] Although the average time spent traveling to the office was twenty-two minutes in 1990, fifty-mile trips are not unusual. In 1980, 1.5 million people traveled that distance to offices, and as people and workplaces scatter farther and farther, that commute will be quite common.[116] Most of the longest commutes are in Edge Cities. The commutes that exceed the national average time are in New York, New Jersey, Massachusetts, Illinois, the District of Columbia, Virginia, Georgia, California, and Hawaii.[117] Much of that commuting is done by automobile, not by train or bus. Several generations have never even used mass transit, since scattered employment and shopping sites may be far removed from any bus line. As affordable housing, offices, and corporate headquarters have leapfrogged to cheaper land on the outer edges of urban areas, travel routes and time to work and shopping have stretched.

Distance

Edge Cities, some of the fastest growing urban developments, represent a new type of conurbation—they are the results of stretched living. These cities are scattered in metropolitan areas, usually hugging major highways. Their development paralleled the move away from the traditional downtowns and the explosion of suburban housing after the Second World War. These new suburban hubs, labeled Edge Cities by author Joel Garreau, grew in response to burgeoning suburban and regional needs and demands. They were not created by regional planners but by random private ventures accumulating into a critical mass of urban buildings like offices, shopping centers and malls, apartments, hotels, stores, restaurants, and varied commercial enterprises.

Shopping malls and centers, not necessarily related to any place other than subregional markets, became the cores of many new Edge Cities, replacing the downtown for both shopping and jobs for millions of Americans. Of the top ten places with the largest number of employees in the early 1990s, nine were city downtowns, led by New York City, followed by Chicago, San Francisco, Boston, Washington, D.C., Los Angeles, Philadelphia, and Dallas. The only Edge City in that top ten was South Coast Metroplex, Irvine, near Los Angeles, and it ranked ninth. However, in the next twenty-five top employment centers in the country, fourteen Edge Cities outranked the traditional downtowns: Schaumburg Area and O'Hare Airport Edge near Chicago, King of Prussia near Philadelphia, Galleria/LBJ Freeway near Dallas, and Santa Clara in California. These conurbations have become major commercial hubs employing hundreds of thousands of people, many in small companies. In 1990, the ten areas with the highest percentage of companies with fewer than fifty employees were all Edge Cities, four of them outside San Francisco, along with Tysons Corner in suburban Washington, D.C.; Southdale, south of Minneapolis; Perimeter Center, twelve miles from Atlanta; Bellevue, Washington, near Seattle; and Parkway Center, near Dallas.[118]

The car rules in the stretched world of Edge Cities. Hence its landscape is dominated by the car: multilane roads, acres of flat asphalt parking lots, usually free parking punctuated by low-rise malls and shopping centers and scattered office buildings, hotels, and apartment buildings, all sited near major highways. From a distance these Edge Cities appear to be clustered commercial buildings, but that is deceptive because the spaces between buildings are vaster than first appears, due to the sprawled scale of these areas. They are not geared to the pedestrian. Sidewalks do not exist, and traffic lights are not synchronized to allow pedestrians to cross the six-lane highways that often abut or are inside Edge Cities. One cannot even walk from one shopping center to another in Tysons Corner, Virginia. Edge Cities are seldom destinations for public transportation. What planning took place was oriented to the car.

Once in the Edge City, half of the workers left the building at lunch, and half of those trips were within the Edge City for lunch or work-related purposes. "Dispersion of uses—a restaurant here, an office building a fair distance away—forces people to get into cars to even travel short distances," according to the Tysons Corner Task Force's draft plan.[119] Bellevue, in the environmentally conscious Seattle metropolitan area, was a striking exception in providing pedestrian facilities, which resulted in 25 percent of the workers making that midday trip by foot.

Many activities formerly found in downtowns have appeared in Edge Cities. The ten places with the largest numbers of ethnic restaurants are no longer in inner-city ethnic neighborhoods but in the 1990s in Edge Cities—with seven of them in California, according to *American Demographics*. And eight of the top ten "restaurant rows" were in Edge Cities rather than in downtowns, according to the same *American Demographics* study. Nightclubs formerly associated with the Great White Ways of cities are also found in abundance in Edge Cities, with Edge Cities in Texas taking the lead, followed by those in California.[120] Now theaters, dance groups, symphonies, and other major cultural institutions, once found only in center cities, can be found in Edge Cities and the suburbs.

Tysons Corner, which grew with the sprawl of the suburbs, is a prime example of stretched commercialism. Located on the highest elevation in Fairfax County, this 1,700-acre area boasts office complexes, hotels, two super-regional malls and many smaller shopping strips and centers, lone office buildings, Big Boxes, and Category Killers, as well as a handful of apartment buildings. It sprang in the early 1960s from a rural crossroads into one of the country's large Edge Cities. After downtown Washington, Tysons Corner is the largest center for business and commerce in the region—not as the result of a carefully considered public planning process but rather as the accumulation of different private development schemes, all aided by massive public expenditures for highways and highway improvements, and the public infrastructure necessary for such large-scale development. Viewed as Fairfax County's downtown—with 30 percent of the county's office space for white-collar professionals, six of the county's hotels, and more than 20 million square feet of office space, the overall image of Tysons Corner remains scattered buildings, wide, congested highways, low-slung shopping malls and centers, and a never-ending strip of automobile dealers.

This growing and important commercial hub in Washington's metropolitan area is typical of most Edge Cities—random siting of commercial and some residential buildings coalescing into a critical mass, accessible primarily by automobile, with little attention paid to how all the parts interact, how they function as a whole, and how people move around within them. If you want to get there, you have to drive; if you want to get from one building to another you have to drive; and if an office worker just wants to have lunch out, he or she is likely to drive. It is a stretched commercial area, a "dispersion of uses," as a Fairfax County report on Tysons Corner diplomatically described it, with "no sense of place."[121] A variety of stores, restaurants, offices, and commercial establishments may be there, but there is no civic glue to hold them together and make them a place. The car is the only connector.

Although Edge Cities are the most concentrated conglomerations of commercial and urban activities in many sprawling suburbs or on the peripheries of major cities, they serve the decentralized world and are decentralized within themselves. They represent stretched spaces and functions.

Shrinkage in the Stretched World

The stretching of the world we live in—whether of our expectations, resources, money, time, distance, and longevity—is showing signs of wear. In fact, a striking paradox is emerging. Shrinkage is appearing in many social and economic activities affecting home life, the workplace, social relationships, the community—and shopping. For example, one can communicate instantly by fax or e-mail with almost any corner of the world in a phenomenal stretching of communication capability, yet at the same time that communication can be an isolating experience as one works at the computer alone at home in a remote suburb instead of having face-to-face communication at the office. The rampant consumerism of the 1980s and 1990s, a glaring example of the stretching of expectations and money, is facing shrinkage as interest in downshifting catches on with those ideologically attracted to simpler living, and for the many with uncertain economic futures.

In the yin and yang of economic behavior, "less is more" may be the new slogan influencing how people will live in the early twenty-first century and beyond. The paradoxical stretching and shrinking are critical bits in the kaleidoscope of shifting values, tastes, and mores. The early glimmerings of shrinkage or scaling down, now noticed only in certain pockets, may be increasingly important determinants of the dominant cultural environment influencing the way we live, work, and shop.

The Isolation of Cocoon Living and Working

As development has stretched into the suburbs, exurbs, and beyond, life at home and in the community has shrunk. In the early suburbs, there were still ties to jobs, friends, doctors, and clubs in the center city. Then, as suburbs became more self-sufficient, residents grew more divorced from the diversity of people and activities of the city. Now, with the stretching of suburban life and the availability of home entertainment, suburban neighbors are isolated even from each other.

Instead of going to the local movie theater or catching up on the news at a local diner, one stays at home and operates machines alone—playing games on the computer, viewing a movie on tape, talking on the telephone, or watching one of the countless television channels available on cable TV. In a 1995 to 1996 *Washington Post*/Kaiser Family Foundation/Harvard University national survey of 1,514 people, 80 percent of the respondents said that they did not regularly attend or participate in any civic organization or service club (Chamber of Commerce, PTA, Kiwanis), and 63 percent of the respondents had lived in their present community for more than ten years, 28 percent for more than thirty years.[122] The home is where the action is. Although cocoon living has many benefits, it puts the family under new pressures, as so many family activities are conducted within the house. Only a few activities—like those of school-age children, church, and shopping—take one out of the home. Otherwise, the family is focused inward. David Riesman observed in his 1964 article "Abundance for What?" that the "home itself, rather than the neighborhood, becomes the chief gathering place for the family—either in the 'family room' with its games, its TV, its informality, or outdoors around the barbecue." And those observations were made before VCRs and computers converted the home into an even more entrenched fortress of electronic machines.

The same equipment that provides entertainment at home enables some to work at home, adding yet another layer of isolation to the cocoon. Some opt to work at home for the flexibility and freedom, while others are being forced into it. In the New York metropolitan area, 750,000 people are likely to be telecommuting, according to the Regional Plan Association's 1996 Third Regional Plan's estimates of the "next 2.75 million payroll jobs," based on 1995 to 2020 regional job formation.[123] As corporations have cut down on their overhead and reduced their office space, employees find themselves without a desk or even a shared workspace, so the home workspace seems inviting. When Lexis-Nexis reduced its Washington office expenses by 45 percent, it gave each employee a $500 allowance to furnish a home office, as well as a telephone, a laptop computer, and a combination printer/copier/fax machine—and their old Herman Miller chair for $50—in order to work at home. Travel time and costs were cut, and for many the ease of working at home was welcomed, although a new self-discipline was needed.[124]

Public agencies, so often pictured as sluggish in adapting to change, also are converting to telecommuting operations. In Loudoun County, Virginia, telecommuting has proved "efficient," according to Russ Blackburn, former assistant administrator of this fast-developing Washington, D.C., county, which by 1997 had 200 deputy sheriffs telecommuting, as well as the division of mental health and retardation. The mental health workers have the opportunity to work at "customer sites" or at home with the assistance of a laptop, a beeper, and a county car stationed at city facilities near where they live. Once a week they go to the office for group meetings, which provide a "lifeline for communication," says Blackburn. The success of these telecommuting experiments led the county to develop its new office building in downtown Leesburg and a future office building in the eastern part of the county on the "hoteling" model, where employees have no fixed offices but instead telephone in to reserve a "workspace," as Xerox and other large corporations are doing, Blackburn reports.[125] Interest in telecommuting in the county continues. "Loudoun's office space is getting very, very tight," noted county policy analyst Jules Withrow in 2001, "and we are planning on looking more actively into telecommuting."[126]

With its flexibility for the employee and its efficiencies and economies for the employer, telecommuting is becoming increasingly popular. Yet random encounters at the water cooler, the spontaneity of lunch engagements, and the exchanges at daily meetings of the old office life are missing in the new cocoon offices.

Computers make cocoon living and working possible. Paradoxically, they open windows in the vast world of communication even as they shrink people into solo operators of electronic machines. An employee working at home sends e-mail messages to people who might otherwise have been seen at the coffee machine or at lunch—and who might impart random news and information or convey by a facial expression something one might not otherwise have considered. A nonworker intrigued by games and puzzles can spend hours playing chess not with an old friend but against a computer program. Innumerable communities on the Internet connect people and provide information in ways never imagined a few decades ago, yet these are remote cyber communities. The paradox of expanding opportunities that simultaneously contract opportunities is at the heart of much of stretched living.

The computer has transformed not only our business and home lives, but also how we think—or so its advocates boast. "The Internet is, by far, the greatest and most significant achievement of mankind," according to Osbourne's *Internet Complete Reference.* "What is amazing is that, within a few short years, the Internet has changed our civilization permanently and has introduced us to . . . completely unexpected ideas." The power of the computer to connect with networks and to communicate "create[s] something that is much more than the sum of its parts."[127] This book provides a glimpse of the excitement of one Internet user, an author of this volume, Harley Hahn, in looking ahead to what Internet offers the world.

For those who spend hours and days looking at a computer monitor, "cyberspace had a presence as real and as full of promise as the lights of Broadway," Paul Goldberger said. "It is monumental, and noble and intimate, all at once." It is also empowering, as the computer operator feels as though he or she is keeping abreast of the times and is well launched into the twenty-first century. And this cockiness is compounded by the fact that one suddenly feels as though one can communicate with anyone about anything, anywhere—and instantly. Paul Goldberger described it well as feeling "like being dropped in the New York Public Library without a card catalogue; you know everything is there somewhere, but getting to it is quite another matter." Yet all this cyberspace is private and lonely: "It is a set of silicon bubbles, not a town square or soapbox. In cyberspace people are alone, pretending to be in public. In real public space they are physically together."[128] The cyberspace community will never be the town square, but, like the telephone, it is an easy and quick way for people to connect with worlds beyond their own, and for many it may be the best community they can find in this stretched living.

Brain Workers and New Individualism

The navigator on the Web, the physicist working in Silicon Valley, the Wall Street merger expert, and even Boopsie and her consumer friends share many of the same values of the new individualism, a contemporary version of "virtuous materialism." They are smart operators relying on their own intelligence and ego, rejecting support from the corporation, government, and union; yet those institutions, considered necessary and helpful not too long ago, are seen as burdens. Today's virtual office of the agile company is the environment of the new individualist, whose values and attitudes reflect a new order and a sharp break from the group-bound values of the organization man. The new worker is an updated version of R. H. Tawney's brain worker, who was born "from the developments springing from the applications of science to industry."[129]

Alpha I Biomedicals, Inc., is a good example of an agile company and its brain workers. Located in suburban Maryland, not far from the National Institutes of Health, Alpha I has a total staff of five administrators of one sort or another to work on new drugs for cystic fibrosis. Most of their work is farmed out by contract: three universities work on research, three commercial laboratories work on toxicology studies, and three different drug companies work on production of the drug. Once a traditional company with twenty-nine employees, Alpha I lost money after developing a hepatitis drug that proved ineffective, so it transformed itself into a "virtual" company, which has greatly reduced its overhead and operating costs. But such a company has to stay on top of all its diverse contractees by visits, phone calls, and computer contact. "You lose control and communication with those carrying out the tasks for you, so you have to work extra hard, spending more time on the phone and traveling to see suppliers," said Alpha I's CEO, Michael Berman. For Alpha I, this is hard-nosed, bottom-line administration, and for the contracted employees, it is intellectual piecework that doesn't encourage loyalty or a sense of collegiality with Alpha I's administrators.

The virtual office of a high-tech firm like Alpha I, located far from downtown, with a bare-bones staff that "outsources" its work, is like many other small companies that opted for agility. These small "virtual" enterprises focus on what they can do best and bring in specialists to do what they do best, according to James Brian Quinn, management professor at Dartmouth's Amos Tuck School.[130] Unlike the traditional corporation, with its large and loyal staff, the agile high-tech firm trades on its ability to pull in the right mind for the right task, keeping office overhead to a minimum. Now transfixed by the bottom line, all types of corporations aim to be lean and tough, firing thousands of employees and destroying the last vestiges of loyalty. For the assistant vice president who traded security and benefits for a stagnant salary, the pink slip was a rude awakening to the fact that loyalty to the corporation was a thing of the past. The individual now has to go it on his own, and for many not attuned to the agility of the new individualism, it has been a very rough time.

Sharpness and intelligence, not loyalty and conformity, are the ingredients needed to succeed. In the extreme, these qualities stoked the operations of those manipulating mergers and buyouts where quick billions seem to be made with hardly a public murmur about anti-trust legislation. But the mainstream image of these new workers grew out of the computer industry.

Small Silicon Valley computer companies with bright employees hopping from one high-tech firm to another, carrying intellectual secrets to expand the information highway, are today's role models for workers. Their loyalty is to themselves, not to the company. They are not interested in going up the corporate ladder but in having flexibility and freedom to invent. The middle-aged corporate vice president in a gray flannel suit was replaced by a young MIT graduate in blue jeans and a sports shirt, and at Apple he or she doesn't even have to wear shoes. The vitality of the high-tech firm seems to derive from the restless vitality of its workers, who switch from one firm to another and produce a kind of synergy, the antithesis of the stability of the workers and the corporation of the 1950s. The intellectual arrogance driving these high-tech workers—or even the corporate maneuverers in the takeovers and buy-outs—is both product and producer of the new individualism.

Gone are Whyte's fears of the individual surrendering his individualism to the corporation's "constant and powerful" demands. In 1956, when Whyte wrote *The Organization Man*, he was on the staff of *Fortune* and had previously worked for a major corporation, so he understood the pull of the organization. "The more he [the organization man] has come to like the life of the organization, the more difficult does he find it to resist these demands, or even to recognize them."[131] But that organization life has been shattered, and an era of self-promotion, aggrandizement, and self-fulfillment dominates. It is not surprising, therefore, to see the rise of a new individualism, with its stretched personal freedom and often shrunken personal perspectives.

While the new individualism is most apparent in the business world where a radical change in corporate ethics has taken place, individualism pervades our culture—and has stimulated much of the heady consumerism of recent decades. The country's value system has changed along with attitudes toward community, government, and fellow human beings. Consumption has been a hallmark of this "me generation," whether in acquiring large houses, many cars, vast wardrobes, gourmet foods, or in taking jetsetting weekends or exotic vacations. Material goods are ways to express one's ability—as well as capacity—to choose, and hence they indicate one's success. Groups like the innumerable support groups for women and for victims of various diseases are listed in most daily newspapers, and many others, like Alcoholics Anonymous, exist for the individual's benefit. Networking is not for frivolous socializing but for job seeking, information gathering, and promotion. As in most of the activities of the new individualist—whether working in one of these agile companies or cruising outlet stores, individuals have stretched themselves out of the constraints of yesteryear's conformities and institutions but have also narrowed their focus to what's best for themselves; the stretch/shrink syndrome again. These attitudes and values of the whiz kids of the 1990s, as revered as those of the organization man of the 1950s, affect how we live and how and why we shop.

Cracks in Consumerism

Cracks are appearing in the world of the new individualism—and they can have dramatic impact on both consumption and community. The effects of buyouts, bottom-line corporate policies, downsizing, a shaky stock market, serial jobs, and careers have been felt. Who is going to buy a house, a new winter coat, or a new car when one is uncertain whether one will still have a job in a year, and if one has a job, what benefits will exist? Some people, even those who have been secure, are beginning to wonder whether it is necessary to have twenty-two pairs of shoes, ten power suits, yet another sports car, and all those endlessly accumulating gadgets, like salad shooters.

The idea of a simplified life, with less consumption as a way to a more satisfying, less stressful, and often more creative existence, has emerged from different corners. The Green movement among environmentalists in the Pacific Northwest and the trust-fund kid or early retiree in pockets of New England have been joined by those who have tired of the work-spend treadmill, by those who are attracted to a simple style of living, and those who haven't profited from the economic boom times or reckon that good times will not last.

This movement comes under different names—Voluntary Simplicity or Downshifting. Ever since the 1960s, dropouts from the mainstream have been living simply—raising their own foods, making their own clothes, and ignoring the advertising pressures of the consumer economy. But now their numbers are increasing. Information about this movement has become increasingly available in such books as *Your Money or Your Life* by Joe Dominquez and Vicki Robin, *The New Road Map Foundation* by Michael Fogler and Elaine Stover, research by the Merck Family Fund, predictions from the Trends Research Institute in Rhinebeck, New York, and conferences, newsletters, study groups. The competent research of Harvard economist Juliet Schor in her *Overworked American* (1991) and *Overspent American* (1998) has stimulated considerable interest in the American work/spend cycle, in consumerism, and in downshifting. Accounts of the growing numbers of people opting out of the consumer mainstream have appeared in syndicated newspaper columns and even in front-page features in the *New York Times*. And newsletters like *Tightwad Gazette*, *Penny Pincher Times*, *Living Better for Less*, and *Quality of Life Unlimited* offer practical advice to the downshifters. At www.newdream.org, the Center for a New American Dream of Takoma Park, Maryland, provides a range of information on new attitudes about materialism, consumption, and the environment as well as ways to foster simpler living through sustainable households, communities, and businesses. For ten dollars you can buy the "Simple Living and Earth Saving Action Kit" from the center, whose board comprises some of the country's leading environmentalists from organizations like the Natural Resources Defense Council, respected academicians like Donella Meadow and Juliet

Schor, and key leaders in the Simple Living Movement. One can get bumper stickers—"The more you know, the less you need"—to adorn your car.

The message from this growing movement is: Shop for what you need. Do not shop for entertainment. "Choose the quality of life over the standard of living." Keep only one credit card and avoid debt. Move to a smaller place, cook at home, plant a garden, use things until they wear out. Get out of holiday gift-giving if it has become "oppressive." And save—saving is a cardinal rule for these simplifiers, as Vicki Robin, coauthor of *Your Money or Your Life*, states on a highly popular 1997 segment of National Public Radio's Morning Edition. "First, save money. . . . Teach people how to live well on less." She continues: "Saving up for things has tremendous value, both in moderating what we will buy, because if you have to save up for something . . . it's going to increase the importance of that item to you."[132]

These soundings of a movement have been confirmed in a survey and conference sponsored by the Merck Family Fund, a foundation concerned about the United States following an "unsustainable path—one that robs resources from future generations, generates far too much waste, and undermines community and family alike for many Americans." In a 1995 survey of Americans "from all walks of life" conducted for the Merck Family Fund by the Harwood Group, 62 percent of those surveyed agreed with the statement, "I would like to simplify my life." Americans were found in this survey to believe that "materialism, greed, and selfishness increasingly dominate American life, crowding out a more meaningful set of values centered on family, responsibility, and community." One respondent to the survey stated, "We've become far more materialistic. . . . Things have become so important to us that things and the acquisition of things run our lives and our relations with others." Criticism of the materialistic ways of our society was substantiated by the survey:

- 82 percent of those surveyed agreed that "most of us buy and consume far more than we need; it's wasteful"
- 86 percent agreed that "today's youth are too focussed on buying and consuming things"
- 89 percent agreed that "buying and consuming is the American Way"
- a whopping 91 percent agreed that "the 'buy now, pay later' attitude causes many of us to consume more than we need"
- only 51 percent agreed that "material wealth is part of what makes this country great."[133]

Although the respondents saw the "material side of the American Dream 'spinning out of control'" and the "effort to keep up with the Joneses . . . increasingly unhealthy and destructive," they were ambivalent about what to do about such a global problem. Also, many respondents had difficulty reconciling their satisfaction with financial security and its material comforts with their deep-seated, nonmaterial aspirations. The conflict between "their condemnation of other Americans' choices on consumption with their core belief in the freedom to live as we choose" emerged.[134] The ecological impacts of consumerism, according to this survey, have not been fully comprehended, nor the connection between their consumption and their concerns about environmental damage.

A strong current throughout these Merck studies is a concern for the family and particularly for children. "Skewed values are destructive of family life, having an especially negative effect on our children," according to the survey summary. Indeed, discussion of children and future generations aroused the most serious involvement of these respondents in the interrelationships between materialism, consumption, and environment. When faced with future problems stemming from materialistic consumption, respondents seemed interested in thinking about change. Yet one woman, faced with working overtime to meet her children's request for expensive sneakers, went along with keeping up with the neighbors. "Somebody down the block got the new Jordans [sneakers] and my kids want Jordans too, and I want them to have them."[135]

People are clearly torn about adapting to the expanding American Dream of more and bigger things and of choosing to live more simply. Seventy-seven percent agreed that "if I wanted to, I could choose to buy and consume less." It is easier to step off the treadmill of consumerism if one's appetite for material goods has been satiated. For many who have not been able to fully enjoy the materialism of the American Dream, cutting down on consumption represents a formidable challenge. As one woman stated, "It depends on how much money you have whether you can slow down or not."[136]

Yet downshifting is occurring. Millions of Americans have started to downshift by scaling down their salaries and altering their lives to jibe with new values and priorities. A Yankelovich Monitor study found that 76 percent of 2,500 Americans surveyed in 2000 are increasingly looking for a way to simplify their lives.[137] In the Merck survey, 28 percent of respondents indicated that they had "voluntarily made changes in their life which resulted in making less money" in the five years from 1990 to 1995. The major reasons given for these changes were to balance life (68 percent of downshifter respondents), to have more free time (66 percent respondents), and to live a less stressful life (63 percent). These downshifters were younger respondents, often with children; in fact, 60 percent were women, and more than half the respondents downshifted to have more time to care for their children. Those who downshifted were overwhelmingly (almost 90 percent) happy with the change. One respondent left a "job making three times the money that I'm making now; but by the same token, I've got more time with my family." Another respondent climbing the corporate ladder found herself working harder and harder and "hating it more and more . . . I was already hiring people to clean my clothes, watch my kid, and now clean my house. I sold the car and I bought a '65 Falcon. . . . I'm much happier. I work two blocks from home and I'm doing something that I really enjoy."[138] And that was confirmed by all the interviews—and the high level of listener response—to a two-part series on voluntary simplicity on National Public Radio's Morning Edition in February 1997.[139]

While more individuals are scaling down, it seems to remain an individual choice despite the recognition that consumption and materialism are problems of society at large. How to translate these individual concerns into compelling collective action for change has not been resolved. Whether due to the new individualism, the current disdain for public governance, or other reasons, basic social problems such as racial justice, housing inequities, or long-term conservation measures do not command public attention today as they did in the 1960s and 1970s. When specific policy changes were presented in the Merck study, about half the respondents agreed that limiting advertising on prime time, and changing the tax structure to reduce taxes on savings and increase taxes on consumption, would be good ideas. Some respondents recognized that individual action was their main way to demonstrate their commitment to changing priorities. And that is how movements get started. Ideas percolate, trickle down, and spread out in many different ways, and if the time is right, the conditions are fertile, and people are receptive, movements become energized and social changes like women's rights or civil rights occur. Such changes take time. It took almost a century to achieve basic civil rights for African Americans.

What is significant is the fact that so many people are trying to break out of the spend-work cycle and lead a less stressful life with less consumption and less competition. And then many women, who do lead stressful and overcommitted lives as they juggle jobs and families, are becoming more deliberate, rational shoppers, dashing the image of the frivolous woman shopper exploited by contemporary consumerism. Yet despite these cracks, materialism has always been a part of American life. As Tocqueville noted, "The love of well-being is now become the predominant taste of the nation; the great current of human passions runs in that channel, and sweeps everything along in its course."[140] But the stretched living of new individualism and the frantic spend-work cycle have boosted consumerism beyond Tocqueville's imagination and beyond the sensibilities of many Americans. As the pendulum swings with changing values about consumption, self, and ways of living, and as a commitment to a less consumptive life becomes more pervasive, the retail world, whose survival depends on satisfying consumer demands, will have to respond.

CHAPTER FOUR

What's in Store?

Shopping in the Future

When a retail store executive reported that shopping changes as quickly as the flash of a firefly, he was correct in recognizing the inherent volatility of retailing. To stay ahead of competition, the stores and their suppliers, all operating on a thin profit margin, must keep abreast of ever-changing fads. Many customers' needs and desires are swayed by unpredictable changes in fashion, as well as by unpredictable pressures from peers and advertisers. For this industry, assessing market trends is indeed a risky business. In the 1980s and 1990s, when retailing was on a high, malls of every size, Category Killers, Power Centers, outlet "villages," and revamped commercial strips were popping up everywhere, so by the beginning of the twenty-first century the United States was supersaturated with stores. With twenty square feet of retail space for every person, it was not surprising that malls were dying, stores were in and out of bankruptcy, and that 20 to 30 percent of existing retail was estimated to be redundant.[1] This is retailing's fickle side.

Less fickle but perhaps more jolting have been the technological innovations that throughout history have radically altered how retailing works. The introduction of rural free mail delivery (1896) and then parcel post (1912), enabling mail-order houses like Montgomery Ward to reach distant customers, and refrigerators (1920s) and freezers (1950s), eliminating the need for daily marketing trips, and, most recently, automation and the computer are among the technological innovations that produced seismic changes in shopping. These changes are part of the volatile and fascinating nature of retailing. On the other hand, pervasive cultural forces—attitudes about debt, luxury, women, and self-fulfillment, for example—inject some longer-term elements into shopping and undermine the impression that retailing fluctuates solely with the whims of customers, the dreams of inventors, and the vagaries of the marketplace.

Forecasting the future of shopping remains daunting. Nonetheless, some trends point to types of shopping that are likely to continue or even become more popular than they are today. Understanding these trends and their possible impacts should help the planning, development, and maintenance of shopping, which could benefit communities and quality of life. Public agencies, often not fully recognizing the social and even the economic functions of shopping in communities, tend to leave decisions about the timing, types, and locations of real stores to the entrepreneur. That public agency passivity, combined with retailing's low class/trade image, has created a hands-off environment for this important activity, which allows retailers to enjoy a relatively unfettered laissez-faire world. Retailers' plans are too often accepted without adequate public agency analysis and community scrutiny. By the time the public has become aware of major retailing decisions, building permits have been applied for and all the political circuitry has been wired. The public, frustrated in its attempts to participate in the decision-making, then finds it necessary to use legal means to prevent or slow down projects. Such a litigious atmosphere can make objective decision-making extremely difficult. Exploring trends in shopping, as well as the forces propelling those trends, is essential if we want to match retailing opportunities with the needs of both individuals and communities.

Among those changes, advances in communication technology are clearly the most revolutionary, as more and more shopping will be done remotely by telephone, fax, and computer. Internet retailing may well be the fastest growing way to shop. Sales from Internet retailing, still in its infancy, reached $20 billion in 1999, ten times the 1997 sales.[2] In just over two years, the bookseller Amazon.com reached more than a million customers. As more mass marketers set up websites to capture markets and loyal customers, consumers will find a dazzling array of shopping opportunities for almost anything, from books to cars, which can be purchased at any hour of day from any place with a computer and a credit card.

In contrast to this highly publicized remote shopping, real stores will continue to exist, but with added emphasis on personal and creative shopping, whether more service in traditional stores, increased use of "personal shoppers" in high-priced department stores, specialized boutiques, or more shopping at farmer's markets, public markets, and flea markets. Such personalized shopping will involve face-to-face contacts and more attention to quality, personal tastes, authenticity, and personal service—a refreshing contrast to the anonymity and isolation in so many aspects of working, living, and mainstream shopping today.

One of the most significant changes in the world of retailing has been the slowdown in the raging consumerism of the 1980s and early 1990s. Many factors have accumulated to diminish the all-consuming passion of shopping. Just the overkill of advertising and the insistent pressure to shop, which invade every phase of life, whether on the computer screen or on television, in magazines, newspapers, bus stops, airplane streamers along beaches, and even airports like Pittsburgh's, which is advertised as a mall, can quell some people's desire to join the consumer world. Many people are worn out by the shop-spend cycle. The scarcity of free time to shop, diminished personal satisfactions derived from shopping, a surfeit of possessions, and rising personal debts force one to reconsider how, when, and for what one shops. When these concerns merge with a mounting realization that accumulating goods can be a physical, financial, and moral burden, shopping may drop from the top of the list of personal priorities for many Americans.

Many children of the baby boomers are turned off by shopping. Thirty-year-old Liz Clark of Oakland, California, has a style of dressing that she likes, and she can get what she wants from catalogues or thrift shops. When Tobie Cornejo, a recent college graduate, worked at the Federal Reserve Bank in Washington, D.C., she picked up what she needed near her apartment, never went to malls, and avoided shopping almost entirely. These women are not seeking an alternative life style; they just find shopping "boring" and a waste of time. While the downshifters and anti-shoppers may be a small percentage of the public, they could be in the vanguard of a movement that will affect the future of shopping.

Trends

Looking ahead, the following shopping trends appear most significant:

Fast-and-Easy and Bargain Shopping

With less time for shopping and less interest in it, people will shop where they can get in and out quickly. That rules out the massive malls of the 1980s and makes neighborhood stores and remote shopping, especially catalogues and e-commerce, inviting retail destinations. For bargain shopping, the variety of brick-and-mortar discount stores as well as e-commerce will continue to be popular.

As both bargain and fast-and-easy retailing rely heavily on "branded" products and stores, a sameness will permeate shopping. With fewer conglomerates owning more chain stores, stores like The Gap are now spreading from the malls onto city avenues and small-town streets. A single Internet company like America Online can reach 55 million people. With national advertising on television, on radio, online, and in the printed media, it is no surprise that sameness is increasing. At the same time, many small, independent operations are being priced out by wholesaling and distribution operations, high rents, and backward business practices.

The massive mall is becoming a dinosaur. Its intimidating size, vast array of mostly franchised stores, large parking areas, and remote locations—all initial attractions—today are liabilities, especially for those with multiple jobs and limited leisure time. Entertainment attractions such as multiplex theaters, themed restaurants, and sports bars are being introduced at malls, but that is not enough to sustain them in the long run. To remain major shopping destinations, malls will no doubt be blending in more accessible civic activities and public institutions, making them a real alternative to the old downtown, as envisioned by early mall planners like Victor Gruen.

Remote Shopping

As clerks disappear from department stores and tellers from banks, customers have been learning to cope with reduced service. These changes, first propelled by automation and now by the Internet, have immersed the consumer in an increasingly remote world, often efficient and fast but sometimes exasperating and inefficient. For retailers, usually operating on a very thin profit margin, automation provides ways to cut operating costs and to streamline inventory, warehousing, and shipping activities. For community and civic life, remote shopping and the world of the Internet may further isolate us from each other, despite the popularity of online "communities." While the excitement and novelty of e-commerce has added élan to shopping, it is really one more important and remote way to shop.

Tourism and Entertainment Shopping

Tourism is here to stay, but more than franchised shops and festival marketplaces will be needed to satisfy the tourist shopper. Authenticity increasingly will be the byword as tourists seek culturally and regionally distinctive products that are individualistic, creative, and functional.

Theater has always been part of retailing, but the staying power and the pizzazz of the packaged marketplace—the entertainment shopping center of the 1970s, 1980s, and 1990s—and current entertainment retailing are slipping. To survive, entertainment retailing needs to blend authentic tourism and interactive, museum-type entertainment into its shopping theater.

Sociable, Service, and Communal Shopping

As an antidote to the sameness, remoteness, and heavy-handed commercialism of so much of shopping, consumers will seek friendly, communal, and face-to-face retail operations, whether in coffee houses, friendly bookstores, health food stores, service-oriented department stores, small specialty shops, flea markets, or farmers' markets. Such personal shopping will be increasingly important for the products and services provided, as well as for its personal attention and sheer friendliness.

Bargain Shopping

Saving money has been a necessity for many shoppers and part of the game of shopping for others. In the past, buying discounted goods often carried a stigma: you could not afford full-priced items. That is no longer true. "In fact, it is in vogue to search for good value," as Standard and Poor's reported in 1999.[3] Upscale buyers are becoming solid discount store patrons at the same time that discount stores—like Target with its Michael Graves designs and Kmart with its Martha Stewart products—are reaching out to more upmarket, sophisticated patrons. Bargain hunting is now for everyone, every day.

In the past, the shopping year would be punctuated with white sales, post-Christmas sales, pre-school sales, and end-of-season sales at traditional department stores. Then some stores, like Klein's in New York, offered solely lower-priced merchandise. Others had bargain basements; perhaps one of the best known has been Filene's Basement in Boston, a ninety-year-old institution attracting 15,000 to 20,000 customers per day. Its legendary wedding gown sale at the Boston store, celebrating its fiftieth anniversary in May 1997, drew hundreds from all over the East Coast, some of whom lined up at 3 a.m. for the 8 a.m. opening. After a 1999 bankruptcy, the Filene's Basement chain declined from fifty to fourteen stores scattered across the country. (Since 1988, when Campeau bought Filene's and sold the Basement to raise cash, the Basement has been a separate corporation.) And now like other discount stores, Filene's Basement can be found in choice center-city locations, where turnover is faster than in the suburbs. Marked-down, discontinued, overrun, and last season's items, once found at dramatic savings in stores like Loehmann's in the Bronx, where in the 1950s Upper East Side matrons would find glamorous evening dresses for their charity balls, now are available in stores all over the country.

In the early 1960s, discount stores—some from the city and others altogether new businesses—appeared on highway strips outside major cities—for instance, Route 4 beyond the George Washington Bridge in northern New Jersey. As the prices of everyday items in regular stores soared with designer labels filling the racks, discounters proliferated. Loehmann's, Alexander's, and Filene's Basements moved out of city centers to be joined by an array of discounters—including T. J. Maxx, Syms, Kmart, and Marshall's—that were expanding in number, size of operation, volume of products, and specialization. While some individual stores remained in detached sites on suburban arteries, many clustered in strip shopping centers on those same arteries, and others were built in Power Centers or discount malls, often on or near interstate highways. Traditional department stores responded to the pervasive markdowns by jamming their once-elegant stores with a dizzying array of sale merchandise. Bargain shopping seemed to be everywhere, and it was paying off as discounters' share of apparel sales reached a remarkable 20 percent in 1999.[4]

The very proliferation of these discount stores indicates their success in filling a gap in the market. The major categories of these discounters have been:

1. Such stores as Marshall's, T. J. Maxx, Loehmann's, or Syms, which sell discontinued items from a wide range of manufacturers.
2. Outlet stores for manufacturers, like London Fog, Maidenform, or Coach, or single stores, like Brooks Brothers or J. Crew. Often called factory outlets, these are more likely to be in stand-alone locations or in outlet shopping centers in places like Manchester, Vermont. Ironically, they are rarely near factories, especially as their factories may be in Southeast Asia.
3. Category Killers such as Toys "R" Us, Sports Authority, or Home Depot, which concentrate on a particular line of products and often kill their competitors.
4. Superstores or Big Boxes—like Wal-Mart, Kmart, Target—carrying an array of goods at reduced prices in vast, low-slung buildings usually in isolated locations, sometimes as lone wolves preceding other retail development, sometimes with other superstores in Power Centers.
5. Warehouse clubs like Costco's Price Clubs and Wal-Mart's Sam's Clubs, with industrial warehouse interior ambiences of wide aisles and tall stacks of merchandise, where forklift vehicles commingle with customers making volume purchases.
6. Small retail discount stores, often concentrating on such home goods as tile, carpets, plumbing and electrical supplies, which have popped up in low-rent commercial-industrial areas on the edges of cities.

Wal-Mart has come to symbolize mass discount retailing in America. Its "everyday low price" retailing is steamrolling its way into small communities in suburban and exurban areas and now into towns and city centers. It is the ultimate blockbuster discounter in the United States today, number two in *Fortune's* 2000 list of the 500 largest U.S. corporations, with 2000 revenues of over $191 billion. There are 3,102 Wal-Mart discount and supercenter stores and 497 Sam's Clubs in all fifty states and eight foreign countries, with more than 1 million employees—or associates, as Wal-Mart calls them.[5] Starting in 1945, with a franchise for a Ben Franklin store in the cotton and railroad town of Newport, Arkansas (population 7,000), Sam Walton expanded his variety store business by taking over other variety stores in Bentonville and Fayetteville through the 1950s until 1964, when he opened his first Wal-Mart in Rogers, Arkansas.

Wal-Mart's public image is mixed, as its size and skills have produced a wide range of goods at low prices in areas where shopping options often had been limited. But those very features have also made Wal-Mart an eradicator of the stores on Main Street and a redesigner of the social structure of small towns and rural America. Just the mention of Wal-Mart arouses love-hate emotions. Towns like Greenfield, Massachusetts, states like Vermont, and national organizations like the National Trust for Historic Preservation have waged fierce campaigns to prevent Wal-Mart from encroaching on their turf. Spirited local citizen groups in communities all over the country, helped by outside organizations like the National Trust and consultants, have had some dramatic victories in warding off Wal-Mart stores and their threats to downtown centers, community spirit, and retailers. On the other hand, local governments often lust for the tax revenue and jobs that a Wal-Mart usually promises, while many customers enjoy the variety and low prices of its merchandise, as well as the store's efficiencies and accessibility.

Small-town America has always been at the heart of Wal-Mart's operations. "Our customers in smaller markets and rural America . . . represent our roots," states Wal-Mart's 1995 *Annual Report*.[6] Sam Walton himself describes how important his small-town beginnings were in shaping his company. Starting out "underfinanced and undercapitalized in these remote, small communities, contributed mightily to the way we've grown as a company," according to Walton. "Had we been capitalized, or had we been the offshoot of a large corporation the way I wanted to be, we might not ever have the Harrisons or the Rogers or the Springdales and all those other small little towns we went into in the early days. It turned out that the first big lesson we learned was that there was much, much more business out there in small-town America than anybody, including me, had ever dreamed."[7]

Yet Wal-Marts are seen by many as unsightly and unfriendly neighbors creating a host of economic, environmental, and social problems. Located in big one-story industrial buildings, they sit on at least two acres of land with many more acres of asphalt parking lots, often alone on a major highway and usually outside the settled area of a town (fig. 57). Their out-of-town locations, accessible primarily by car, increase air pollution, make shopping difficult for those who cannot drive or do not own cars, and encourage further centrifugal development—and erosion of the vital social and economic life of Main Street.

Some of the earlier chain retailers, like Sears and J. C. Penney, tried to complement rather than eradicate Main Street businesses, but Wal-Mart, because of its large scale of merchandise—drugs, hardware, clothes, food,

57. Wal-Mart near Troy, New York, where a farm and its silos are visible behind the store, 2000

appliances, computers, linens, jewelry, furniture, and more—can wipe out all of the independent and small chain stores on Main Street in one fell swoop. It also converts those former storekeepers into Wal-Mart "$5 an hour clerks," according to Kenneth Munsell, head of the Small Town Institute.[8] Only associates "in supervisory and management positions are compensated on a salaried basis"; managers receive extra compensation based on their "unit's profits," and all other store associates are "compensated on an hourly basis," with maybe a little more, "depending upon the Company's productivity and profitability."[9] The impacts of the big discounters, like the earlier shopping centers, cut into the economic heart of the downtowns. Kenneth E. Stone, an Iowa State University economist, has found in his studies of small Iowa towns that the loss of business from a mega-discount department store like Wal-Mart has a ripple effect that reaches well beyond the host town. The effects of these large discount department stores on existing commercial towns and their neighboring communities are as devastating as impacts of the earlier out-of-town shopping centers, which have been documented in studies of Plattsburgh, New York, and Hagerstown, Maryland, where downtown retail sales and commercial real estate values dropped slightly more than 30 percent in the 1970s.[10]

Countering these charges, Wal-Mart has tried to convey the impression that it is community minded. "Community service is part of the mindset of Wal-Mart Associates," states the 1995 annual report, whose theme is "Giving Back to the Community." Wal-Mart associates in Fresno, California, plant trees along city streets; in Pasadena, Texas, they clean up a parkway

58. Wal-Mart, Bennington, Vermont, in the shadow of the Bennington Battle Monument

and eventually "adopt" a highway each year; and in Yuma, Arizona, they raise money for the local hospice. These projects by Wal-Mart associates, which totaled $127 million in 1999, made the company the "largest charitable fund-raising force in the United States," according to the 1999 annual report, as well as "good neighbors to the nation."[11] Wal-Mart's efforts to be a good neighbor are especially interesting in one of its most contested locations, the state of Vermont, where a national campaign was mounted to keep Vermont Wal-Mart free.

However, on September 19, 1995, Wal-Mart's first Vermont store opened in Bennington in the 50,000-square-foot former F. W. Woolworth store in Monument Plaza shopping center, a site approved by Governor Howard Dean. "Wal-Mart officials have worked with the Town of Bennington," the Governor said at the store's dedication, "to bring new jobs (70 percent full-time and 30 percent part-time) to the community while siting their store in existing retail space. I appreciate Wal-Mart's willingness to look at downtown sites for their Vermont locations. Revitalizing downtowns is an essential ingredient for economic growth that respects and enhances the unique charm of Vermont" (fig. 58). To foster a friendly relationship as a "caring corporate citizen" in Bennington, Wal-Mart offered more than $15,000 to such "area organizations" as the Molly Stark Elementary School and the local anti-drug group, and another $10,000 to the town of Bennington to "enhance the downtown area." To remain on good terms with Vermont, Wal-Mart's Bennington store was to "feature many Vermont-made products . . . some of which are sold in Wal-Mart stores across the country," said Larry Fennell, Wal-Mart's regional vice president.[12] Rutland, Vermont, followed suit as the second Vermont site. There Wal-Mart, encouraged by the mayor and local officials, has located downtown in a renewal site formerly occupied by Kmart. Eighty new jobs have been provided, as well as a much needed centrally sited department-like store, which has become a magnet drawing people downtown.

Wal-Mart's patriotism, with its "Buy America" program, its use of the American flag in its print advertising, and its identification with the small town, along with its collegial work environment, including folksy associates and greeters—known by their first names and appearing like hometown neighbors—resonates in Middle America. Wal-Mart is not alone in trying to "present themselves as members of the community."[13] PetsMart, a Category Killer for pet supplies, encourages customers to shop with their dogs, leases spaces for local vets, and offers dog training. Home Depot, a home supply Category Killer, has how-to seminars for its customers. Skillful promotion and marketing are necessary for survival in one of the country's most competitive fields.

To stay on top requires close attention to detail. Although it prides itself on its uniform prices, Wal-Mart admits that it veers from that practice when necessary to meet local competition. While its efforts to meet competition have involved shrewd distribution, pricing, and many targeted programs, "there is no assurance that this [success] will continue," a 1995 Wal-Mart report to the Securities and Exchange Commission honestly states. Uncertainty is inherent in this highly competitive business, which relies on the thinnest of profit margins. Wal-Mart made the number two spot for revenue on the Fortune 500 list in 2000, but it ranked only fifteenth in profits. Other corporations in the top five of that list ranked first, second, third, and sixth in profits. Although on top now, Big Boxes face an uncertain future. Wal-Mart is adapting to e-commerce, with its online connections with AOL, and also is recognizing the popularity of smaller stores as it experiments with a handful of 40,000-square-feet Neighborhood Markets, which offer food and drugs in supermarket-type stores. Wal-Mart and other discounters could be easily knocked off their feet by an unforeseen competitor, calamity, or misjudgment. That could be disastrous for communities and their environs because such megastores have become major determinants not only of shopping patterns but of the quality of life in a wide circle of communities. When the giant has stamped out all the local competition and then dies itself, a community is in trouble. Thus, public concerns about the megastores like Wal-Mart deserve careful attention.

Another variant of these discount department stores is the warehouse club, including Sam's Clubs and Costco's Price Clubs. Price Company, the originator of warehouse shopping, merged in 1993 with Costco, a wholesale retailer, to produce its high-volume and low-profit (1–9 percent) Price Clubs in 1999, with more than 308 stores worldwide and 70,000 employees. Most of these warehouse clubs, which have limited lines of goods but wide variety, require thirteen to fourteen acres in flat sites easily accessible by car. Costco, however, pioneered with city stores as early as 1993 with a five-acre site in a San Francisco redevelopment project in a city factory building with roof parking. By 1999 New York City alone had three clubs, with another planned just for food in Manhattan.

Price Clubs are warehouses with bare cement floors, eighteen-foot-high shelves piled with "super deal" volumes of fifty diapers, twelve-can cases of motor oil, packages of twenty-four rolls of toilet paper, and upscale wine, vinegar, and gourmet food; some of these items may be procured only by forklift. And there is no sales clerk to help. Costco continuously changes the merchandise, so there is always an element of surprise. The customers—members, who pay an annual fee of $35—can enjoy a food court, as in a mall, but the club is meant for serious buying. Many customers ring up at least $100 a trip, and then they have to find storage space at home for the big-volume packages.

This buying in bulk contrasts with an earlier shopping pattern, in which frequent small purchases were made in independent stores or in department stores with the thoughtful advice of trained clerks. Now all the responsibility of selection has been given to the shopper. Costco has narrowed the options. "It's the good deals that win me over," said Elizabeth Clark, a veteran shopper visiting the Price Club outside Washington, D.C., near the Pentagon. "While they have a lot of some things, it is not overwhelming. In fact, it's easy decison-making. I don't want a clerk hovering over me. I want to make my shopping decisions independently."[14] The straightforwardness of this type of shopping—bare interiors, no hype, no coupons, no deals, and plenty of bargains—is popular. Like many brick-and-mortar stores, Costco also offers online shopping.

Another type of discount shopping that is attracting customers and retailers is outlet shopping, which is seen as a growing market in the shopping center world. That seems to be confirmed by outlet stores' sales figures, which almost doubled from $6.3 billion to $11 billion from 1990 to 1994, with clothing the most popular type of merchandise. In the Washington, D.C., area, 33 percent of residents shopped at outlet malls or centers at least once a month.[15] While most of the merchandise comes from manufacturers' excess, which is not sold in regular stores during slow economic times, some merchandise is made expressly for outlets.

Outlet stores have moved from small buildings adjacent to the factory to stand-alone locations to strip malls often devoted to outlets, or to clustered, villagey malls in remote, tourist-oriented sites. Conglomerations of outlets have converted some communities into major tourist attractions. Freeport, Maine, home of L. L. Bean, the progenitor of sporting goods mail-order houses, has become a mecca of upmarket outlet stores, with over 185 retail establishments employing more than 6,000 people in the peak season, half of them Freeport residents. Vacationers in Maine, who once stopped in Freeport to buy fairly priced outdoor gear like hiking boots or down jackets in the legendary L. L. Bean store, now can spend a day—and lots of money—in what has become a major tourist attraction. An estimated 4 million people visited Freeport in 1999 (fig. 59).[16] L. L. Bean opened its first outlet store outside New England in May 1995 in an outlet center, one of many, at Rehobeth Beach, Delaware. Rainy days bring bored beachgoers and stray tourists to these outlet centers. "We look for locations that are heavy tourist areas," said Beth Fisher, the marketing director of Fisher Development Company of Lancaster, Pennsylvania, which runs the outlet center in which L. L. Bean is located, as well as other outlet malls in Lancaster and Sarasota, Florida.[17]

Manchester, Vermont, a century-old tourist destination near Mount Equinox, the ski resorts of Bromley and Stratton Mountains, the elegant Equinox House hotel, and Orvis, the well-known fishing gear manufacturer and store, has been transformed into another major outlet center. Its roads are lined with strips of outlet stores, some in new quiet gray frame buildings, with all the upmarket regulars—Coach, J. Crew, Brooks Brothers, Dana Buchman, and others—in detached and sometimes isolated buildings. These strips of stores, once just a retreat for condo renters frustrated by poor snow conditions, have become so popular that they almost overwhelm this once classy small town with tourists and traffic jams in all seasons. The town of Manchester has tried to capitalize on the positive features of such shopping: its economic multiplier benefits, the rehabilitation of downtown buildings, and even a local sales tax, which brought in $1 million in 1999. The stores have helped finance various town projects, such as construction of a needed traffic roundabout, which has calmed traffic and signaled the entrance to the town, and of a river walk and pedestrian bridge. Recognizing that outlet shopping could easily fall from favor, the town's planning required that well-constructed, attractive buildings be built to the sidewalk with parking behind. This design fits into the townscape and also is adaptable to alternate future uses (fig. 60). As the town planner, Lee Krohn, said, the buildings are designed to be "community assets."[18] In the meantime, Manchester's stores are destinations for thousands of tourists; the Chamber of Commerce generously estimates 3 million visitors.

The newest generation of outlet malls are "whoppers," attracting tens of millions of shoppers. Potomac Mills, a mega-outlet mall south of Washington, D.C., boasts that it is Virginia's top tourist attraction. Mills Corporation—which runs Potomac Mills, as well as Gurnee Mills near Chicago and Milwaukee, Franklin Mills near Philadelphia, Sawgrass Mills near Fort Lauderdale, Florida, and others near Nashville, Dallas, and Tempe, Arizona—follows the same formulae as the massive enclosed regional shopping malls of the 1980s. Big anchors, hundreds of stores, a sea of parking, play

59. Outlet shopping in Freeport, Maine, 1998

60. A few outlet stores in Manchester, Vermont, 2000

areas for children, and food courts—all the ingredients of the massive mall—are here in these discount malls. The only difference is the tenant. Instead of Saks Fifth Avenue there is the Clearinghouse Saks Fifth Avenue, and instead of Neiman Marcus there is the Last Call From Neiman Marcus. But these fancy stores are blended in with hundreds of discounters (Marshalls, Burlington Coat Factory, Loehmann's and T. J. Maxx), outlet stores (J. C. Penney Outlet Stores and Spiegel Outlet Stores), and Category Killers (Sports Authority). These malls are for the bargain hunter willing to devote long and hard hours to a shopping trip.

An often unrecognized and understudied type of merchandising is the low-overhead incubator retailing appearing on the edges of cities in areas zoned for industry and commerce. Operating off the beaten path in unprepossessing buildings, these stores sell carpets and flooring, pool supplies, roofing, tiles, and plastics. Some are offshoots of wholesale companies, but usually they are small, independent retailers specializing in household and office supplies, not clothing. In Markham, Ontario, a rapidly growing suburb of Toronto, a large new commercial-retail town has been built. However, across the road in a commercial warehouse area, incubator retailing has mushroomed in one-story buildings meant to house offices of small companies. White-collar trade had been anticipated, but the low rents attracted these upstart retailing operations.

Rabbit warrens of such discounters are tucked into the backs and sides of buildings in Rockville, Maryland, near Washington, D.C., in the sprawling industrial-commercial sections off Rockville Pike, an artery now lined with shopping centers. Rents here are one-third those of the retail sites on main roads.[19] The shopper can find almost any household item here for considerably less than in the big hardware stores. Because they operate, like most discounters, on a low profit margin, these retailers gravitate to such low-rent areas. Current zoning in Montgomery County, where Rockville is located, allows retailing in warehouse areas only for those that sell building materials or auto parts, or for those that serve the industries in the area, such as day care centers and sandwich shops (fig. 61). The shops that located in these districts prior to the restrictive zoning are allowed to stay.[20] This retailing proliferation is yet another example of the segregated single-use district, which planning and zoning have promoted in this country.

Bargain shopping will exist in many different forms in the future. Already overstored, as the trade refers to the current saturation, and operating with very narrow profits, discount retailing faces severe competition not only from its wild overgrowth but from e-commerce. In regions overloaded with bargain shopping opportunities, from the isolated discounter to the outlet center to the massive outlet-discount mall, there will be disruptions as discounters merge, expand, and contract, and as bargain shopping permeates more of traditional shopping, right down to supermarkets, with their coupons, discounts, special buyer cards, and even volume bargains. The large-scale internalized discount malls in saturated areas of some of the most populous metropolitan areas—Philadelphia, Chicago, New York, Washington, D.C.— seem most vulnerable. As the internalized shopping mall reinvents itself as revenue slows, the whoppers of discount malls in saturated areas may face the same challenge. E-commerce is a serious threat to the discounter, as online shopping offers many of the same products as the discounters but with the advantages of easy comparison shopping in one's home at one's leisure.

In regions that have not experienced bargain shopping saturation—

61. Warehouse retailing in Rockville, Maryland, 1999

often smaller metropolitan areas or rural areas—the invasion of discount-bargain stores will no doubt continue. In Vermont, Bennington welcomed the state's first Wal-Mart in a shabby shopping center, if only because this South Shire town is less tony than Manchester. The Bennington Wal-Mart has been considered successful by the town government, the majority of shoppers, and some nearby retailers, like the established Bellemare Furniture Company, despite vigorous opposition from national, regional, and local groups. The upscale outlet shops in nearby Manchester and an earlier outlet center in abandoned mills in Cohoes, New York, do not appeal to the family of four struggling on an income of $20,000. Nor does the Mills Corporation see rural areas like Bennington, with its thin population, as promising sites for its whopper discount malls. But the areas with less affluent shoppers may need to attract more bargain warehouses, smaller-scaled and lower-priced outlets for their shopping.

Discount retailers, especially the blockbusters, will adapt to meet changing market situations. As the early enclosed malls and fast-food restaurants adapted to new consumer and community needs, so will the big discounters. The fast-food restaurants now feature salad bars and fish sandwiches to meet the desires of health-conscious customers, and their architecture can blend in on High Street in Oxford, England, on the boulevards of Paris, and on town and city streets in America. The early malls revamp themselves with new stores, customers, and interior designs. Discounters are now online and becoming more urban. Some, such as Loehmann's, Syms, and Marshall's, are starting to move into the center city, whether 17th Street or Park Avenue in New York City or Boylston Street in Boston, and they are finding it a lucrative move. Loehmann's, already in Boston and San Francisco, opened its Manhattan store in November 1996 and in its first five days sales reached almost $2 million, three times better than similar five-day tallies at its other stores.

Thus, the discounters, like the malls, fast-food operations, and many retailers, are adapting to new urban situations and new technology. It seems as though only the big ones, like Wal-Mart, get bigger as the smaller chains, such as Bradlee's, Jamesway, and Caldor, liquidate or go into bankruptcy. Whether there will be systemic modifications in the discounters' distribution system, the backbone of their operation, against which independent retailers have trouble competing, is less probable. But that might change if the downshifters, and others interested in community responsive retailing gain influence, as the environmentalists have done in the last few decades. Change is the only certainty.

The Pall of Malls

The shopping mall is facing hard times. This "mega industry is on the brink of a mega decline," Francesca Turchiano predicted in 1990 for *American Demographics*.[21] Standard and Poor's goes a step further and states that malls will be obsolete by 2010.[22] By 1999, the respected Urban Land Institute Council members were ranking regional malls at the bottom of the list of income-producing properties (fig. 62).[23] And indeed, dying or dead malls are so common that redevelopment of mall sites has become a specialty for planners and developers, and it was even a class topic in the spring of 2000 at Harvard's School of Design.

62. Kent Narrows Sportsmans Center, Kent Narrows, Maryland, 2000, bypassed by newer and larger centers, has been awaiting resuscitation for years

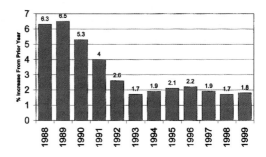

Growth Rate in Number of Centers

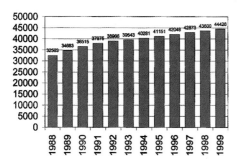

Number of Shopping Centers

63. The development of new shopping centers slowed down dramatically in the 1990s, as the annual growth rates indicate. Source: International Council of Shopping Centers

64. Number of shopping centers

Shopping malls have been a mega-industry, with 8 percent of the American labor force working in shopping centers in 1987, which generated that year $586 billion in sales, or 13 percent of the Gross National Product.[24] Yet the number of enclosed malls opened in the United States has dropped steadily from 106 in 1970–74 to 36 in 1990–1992.[25] Only two malls with more than 1 million square feet were built in 1994, compared with twelve in 1988 and seventeen in 1989.[26] Another set of statistics, prepared by the National Research Bureau, shows that between 1988 and 1992 new shopping center construction dropped by 59 percent while shopping center renovations increased by 15.7 percent. And mall shoppers have decreased. *American Demographics* found that the number of adults shopping in malls dropped 6 percent between 1987 and 1991 and, according to a Roper survey, only 50 percent consider malls a "pleasant place to shop."[27] By 1997, Standard and Poor's found that mall trips had declined by more than 50 percent from the early 1990s and that the number of stores visited was down by two-thirds.[28] And those visits only averaged one hour, according to PricewaterhouseCoopers/Lend Lease's report on trends for 2000 (figs. 63, 64).[29]

Malls have been overbuilt; retailing has shifted away from the traditional retailers to newer bargain stores, electronic shopping, and faster shopping; and some of the very problems of the inner-city stores, like traffic, parking, and crime, from which mall builders had hoped to escape, have followed them to their suburban locations. A stultifying sameness, a McDonaldization, permeates malls, no matter how they have been spiffed up.

Most important, women have less time for shopping, as more of them work; some hold down multiple jobs. When these time-pressed women shop, they are not leisurely cruising the malls but are "precision" shopping, as the trade calls it, zeroing in on exactly what is needed. By 1997, the number of shoppers going to malls declined by more than 50 percent, and the number of stores visited went down by two-thirds, Standard and Poor's reported.[30] Not surprisingly, these changes are "substantially shifting the industry's real estate requirements," according to a 1994 Urban Land Institute report.[31] There are exceptions. In August 1996, Park Meadows opened in Denver, and Cottonwood opened in Albuquerque, the first mall on the western side of the city. Not only is Cottonwood Mall large (over 1 million square feet), but, unlike many eastern cities, where the traditional department stores are vanishing, it has five department stores, as well as 135 other stores. In areas with growing population with few large shopping centers, new malls are being constructed and older ones refurbished. In the heart of New York City a Power Center is planned for East Harlem, and, in Queens, the twenty-seven-year-old Queens Center Mall has become so popular that it is being enlarged. Such malls are convenient and offer stores not previously available in those areas. However, the overriding fact is that many areas are saturated with malls such that some are being killed by retail Darwinism. In a 1996 survey by the National Main Street Center of nationwide downtown development trends, 22 percent of the small rural town, suburban, and midsize cities in the Main Street program reported dying malls, with the highest, 34 percent, in the midsize cities.[32]

The demise of the anchor department store poses another problem. These big department stores, considered linchpins for the success of shopping centers and malls, are disappearing or scaling down through buyouts, bankruptcies, and falling popularity in city after city. In Washington, D.C., Garfinckel's and Woodward and Lothrop have been replaced in their anchor sites at malls by J. C. Penney and Hecht's. In the late 1980s and early 1990s, the Mall at Short Hills in Millburn, New Jersey, an upmarket shopping center, lost two of its anchors, Bonwit Teller and B. Altman, both New York department stores, when they "went out of business"; then two other department store tenants, Abraham & Straus and Bloomingdale's, fell into bankruptcy. Those department stores that remain have shrunk and downgraded with deskilled labor forces. When a mall's anchors disappear, "the center often requires repositioning, and renovations frequently accompany this repositioning," the Urban Land Institute diplomatically states.[33]

The blockbuster mall of the 1980s, with its time-consuming mode of shopping—long trips on traffic-clogged roads to arrive at the mall and then walks from the car to the mall, equally long walks within the mall from store to store, will soon be a dinosaur, unless it adapts to a faster way of shopping. While renovating malls with enclosed parking, airier interiors, skylights, plants, and soothing colors has been seen as a high priority in mall management, there is still the basic problem of the inherent scale of malls. "Much of the huge stock of shopping centers built in the 1960s, 1970s, and 1980s is fast becoming outdated," the Urban Land Institute's *Remaking the Shopping Center* states. Putting a positive spin on these changes, the Urban Land Institute sees the "trend toward the remaking of older or underperforming centers . . . offering the industry a chance to reach a new level of maturity."[34] The Urban Land Institute reports on a myriad of ways that malls can be redesigned: skylights and lighting, flooring, graphics, art and sculpture, food courts, circulation patterns, restrooms, security for the interior, signs, expansions and contractions for the exterior facade. Advice for redoing the site plan and suggestions of ways of dealing with tenants, marketing, and management are part of the Urban Land Institute's ideas, along with case studies of renovated shopping centers from all over the country. And that advice seems to have been heeded as the trade organization for shopping centers, the International Council of Shopping Centers, reports that "developers are enhancing existing centers rather than building new ones" and that 2,586 "expansions and renovations of existing centers" were begun, compared with 1,511 new centers between 1993 and 1995.[35]

Adapting shopping malls and centers to changing times is the name of the game from La Jolla, California, to Orlando, Florida. In the Washington, D.C., area, five malls are being revamped. The tony Mazza Gallerie in Chevy Chase, with upmarket tenants like Neiman Marcus, once sealed off from the street with formidable marble walls, opened its facade to the outside world with traditional store windows and street entrances. One of Washington, D.C.'s earliest centers, Seven Corners, in the inner suburbs of northern Virginia, has undergone several radical renovations. Begun as a shopping center, Seven Corners was converted to an enclosed mall, and in the late 1990s it returned to its original shopping center operation—all with the same overall block-long building layout. Built in 1955–56, Seven Corners Shopping Center followed the dumbbell layout, with two department stores, Woodward & Lothrop and Garfinckel's, anchoring the ends. In between were forty smaller stores selling goods in every price range—including several candy stores, Brentano's, Singer Sewing Machine, Edmond's Opticians, and Cavalier & Buckley leather goods—on two levels; there was parking for 2,200 cars on both sides. To make shopping a one-stop experience, a detached supermarket was built on the periphery of the western parking lot. In its early days, Seven Corners was exceedingly successful and, in fact, outperformed other shopping centers. But when half a dozen new shopping centers appeared in the metropolitan area during the 1960s, Seven Corners' business started to slip. Remedial actions were sought. The answer was transforming the shopping center into a mall with an interior common space, the popular style of shopping emporium in the 1970s. But not even that new configuration could stem the retailing problems of Seven Corners. Most of its upscale shops disappeared, as did the two store anchors, due to bankruptcy and takeovers. Seven Corners' clientele evolved increasingly into lower income, immigrant, and elderly customers, and Big Boxes, Category Killers, and large discounters commanded an increasingly important role in the mall's shopping mix.

In 1995, after the Washington real estate firm B. F. Saul acquired the dying mall in 1994, Seven Corners was returned to its early shopping center operation while retaining the same footprint. Located in an area with a growing low-income Asian and Hispanic population and an oversupply of Big Boxes and Category Killers, market studies concluded that its "highest and best use" was no longer as a mall. Today, the interior open space is gone so that stores can be approached only from the exterior, as in the original shopping center. There is now no need to wander down long, plant-filled atria seeking a particular store, because you can drive almost to the doors of these stores, identified by large signs visible from the highway (fig. 65). But unlike its shopping center predecessor with top-line stores, now discount and Big Box stores, like Ross-Dress-for-Less, Barnes and Noble, and Home Depot, are the major draws. The reversion of this tired mall to its former shopping

65. *Seven Corners Shopping Center after its renovation in the 1990s, Falls Church, Virginia, 2000*

center configuration reflects one developer's response to new times and attitudes about mall shopping.[36]

It is not just in tired malls like Seven Corners but in malls everywhere that the sameness of layout, design, choice of stores and products, and management policies are dampening shoppers' enthusiasm, as well as the malls' economic vitality. Some of the tedium derives from a lack of individuality in malls and the tight control of retailers and shoppers exercised by mall operators swayed by the latest behavioral science findings. How can individuality thrive in a business in which conglomerates—like the big department store holding companies of May and Federated—control so many stores, where chains like Gap and Benetton are everywhere, and where one mall developer like Simon de Bartolo runs so many malls? The deadening bigness, sameness, and security contribute to the pall of the malls. This, combined with the overriding control of mall shopping by single mall operators—whether edicts on curfews or on what clothes can be worn by patrons, or the more subtle management decisions based on behavioral science—kills much chance of experiencing the pleasurable serendipity once associated with shopping.

For these shopping malls to function profitably, they will need more than retailing, entertainment, and architectural overhauls. They must metamorphose into the community centers that visionaries like Victor Gruen hoped they would become. The fact that some new malls are now being named "town centers," like Dulles Town Center in Loudoun County, Virginia, would indicate that developers want their malls to be seen as more than blockbuster buildings with stores. However, civic functions need to be incorporated in those malls if they are to be true town centers. And if they are, the malls' life spans can be extended for many segments of the population, including the growing ethnic groups and the ballooning numbers of elderly, many of whom welcome malls' climate-controlled environments, according to the Rouse Company's vice president for community development, Alton Scavo, a former native of New Orleans with a sensitivity to the effects of intemperate weather conditions.

The superstores and Big Boxes, which have been locating beyond established retail districts and far from the old downtowns, need not be lone wolves in isolated locations. They, too, can be communally oriented. As the Regional Plan Association (RPA), a respected private-planning think tank in the New York metropolitan area, stated in its 1996 *Third Regional Plan*, the challenge is to see "how to site, design, and operate them so they reinforce rather than undercut the region's downtowns." While recognizing that different types of superstores have different requirements and markets, like large hardware–home improvement stores suited to commercial or industrial areas, RPA urges that discount department stores and Category Killers and other superstores that can be "incorporated into or can adjoin established downtown retail districts" should be located in existing shopping areas.[37] As Costco discovered in San Francisco, some superstores can successfully adapt to downtown multi-story industrial and warehouse buildings with convenient public transportation or structured parking. The RPA recommends zoning rules that allow this popular large-scale discount retailing to be incorporated into existing shopping districts, as is being legislated in several foreign countries. Indeed, as malls are named town centers, are made to look more like Main Streets, and are lured to locate in city centers, retailing may be "coming full circle," as discussed in *Shopping Center World's* millennial December 1999 issue. It's "from Main Street to malls and back again."[38]

Fast Shopping

Fast and convenient shopping has become a priority for many time-pressed dual-earner families, multiple job holders, and working women, and its popularity seems likely to continue. The proportion of married women in the workforce with children aged six to seventeen, up from 39 percent in 1960 to 77 percent in 1998, certainly accounts for much of this interest in convenient and quick shopping.[39] As mall shopping has decreased, a significant increase has occurred in shopping close to home or on the way home from work in shopping centers where one can quickly buy food, get clothes cleaned, rent videos, or buy pizza. The neighborhood convenience store, once the city corner store and now most likely a chain store like 7-Eleven, continues to be a major fast shopping stop, as is the strip shopping center, which is being resurrected. Neighborhood and strip shopping outdid all other types of shopping in per-square-foot revenue in 1998, according to the Urban Land Institute.[40] And Census statistics show that the number of convenience stores and their dollar sales both grew from 1990 to 1997.[41]

The rebirth of the once-denigrated strip shopping center, left over from the 1960s and 1970s, is one of the success stories in the shopping world and an indication of the enthusiasm for fast and convenient shopping. These centers, in fact, have become the "bread and butter of the trade," according to Mark Schoifet of the International Council of Shopping Centers Council.[42] These one-story centers, stretched out with a couple of large stores and a raft of smaller ones, usually have a canopy covering a walkway along the entire length of the shops; bear signs and entrances visible from a parking lot in front of the center; and can be found on commercial arteries, often near older residential neighborhoods (fig. 66). Now reeking of age, bypassed commerce, and poor maintenance, many are candidates for renewal. The trade recommends "remaking" them at seven-year intervals, and, indeed, a 1992 study by the Urban Land Institute found that more than 70 percent of them are over seven years old.[43] To help potential redevelopers of these faded centers, Urban Land Institute has held workshops titled "Shopping Centers: How to Build, Buy, and Redevelop," featuring "How to remerchandise a

66. *Cloverly Village Center, a spruced-up strip shopping center, Cloverly, Maryland, 2000*

'tired' project,'" with case studies on renovating, redeveloping, and remerchandising a 1960s neighborhood center for the twenty-first century.

Shoppers like centers that are accessible and friendly and have the necessities, according to studies. Eighty-nine percent of adult shoppers patronize strip malls, and 24 percent shop only at strip malls, according to a 1991 *American Demographics* article. In a nonrandom study for *American Demographics*, 72 percent of the frequent strip mall shoppers were women, 62 percent of them married and 50 percent with "children in the household." That such shoppers want speedy service is also borne out by a 1990 National Benchmarks study, which found that from 1982 to 1990 shoppers visited fewer stores (down from 3.6 stores to 2.6 stores per visit) and spent less time shopping (down from ninety minutes to sixty-nine minutes).[44]

Shoppers' interest in fast and convenient shopping was also confirmed in a study of designs for the most marketable strip shopping center, undertaken for a 1984 dissertation by Lori Ann Pristo. Pristo found four of the five key design attributes related to accessibility and convenience:

1. convenience as "size of the center, being able to shop without reparking, the mixture of stores in the center and the layout of the center";
2. access and visibility as "the shoppers' perception of the ease of drop-off at the center, the visibility of the center to passing traffic, the ease of getting to the center, and the visibility of the merchandise through the window";
3. entry into the center as "a combination of perceptions of the ease of entry and exits, and convenience of shopping in bad weather";
4. and parking as "perceptions of convenience of the parking facilities and the safety of shopping at the center."

The only attribute not directly related to convenience in this study was image—the "shoppers' perception of the center's personality," including "store management, design of the storefronts, signage, and cleanliness."[45]

The findings of this study, undertaken at a time when developers' sights were still set on the large enclosed malls, and of surveys, undertaken in the 1990s, have been validated by continuing customer and developer interest in such strip centers in the early twenty-first century. The small scale of the strip center can offer the busy shopper service and sociability, called "relationship merchandising" by some in the trade. The clerks get to know the shopper and what the shopper likes. Familiarity can develop to the point where customers are called by their first names. That familiarity, along with computers and survey research, makes it possible to keep tabs on what merchandise is popular with the community. Seasoned merchandisers may call key customers when something is in stock that they know a customer wants. Small can be beautiful for both the customer and the retailer—and convenient shopping in the small strip center is being sought by more shoppers as developers and retailers recognize their popularity.

The convenience store, like the strip mall, has suffered from a low-class image, but it too has gained new respect as an important fast shopping destination. Stores like 7-Eleven, defined by the Department of Commerce as a "small grocery store selling a limited variety of food and non-food products, typically open extended hours," are convenient not only for the range of goods they sell and the hours they keep, but often for their ubiquitousness.[46] The stores seem to have a little bit of everything—aspirin, toothbrushes, cooked hot dogs, coffee, soft drinks, magazines and newspapers, candy, canned items, and, of course, the basics—milk, eggs, butter, bread, coffee, and sugar. This variety, as well as the service, embodies the convenience store's strong points, according to Marshall Dowdy's 1994 dissertation on convenience store patrons. Many are franchised, unlike the old street-corner mom-and-pop stores or the general stores in the country. It is commonly thought that convenience stores provide "fill-in" shopping. But Dowdy found that 85 percent of convenience store customers patronize the supermarket for their fill-in shopping and use the convenience store for ancillary grocery shopping.

While a frequent convenience store shopper was found by Dowdy to be susceptible to impulse buying, that patron also had strong feelings of "personalization and socialization" with the convenience store. "Socializing shoppers are defined as receiving gratification from being waited on by store personnel and affiliating with other shoppers," Dowdy reported.[47] Policemen get their coffee, neighbors exchange gossip, and truck drivers find someone to talk to—just like at the old general store but without the credit operation. The familiarity and informality of small stores are critical to their success, especially when shopping in the supermarket means investing time and energy just to cruise the vast aisles, with little opportunity for a social relationship with the clerks, most of whom shift from job to job within the store or checkout counter.

In city neighborhoods, suburban areas, and rural regions, the small, independent convenience store, often in the guise of a corner store, has been a community necessity (fig. 67). "Many corner grocery stores became the social and physical anchor of an intersection or neighborhood," stated Ellen Beasley in her informative book *The Corner Store*, about the 103 corner stores in Galveston, Texas.[48] In the past, independent stores in cities, often operated by immigrant families, many of them Jewish but more recently Asian, Middle Eastern, or Indian, have provided an array of food and household

67. Corner store, 34th Street NW, Georgetown, Washington, D.C., 1999

items, as well as lucrative beer and wine, if state law permits their sale. As the survival of the independent grocery was threatened by the chain store, the independent neighborhood convenience store has been threatened by the chain convenience store. The sheer ubiquitousness of a chain like 7-Eleven—with 500 or so stores in the Mid-Atlantic region and 236 in just the Washington, D.C., metropolitan area—threatens the independents, especially when combined with the chain's modern inventory, delivery, and merchandising methods.[49] Advertised specials with reduced prices induce patronage as well as standardization, as did the old Howard Johnson's motels and restaurants on the highways. Despite the efficiency or economy of scale enjoyed by the chain, local mom-and-pop stores often can be as fast as the chain competitor while also offering friendly, localized service, like ethnic specialties made by the owner or special orders for customers.

Convenience stores are scattered in rural areas as well as in city and suburban neighborhoods. Route 7 in Vermont is dotted with independent convenience stores, which have evolved into popular shopping and social stops for nearby communities, after their general stores were replaced by supermarkets, often tens of miles away. A chain out of Saratoga Springs, New York, Stewart's, has appeared in southern Vermont and nearby New York State with not only convenience items, but with inexpensive gas, providing tough competition for the local independents—and also evidence that a strong market exists for rural convenience stores. Whether part of a chain or an independent, the convenience store offers fast shopping—and with stretched lives, that is increasingly important.

Fast shopping also extends to prepared food and meals, which can be selected on the spot or ordered by telephone, fax, or e-mail. Increasingly supermarkets, specialty stores like the delicatessens or gourmet food shops, and even restaurants now sell meals and parts of meals to customers living on a fast track. The working mother can pick up a large and nutritious meal for the family on her way home from work, and the busy young office worker can get a fancy, gourmet meal for himself and his girlfriend at Dean and Delucca after he leaves work. Where once only pizza, fried chicken, and food from the local Chinese takeout were delivered, urban and many suburban residents can now choose meals from their favorite restaurants. A holiday meal, like Thanksgiving dinner, need not take hours of preparation; it can be ordered by phone from the local supermarket or a gourmet store. If you would like spiced roast loin of lamb with braised salsify and sweet potato confit for a special dinner, you can get it in New York from Daniel Boulud, a chef and restaurant owner who set up an "off premises catering" service for those who want to serve his food in their homes.[50] Where supermarkets once had just salad bars, prepared soups, and rotisserie chickens, now whole meals or parts of meals are available—and some supermarkets are delivering meals. The successful Wegman's supermarkets in Rochester, New York, find their grocery sections shrinking as their prepared and fresh food sections expand. As more women work and more people are on the fast track, the convenience and options of remote shopping, including prepared foods, will no doubt increase.

Shopping for ready-made meals is becoming popular around the globe, even in gourmet capitals. In London, Pret à Manger stores are cropping up all over (fig. 68). In Paris, the proverbial long lunches with wine, fine food, and good friends now are thought by some to take too much time and cost too much, so carry-out food, from drive-through McDonald's to the local bakery, is becoming more popular. Whether from the Safeway in Annapolis, Maryland, or from Le Crior bakery in Neuilly-sur-Seine, near Paris, prepared food and meals are becoming increasingly popular with time-pressed shoppers.

Remote Shopping

Shopping has become remote in many ways—you can shop by telephone, fax, or Internet. Even if you do go to a store, the likelihood is that its owners are states away, that the clerks are part-time, short-term employees, and that the store's policies are dictated by a regional headquarters. Even that commercial establishment where you entrusted your money and received judicious advice,

68. Pret à Manger, London, 1998

the bank, has gone the remote route, making the traditional trust between customer and bank officer a thing of the past. Most bank transactions now can be done by machine, and if you have a more complicated dealing, you may see a teller in some banks for a fee. Even banks that still have free tellers run most of their operations remotely. My bank in Washington, D.C., is owned by a bank in Charlotte, North Carolina. Many functions formerly undertaken by the branch staff are now transferred to headquarters or handled by machines. Managers, who came and went, have disappeared completely; now all-purpose "financial center managers" run the branches at a "service" counter. Thus, no long-term relationships form between clients and bank employees, which are useful when difficult problems arise. When problems do arise, you may finally reach someone in Charlotte if you have the patience to cope with the telephone's mechanical voice instructions.

Although remote shopping seems very contemporary, it is not new. In the 1900s, mail-order retailing, like the Sears Roebuck and Montgomery Ward catalogues, brought the world of retailing to isolated rural folk, who could not easily get to city stores. "Catalogs were, in essence, an early equivalent of today's virtual department stores," according to Harvard Business School professors Clayton Christensen and Richard Tedlow.[51] Mail-order shopping, or catalogue shopping, became universal for city, rural, and suburban customers who did not want to go to a store, did not have the time to shop, or could fulfill their needs through particular catalogues. In 1948 there were only 239 catalogue and mail-order houses employing 70,998 people; by 1996 the number of mail-order houses had swelled to 8,200, with 180,000 employees. The quantum leap in the number of retailing operations came in the 1950s and 1960s, when the total jumped almost fifteen times and the number of their employees almost doubled. Since then there has been a steady increase in the number of stores and employees.[52] Sales increases have been equally dramatic. From 1990 to 1999 consumer catalogue sales increased from almost $30 billion to $67 billion, according to the Direct Marketing Association.[53] Catalogue retailers are the largest part of this industry, but other nonstore, specialty, and general merchandise companies are branching into catalogue selling. As catalogue companies prospered in the 1990s, it is ironic that America's venerable and first catalogue company, Montgomery Ward, faltered and eventually died in 2001.

The growth of one mail-order company, Lands' End, illustrates the popularity of specialized catalogue shopping. Started in 1963 in Chicago by an advertising copywriter and sailor to sell sailboat hardware and equipment by catalogue, Lands' End has expanded continuously, becoming a public corporation in 1986 and achieving sales of $1.3 billion in 1999.[54] More than 250 million catalogues were distributed in 1998; 15 million people called its toll-free number, which functions 364 days of the year.[55] Casual and tailored clothing, shoes, luggage, and bedding now overshadow sailing gear. Its Oxford button-down shirt is so popular that one Lands' End employee boasted that 26 percent of the white and light-blue button-down Oxford shirts worn by men in the United States in the mid-1990s were purchased at Lands' End. Located since 1978 in an industrial park in rural Dodgeville, Wisconsin, forty miles southwest of Madison, every phase of the Lands' End operation has swelled: it now boasts two distribution centers, one of them the size of sixteen football fields; in 1993 a warehouse and phone center were established in England, in 1994 in Japan, and in 1995 an Internet home page was created, which had 15 million visits in 1998 and $138 million in sales, seven times the sales of 1993.[56] Online services include "Shop with a Friend," where two people can browse simultaneously, "Lands' End Live" with a split screen for direct communication with a sales associate, and a digital dressing room with a 3-D model. In 1999, 20 percent of the online shoppers were new to Lands' End.[57]

The guideline of the company's founder, Gary Comer, is reminiscent of retailing in years gone by: "Don't worry about what is best for the company—worry about what is best for the customer." Sales representatives are well trained and knowledgeable, and there is fast delivery. In-stock merchandise orders leave the warehouse on the day they are ordered, with 90 percent of sales achieving "initial fulfillment," meaning that the goods are in stock. Newsy catalogues feature articles on Ireland and Scotland, where some of the clothes are made, or stories of country ways by authors like Garrison Keillor.[58] These selling methods appeal to the educated (88 percent with college education), to those in professional and managerial positions (66 percent), and to the 35-to-54 age group with a median household income of $60,000.[59] This is just one catalogue retailer, which, like most retailers today, has diversified. Lands' End now has online services, seventeen stores in the United States and three in the United Kingdom, as well as its direct-marketing operation.

The overwhelming number of unsolicited catalogues in everyone's mailboxes confirms the large numbers of mail-order houses, as well as their many mailings. In 1999, L. L. Bean produced 70 different catalogues, and more than 200 million copies were distributed.[60] Orvis, which had been primarily a store for fly fishermen, now issues catalogues that barely mention fishing equipment in its pages of clothes for the suburban housewife and her outdoorsy husband. Gardening equipment, flatware, fancy cookware, inexpensive underclothes and stockings, stationery, plants, art supplies, museum store items, shoes, you name it, can be found in an Orvis catalogue. While ordering is simple, receiving is another matter, especially for home deliveries. Commercial delivery services, which most mail-order houses use, require that a package be picked up at some distant warehouse if you are not home to receive it on several delivery attempts. Once received, ordered items are often not as pictured in the catalogues: colors, sizes, textures, shapes, durability, and ease of operation may differ from advertisements.

Despite problems with catalogue shopping, many people consider it easier and more efficient than e-commerce. After frustrations in ordering from virtual companies' checklists, people are finding the user-friendly telephone ordering system of mail-order companies to be time-saving, informative, and responsive. You can ask questions of real people and receive immediate responses.

Direct-selling companies, like Avon Products, Tupperware, Amway, Mary Kay, and Fuller Brush, are adapting to the cyber age. Several of these—like Avon, Fuller Brush, and Tupperware—sell products online to the wired generations as well as through traditional face-to-face selling. Tupperware, recognizing the need to stay abreast of contemporary retailing, sells directly online and also offers online help for organizing selling parties, which remain the backbone of its operations. "At a party, you see more, feel it, understand it," states Lawrie Hall, a Tupperware spokesperson.[61] Although the direct marketing industry does not want to undermine its sales people, who function as its distributors even though many may be short-term employees, the industry also does not want to be left out of twenty-first century retailing.

"Teleshopping" is yet another variant of remote shopping. Instead of going to the supermarket or wholesale club for volume purchases—even for staples like toilet paper, soap powder, and branded products like Coca-Cola—you can telephone orders to a warehouse for home deliveries at an appointed hour. Some foresee brand-name packaged goods like Corn Flakes being delivered directly to the consumer, hence avoiding any middlemen, according to an article in *Adweek's Marketing Week*. Most shoppers, the article found, do not like everyday supermarket shopping, so marketers are thinking of ways to make shopping more "fun" and to eliminate its tiresome aspects. Teleshopping is one answer. Another is reorganizing the supermarket. Arranging items in a supermarket by function — like displaying all spaghetti-making ingredients together — is a first step already being tested. "Supermarkets will become true marketers, rather than marketers that act as distribution centers."[62]

But the big leap in remote shopping is electronic shopping — which employs computers and television. In 1988, Ross L. Davies of the Oxford Institute of Retail Management in England stated that "it is not so much a case of whether teleshopping will happen, but when."[63] That time arrived a decade later.

Television Shopping

Television home shopping has not taken off as expected. This emerging technology has suffered from a low-class image owing partly to its seemingly endless advertisements for gaudy jewelry and other downmarket apparel. That impression has clearly worried the industry. Fred Siegel, the vice president of cable shopping channel QVC, told the *New York Times* that "less than a third of our air time is devoted to jewelry and less than 5 percent of our jewelry is cubic zirconia," the fake diamonds that seem to fill the home shopping screens.[64] QVC, which stands for Quality, Value, and Convenience, launched a campaign to broaden its market appeal. It began offering products for a wider spectrum of viewers, made new commercials, and spruced up its interactive technology with an online service developed by Microsoft. QVC had tried advertising with entertainers, including "new generation" country performers, to reach a younger audience, and its programs targeted those interested in arts and crafts. In 1995, when QVC featured exemplary crafts from different states, David Gil of the Bennington (Vermont) Potters selected to represent Vermont, saw his 3,000 pieces of pottery snapped up by these television buyers in three and a half minutes. Clearly, QVC appeals to more than those interested in zirconia. This twenty-four-hour network, with its folksy, friendly tone, offers a range of merchandise and a type of visual, interactive entertainment not available on the Internet.

Most television home shopping consists of scrolling through illustrated lists of products. Teleshopping also is used to provide information — and lure clients — as in the case of the Washington, D.C., real estate company Shannon & Luchs, which displays its listed houses for sale. Major department stores, such as Macy's and Marshall Field, as well as catalogue houses like Lands' End, had considered teleshopping before opting for the interactive technology of the Internet.

Internet Shopping

Internet retailing — known as e-retailing, e-commerce, or online shopping — is the most significant recent development in retailing. In the parade of changes in retailing, shopping on the Internet ranks with other revolutionary techno-

logical and cultural innovations, like mail-order retailing and the early department store. Such a change, categorized as a "disruptive technology" by Harvard
Business School professors C. M. Christensen and R. S. Tedlow, introduces a
distinctly different way of shopping, as compared to a "sustaining technology,"
such as the change from supermarkets to shopping centers to malls, which represents larger models of the same type of business practice.[65]

Internet shopping is, indeed, a whole new ball game in the world of
retailing. The capabilities of the Internet to connect people to people, or people to institutions, to commerce like retail stores, to information sources, or
to entertainment open incredible opportunities that are just beginning to be
tapped. The soaring sales figures of early e-retailing indicate the popularity
of this new type of shopping. In 1997, Internet retail sales had reached $2.4
billion; by 1998 they had swelled to $8 billion; and by 1999 they had reached
$20.2 billion. Standard and Poor's estimates that online sales will reach $41
billion by 2002.[66] Whatever the exact figure, it is clear that e-commerce is
growing fast and fitfully.

The popularity of e-commerce can be explained as it meets the needs
and desires of many who want ease in shopping; it offers easy means of comparing prices to select bargains and provides a wide range of choices, as well
as entertainment. That was confirmed in a study by Forrester Research, a
Cambridge, Massachusetts, research firm that tracks e-commerce, which
found users citing convenience and ease of research as the most important
reasons for choosing online vendors.[67] The future of e-commerce lies not
only with the retail shopper but with the enormous business-to-business
world. All that is needed for e-commerce transactions are a computer
with access to the Internet and a credit card. Indeed, "this is the future," as
Jack Clarkson, marketing director of the online funeral website Heavenly-
door.com, stated at the 1999 National Funeral Directors Association
convention.[68]

The explosive interest in e-commerce also reflects the phenomenally
rapid growth of ownership of computers, use of the Internet, and development of dot.com/e-commerce companies. In 2000, 51 percent of American
households had computers and 42 percent were online, with Internet use
divided equally between men and women, according to the Department of
Commerce.[69] That's 150 million Internet users, according to the respected
Mary Meeker, an Internet analyst at Morgan Stanley. And it took only five
years for the Internet to reach 5 million users, compared with thirty-eight
years for radio, thirteen for television, and ten years for cable. "The market
for Internet-related products and services," Meeker ventures, "appears to be
growing more rapidly than early emerging markets for print publication, telephone, film and TV."[70]

The rapid acceptance of the computer and the Internet has only
fueled excitement about this novel way of doing business. And, in turn, the

euphoria about e-commerce in its heady, early days has produced extravagant and often misleading impressions about the future of online shopping.
This newcomer to retailing is not necessarily the death knell of real stores
and other types of retailing, as might have been implied by early publicity.
As a Standard and Poor's report states, "Although many industry pundits have
predicted that Internet commerce will lead to the demise of traditional retail
stores, this is not likely to happen."[71] For Christmas 1999, despite predicted
e-commerce sales of $13 billion, the Department of Commerce reported hol-
iday sales (October to December) totaled $5.3 billion. While $5.3 billion is
a hefty figure, it made up only 0.64 percent of all retail sales.[72] Future online
sales are optimistically predicted to move up e-commerce to 10 percent of
total retail sales. Although there is no question that online shopping will be
an increasingly popular way to buy goods, it will be just one more way to
shop. It will coexist with catalogue shopping as well as real-world stores,
referred to by the e-commerce world as "brick and mortars" in the same disparaging tone as "snail mail."

   With a few clicks of a mouse one can order books, clothes, hardware,
CDs, groceries, drugs, flowers, art, crafts, furniture, cars, or grave sites at any
hour of the day or night. For the comparison shopper, the seeming universality
of e-stores provides unbounded chances to browse and compare prices, so
much so that many retailers fear that shoppers will spend their online time
searching for the best bargains for goods that they may then purchase in a real
store, where they can see, feel, and test an item. No longer do consumers have
to rely on a salesperson for product information. Car dealers, for example, are
finding potential buyers far better informed on what they want and on the
attributes of different cars—customers have searched the Web for information. As many cars are similarly equipped and styled, consumers do not need
to see, touch, and feel cars as much as they did in the past, dealers report. Nor
do they need face-to-face negotiations with the car dealer. A prospective car
buyer can now go online to gather information, make a decision in the peace
of his or her own home, and then take the plunge of ordering online a car that
will be delivered to a local dealer. With the ease and convenience of the Internet for comparison shopping, the consumer can save time and avoid the has-
sle of driving to the store, waiting in lines, and dealing with clerks, especially
for branded products, which do not require qualitative decisions on factors
like color, thickness, sturdiness, size, sound, and weight.

   The process of ordering seems almost effortless and money-free for
the technically confident. Differences in the level of skills and familiarity
with computers clearly influence who is and who is not shopping on the
Internet. For the computer literate, navigating interactive shopping is easy,
but for a less adept, often older computer user, the interactive world and its
pinball-type of operation can be daunting. But computer ownership and use
by the elderly is increasing. Government figures show that individuals fifty

years old and older experienced the largest percentage increase of Internet usage in 1999 and 2000.[73] Older adults, according to Jupiter Communications, spend more hours online than any other age group. Even if octogenarians do not own computers, they may well be working the Internet alongside teenagers on the local library computers or in the computer rooms of retirement communities. In fact, educated and moneyed oldsters are seen now as good candidates for e-retailing.

Income, race, and education seem to determine computer ownership and use, which in turn determine who will be e-shopping. An elite group of "High Income Optimists," who have a median income of $59,000, two years or more of online experience, log onto e-mail daily, and have owned at least three personal computers appear to be the early e-shoppers, according to a 1999 Forrester Report.[74] This group, enjoying the new technology with constantly upgraded PCs and hardware, accounts for a small portion of North Americans—only 5 percent in 1998—Forrester reports. The Department of Commerce found in 2000 that high-income and well-educated households owned the greatest number of computers. Seventy-eight percent of American households with computers had incomes of $75,000 or more, and 70 percent of households headed by someone with a college degree had Internet access. On the other side of the digital divide are low-income, poorly educated, single-parent, and minority households, especially blacks and Hispanics. This divide is narrowing, however, as more people of all colors and ages in all locations acquire computers and get online. In 2000, 33 percent of black and Hispanic households owned computers, compared with 51 percent for all American households. Internet access for both blacks and Hispanics rose to 24 percent from 1998 to 2000, a 100 percent increase. But most dramatic has been the increase in rural households' access to the Internet, which reached 39 percent in 2000, only slightly lower than the 41.5 percent national Internet usage. But whatever the increases in computer ownership and use, large segments of the American population are lagging behind in the digital age and will not be participating in online shopping in the near future.[75]

In the early, exciting days of online shopping, new e-commerce companies have been popping up at a staggering pace, and massive operations like AOL and Amazon.com are evolving into all-encompassing cyber-corporations. At the same time, old-line department stores, newer discounters, and mail-order houses are setting up their own online stores. There is a lot of "noise" from the hundreds of e-commerce companies trying to be heard, according to Richard Sabot, chairman of e-Ziba, an online company selling authentic crafts from around the world.[76] "Getting heard" means attracting customers and capturing their loyalty to these dot.coms early on, similar to Bon Marché in the nineteenth century seeking a "*clientèlè fidele.*" If a shopper finds a website, gets accustomed to it, and trusts it, many in the industry believe that a customer will continue to use the website and, if all goes well, will sustain a loyalty to it, as one would to a brand-name product. Thus, creating a user-friendly website and a "web of trust" are critical initial steps for an e-commerce company. The early success of Amazon.com and AOL has been attributed to their easy, efficient web pages.

In the cornucopia of goods available online, books, music, airline tickets, toys, videos and DVDs, software, flowers/cards, and financial services have ranked high with shoppers, according to market surveys of early e-commerce. Two important areas of shopping—food and clothes—have not fared well in these early days, and their problems reflect troubling inadequacies of e-retailing.

Many companies—like Peapod.com—have been trying to capture an affluent market of people who do not have time or who do not like to shop for groceries at supermarkets. Many others have fallen by the wayside. In Washington, D.C., alone, All Things Delivered, Shoppers Express, and Shopping Alternatives have disappeared. While the supermarket is an enticingly large $450 billion business per year (with only a 2 percent profit margin), it is difficult for remote companies to garner enough volume to be successful. Online grocery shopping, advertised by Streamline.com as the "final evolution of the supermarket," is estimated by Jupiter Communications to grow almost thirty times from 1999 to 2003, with sales hitting $7.5 billion, but that is only 1 percent of the total market.

Arrangements for ordering, delivering, and payment vary. Most charge a monthly fee, often in the $25 to $45 range for weekly deliveries. Some charge by delivery, and others have an extra charge for a refrigerated garage container. Coping with the many fulfillment problems, especially for perishables, has been a major hurdle for online food shopping. Also, these early food e-retailers' warehouses are not as fully stocked as traditional stores, so selections are limited. However, for branded products and many staples, online shopping is promising, especially for those who can afford the extra charges for their services.

Where online food and other e-shopping fails is in the quality/selection decision-making. How ripe do you like your bananas? How lean do you like your roast beef? There are also people who like the serendipity of supermarket shopping, finding the right food for the right occasion, seeing neighbors, and feeling part of the community. "As much as I hate supermarket shopping, I'll never stop going altogether," commented Frances Whittlesey. "Sometimes I need visual inspiration to come up with a new dinner idea. I like bumping into neighbors and chatting about the kids. And I'd rather give business to local merchants . . . who enrich the community and treat me as a friend, rather than to an anonymous entity."[77] Despite these hurdles, interactive food shopping will no doubt improve its fulfillment process and increase in popularity as it eliminates some of the drudgery of store shopping and provides fast and convenient service—often at a high charge.

Buying clothing online has been another disappointment for e-commerce. Almost half of Internet users in a 1999 survey of 2,399 people indicated that they were not planning to buy any clothing online. More than 40 percent of those surveyed who had bought apparel online reported that they would not buy clothing on the Internet because they wanted to be able to try it on (85 percent of the respondents) and because they were concerned about returning items (70 percent).[78] Concern about trying on clothes may be more of a problem for women than men, as women's clothing does not have standardized sizes. Women will, no doubt, be cross-shopping between real and virtual stores; real stores for quality selection and often online for items that cannot be found on real store racks. However, to counter consumer resistance to online apparel purchasing, e-retailers have been experimenting with techniques to personalize online shopping—like the Lands' End's "digital dressing room," My Virtual Model, which allows the shopper to try selected clothes on a 3-D paper-doll-like form configured to the shopper's approximate shape. This can help the shopper choose between an ankle-length skirt and a short one, but it fails in all those quality decisions of color, fabric texture, and true size, often critical for the final decision.

E-Commerce Companies That Work

Of all e-retail pioneers, Amazon.com may be the best known and one of the most successful in attracting customers, handling the mechanics of the purchase and delivery, and expanding its empire. Started in 1995 in the Seattle garage of its president, Jeff Bezos, Amazon.com in five years has grown to a company with $1.64 billion annual sales in 1998, 7,000 employees, seven massive distribution centers around the country, and multiple online stores under the umbrella on its website.[79]

The slogan "The World of Books Is Just a Click Away" was rapidly transformed into "The World's Largest Bookstore." And now Amazon is the Web's biggest store—a cyber-mall for its 17 million customers that offers music, electronics, software, toys, tools and hardware, auctions, gifts, and, of course, books. Most of these items are branded goods or books and music. Even its Sotheby's auctions trade on the reputation of Sotheby—a form of a brand. Its "zshops," with products from over 3,000 merchants, do not rely on brands but produce cash from commissions on each sale and a rental fee, as well as information on who is buying what.

Its website is easy to navigate, information is readily accessible, transactions can be quickly negotiated, and—the final test—purchases arrive when expected. For the e-shopper, Amazon.com's system has worked. For those tracking books, Amazon.com's early and maybe its most faithful customers, book reviews and suggested books on similar topics add an educational element to an otherwise mechanical mouse-clicking operation.

In the critical early testing period for e-commerce, the 1999 Christmas holiday season, Amazon.com had more visits by far than did any other e-retailer (33.1 million visits compared with 11.1 million to its closest e-commerce competitor, eToys.com, between November 15 and December 19). And, of those visits, 42 percent materialized into purchases, compared to 20 percent for eToys.com, and 2.5 percent for Gap.com and Wal-Mart.com.[80]

Despite the laid-back and almost funky ambience that Bezos has created, the actual operation of Amazon.com is highly efficient. Henry Ford would be impressed with the sophisticated distribution centers' assembly lines. Starting out with one 93,000-square-foot warehouse in Seattle, Amazon.com had seven warehouses by the end of 1999, five of which were opened in 1999, each larger than the last. That infrastructure—the planning and operation of the distribution system—is run by a large blue-collar contingent, 40 percent of the company's total staff, in striking contrast to the young computer whizzes in the front office. Fulfillment can make or break a retailing company, and success requires efficient blue-collar distribution assembly lines. After meeting its first big test in e-commerce by capturing early online shoppers, Amazon now must retain these shoppers' loyalty for a wider range of future purchases—and become profitable. In a country where television was feared to be the demise of book reading, it is ironic that the giant of e-commerce emerges from an online book seller.

Other early e-commerce successes have been the online auction and bargain centers. The popularity of this type of e-commerce indicates not only the incredible number of bargain hunters and auction aficionados lurking out there, but also how effectively the Internet connects people and things. E-Bay.com, started in 1995, has become "the world's largest person-to-person trading community," with 19 million registered users in 2000.[81] In one week before Christmas 1999, eBay had more than a million visitors.[82] Old and young, professional and amateur, voyeur and participant click on e-Bay.com; "individuals—not big businesses—use eBay," the company stresses.[83] For some people an online auction is sheer entertainment, for others it is a business or a way of getting rid of unwanted possessions, and for some it is addictive. Basement.com, another variant of bargain buying, makes a "Vegas-worthy game out of buying stuff" and can be as addictive as a slot machine, a psychologist observes. Items sold get continually cheaper until they are sold out, so it becomes an "inventory liquidation service . . . and a fascinating experiment in retail psychology."[84] Whatever the psychological implications, the bargaining at remote auctions is exceedingly popular.

Problems

Placing the order may be the swiftest and most gratifying part of the online shopping transaction. The ultimate gratification of physically possessing the purchase is postponed in online retailing (fig. 69). For many avid shoppers, the

69. New Yorker, *May 29, 2000*

disappointment of "delayed fulfillment," what happens between clicking on your intended purchase and receiving it, prevents them from shopping online.

What savings may have accrued in the online purchase can often be offset by shipping and handling charges. Although sales taxes are not assessed for online purchases, that may change. A 1999–2000 congressional advisory commission tackling this issue ended up in an acrimonious stalemate as the anti-tax members of the commission, including its chairman, Virginia Governor James Gilmore, fought to protect burgeoning Internet companies from the burden of such taxes, while other commission members, including governors, business owners, and consumers, sought a level playing field. States worry about the loss of potential revenue, and businesses with real stores required to charge sales taxes want equity. AOL's chairman, Steve Case, agreed with the sales tax supporters: "It is wrong for the Internet to be a tax haven."[85] When the playing field is leveled, online purchases will be subject to sales taxes, and those taxes will add to the cost of fulfillment for the customer.

Receiving the purchases is another problem. Some are shipped by mailing services like United Parcel Service, others by the U.S. Postal Service, but by whatever means, where are packages to be received when one is not at home? At the office? At the apartment building's front desk? At the back door? In the garage? Different arrangements are being considered, like timed deliveries, and others, challenging the most imaginative inventor, like boxes with special codes placed in garages or windows, some with refrigeration for perishable goods.

Returning unsatisfactory purchases is always a nuisance for the disappointed buyer, who has to repack the item and take it to the post office or mailing service. Returned items are also troublesome and expensive for the retailer, who has to cope with physical, inventory, and credit problems. For remote retailers, this is an important activity. In 1998 L. L. Bean had a staff of 375 in its return section, more employees than on the entire staffs of some mail-order houses.

Credibility, Security, and Privacy

The underlying problems of credibility and privacy haunt online companies in this era of wild and unregulated growth. For this new industry to prosper, it has to instill and maintain confidence in its customers. Yet few users of e-commerce know who is running the website, how online information is gathered, how reliable it is, and who is watching electronic actions. Even in e-mail, there are privacy concerns. Former President Bill Clinton's worries about the insecurity of cyberspace prevented him from corresponding by e-mail with his daughter, Chelsea, while she was at Stanford. Credibility is another concern. When DrKoop.com was found to be promoting products for which Dr. Koop had been receiving commissions without any disclosure of these arrangements, the public was awakened to the hard truth that even a reputable doctor could mislead the public and that conflicts of interest might mar the credibility of online commerce. The nature of online business is to capture consumers by telling an enticing story, and that can often lead to misrepresentation. Concern mounts that a naive public is being engulfed in half truths, where it is difficult to decipher what is actually advertising.

With the excitement of the speed and novelty involved in e-commerce, users are not likely to scrutinize the reliability of the companies with which they are negotiating. However, many people balk at giving their credit card numbers to unknown, unseen online operators and are fearful of this invasion of their privacy. To counter that fear, online companies are taking precautions to protect the privacy of their customers through "self-regulation" and enforcement programs. More should be done, however. As former Commerce Secretary William Daley stated, "more companies must put privacy protection in place, and those protections must provide real notice and choice for the consumers."[86]

Likewise, the systemic problem of misrepresentation and basic business ethics of e-retailing have not been adequately addressed, even though several groups have been formed to tackle these very serious problems. Other media have adopted standards and practices so that one knows what is paid advertising and what it is not—and where conflicts of interest might occur. Although the industry has benefited from an unfettered business environment, its future depends on trusting and loyal customers who assume that e-commerce is guided by traditional business ethics.

The Buyer's World

Online shopping offers significant social and cultural benefits for the individual and society, of which the most important is the powerful democratization involved in many aspects of this new interactive technology.

Online retailing empowers the buyer as never before. With quick online access to enormous reservoirs of information, the consumer can choose the attributes and prices of potential purchases from an array of competitors at his own convenience. In its interactive ways of bringing buyers and sellers together, e-commerce is creating a "massive shift of power away from sellers to buyers—buyers in the consumer world, buyers in the business world," according to Kim Clark of Harvard Business School. "Buyers," Clark continues, "have enormous power they didn't have before."[87] Already shoppers can design online their Dell computers, Mattel Barbie dolls, and Chipshot.com golf clubs. This is just the beginning of a new era of interactive shopping, according to Adrian Slywotzky of Mercer Management Consulting, who foresees the use of "choiceboards," an interactive, online system in which a customer chooses attributes, components, prices, and delivery options by clicking through a menu of options.[88] Thus, the consumer could design exactly what he or she wants. Whether choiceboards become a reality for the average consumer, there is no question that the Internet empowers the consumer with information and further democratizes shopping.

The anonymity of e-retailing can be seen as another democratizing factor. In the late nineteenth-century department stores, customers were seen as equals at the counter. And in the virtual store, no clerk is looking at the color of your skin, your slightly tattered pocketbook, or your wrinkled face, nor making any other judgment about you. You are the same as any other "hit" at an online company, regardless of your sex, race, or age. Thus, the social discrimination of shopping in real stores, whether real or perceived, is eliminated in the virtual world. Economic discrimination, however, persists for the many without access to the Internet and credit cards.

E-commerce has democratized shopping in another way as well: its interactive capabilities open up a vast range of retail opportunities to those previously excluded. For those living in isolated locations, or for the handicapped, or even for those simply beset by overcrowded schedules, online shopping makes its possible to buy things that might not have been readily available in the past. Mail-order companies previously widened such shopping opportunities, and now e-commerce further expands them.

For the consumer, e-commerce's seismic jolt to the industry, producing more and different ways to shop, has intensified the intrinsically competitive nature of retailing. Traditional stores, direct marketers, mail-order houses, discounters, and e-retailers are all scrambling to capture the consumer, and the result is that many retailers run hybrid operations, incorporating real stores, catalogues, and e-retailing. Each type of retailing has its advantage. The brick-and-mortar stores, often viewed disparagingly by the online set, have a high cost structure, with clerks and warehouses, but they also have an operating warehouse-distribution system, which the dot.coms are struggling to set up. As these traditional stores get online and also send out catalogues, such mail-order houses as L. L. Bean, Williams-Sonoma, and Harry and David, and online companies like Gateway, have been setting up real stores. Gateway, established in South Dakota as a virtual company, is one example of a "click and brick" retailer, as it had two real stores in 1998, 185 by 1999, and 275 in 2000. The retail stores are not fully stocked with products, which you can buy on the spot, but rather are showrooms displaying machines so that prospective buyers can see, feel, and lift them, question the "associates," and place orders.[89] L. L. Bean, long known for its Freeport, Maine, store and its catalogues, whose telephone orders account for almost 90 percent of its total orders, is another example of a hybrid retailer. L. L. Bean went online in 1995, and it opened, in July 2000, its first full-price retail store outside Maine, in the Tysons Corner shopping center outside Washington, D.C. (fig. 70). The company opened another real store in 2001 in Columbia, Maryland.[90] As retailers play musical chairs, with some remote

70. Outfitted in Bean hunting boots, Lincoln was prepared for the arrival of an L. L. Bean store in a mall outside Washington, D.C., Tysons Corner Center (advertising mailing, 2000)

L.L.Bean is coming to Washington
GRAND OPENING JULY 28, TYSONS CORNER CENTER

retailers moving into actual buildings and many brick-and-mortars getting online, the consumer ends up with more shopping options.

A New Respectability

The cloak of contemporary technology permeating e-commerce adds a new respectability and panache to retailing, so often considered a low-class trade associated with those losers of small shopkeepers buffeted by the "gale of fate," like H. G. Wells's Mr. Polly. For retailing as a whole, even the press coverage of e-commerce has helped to elevate retailing to a more prominent place in the world of business. When I began my research in the early 1990s, the Harvard Business School had very little course work relating to retailing; e-commerce has radically changed that. Now the Harvard Business School offers courses, runs seminars, and publishes research papers on online retailing. In fact, an article in Harvard University's alumni magazine on a panel discussion of the Internet and e-commerce by Harvard Business School professors was one of the most insightful analyses on the topic I have read.[91]

The élan of the high-tech world extends to entrepreneurs in the many start-up e-commerce companies—and even in the mega-corporations like AOL. These new entrepreneurs are not the robber barons of yesteryear but rather admired innovators and leaders. Amazon.com's Jeff Bezos has become a folk hero, featured as *Time* magazine's 1999 Man-of-the-Year. E-commerce is seen as a contemporary and relevant industry being run by smart, forward-looking people.

The individual shopper also benefits from the élan of the high-tech world. Using the computer to buy goods and services helps to transform shopping into a more rational and deliberate process than it has been traditionally portrayed, especially for women. E-commerce shopping begins to erase the stereotypical image of the serendipitous woman shopper. This modern technology, in fact, makes her seem modern—and a responsible decision-maker relying on her brains, not her heart. Boopsie is replaced by a smart businesslike woman and shopping becomes more respectable—and the shopper more respected.

Easy Entry

One of the revolutionizing—and democratizing—aspects of e-commerce has been the ease, speed, and often low cost of starting up a new company, or "ramping up a website," as the trade puts it. These emerging online companies are neither location nor heavily capital dependent. Many are run from garages, bedrooms, or small Main Street stores. A Williams College student, interested in fine violins and bows, set up, with the help of well-known violin experts, an online auction via a web page with images and information on antique violins. The first auction grossed $860,000, and the second auction grossed $2.3

million, with one viola selling for $750,000. Other students are postponing going to business school in order to get on this e-commerce bandwagon.

For small businesses, especially specialized or "niche" operations, the Internet can help them better service existing customers, as well as reach new and distant ones. Almost a million e-businesses with fewer than a hundred employees were estimated to exist in 2000. For the store owner or businessperson who wants to live and work in a small place like Montpelier, Vermont, or Fairfield, Iowa, e-retailing may be the answer. Success stories abound of out-of-the-way book sellers, craftspeople, antique dealers, collectors, horticulturists, and designers whose commercial vistas expanded once they went online. With overnight postal and other delivery services combined with the Internet, many Main Street businesses are coming to life, with 20 to 40 percent of their sales online, according to Kennedy Smith, director of the National Trust for Historic Preservation's National Main Street Center. Bette Sherman, owner of the Longhorn Gallery in Denton, Texas, said, "The web is the marketplace of the future, and to not have a presence would be a retailing mistake." Not only do individual stores benefit from expanded sales and improved public images, but a town's commercial district benefits when more people are employed and more use the local restaurants, stores, and services, and more buildings are better used as online companies occupy upper floors.[92]

Despite the relatively easy entry for startup companies, especially when they hitch up to engines like Yahoo, which enables newcomers to become Yahoo stores for $100–$300 per month and be exposed to Yahoo's 100 million viewers each month, many stumbling blocks lie ahead. How is information to be conveyed? What image is to be projected? How are inventory and fulfillment to be handled, and how can growth be accommodated? Easy entry into e-commerce and early promises of a robust business do not guarantee long-term success, as many entrepreneurs have discovered. Positively-You.com, an online bookstore operated by a Cedar Rapids, Iowa, professor from his home, did so well initially that Professor Bowlin left teaching, rented an office, hired staff, and tried to compete with the big operators, like Amazon.com. After a year, Positively-You.com was out of business. Professor Bowlin learned that an established business with loyal customers has a bigger chance of online success than does a strictly online company, which is always looking for new customers. For many e-commerce pioneers, entry may be the easiest part of the venture; after that, trying to survive is harder, but staying focused and small seems to be the important lesson.

In Perspective

Online shopping works best for brand items, for which little selectivity or decision-making is needed. It provides endless opportunities for browsing and comparison shopping. However, as many consumers want more service, authenticity, ambience, and sociability in their shopping than e-commerce offers, tomorrow's shopper will be cross-shopping to take advantage of what real stores, e-retailers, and catalogues have to offer. The shopper's basic human desire to see the true color, smell the scent, feel the texture, test the ripeness, see how it fits and feels, seek advice, or just contrast different brands means that real stores with real clerks are here to stay.

Despite all the latest sophisticated technology and the varied means of establishing trust and online communities, the social function of face-to-face shopping endures. As Esther Dyson, considered a doyenne of cyberspace, said, "People will go shopping in stores as a social activity."[93] Standard and Poor's 1999 analysis of current retailing concurred: "There will always be a core of shoppers who enjoy the social interaction involved in going to a retail store."[94] And that core is a deep and lasting one. In the Harvard Business School professors' discussion "Wired Society," Dean Clark stressed that "people seem to value highly personal contact with real human beings. You have this weird interplay going on where, yes, electronics is great and it is nice to be online, but sometimes you like to talk to a real person and have a real . . ." "Connection," interjected Professor Koehn. And Dean Clark confirmed, "A human connection."[95]

Face-to-Face—and Friendly—Shopping

As remote shopping and remote living continue to take hold with all the seeming speed and modernity of the latest technology, as evidenced in virtual shopping, a counter movement of personal, specialized, friendly, old-fashioned, and natural shopping has gained popularity. Sometimes it is found in large department stores like Nordstrom, in chain stores like Fresh Fields, or in small boutiques, farmers' markets, or flea markets. Shoppers are seeking honesty, authenticity, and directness. They want organic and healthy food; they want personal attention; they want quality goods; and they want a friendly, nonmanipulative, noncorporate environment for their shopping. This might sound like a throwback—and it is. These qualities, once so common that they went unnoticed, are now considered affordable only by those in upper income brackets. This is often referred to in the trade as niche shopping.

This interest in stores with distinctiveness, character, and integrity is partly a reaction to the sameness that permeates today's retailing. While malls have become numbing environments for many, so have all their franchised tenants. Even relatively new stores like the Museum Company, offering items sold in museum shops around the country, lose their individuality when their numbers expand and they move into upscale shopping malls and districts. Window shopping pales when the products are predictable and the displays repetitive. The quest for things that are "interesting" and not mass-manufactured has spawned the development of individualistic boutiques. There is also a sentimental—and practical—yearning for the straightforward, functional shop like the hardware store, the shoe repair shop, the watchmaker's shop, and magic weaver. The once prosaic bakery, which now sells dozens of different kinds of bread—containing raisins, nuts, multiple grains, olives, or cranberries—is so popular that its loyal customers are willing to wait in long lines. They make good bread, and their products have been unavailable in supermarkets. Health concerns and gourmet cooking have combined to produce a rash of health and gourmet food stores, and special sections in supermarkets display organic foods, like Happy Hen eggs.

Service, thought to have vanished with automation and business efficiency, is having a comeback, as stretched families need all the help they can get. For those who can afford it, stores like Neiman Marcus, Nordstrom, Bergdorf Goodman, Macy's, and Saks Fifth Avenue find new interest in their personal shoppers, sometimes called "wardrobe consultants." Saks Fifth Avenue's flagship store in New York has eleven personal shoppers, 80 percent of whose clients are termed career women. Nordstrom's reports that 90 percent of its personal shopping clients are career women, and Neiman reports that about 50 percent are.[96] These clothing advisers and shoppers for busy women and men operate on commission, earn good salaries, and provide useful services to their customers. They also instill customer loyalty to a given store. They advise on wardrobes, select clothes, and wrap and send things. Such shopping is usually for upscale customers in upmarket stores, but personal service, which has been the hallmark of Nordstrom, is being recognized as a way for stores to stay alive. Loehmann's, founded in 1921 in the Bronx, operates sixty-nine stores in twenty-three states and offers off-price clothing to affluent shoppers. The company has added some personal services to its no-frills operation. The Insiders Club provides its most loyal 1.2 million customers with mailings of specials, discounts on their birthdays, and even telephone calls if something requested comes in.[97] This sounds like the old days, when department store clerks notified customers of their special requests or held items for them, no matter how small. In 1893, Woodward & Lothrop wrote a customer that the store was out of the requested pins but would inform the customer when they came in.[98]

Public and Farmers' Markets

Another type of personal and in some cases specialty shopping that appeals to many turned off by the impersonality of mainstream shopping is the public market, farmers' market, and flea market. Once considered offbeat nuisances by municipal governments, retailers, and much of the public, this kind of shopping has become popular with a range of people: some interested in fresh and natural products, some in bargains, some in the adventure of being a free agent, and others in warm and friendly social interactions.

Public and farmers' markets are usually in or on public property, such as a municipal parking lot, while the flea market can occur in many different places—from a town, city, or regional market to a front lawn, sidewalk, or alley. All produce spontaneous, lively places with intriguing sights, smells, colors, and sounds—perhaps the American version of the bazaar.

Public markets have existed since the earliest colonial settlement on the North American continent so that farmers, fishermen, and other vendors could sell their produce and goods. Every city had them. In Hartford's first decade (1643), the Connecticut General Court established a weekly market "for all manner of comodityes that shall be brought in, and for cattell, or any marchandise whsoeuer."[99] The public nature of these markets has made them enduring democratic institutions in city after city. They have been located on public space, have had public goals, and have provided a place for people to buy fresh food without regard to the shoppers' different economic and social distinctions, as Eaton observed in his 1814 "Review of New York."

> The place where no distinctions are,
> All sects and colors mingle there,
> Long folks and short, black folks and gray,
> With common bawds, and folks that pray,
> Rich folks and poor, both old and young,
> And good, and bad and weak, and strong,
> The wise and simple, red and white,
> With those that play and those that fight,
> The high, the low, the proud, the meek.
> And all one common object seek:
> For lady, belle, and buck, and lass,
> Here mingle in one common mass,
> Contending all which shall be first,
> To buy the cheapest, best, or worst,
> In fact their object is to get
> Such things as they can 'ford to eat.[100]

Almost every city had them. New Orleans had twenty-three, New York thirteen (in lower Manhattan), Baltimore ten, and Washington, D.C., five. Philadelphia's famous High Street was renamed Market Street for the long line of vendor stalls located in the center of the street, stretching from the Delaware River to almost City Hall. These public markets came in many forms: some open air, some with shed roof structures, some in permanent market halls, and others in market districts (fig. 71). Few of these markets remain in cities, as the neighborhood store, then the chain store, and later the supermarket grabbed more and more of the food marketing, partially because urban populations and their disposable incomes shrank and locations of wholesaling and distribution moved out of the cities' downtowns.

71. The crowded public market in Albany, New York's Market Square, Grand and Beaver Streets, 1905. Now the site of the Pepsi Arena (collection of the Albany Institute of History and Art)

Urban renewal efforts to "upgrade" downtowns, along with truck transportation requiring vast and often outlying locations, doomed many of these markets. That any survive is due to the extraordinary efforts of individuals, groups, and sometimes city officials who fought tenaciously for them. New Orleans' French Market is the oldest American market in continuous operation. However, its meat, fish, and vegetable selling has been dwarfed by tourist-oriented flea markets, although recently a farmers' market was reintroduced. Louis Pressman, Baltimore's comptroller from 1963 to 1991, retained the city's remarkable five neighborhood markets by preventing city funding for cost-analysis studies of the market system, fearing that such studies would indicate their obsolescence in the late twentieth century — and the need to close them. Today the city's markets, as well as the large downtown Lexington Market, which is operated by a public-private board, are still serving their neighborhoods, as well as tourists and people from other parts of the city. In Seattle, Victor Steinbrueck led the successful referendum in 1971 to prevent urban renewal from razing the Pike Place Market. That market continues to function as a citywide farm and fish market, a tourist attraction, a stimulant for regional farm preservation, and an anchor in an imaginative downtown redevelopment project.

Of Washington, D.C.'s five markets, only the Eastern Market near the U.S. Capitol still operates; its welfare had been a constant community concern. There were threats to eliminate it or to modernize it, which would have radically altered its vendors and character. Washington's major fish market, which lined its Southwest waterfront with buildings and boats, was threatened with closure for decades, ostensibly for health reasons, and finally evicted for 1960s urban renewal motels and tourist restaurants. But that did not kill the market. Although it is now in a less desirable place on the waterfront with no boats (the fish is trucked in), it has become a popular market jammed on the weekends with both natives and tourists.

In New York, the Fulton Fish Market is all that is left of its old public markets. It remains on its East River site near Wall Street, thanks to the efforts of a Mafia syndicate that prevented its move to the large wholesale fruit and vegetable market in Hunts Point, the Bronx, another part of the syndicate's turf. While the city has had skirmishes with the market's labor unions and syndicates, this working fish market has survived, even though it is a stepchild in the South Street Seaport entertainment district. The district is a public-private venture with five different participants: the Rouse Company, which operates the Festival marketplace, the Seaport Museum, the city, the neighborhood, and the original occupant of the area, the Fulton Fish Market.

Philadelphia's Reading Terminal Market, known for its Pennsylvania Dutch farmers' stalls, survived two major threats: first, the Reading Railroad terminal's threat to replace it in the 1890s and, more recently, the city's convention center. Farmers from the heart of Pennsylvania Dutch country supply thriving and longstanding public markets in downtowns of cities like Lancaster and York, Pennsylvania.

Cities, after years of neglecting and scorning markets, have come to realize that these public markets are not only visible landmarks but also are popular marketing tools—in many cases even tourist attractions. In a report on public markets undertaken by the Project for Public Spaces, an organization interested in making public areas more active and enjoyable, markets were found to be "valued because they create common ground in the community, where people feel comfortable to mix, mingle, and enjoy the serendipitous pleasures of strolling, socializing, people-watching, and shopping in a special environment."[101] Neighborhood shoppers love them, farmers find them excellent ways to sell their goods, and cities see them as providing an essential sense of integrity and place augmenting their quality of life, a major selling point for cities today. While more eating places have been added, so have new types of vendors, as in Charleston, South Carolina, where crafts, tourist items, and flea market wares mostly replaced farmers' produce. These markets, however recast, continue to provide needed goods as well as the life and color so often missing in the homogeneity of contemporary franchised stores. For the conventioneers at Philadelphia's convention center they offer a welcome relief from the tedium of meetings in hotel rooms.

The history of the Reading Terminal Market, a landmark in Center City Philadelphia, provides a glimpse of how one city's major farmers' market has survived more than a century. As in many cities, the early selling of farm produce, fish, and meat was highly unorganized; farmers, fishermen, and hunters gathered in Philadelphia's earliest days to peddle their produce on a patch of open land near the Delaware River. In the late 1600s, William Penn's managers pulled the peddlers and hawkers together into a single market, called the Jersey Market, on the then High Street. From that time until the mid-nineteenth century, as the city's commercial district inched into what is now known as Center City, markets continued to spread in long colonnades for six blocks in the center of High Street, appropriately renamed Market Street. The nuisances of these scruffy, noisy, smelly market operations aroused so many complaints from adjacent neighborhoods in the mid-nineteenth century that the markets were closed down.

However, they reemerged in new locations in Center City. Two of the most prominent markets, the Farmers' Market and Franklin Market, were constructed on or near Market and 12th Streets, where they remained until the early 1890s, when the Reading Railroad decided to build its terminal there. After negotiations between the property owners and the railroad, the railroad agreed to construct and operate a single market under the train shed for both the Farmers' and Franklin Markets. The Reading Terminal Market, as the new 78,000-square-foot market was called, opened in 1892, and soon almost 500 vendors, some of them descendants of the early marketmen, filled its twelve aisles of stalls (fig. 72). Under able management by George H. McKay, a strong market advocate who held the job for thirty years, the railroad was convinced that "running a good market was just as important as running a good railroad."[102] The railroad did just that for both city and suburban customers. Suburban housewives could order food from the market, which would be placed in baskets and put on trains headed for suburban stations, where it would be held until picked up. For city residents, not only did the market offer seafood from Chesapeake Bay and a wide array of fresh produce from the rich Pennsylvania Dutch farmlands, but also a variety of eating places.

By the 1970s center cities and railroads were in trouble—and so was the Reading Terminal Market. But unlike most cities, this market did not fall prey to the bulldozer. In 1971 the railroad went into bankruptcy, yet the Reading Company continued to hold onto the terminal building, a major real estate asset. Leased to a local speculator in the late 1970s, the market was kept alive, though in poor repair with a defunct central cold storage facility, inadequate wiring and plumbing, and faced with thinning customers who were moving to distant suburbs or patronizing one-stop supermarkets. While

72. *Reading Terminal Market, Philadelphia, c. 1890 (collection of John E. Thompson)*

a shadow of its old self, the market become a source of speciality items appealing to different ethnic groups and to the growing number of gourmet cooks.

The future of the market seemed uncertain again after 1985, when commuter rail lines bypassed the terminal, making it redundant. This centrally located real estate again came to life in 1990, when the Pennsylvania Convention Center Authority, after tough haggling with the merchants, decided to develop the city's major convention center on the upper level of the terminal and to locate the market on the ground floor—this time with modern electricity and plumbing. Despite disruptions during reconstruction and then fears that its gritty flavor would be lost, the market not only survived but became a sounder, healthier, and cleaner place for both old and new vendors. Of the seventy-eight vendors now in the market, more than six have been there for several generations—like Bassett Ice Cream, begun in 1861. Nine Amish stall holders and four old-time meat purveyors sell alongside merchants at Asian produce stands, sushi bars, an African craft shop, and a cookbook stall, which has been in the market for fourteen years.

Even though it attracts tourists and convention-goers, the market continues to retain its gritty working-market atmosphere, with authentic products and honest-to-goodness vendors selling native scrapple, pretzels, and sausage. The babble of conversations between merchants and customers seems a sharp contrast to the quiet of supermarket shopping, observed Betty Kaplan of the Cook Book Stall—and a heartening sign of the timeless communality of shopping.[103] That Philadelphia has maintained this down-to-earth market is remarkable, especially as one surveys the handful of remaining American center city markets today. The market's survival is due to many causes: the Reading and Philadelphia Railroad held on to the property as a good long-term investment; the railroad's management and the values of the city, which no doubt reflect a Quaker heritage of straightforwardness, directness, and plainness; and the merchants themselves, who were able to work over the years with the railroad, the market managers, the leasor, and the convention center promoters to sustain this important urban institution.

Another type of market, the open-air farmers' market, is becoming increasingly popular all over the country. The U.S. Department of Agriculture's 1998 National Farmers Market Directory reports that there are 2,746 active markets, as listed by state departments of agriculture.[104] That number of markets would probably be doubled if locally formed markets were included, according to the U.S. Department of Agriculture. Not only do these markets enable many otherwise threatened small- to medium-sized farmers to stay in business, but they also provide fresh fruit and vegetables to inner-city residents whose neighborhoods are often lacking supermarkets. New York City alone had forty-four farmers' markets in 1999; twenty of them, relying on the produce from 200 family farms, are operated by Barry Benepe, director of Greenmarket, a project of the New York City Council on the Environment.

Farmers' markets are often informally operated, but many are located on public property and sometimes in prominent downtown sites—the town square, the courthouse, a school parking lot. The level of public supervision varies. Some communities check to ensure that the products are raised on farms and that the goods are baked at home, as in Arlington County, Virginia. Whatever the arrangement, farmers' markets have become places where people buy fresh, wholesome fruits and vegetables and meet neighbors and strangers as well as the farmers themselves in a refreshingly friendly environment (fig. 73).

"Customers shop the [farmers'] market frequently," according to research by Urban Marketing Collaborative. They are looking for "choice, atmosphere, quality and homegrown foods, rather than convenience and price." Maureen Atkinson and John Williams, in an article in *Public Management*, found that much of the new interest in farmers' markets was a reaction to an "increasingly depersonalized atmosphere in large-scale operations."[105] Studies of farmers' market and supermarket customers over the past twenty years by psychologist Robert Sommer of the University of California at Davis indicate that customers of farmers' markets value the "friendly, personal, rural, smaller, happier setting" of those markets, where far more social encounters between customers occur than at national chain supermarkets. In observing nine farmers' markets and twenty-six national chain supermarkets in ten California cities, Sommer's studies found that "there were about two and a half times as many encounters per person at the farm-

73. Farmer's market in Palermo, Sicily, 1999

74. Greenmarket at Union Square, New York, 2000

ers' markets" than at the national chain supermarkets. A supermarket customer had "less than a one in ten chance of a social encounter with another
customer during a single visit to a supermarket."[106] The farmers' market shoppers not only had more social encounters with other shoppers but also four
times as many encounters with sellers or employees than did the supermarket customer. This contagious sociability combined with Americans' growing
health consciousness and interest in farmland preservation has helped make
the markets successful in city after city. In fact, many markets are now considered "community builders."

Union Square in New York City for years was a drug-infested area
where it was dangerous to walk. In 1977 the greenmarket transformed the
area four days a week with farmers' produce, attracting 20,000 shoppers in a
summer week. The square now is crowded with people from all over the city
buying quality farm goods at a well-run, clean, safe, lively market that grosses
$9 million a year (fig. 74). Even the surrounding streets have benefited.

Instead of the old discount stores associated with 14th Street, the area now has choice restaurants and popular stores like Paragon Sports and ABC Carpets, making Union Square a much more desirable—and high-rent—location. "The more that Greenmarkets become fixtures in city neighborhoods," according to Molly O'Neill in the New York Times, "the more they resemble the proverbial backyard fence where neighbors meet to exchange recipes and gossip. . . . The markets are meeting places for children's play groups, dissemination points for public education and community organizations, platforms for local politicians and stages for concertina players and performance artists. . . . They sell fresh food, but they promote community."[107]

In southwest Philadelphia, an area packed with public housing projects and minorities, a farmers' market now provides fresh vegetables and fruit through the efforts of the Merchants Association of the Reading Terminal, which recognized the need for inner-city neighborhoods to have access to fresh food. This part of the city had been without supermarkets as chain stores consolidated and abandoned crime-ridden inner-city neighborhoods. With $50,000 raised by the Merchants Association, a farmers' market was established with food bought at wholesale from the Reading Terminal Market, much of it from the thriving Amish farms west of the city. The produce is sold for slightly higher than wholesale prices, although seconds are often given away. For the 2,500 or so people living in the dreary brick bungalows of the Tasker Homes project, the market upgrades their diets with fresh fruit and vegetables, some of which, like asparagus, they had never seen. Like other farmers' markets, this one has become an important spot for neighbors to gather, share gossip, have a cup of coffee, buy fruits and vegetables, and exchange recipes, especially at the beginning of the month, when welfare checks and food stamps are issued. The popularity of this market has spurred the opening of other farmers' markets in other parts of Philadelphia. In fact, a Farmers' Market Trust of the Reading Terminal Market has been set up to coordinate the outreach and satellite farmers' markets.[108] These markets need not be just for affluent shoppers looking for organic produce and specialty items; they can also serve many city neighborhoods and suburbs—and their varied populations.

Garage Sales and Flea Markets

The most diverse and offbeat variant of "personalized" shopping is the flea market—"penny capitalism," as it has been called—which operates on the idea that one person's trash may be another person's treasure. Millions of Americans shop at millions of flea markets, garage sales, tag sales, rummage sales, and swap meets, where they find everything from old baked-bean pots, television sets, and rocking chairs to books, postcards, flower vases, and computers. While it is hard to categorize flea markets, the garage sale is often just

75. *Yard sales on an autumn day, Pullman, Illinois, 1996*

a table or two on the front yard laden with things cleaned out of the attic or cellar; others are organized multi-family sales held on multiple front lawns. And bigger neighborhood or town sales might take place on the town green (fig. 75). Stephen Soiffer and Gretchen Herrman, who studied more than 500 garage sales in the Ithaca, New York, area, estimate there are 6 million garage sales a year bringing in $1 million to $2 million.[109] The larger operations of hundreds of individuals and dealers selling to hundreds and sometimes thousands of buyers are the true flea markets, reminiscent of the well-known Marche aux Puces in Paris. Often what might be called antiques are displayed on tables beside the sellers' trucks or station wagons, which are lined up on temporarily laid-out avenues on farm fields, high school parking lots, or even unused freeway property (figs. 76, 77).

The garage sale, called a rummage sale in the winter in New England, is usually held in middle-class neighborhoods, as the "used goods are too used to be reused" in lower-income neighborhoods, according to Marcella Mazzarelli, a professor of anthropology.[110] (Her academic field is one of several— along with sociology, geography, history, economics, and fine arts—that have taken up the study of this rich field of flea markets, or "material culture.") The garage sale, which is more informal, smaller, and less organized than the flea market, has become a survival strategy for many buyers and sellers, according to Soiffer and Herrman. Two major types of garage sale attendees predominate: people who need objects on sale, and those who attend for social reasons. But Soiffer and Herrman developed a more refined typology of garage sale shoppers to display the breadth of shoppers and their needs and desires:

76. A flea market in a large field, Rowley, Massachusetts, 1996

77. A roadside flea market in Searsport, Maine, 1997

1. Retailers, who operate stores selling used goods.
2. Habituals, who purchase a large percentage of what they need at garage sales.
3. Economic transition shoppers, who are living beyond their means.
4. Specific need shoppers.
5. Child-item shoppers, who are trying to meet short-term children's needs.
6. Movers establishing a household.
7. Collectors.
8. Bargain hunters, browsers, bored people.
9. Buyers out to mingle with friends and even sellers.[111]

For these shoppers, garage sales and flea markets, with all the attendant searching, hunting, bargaining, haggling, hoping, winning, buying, and losing, have some of the serendipity and liveliness of the old bazaar, which are missing in most mainstream shopping.

And the excitement of the treasure hunt, which permeates garage-sale buying—and browsing—stimulates many customers and humanizes these "bazaars." The humane shopping environment appears as a constant theme in studies of garage sales. A Williams College undergraduate, Michelle Lebovitz, wrote in a class paper in 1972 that "meeting with other people, both other buyers and salesmen and haggling for prices, helps fight the impersonality of the modern commercial world."[112] And Soiffer and Herrman state that "the shopper takes advantage of a more humane atmosphere, one in which he or she is not a passive consumer of the standardized items of the department store, but a hunter stalking the wild pressure cooker, or adventurer after buried children's clothing."[113]

Flea markets, especially the large ones, have emerged as mass markets for selling and buying collectibles and antiques. They attract nomadic dealers, serious collectors, obsessive buyers, and the stray and the curious. Sellers can spend $5 to $50 to rent space large enough for a table or two and a chair, mostly in outdoor space and often on public land. Admission is usually free, although some charge a nominal fee, as does one of northern California's largest flea markets, in Alameda. It charges its 7,000 to 9,000 customers a 20-cent admission fee and an "early buyer's" fee, which can be $5 a person or even $40 a car for up to four people.[114]

In a metropolitan area, like Washington, D.C., nine major flea markets are scattered through the region—two are in the city, four are in inner suburbs, and two are in the outer ring of suburbs. Some flea markets in distant spots have clustered, just as antiques stores have clustered in places like Nyack, New York, New Market, Maryland, and New Hope, Pennsylvania. One area with a growing number of flea markets, some with more than a thousand dealers, is in the Pennsylvania Dutch country near Adamstown along a five-mile stretch of Route 272. This is for the serious and energetic flea market shopper, as hours of travel time are needed to get there from Baltimore, Washington, Harrisburg, or Philadelphia, and then stamina is needed for the stalking. These are serious stalking grounds attracting collectors in every speciality: corkscrew, postcard, model train, doll, salt cellar, and animal painting, to name but a few. The searching, discovering, and haggling are all part of the game. It is a means of self-expression and fulfillment, according to Robert Maisel, who sees flea market shopping as a leisure activity supplying some of the satisfactions that work once provided.

But not all flea markets are for closet antiques dealers. The country's oldest flea market, or at least open-air market, was Chicago's Maxwell Street Market, held on four acres of land with 1,000 to 2,000 vendors and crowds of

20,000 each Sunday. Begun 125 years ago by Russian Jews peddling their wares from pushcarts, the market became a place where the city's disenfranchised immigrants, or recent arrivals like blacks and Hispanics, met and traded. This massive business incubator for the poor, which has been estimated to involve almost $50 million for vendors, was killed in April 1994 when Chicago's City Council voted to move the market so that the land could be sold for $4.25 million to the University of Illinois in Chicago for research and recreational facilities.[115] Like so many markets, this scruffy, smelly, and bustling operation did not fit the image of an upbeat twentieth-century American city. Nor did these poor vendors and shoppers have the political clout to fight City Hall. The city has provided a smaller, more sanitized location several blocks from its original site for only 450 vendors and doubled fees and tightened vendor entrance requirements. It is not the same. The huge numbers of shoppers who relied on the market, the vendors whose livelihoods depended on their sales, and the city whose cultural diversity thrives on the mix of unplanned and unsanitized activities all lost out. The junk that was sold—the hubcaps, tires, scrap, trinkets, pots and pans, worn electrical appliances—might seem unsightly to some, but to the poor they were essential. It was also a community. Many of the vendors had been regulars at the Maxwell Market for tens of years. Joe Henderson has been making a bigger profit at the market on Sundays than he makes in his record store the rest of the week.[116] Jack Cohen set up his first stall, selling shopping bags at a penny in 1939, and now owns eight pawn shops but still comes to the market every Sunday to sell jewelry.[117] This market does not have the tone of a greenmarket nor the moneyed customers of some antiques-oriented flea markets, but it was a popular market serving inner-city sellers and buyers.

Craft markets and fairs, another type of personal shopping, have captured the interest of so many people that they have become major local and regional events. Sometimes part of farmers' markets (as at Washington, D.C.'s Eastern Market), crafts can also be sold at flea markets (Washington's Georgetown Flea Market) or at combination farmers'–flea markets (Charleston, South Carolina), at massive regional craft fairs, which can also fill up large county fairgrounds (Rhinebeck, New York), or at a city's convention center (Baltimore). One "chain" of craft fairs, Sugarloaf Craft Festivals, sponsors sixteen festivals a year, each featuring hundreds of artisans and attracting tens of thousands of visitors; six are in the Washington, D.C., area, and the others are in places as scattered as Atlanta, Georgia, and Novi, Minnesota. In Eugene and Portland, Oregon, hundreds of craft vendors sell at their weekly Saturday Markets, now immensely popular civic occasions (fig. 78). Some of Portland's Saturday Market is held under a highway approach to a bridge, but most of the vendors sell in the open air from booths with homemade canopies. A sprinkling of food vendors, often peddling fruit juices and organic foods, can be found at these Saturday Markets; 20 out of an average of 240

78. The popular Saturday Market, Portland, Oregon, 1997

vendors sell food each week in Eugene. Jewelry boasts the largest number of vendors at Eugene's market; ceramics, mixed media, and handsewn clothing are the next largest, and then artwork, beadwork, wooden items, fiber goods, glassware, leather goods, herbal products, varied types of clothing, toys, furniture, metalwork, and candles.[118] This mixture of crafts, art, and food makes for unusually festive markets, and they are occurring all over the country and attracting thousands of natives and tourists of all ages.

In a time when remoteness, stretched living, and cyberspace are reducing opportunities for face-to-face activities, these personal types of shopping, which "cut across traditional social lines . . . and emphasize experiences," will become increasingly important.[119] The public's quest for quality, nonstandardized goods, the satisfactions of direct human contact, the excitement of negotiating, and all the spontaneity, noise, smells, and action far from the commercial mainstream may influence future retailing to meet a very basic and growing need for personal shopping.

Tourism and Entertainment Shopping

The 217-store discount shopping mall Potomac Mills, south of Washington, D.C., is touted as Virginia's biggest tourist attraction. Whether a visit to a mall can be considered a tourist visit is questionable, but attempting to count shoppers as tourists exposes retailers' efforts to broaden the shopping experience to appeal to more than just local shoppers. A tourist is defined as someone who has traveled a distance to a shopping facility; and that distance is defined differently by major retailers, but 150 miles for the huge Mall of America near Minneapolis is among the longer distances. To make that trip worthwhile and to captivate shoppers so that they will linger, and spend, entertainment is seen as an "operational requisite for shopping centers and an essential merchandising element for retailers," according to a special entertainment edition (fall 1995) of the International Council of Shopping Centers' *Research Quarterly*.[120]

Entertainment has always been an ingredient of shopping. Aristotle Boucicaut's Bon Marché, Marshall Field, and every department store in the early part of the century offered fantasy and excitement to lure shoppers, very much as the Nike Store uses contemporary electronic entertaining today. Gordon Selfridge's community center of a store was an escape into the world of luxury, where shoppers, especially women, were treated as royal visitors—and entertained. Looking at store window displays or wandering aisles ornamented with seasonal decorations and overriding opulence was entertainment—and still is for some. Yet today's entertainment is increasingly interactive and electronic.

Shopping centers, then malls, then festival marketplaces, and then later megamalls were designed to offer an enticing environment, with entertainment progressively being defined more and more literally. "The very idea of a shopping center to some degree implies entertainment," according to the International Council of Shopping Centers.[121] At first benches, Muzak, potted plants, and occasional performances like fashion shows were adequate entertainments at shopping centers and malls; then food courts and movie theaters were added. But festival marketplaces introduced a new level of planning of events and entertainment. Rouse's marketplaces were meant to be fun and safe destinations luring wary suburbanites into the bowels of the cities. Boston's Faneuil Hall Marketplace and Baltimore's Harborplace, with their flags and kiosks and mimes and clowns, launched a new type of entertainment shopping. One went there not just to shop, but to eat, watch, socialize, and be where the action is. Another leap has been taken in providing immersive, interactive, and technologically advanced entertainment, as theme park scenarios try to revive fading shopping malls and introduce new life to new malls, like the Mall of America.

The entertainment quotient of the American public has been stepped up so that visiting Santa Claus or watching a choral group perform at a shopping center seems pretty tame. "When the consumer has been everywhere, seen everything, and done everything," the Urban Land Institute's 1998 report on urban entertainment centers states, "the old entertainment options simply will not do anymore."[122] Shoppers want to play, touch, listen, eat, drink, and learn—and now there are many ways they can do these things in shopping centers. Megaplex theaters, which have almost become anchors in many centers, are now in competition with the 3-D interactive experiences being developed by companies like Sony. Large themed restaurants–bars–adult entertainment centers, like Dave and Buster's, occupying 60,000 square feet at White Flint Mall in Bethesda, Maryland, and touted as "the largest dining and entertainment extravaganza in Maryland," offer an array of virtual reality games, as well as food and drink.[123] The Sportsplex mall in Scottsdale, Arizona, will have eight sections, each bearing a sports theme, so flycasters can cast into a small pond and golfers can putt near a replica of Scotland's St. Andrews clubhouse. You can swim in the waves of the five-acre pond at West Edmonton's mall in Alberta, Canada; play golf at the Mall of America; and hear robotic statues speak on the hour, as well as view a laser light show, at the Forum Shops at Caesars in Las Vegas. For children there are Lego parks, Camp Snoopy, simulated rides, and, of course, interplanetary laser warfare games. The Recreational Equipment, Inc. (REI), store in Seattle has even adopted interactive retailing with its "try it, you'll like it" sixty-five-foot climbing pinnacle.

The scale and sophistication of these entertainments differ considerably from the entertainments traditionally associated with shopping. The early department store created a fantasy experience, but those stores were part of a vibrant city or town, which had developed incrementally and boasted many different activities, owners, developers, and stores. The identities of department stores were tied to the larger city, as was the case with Wanamaker's in Philadelphia. To jazz up an image in fading older cities, or to create one in a place like Las Vegas or in an isolated shopping mall, entertainment took on a new role. Creating the desired images, excitement, and entertainment in a mall has been possible with the omnipotent mall developer/manager, who controls the siting, the development, the types and layout of stores, the atmosphere, and the security. And many malls, especially such megamalls as the Mall of America or West Edmonton's mall, and entertainment malls like Universal Studios CityWalk, try to be all-encompassing environments that mimic the real city. Following Disney's example, these malls are safe, clean, and inviting imitations of once-vital downtown city streets. Small-town streets lined with shops and restaurants, just as people imagine they were, come in many different scales, styles of architecture, and levels of technology. These theme parks, called urban entertainment destinations by the trade, may be as short-lived as the Cabbage Patch Kid.

The fizzle of a proposal for a whopping entertainment-retailing mall, modestly called Dream of America, in a flagging commercial section of Silver Spring, Maryland, may be a harbinger of the decline of the mega-entertainment mall. The Edmonton Ghermezians company, Triple Five Group, wanted to cover twenty-seven acres of this close-in suburb of Washington, D.C., with indoor wave pools, skating rinks, a twenty-five-screen movie theater, fresh food markets, nightclubs, restaurants (many of them themed), a hotel, food court, "family entertainment," and, of course, shops. The goal was to attract an estimated 20 million people a year, twice as many as visit the Smithsonian's most popular museum, the National Air and Space Museum. Doubts were raised about the likelihood of the economic and social benefits outweighing the costs, about whether this type of retailing would be short-lived, and about whether the resuscitation of Silver Spring would have been helped or hurt by the development. Those doubts were confirmed when the developers were unable to raise the necessary private financing and the project died. In its stead, a community-supported development is under way, with an existing art deco movie theater functioning as an anchor for the American Film Institute, which will be located in an office building within the project. Stores will include a popular local hardware store, a Fresh Fields/Whole Foods organic foodstore, restaurants, office buildings, and a cluster of townhouses.

Although this Moby Dick of a mall never materialized, old and new malls are adopting entertainment retailing. Park Meadows, which opened in Denver in August 1996, is actually not a mall but a "retail resort," according to its developer, the Hahn Company. Countering the overwhelming scale and anonymity of massive shopping malls, Park Meadows, like Wal-Mart and other shrewd retailers and developers, has tried to create a warm and cozy feel. Shoppers are "guests in our home"; the cafeteria in the food court is a "dining hall"; the management office is a "hospitality suite."[124]

The entertainment retailing strategy is also being used to rejuvenate tired downtowns in major cities, including New York and Washington, D.C. A task force in Washington hopes to "reposition" the nation's capital as a "world class" city with entertainment retailing, according to Herbert Miller, chairman of the city's Interactive Downtown Task Force—and also developer of Georgetown Park and Potomac Mills. Washington, Miller states, is "on the leading edge of major economic change," where "entertainment, tourism, and information" can transform it into an exciting "interactive" place bursting with UEDs (urban entertainment destinations) like Universal Studios CityWalk in Los Angeles. The new heartbeat of the city will be shopping, eating, and virtual machine playing, with "state-of-the-art" stores blended into new and old museums amid government buildings—and, of course, sports arenas and convention centers. The existing and planned museums and stores in the area will be dwarfed by such blockbuster entities as Toys "R" Us and "sports-related retailing and dining," such as Niketown and the Original All-Star Cafe ("thematically" tied to a proposed American Sports Museum), if Washington's interactive committee's recommendations are followed.[125]

No one wants to be left out of the popular interactive entertainments of the twenty-first century, yet, as this new overlay of commercialism is being proposed to rejuvenate old downtowns, serious questions arise about its long-term benefits and costs for cities. Perhaps flashy entertainment is a way of transforming New York City's tawdry Times Square into an exciting and vital part of the city, but even there its once resident serious theater has vanished to other sections of the city. For the hearts of cities with comatose commerce, this entertainment/retailing/interactivity might produce some quick fibrilla-tions, but then the heart might fail again. "If downtown is just the Urban Land Institute flavor of the month, then it runs the risk of every real estate fad since urban renewal," according to Rick Cole, the former mayor of Pasadena, California. "In the end, people simply won't care about it as a place."[126]

For these resuscitation schemes to work, "entertainment has to tap into what is unique about each community," observes Nina Gruen, a well-respected and highly experienced consultant on downtown revitalization.[127] Downtowns have an intrinsic sense of place and of history with centuries-old activities, buildings, libraries, and museums; truly diverse people, from the homeless to dowagers; and also many tired and messy places once con-sidered such liabilities that commercial developers wrote them off altogether. Yet the theme-park activities of entertainment retailing, complexes with twenty movie screens, and sports arenas can be anywhere, while the real-world drama of downtown life can never be replicated.

Certainly entertainment in one form or another will continue to be a part of retailing—and of downtowns—but questions about what kinds of entertainment and on what scale and at what locations are unanswered, as is the question of the sustainability of tourism/entertainment shopping. Such questions are facing communities throughout the United States as this fad of retailing is being promoted by entrepreneurs in retailing, and often subsi-dized or undergirded by cities. All that "new" entertainment can quickly become out of date.

Cultural Tourism

A contrast to these variants of interactive and entertainment retailing is cul-tural tourism, a new type of entertainment–tourism shopping that is growing increasingly popular as travel and education become available to more peo-ple. Cultural tourism, recognized as an integral part of tourism in the 1995 White House Conference on Tourism, involves visiting historic and cultural destinations, real and simulated, and, of course, shopping and eating.

While such unusual places as Charleston, New Orleans, Santa Fe, Georgetown, and Savannah are magnets for millions, every town and city has a story to tell. The history and culture of the town, cities, and regions—their distinctive ways of life and the architecture, industries, commerce, crafts, artists, and other features that create a sense of place—are the attrac-tions. Every place has them. The local cheese factory, weavers' and potters' studios, woolen mills, slate quarries, fish processing plants, or apple orchards are potential tourist lures, as well as places where products can be sold (fig. 79). Many wineries and vineyards have been successful not only in selling their local wines but in making their operations educational and pleasurable experiences, as with the special weekly four-hour intensive tours of the Robert

79. Granville, New York's Slate Valley Museum, interpreting the local slate industry and the Welsh culture of the quarry workers, 2000. Note the patterned slate roof

Mondavi vineyard in California's Napa Valley. This type of tourism has even brought new life to old railroads, which now travel scenic routes during the summer months and foliage season. Local museums are finding visitors interested in their exhibitions—and in their museum shops and catalogues, which sell local crafts, books, and materials. Single dramatic cultural attractions, whether Frank Lloyd Wright's Falling Water house or Los Angeles's Getty Museum, will continue to lure tourists long after anyone has ever heard of Universal Studios CityWalk.

This type of cultural exploring has been associated more frequently with foreign travel, where tourists look at many things that might seem quite mundane at home. But that is changing as people discover interesting places in the United States. Travel sections of Sunday newspapers can make a visit to Cleveland sound as alluring as one to Provence. American cities find that these tourist-shoppers come in vast numbers, providing welcome economic benefits. Santa Fe's Indian Market is said to attract 100,000 visitors a year, and the average visitor is estimated to stay for six days and spend an average of $734 on Indian arts and crafts, according to a 1993 survey for the Southwestern Association for Indian Arts.[128] Not every place has the indigenous appeal of Santa Fe, but towns and regions all over the country are participating in cultural tourism as a means of providing jobs, selling local products, and putting themselves on the map. Weekend sections of city newspapers list increasingly popular walking tours of famous as well as hidden architectural, industrial, park, commercial, and cultural assets. In the tourist magnet of Washington, D.C., a coalition of cultural organizations is promoting "Off the Mall" tours to lure the city's busloads of tourists into the the varied neighborhoods. City life museums are being developed to display cities' mainstream and vernacular history and culture. In fact, cultural tourism has turned into a new kind of economic development.

Maintaining the authenticity of a place is the most basic ingredient for the success of cultural tourism. T-shirts and hamburgers can be bought anywhere, electronic games can be played anywhere, but Charleston's benne wafers and grass baskets can be found only in Charleston, and Crowley's cheeses are made only in Healdville, Vermont. When a place becomes a stage set and loses its authenticity, it shortens its life as a cultural tourist destination. Although authentic and successful cultural tourism differs considerably from the entertainment-driven shopping centers and theme parks, it nonetheless involves shopping. The impacts of tourism and shopping, whether cultural or sheerly commercial, on the host communities present serious threats to the livability of those communities. Hordes of tourist shoppers can create nuisances in neighborhoods, as historic districts like those in Charleston and New Orleans have found; tourist onslaughts can also change the character and types of stores so that instead of serving the residents, they cater to the visitors.

Communal Commerce

Providing ways for the public to meet and socialize has been, and will continue to be, important in our communities. While people have gathered in such public spaces as markets, courthouse grounds, parks, and town squares, equally important gathering places have been commercial establishments: the rural crossroads store, the city department store, the neighborhood coffeeshop, the tavern, the drugstore soda fountain, the convenience store, the English pub, the German beer garden, the French cafe. These "great good places," as Ray Oldenburg describes them in his book *The Great Good Place*, have provided that essential informal public life, but these places are vanishing or changing in character as pervasive social and economic forces have changed the way we live, work, and play.

That basic need for gathering places, for people to see friends and neighbors, persists; that need is just being met in some new and different ways. The French cafe and small stores like the bakery, where one got the daily baguette, are shrinking in number and importance in the lives of French people. The pub remains a major gathering place in many English neighborhoods, but it has a different clientele, hours, and operation. Now the drugstore, with its marble-countered soda fountain, is seen only in museums. The general store has been taken over by franchised stores, and the tavern can be found only in working-class city neighborhoods. However, singles bars, coffee houses, gyms, health food stores, brew pubs, and bookstores now represent some new good places for gathering and meeting people.

Despite the inroads of home entertainment on leisure time—blame television, computer games, and video movies—which caused many to worry about the future of the printed word, books seem to have held their own. The statistics are compelling: book sales have been soaring (up 50 percent from 1992 to 1997), the number of bookstore employees has been increasing (up 33 percent from 1992 to 1997), and the number of bookstores is almost at a record high (down 4 percent from 1992 to 1997).[129] In 1959 there were 1,735 bookstores employing 15,354 persons, and in 1997 those numbers swelled to more than 12,000 stores with almost 120,000 employees.[130] Sales of books reached $12.4 billion in 1997—a dramatic increase from as recently as 1992, when sales were $8.5 billion.[131] The majority of bookstores—about 75 percent—are small, with fewer than ten employees. That was as true in 1959 as in 1997.[132]

The most startling change in bookselling has been the growth of big chains. In 1997, the latest year for detailed Census Bureau retail figures, eleven firms, each with more than 1,000 employees, had almost 4,000 stores and made over $7.7 billion in sales. The sales of this handful of mega-book-selling companies accounted for over 60 percent of the industry's sales, and their stores accounted for almost a third of the total number of the country's bookstores in 1997. From 1987 to 1997 the number of these mega-firms doubled, while the number of their stores increased by 1,464 and their sales quadrupled. In the same period the number of bookselling firms making more than $5 million grew from 74 to 165.[133]

This growth of bookselling is remarkable any way you look at it. The picture of rising sales is projected to continue, with estimated sales hitting $38.4 billion in 2004, up from $23.9 billion in 1994, according to the Book Industry Study Group. This group reported that the number of adult books sold in 1999 had climbed to 1.071 million compared with 1.028 million in 1995. It is too early to tell the full impact of the big bookstore chains, as well as online bookstores like Amazon.com, but in 1999 the Book Industry Study Group found that large chains accounted for 25 percent of adult book purchases, online companies 5.4 percent, small chains and independents 15 percent, and book clubs 18 percent.[134] It is clear, however, that this competition is taking its toll on the independent bookstore. Well-known, independent, and small bookstores like Shakespeare & Co. and Endicott Books in New York City have felt the sting of the new large chains, as have many others in cities where these new chains have located. Aside from being bruised by the discounting and highly automated operations of the chains and more recently by online booksellers, the independent bookstore is also buffeted by rising rents and operating costs, which the large chains can absorb more easily than can the small store.

The surprising popularity of bookstores and the increase in the number of stores and the sales of books are partly due to the communal nature of the stores. The bookstore can be a community gathering place, a safe and friendly harbor in an increasingly impersonal world. Amid automation,

80. *Politics & Prose Bookstore-Coffeehouse, Connecticut Avenue, Washington, D.C.*

sound bites, isolated computer communication, and all the effects of stretched living, the image of a small bookstore with a library ambience, piles of books to explore, helpful clerks to discuss your potential purchases, fellow customers with shared interests, and cozy cafes produces a warm, collegial feeling. These important community institutions, "unlike their corporate counterparts . . . reflect individualized owners and customers."[135]

Washington, D.C.'s Politics and Prose bookstore, started by Carla Cohen and Barbara Meade in 1984 with two telephones, two telephone lines, and one file drawer for three-by-five cards for inventory, is one of Washington's most popular bookstores. Today it has twelve telephones, six telephone lines, two fax lines, an 800 line, a website, eleven computers, thirty employees, 10,000 or so customers (4,000 of whom are clubmembers [3,000 online]), and a monthly newsletter. In expanded space, Politics and Prose now also sells CDs and tapes, posters, cards, and T-shirts (accounting for 5 percent of its business), and runs a relaxed cafe serving soup, sandwiches, desserts, and coffee, making this popular bookstore a single-stop shop. With readings by top-flight writers occurring almost every night, some attracting as many as 300 people, and with 10 book groups (reading groups), comfortable chairs for perusing books, and a very helpful staff, Politics and Prose has become a real gathering place. It fits the image of the friendly independent bookstore meeting the needs of a variety of patrons—and it is also keeping up with the technology of the times. It was no surprise that Politics and Prose was named 1999 Bookseller of the Year by *Publishers Weekly* (fig. 80).

Yet the continued existence of such independent bookstores requires vigilance and promotion. As Carla Cohen says, "We must work to get more people into bookstores. . . . We need to introduce new customers to the pleasures of a physical bookstore. In a physical bookstore people can flip through a book. . . . They can read a few pages from a new novel of a favorite author, look at a book by an unfamiliar writer or simply pick up a book to feel its heft. Above all, they can find community among staff and friends to discuss books."[136]

Politics and Prose is not alone. All over the country many independent bookstores—some small and many not so small—are thriving as key community gathering places trying to ward off the tough competition of chain bookstores, like Barnes and Noble, B. Dalton's, and Borders and online booksellers like Amazon.com. The Tattered Cover, the well-known bookstore in Denver with 300,000 titles; Library, Ltd., in Clayton, Missouri, a suburb of St. Louis, with 125,000 titles, events, readings, seminars, and a cafe; and Seattle's famous Elliott Bay Book Company, started in 1973, with more than 140,000 titles, an experienced staff, cafe, and many events, are just three examples of today's popular bookstore. "More than a store, it's an atmosphere," one library customer stated.[137]

In Portland, Oregon, Powell's City of Books has become such an important institution that it is a stop on visitors' tours of the city. Started as a used bookstore in 1971, Powell's has grown to fill a downtown block to house its 1 million new and used books, which are categorized in 122 subject areas in seven rooms carefully mapped on a large floor plan. Open 365 days a year, from 9 a.m. to 11 p.m., except on Sundays when it closes at 9 p.m., and available on e-mail and the World Wide Web, Powell's also has the requisite cafe in its room with periodicals and gardening books (Portland's weather makes for eager gardeners). It hosts a series of readings and events, including musical performances and weekly programs of local actors "presenting the writings of celebrated authors." That's just in its downtown store. There are six other Powell's bookstores—some specialized for technical, cooking and gardening, and travel books—and other neighborhood, mall, and airport stores. The test for me is the section on urban affairs, which is often stocked primarily with architecture books. But Powell's ranked high, with its unusually comprehensive selection of books from sociology, design, anthropology, and engineering. It also ranked high as a communal "good place," making even the outside gray, drizzly skies seem warm and friendly.

The large chain stores, such as Borders and Barnes & Noble, recognizing the commercial value of the collegial feeling of the independent bookstores, are trying to reproduce it in carefully designed and managed stores. At these new Borders outlets, you can browse at length, look at magazines, sip cappuccino, look at paintings by local artists, attend a reading, listen to string quartets, or join a book club. And unlike many small bookstores, whose intellectual elitism can seem intimidating, the chains have made their stores and books accessible to anyone.

Started in Ann Arbor in 1971, Borders—"with its coffeehouse atmosphere in large quarters," according to *Publishers Weekly*—has expanded to

81. The busy cafe at Borders in the Crossroads Place Shopping Center, Falls Church, Virginia, 1993

277 stores around the world, is online, and is listed on the New York Stock Exchange.[138] Taking advantage of high-powered management and sophisti-cated computerized-tracking, permitting access to 3 million titles, these stores are found in large cities, inner and outer suburbs, and small cities like Saratoga Springs, New York, where Borders has built a store on a prime Main Street location. Borders' sophisticated technology is not apparent to the browser who happens upon a group performing traditional Irish songs on harp, guitar, and hammered dulcimer on St. Patrick's Day, or the espresso bar manager's demonstration of how to make Easter breads, or the twelve oil paintings of the "Icarus Cycle" by a local artist. While readings at bookstores are common, these events add many dimensions to the store. Young and old gather for these events or just to talk at the cafe. They have provided a sense of community in many suburban areas where community has been missing and where there were often no bookstores. In northern Virginia at Bailey's Crossroads, a major traffic intersection surrounded by Category Killers, shop-ping centers, and the twenty-five-story apartment towers of Skyline City, Bor-ders has become the cultural hub, attracting all ages from a large radius of the lower middle class, as well as a mix of ethnic populations (fig. 81). In the heart of Washington's Connecticut Avenue business district, Borders draws big lunchtime as well as evening and weekend crowds with its books, atmos-phere, events, and local art, which is selected by an in-house "curator," Michael Utter. These stores have become "community resources" as well as "destinations to inform and enrich," as the company planned.[139] "In many

markets our stores have become neighborhood gathering places," says Nancy Levy, marketing director of Borders Bookstores at the Ann Arbor headquarters—and strong advocates of community involvement, too. "We feel it's important for a Borders . . . to be more than a retail store, but also part of the community," Levy continued. "Since the products we sell, books and music, are such an important part of our cultural life, events are a logical part of our marketing strategy. We have events in stores to bring more customers in more frequently, so naturally our stores host events people in their particular market are interested in. Our policies are to have some type of event happening at the store every day; to create events which appeal to many different types of people in the community; to create events which feature various aspects of the store."

Borders boasts a long history of sponsoring events in both its city and suburban stores. "Early on we began building stores in the suburbs," states Levy, "and saw the need for cultural activities in those markets," of which Bailey's Crossroads area is a good example, as few cultural institutions, bookstores, dance studios, or galleries exist in such strip mall environments. "Our stores provide a comfortable atmosphere and also a place for people to meet and talk. Based on this fact, we've found the best way to relate to the community is have a person at each store whose job it is to determine what local people are interested in and create an atmosphere that appeals to those interests." That community event manager for each store is called a community relations coordinator (CRC), trained by Levy. The CRC strives to "discern the interests and tastes of people in their particular community" and also "respect the diversity of opinions and people within the communities."

According to Levy, "there is a basic template" for the design of the stores, but "there are variations from store to store based on the characteristics of the area; for example, our store in Anchorage includes a working fireplace." The ambience of Borders bookstores, which has been one of the chain's distinguishing features, derives from a "combination of factors, interior design, merchandising, and the store's staff," Levy states. "Much of the Borders ambience stems from our customer service. Book and music sellers are always available to help customers, but we'll also leave you alone and let you browse."[140]

The success of stores like Borders and many independents shows how booksellers can capitalize on communal benefits as well as on the cultural nature of their wares. It is also an indicator of popular interest in books, music, and culture. But the popularity of these stores results from the work of managers who carefully oversee operations, from book selection to operation of the cafe, to create a friendly and interesting ambience. Whatever the formula for success, many bookstores are meeting places for singles. An NBC television program showed how a young woman dropping a book in one of these friendly bookstores might find a man who not only would pick up the book but would invite her to the bookstore's cafe—and then who knows what next.

Communally related commercial activity remains a vital part of retailing. The story of bookstores is matched by the story of coffeehouses, in which chains like Starbucks have mastered some of the selling features of independent coffeehouses. Even large superstores like Wal-Mart are learning the importance of communality. In Bowie, Maryland, three dozen senior citizens gather in Wal-Mart's snack bar for their weekly bingo game to enjoy each other's company, the fun of bingo, and the free coffee and prizes offered by Wal-Mart. Bingo brings these individuals into the store, and management hopes they will then do some shopping after their game. As the bookstores and coffeehouses have proved, communal "good places" benefit the community and the company's profits.

Retailing in the beginning of the twenty-first century has similarities to Emile Zola's description of retailing in Paris in the late nineteenth century, as it reflects many of the conflicts and challenges facing society: ever-advancing technology making standardized products available for mass-marketing through sophisticated advertising at affordable prices in a variety of remote ways. Today, two very different paths of retailing have developed.

One path is characterized by the Big Boxes, superstores, discounters, and the growing nonstore types of shopping, especially Internet retailing, which all depend on mass production and automation to quickly provide inexpensive and standardized goods to almost any location. Technology will refine and no doubt improve the production, inventory, delivery, prices, and selling of such purchases. Concern about monopolistic practices may well arise as the scale and power of some of these retailers continue to grow.

The other path stems from the basic human need for friendly, face-to-face, communal shopping, as well as from the desire for authenticity, quality, and diversity of goods. This timeless type of shopping will become increasingly important as technologically and market-driven shopping continues to expand along with its accompanying remoteness. "Tomorrow's stores will have to be what the Web cannot be: tangible, *intimate*, and local," writes longtime Random House editor Jason Epstein of the future of publishing and bookselling.[141] Today many of these types of stores and markets, such as independent bookstores, public markets, farmers' markets, and even flea markets, are proving to be popular and successful retail activities. The lower prices that the chains, discounters, and Big Boxes can offer customers, which can also kill off local, independent retailers, are not all that buyers seek. "The price isn't everything," as Trish Thomas commented on the demise of Washington, D.C.'s flagship department store, Woodward & Lothrop. Shopping is more than bargain seeking. Shoppers and communities yearn for the individuality, friendliness, color, noise, vitality, grittiness—and soul—that this stream of shopping provides. Big Boxes, tourist-oriented shopping, and now "entertainment" retailing may affect touches of this personal style of retailing, like greeters at the door, but such programmed friendliness misses the essential integrity of the personal style of retailing.

Both the personal, friendly, small-scale, and communal shopping found in the "good places," and the mainstream, technology-driven types of retailing undoubtedly will continue to coexist. They may be on separate courses, sometimes complementing each other and at other times converging and even borrowing from each other. But large-scale, mainstream retailing may dwarf—and kill—personal, friendly retailing unless efforts are made to recognize and promote the public benefits of this type of shopping.

CHAPTER FIVE

Planning for Shopping

An Insurance Policy for Community Well-Being

The contributions of shopping to the sociability and livability of a community have never been consistently recognized by planners and designers. Like
an adolescent whose feelings about his parents fluctuate from disdain to
admiration, many planners and designers vacillate between treating retailing with almost benign neglect, letting the private sector do what it wants to
do, or making it the linchpin of downtown and suburban developments.
Some plans do not even mention retailing.

Developers, on the other hand, as well as investors, retailers, and business groups like the Chamber of Commerce, have been active promoters of
retailing, from the earliest settlements to today's entertainment-retailing projects. Analysis of all the benefits and costs of various types of retailing in different situations—especially small-scale neighborhood businesses, which
Jane Jacobs championed forty years ago—rarely takes place. Communities
usually react to proposals by developers and retailers rather than seek out the
types of and locations for retailing activities best suited to their needs. And in
many cases since World War II, large mall developers have actually guided
the direction and character of new suburban development as they induced

governments to provide the infrastructure—arteries, highway interchanges, and so forth—for their malls, which sometimes preceded residential developments. It was not planners who sited the malls and Big Boxes in Paramus, New Jersey, or the continuous strips of shopping centers along arteries on the outskirts of American cities and towns. These were decisions by developers and investors, who found it cheaper and easier to develop contemporary retailing out of town, where they avoided high land costs, restrictive zoning, and complicated and time-consuming permitting and title searches. Out-of-town locations usually meant easier site preparation, simpler construction, less public and neighbor involvement, and opportunities to build large buildings with ample parking.

Yet after these outlying shopping centers and commercial strips were developed, it was not the developers who had to cope with all the transportation, environmental, social, and economic problems they caused. As Donovan Rypkema commented at a 1998 Vermont conference titled "Making Downtowns and Village Centers More Attractive for Development," developers build outside of towns because they anticipate that the total value of such developments will be greater than their total cost, but they don't calculate all the problems and costs to the community "that building on the periphery creates and that accrue to the community, but are not borne by the property owner."[1] Those problems and their costs are borne by the public.

Retail development has had its own engine, partly because planners were not able to guide, nor were they interested in guiding, that development, and partly because the public has not wanted to be involved in retail planning and retailers have not wanted interference.

Order and Segregation of Uses

Some of the earliest legal decisions on the regulation of the location, hours, and conditions of commercial activities, found in the California Chinese laundry cases in the 1880s, reflect values that have influenced the course of retail planning and have helped build the groundwork for zoning. The attitudes behind these regulations and the later court decisions can often be traced to the old country, to early American settlements, and to the fears and hopes of the nineteenth century. Protection of the sanctity and the real estate values of residential areas was paramount in these early land-use segregation regulations. Encouraging order and avoiding a mix of different kinds of activities—housing, manufacturing, and commerce, for example—has been traditionally seen as a means to protect neighborhoods from nuisances and to promote healthy communities. In the United States, the shopkeeper's family, or those who could not afford better housing in residential areas, lived over the store. In European cities there is no stigma attached to this way of living. In Berlin, people live over stores throughout the city, from the working-class neighborhoods to the upscale Charlottenburg section where luxury apartments are found above the fancy stores on the elegant shopping boulevard Kurfürstendam, which surprised a recent American expatriate journalist, Sarah Defty, since that would not occur in her native St. Louis.

As early as 1883, San Francisco, concerned that laundries were endangering public health and safety, decided to regulate the city's laundries through an ordinance which baldly stated that violators "prejudiced the well-being and comfort of the community and depreciated the value of property in their neighborhood."[2] This ordinance required laundries, three hundred of which were scattered in residential and business districts, to be in brick or stone buildings. Also, due to concern about fire hazards, soapy water in gutters, long working hours, and the unsightliness of drying lines on roofs, the city regulated the activities, sanitation, and hours of the laundries.

Several legal challenges to these restrictions of laundries—all involving Chinese laundrymen—were made on the grounds of the Fourteenth Amendment. Some laundrymen, caught washing during forbidden hours, argued they were being discriminated against—the regulations were forcing them to abandon their trade and only means of livelihood. Were these regulations a discrimination of one business over another, or were they manifestations of prejudice against the Chinese, who found laundries to be a type of work open to them and one that required long hours? While the courts generally supported the ordinances and regulations restricting the location, hours, and operation of these laundries—and, in the case of Modesto, even considered violations to be misdemeanors punishable by fine or imprisonment—the fact that the laundries were run by immigrant Chinese undoubtedly instigated the enactment and enforcement of these regulations.[3] "No variety of anti-European sentiment," John Higham wrote in *Strangers in the Land*, "have ever approached the violent extremes to which anti-Chinese agitation went in the 1870's and 1880's."[4] The racial antipathy even extended to "the fact that the laundry buildings were becoming the clubs of Chinese," W. L. Pollard wrote. Such congregating "added to their objectionable features in the popular mind."[5]

Concerns over fire prevention, sanitation, and health were the overt justifications for the regulations, but laundry location and land use became increasingly important concerns. In Modesto, which developed the United States' first zoning ordinance, laundries could be sited only in designated areas, and in Los Angeles laundries were allowed only with permits and in designated areas. None were allowed anywhere in Napa. San Francisco regulated the operation of laundries on the grounds that their unhealthy conditions were "against good morals, contrary to the public order and decency, or dangerous to public safety."[6] By 1909, laundries in Los Angeles could not be located in buildings used as halls, stores, restaurants, lodging houses, or saloons for fear of the spread of infectious or contagious diseases.[7] Along with public health concerns, protection of residential areas from incompatible uses frequently appeared as the justification for the regulations. Laundries were considered—along with other "noxious" activities like stone crushing, carpet beating, fireworks manufacture, and soap making—inappropriate for residential neighborhoods in Los Angeles. By 1915, all of Los Angeles was covered by the ordinance, making it one large residential district, with only the lightest of industries allowed in certain districts.[8]

Prohibition of businesses from residential districts continued, and the categories of prohibited uses expanded. By the mid-1920s retail stores had become targets for exclusion. Nutley, New Jersey, a small suburb up the Passaic River from Newark, prevented the erection and use of a store in a residential area (in this case, a combination store and dwelling), and when challenged, the courts backed the town, stating that a store in a residential area increased the likelihood of fire hazard, street litter, traffic, and dust.[9] Washington, D.C., feared that stores in residential neighborhoods might spread disease, as flies and vermin landing on the food in the stores would infect the neighborhood.[10]

New York City's early efforts to regulate land use, enact the country's first zoning legislation, in 1916, and cope with sweatshops, pushcarts, and other commercial endeavors deemed deleterious to the health and welfare of the city, dramatically illustrate the forces behind these public actions. These land-use controls reveal the forces that have continued to influence the course of planning and zoning. A sincere interest in ameliorating the living and working conditions of the city's poor propelled the efforts of the social reformers of that era. Squalid, crowded, utterly unhealthy tenements, coupled with equally squalid, crowded, unhealthy sweatshops, aroused public attention and spurred the formation in 1907 of the Committee on Congestion of Population in New York. The committee was run by the single taxer, Benjamin Marsh, joined by well-known welfare leaders Florence Kelly, Lillian Wald, and Mary Simkovitch, and its later chairman, Robert Morganthau.

Health was the primary concern as these reformers grappled with the problems of congested living, tax structure, absentee landlords, and public services. Morganthau stated in a speech in Washington, D.C., in 1909: "There is an evil which is gnawing at the vitals of the country, to remedy which we have come together—an evil that breeds physical disease, moral depravity, discontent, and socialism, and all these must be cured and eradicated or else our great body politic will be weakened. This community can only hold its pre-eminence if the masses that compose it are given a chance to be healthy, moral and self-respecting. If they are forced to live like swine they will lose their vigor." Aside from suggesting better tenement regulations, more playgrounds, and good transit so that people could live outside the city, Morganthau promoted zoning. "We can make city plans establishing factory zones and residence zones, and have every building used for residential purposes so arranged that sunlight can reach some part of the building at some time of the day."[11]

In his proposal, one of many discussed at the 1909 National Conference on City Planning, Morganthau strongly supported the idea of planning zones, which were already established in Germany. The conference recommendations, including Morganthau's support of zoning, exposed deep interest in improving health and living conditions in urban America, and these recommendations planted the seeds for future planning and zoning efforts. Health, light, air, and sanitation remained important incentives for land-use controls by social reformers and visionaries seeking a beautiful, clean, and healthy city. But equally powerful incentives with less humanitarian goals, like the protection of real estate values and exclusion of certain—and usually unrefined—people and activities, drove other promoters of zoning and planning.

The role of these less humanitarian interests in New York's zoning, planning, and regulations can be seen in the efforts to maintain an upmarket ambience on Fifth Avenue by preventing the intrusion of pushcarts and sweatshops. This attitude toward pushcarts reflects the drive to order space by separating activities and people by economic and social class in a hierarchical manner. As elsewhere in the early days of land-use regulation, whether the debate was over the Chinese in California or the Russian Jews on the Lower East Side, "the immigrant is in the fiber of zoning," as Seymour Toll put it.[12] On fashionable Fifth Avenue, the fear of "floods" of workers invading this new shopping district galvanized the Fifth Avenue Association, comprising such prominent businessmen as Elliman, Brentano, Kane, and Knoedler, to lobby for height restrictions that would prevent upper floors from being converted to sweatshops or factories. The association's fear that the upper floors of higher loft buildings would not be rentable for retail use and, therefore, might be taken over by garment manufacturing businesses and their immigrant laborers was so compelling that the city restricted the height of buildings to 125 feet within 100 feet of Fifth Avenue.[13]

This debate over the height and use of Fifth Avenue buildings stimulated discussions about skyscrapers elsewhere, as well as about the development of the city as a whole. The backers of the Fifth Avenue Association, interested in protecting their real estate and businesses from being infiltrated by the wrong businesses and people, became major supporters of the 1916 zoning initiative in their Save New York campaign. This campaign, focused on the problems of factories invading retail areas, called for a boycott of garment manufacturers, even those located away from Fifth Avenue, and also called public attention to these problems through advertisements in newspapers like the *New York Times* in March 1916: "Shall we save New York from what? Shall we save it from unnatural and unnecessary crowding, from depopulated sections, from being a city unbeautiful, from high rents, from excessive and ill-distributed taxation? We can save it from all of these, so far at least as they are caused by one specific industrial evil—the erection of factories in the residential and famous retail section."[14]

This campaign persuaded 95 percent of the manufacturers affected by the boycott to move away from the district, bounded by Third and Fifth Avenues and 34th and 59th Streets. This "great zone . . . affected the very heart of New York, and comprised all that makes the city worthwhile as a place to shop, play, work and live in," stated J. Howes Burton, board member of the Fifth Avenue Association and a force behind the Save Fifth Avenue campaign. The district became New York's first land use zone.[15]

Coinciding with the city's Commission on Building Districts and Restrictions, the creation of this Fifth Avenue zone in protecting businesses from the nuisances of retail factories and sweatshops helped to convince the city's government, newspapers, and citizens that zoning could work to protect all residential areas from intrusions. Thus, social reformers gained new allies—merchants, real estate developers, and architects—who helped them to pass New York's heralded Zoning Resolution in 1916. From the hope of preventing tuberculosis to the desire to protect economic investments, this 1916 zoning plan, designed with hierarchical German land-use principles, offered a formula to make the city beautiful for its natives, its visitors, and its businesses.

While immigrant sweatshops were a primary threat that helped to

82. *Pushcarts in New York's Lower East Side.* Sunday Morning at Orchard and Rivington Streets, New York City, *Bain News Service, 1915 (Library of Congress, Prints and Photographs Division, Washington, D.C.)*

83. Far from the Fresh Air Farm, *painting by William Glackens, 1911 (collection of Museum of Art, Fort Lauderdale, Florida)*

mobilize support for the 1916 Zoning Resolution, another retail activity, pushcarts, produced a different set of public regulations and actions in New York. Many of the same attitudes influencing the passage of the Fifth Avenue regulations were at work in trying to control pushcarts. Specialization, isolation, and containment of single uses were again the issues, this time not in private buildings but on public streets. Although pushcarts were considered an urban blight by many, including Mayor Fiorello LaGuardia, they provided inexpensive foods, clothing, and goods, as well as a first-step occupation for many immigrants and others (fig. 82). In the days of pushcarts, bustling bargaining filled the streets and sidewalks, often to the dismay of the storekeepers. Efforts to control pushcarts, often for the sake of health and sanitation, involved declaring them illegal, segregating them to certain areas on the streets, and developing indoor public markets in LaGuardia's time. These efforts raised policy questions about the uses of public streets, the value of mixing uses, and the whole gamut of views and visions on the uses of public spaces throughout the city. The history of pushcart regulations brings out the clashes that occurred over these visions throughout the years (fig. 83).

The clean-up-and-sanitize approach to urban problems has pervaded zoning and planning since 1916, crescendoing in the 1960s, when urban renewal was seen as a way to eradicate slums. Pushcarts represented an uncontrolled mix of people, goods, dirt, disease, litter, and clutter clogging streets and sidewalks, an image that ran counter to the image of public decorum and social refinement many planners, zoners, and engineers had hoped that cities would encourage. The professionals' dream of free-flowing traffic was dashed by the jumble of pushcarts buying, selling, and socializing. In trying to civilize cities, a Teutonic sense of rational and efficient order took over. The final answer of Mayor LaGuardia, an immigrant himself who saw pushcarts as a symbol of backward ways, was to get them out of sight in market buildings. Now, sixty years later, all that peddling is filling public squares and streets with greenmarkets and flea markets. Even the boutiqued festival marketplaces have carefully designed pushcarts. No longer stigmatized as a low-class, immigrant activity, this small-scale form of selling has joined the upscale commercial world as a vibrant and almost picturesque urban activity, enlivening otherwise dreary city areas, as well as offering opportunities for people to enter the retail world on a small budget.

Through most of urban America, however, the clutter, sociability, noise, bustle, and unorganized nature of the true pushcart has been eliminated through cities' efforts to provide a "modern" system for the operation of commerce—that is, cars and trucks need streets, people need healthy and regulated food, and residential areas need privacy. The true pushcart, a symbol of diversity and pluralism, has been a victim of earnest planners and engineers who, in trying to promote public welfare, decorum, and stability, have often balkanized many neighborhoods, towns, and cities.

Excluding businesses from residential areas provided a sense of order and uniformity in given districts, and this helped to sell enabling zoning legislation to wary property owners, in these incipient days of zoning, according to Edward Bassett, an authority on zoning and planning who was instrumental in establishing New York's 1916 zoning code. "Property owners would have been more hostile," states Bassett in his important Russell Sage study of zoning, "if they had thought that councils could select parts of districts for special favors."[16] Treating all property alike in a district made zoning palatable to suspicious property owners, as uniform-use districts were assumed to stabilize neighborhoods and hence conserve property values—and hence tax revenue for the municipality. In 1903, John C. Olmsted, a stepson of Frederick Law Olmsted and a key member of the Olmsted firm's design team, warned the developer of Atlanta's Druid Hills suburb, Joel Hurt, that incorporating "stores . . . would be an injury to the character of the Company's land."[17] Even Bassett found that "the fair distribution of different kinds of business must be approached through private covenants or some method of trade regulation in the state or city, if any can be found. Zoning, as we now understand it, is not the proper instrumentality."[18] But it is interesting to note that in the famous Cleveland zoning decision *Euclid v. Ambler*, Justice Sutherland stated that "the exclusion of places of businesses from residential districts is not a declaration that such places are nuisances or that they are to be suppressed as such, but it is part of the general plan by which the city's territory is allotted to different uses in order to prevent, or at least reduce, the congestion, disorder and dangers which often inhere in unregulated municipal growth."[19]

The policy of separating land uses and protecting residential areas from perceived nuisances has been one of the constant influences in the development of cities, towns, and neighborhoods—as well as a lasting reflection of American values. Certainly the desire to avoid the vexing problems of the industrial city—its dark, satanic mills, pollution, workers, and traffic—and the honest interest in retaining the simple life of small towns spurred the movement for unblemished residential districts. All cities, not just industrial cities, projected an image of contrasts: opulence and poverty, grandeur and squalor, mansions and tenements, elegant shops and peddlers, safety and crime. The garden suburb, however, was an escape from the jarring contrasts of the cities and a return to the purer values of the small town and the countryside.

The Suburban Ideal

The suburban ideal, following the English Garden City tradition, blended town and countryside, near enough to cities for families to take advantage of urban opportunities but removed from the woes of the modern industrial city. Golders Green was described as a "place of delightful prospects" on a 1908 London Underground poster depicting a suburban backyard with the husband watering a lush garden, his wife sitting nearby knitting, and the daughter holding her yarn—all within sight of the Underground station. A poem by William Cowper, an eighteenth-century poet who extolled the countryside, is printed on this poster:

> 'Tis pleasant, through the loopholes of retreat
> To peep at such a world: to see the stir
> Of the Great Babel, and not feel the crowd;
> To hear the roar she sends through all her gates
> At a safe distance, where the dying sound
> Falls a soft murmur on the 'uninjured ear.'

This quest for a retreat was understandable for urbanites in the Great Babel, with its rapidly expanding populations, unfettered development, and ever-growing industry and commerce. "The urge for zoning . . . has arisen from the desire and the necessity to bring some order out of the chaos that has arisen from anarchistic development of our cities," Gorden Whitnall stated in his 1931 "History of Zoning."[20] For the early settlers in the United States, dislocated from their friends, family, and familiar values and institutions in the old country, and confronting a startling tabula rasa, there was a compelling drive for order as they tried to establish a civilization in a physical, spiritual, and moral wilderness. Some, like Sylvia Fries in her *Urban Idea in Colonial America*, argue that the colonial American city was designed to preserve values and ways of life that were rural in character, since the "countryside . . . was seen by men and women apprehensive of social disorder as a place where traditional social structures and moral control could be best maintained."[21] But whether a revolt against industrialism or a retreat to safe and known values, the ordering of cities and suburbs into districts provided protection from the worst nuisances of cities, as well as a place where the extremes of wealth and poverty could be avoided. The safety of this economic and social uniformity has survived in the American dream of residential purity—and shops and stores have been consistently excluded.

From the early California regulations keeping Chinese laundries out of residential neighborhoods to the more recent establishment of gated communities that seal off intrusions, controlling commercial nuisances has been an important rationale for zoning and planning, which became even more important with the introduction of the car and its potential for generating dispersed development, especially "undesirable" development. "The automobile was upon us," stated Harland Bartholomew in 1931, "and there was a great desire to limit the rapidly increasing number of stores, filling stations, 'hot dog' stands, and what not which were springing up overnight in many desirable residential areas."[22] If not instigated by such negative attitudes, then commercial and retail uses have been treated with benign neglect, attitudes that have followed retail activities through the centuries. Those in "trade" seem to bear a perpetual stigma. And this makes it difficult for retailers to gain adequate recognition, to see how their stores can benefit a community, how their negative impacts can be reduced, and how merchants can be included in a community—and how a community can work with them.

Despite the image of the gaiety of the 1920s with flappers, speakeasies, Dorothy Parker, F. Scott Fitzgerald, and new freedom for women, the decade also focused on such serious matters as the family, children, and community. Academic concern with the careful upbringing of children produced progressive schools, like the Lincoln School in New York, and expanded attention to preventive medicine, healthful cooking, essential play, and exercise. It was in this progressive context that city planning emerged. The American City Planning Institute, started in 1917, attracted idealistic planners and architects interested in making cities and communities both livable and functional. Clarence Stein, George Wright, Clarence Perry, Lewis Mumford, and Benton MacKaye were among the conscientious and idealistic leaders sparking new ideas, projects, and enthusiasm for this emerging field. It is they who produced model

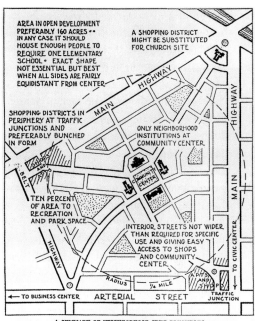

84. Clarence Perry's 1929 plan for a neighborhood and its peripheral shopping

developments like Sunnyside Gardens in Queens, new towns like Radburn, New Jersey, ambitious environmental projects like the Appalachian Trail, and New York's Regional Plan of 1926. The optimism of this era energized planners, architects, and social reformers, who felt that they could better living conditions and plan functional and healthy communities.

Theories on the neighborhood, a basic unit in the community, set the tone for the period and for the future (fig. 84). Clarence Perry's 1929 work at the Russell Sage Foundation, "Planning a Neighborhood Unit," became the guide for neighborhood planning. Perry, oriented to child-rearing families in suburban settings, set forth principles to "give added character, convenience, and safety to outlying sections of cities." The elementary school became the focus of the community. The neighborhood was to be a safe, insulated place with a "residential character" geared to pedestrians, with narrow streets to prevent through-traffic, scattered playgrounds, and small parks occupying 10 percent of the land, and, in its center, a community building for "neighborhood institutions." Local shops were to be located on the periphery of the neighborhood, preferably at traffic junctions, adjacent to similar neighborhoods and not more than a half mile from each "housekeeper." For Perry, in order "to supply parking spaces and service alleys, the neighborhood shopping areas are preferably bunched in form and are best situated adjoining similar districts in adjacent units. Thus placed, the shops are in a position to catch the patronage of through traffic and also serve the local resident conveniently."[23]

This pattern of shops on the edge of residential neighborhoods, as Perry suggested—not *in* those neighborhoods—has persisted in order to assure that the "residential character" of a neighborhood not be violated by the nuisances, litter, and crowds of shops. Placing shops along the edges of residential developments has continued as a dominant pattern, and the result is the seamless commercial strips lining arteries in most towns and cities. For Perry, however, such shopping areas, providing stores for nearby neighborhoods, would be contained and external to residential neighborhoods, usually with parking in front of the stores, which face the street. But these thoroughfare-oriented shopping centers, which could also "catch the patronage of through traffic," according to Perry, became the forerunners of the shopping center in those early days of the auto age.[24]

But it was in the burgeoning urban areas of southern California—especially Los Angeles, with its high percentage of car ownership—that the thoroughfare shopping center, made up of drive-in markets and often built under a single management as a unified group, emerged in the 1920s as a new and important shopping facility. "Drive-in markets had enjoyed an overnight success," says architectural historian Richard Longstreth, "partly because they embodied the still-novel concept of one-stop shopping with individually-run units, each carrying a different kind of food product, coordinated so as to function as a more or less integrated business."[25] These markets became destinations for commuters, Longstreth explains, as they were easily accessible and visible by car and oriented to peak traffic—that is, located on corners facing homeward-bound commuters. An early example of such a drive-in shopping center in the East is Washington, D.C.'s Park and Shop on Connecticut Avenue, recently revivified after demolition threats. Built in 1930 by one of Washington's major real estate firms, Shannon and Luchs, the Park and Shop was sited to catch the patronage of those homeward-bound drivers, as well as to serve the adjacent Cleveland Park neighborhood. This was an automobile-oriented shopping center responding to the challenge of the Motor Age.

A different tack was taken in planning the shopping for Radburn, the New Town for the Motor Age, in Fair Lawn, Bergen County, New Jersey, sixteen miles from the George Washington Bridge. Designed by the New York cluster of urbanists Clarence Stein, Henry Wright, and Frederick Ackerman, Radburn was developed in 1929 by Alexander Bing's City Housing Corporation. Oriented to the community and the pedestrian, Radburn's shopping followed the basic precepts of family and child advocates.

The school was to be within walking distance—no more than half a mile—from the homes, according to Perry, and in Radburn that radius included the stores. "If walking is made safe and attractive . . . by completely separating pedestrian from vehicular traffic, and by paths passing through parks, there will be much less use of automobiles in local shopping," stated Clarence Stein and Catherine Bauer (later Wurster) in their thoughtful study of neighborhood shopping centers. "If residents are to walk to their stores, no home should be more than half a mile from a neighborhood shopping center."[26]

Therefore, instead of facing the street, Radburn's shopping nucleus, the Plaza Building, was oriented to the central park—the community's unifying focus and the heart of its large superblocks—so that shoppers could walk to it on paths from each of the cul-de-sacs penetrating the park and through underpasses from adjacent park cul-de-sacs. This shopping center, the Plaza Building, "will face toward the life of the community which will center around the park," stated Stein and Bauer.[27] Parking was provided, as was service and truck access at the rear and sides of the building; pedestrian paths were totally separate. A play space for children was to be located at the park entrance of the Plaza. Aside from having stores on the ground floor and office space for professionals above, the Plaza Building also had community facilities for adult education, a theater (New Jersey's oldest amateur theater group started here) for discussion groups ("Town Meeting of the Air" originated here), as well as sports events, and other community activities. The Plaza was planned as both a neighborhood shopping center and community center, reflecting the ideals and concerns of thoughtful urbanists who sought to provide affordable housing in a healthful and satisfying community. This was a community driven by ideals as well as by economic and social pragmatism, not by short-term real estate market objectives.

While the Depression prevented the completion of Radburn, the community today is a gem amid sprawling suburbia. Unfortunately, the plans for shopping described by Stein and Bauer could not be fully implemented. But Stein and Bauer offered creative yet practical ideas for strengthening the sense of community in a neighborhood even as they met basic shopping needs. Their underlying premise was that the "economic success of a neighborhood community and the well-being of its inhabitants depend to a great extent on the planning of the neighborhood shopping center."[28] That was a rare admission from planners, who then and now usually let the marketplace shape the siting, functions, and types of retailing.

To create a successful neighborhood shopping center, Stein and Bauer recognized the need to satisfy the consumer, landlord, storekeeper, and local government, which involved scrutiny of the economic dynamics of storekeeping. To avoid the overbuilding of stores and the concomitant struggle for survival of so many marginal shops—which produce the all-too-common situation in which "the great majority of shopkeepers make something less than the barest living and die off like flies before they even get started"—Stein and Bauer worked out a system for analyzing the market and forecasting the number and types of stores required in a community. Their analysis was based on purchasing power and such "modifying factors" as "income, general character, buying habits, location in relation to larger centers, etc."[29]

The Plaza Building still houses shops and offices, but nearby streets are lined with mini-strip shopping centers. However, the ideas from Stein and Bauer's study for planning and developing successful neighborhood shopping centers, their attention to pedestrianization, and their focus on concentrating shopping, "leaving no leeway for shoe-string development," influenced the planning for shopping in the Greenbelt towns of the New Deal, as well as in a later generation of new towns: Columbia, Maryland, and Reston, Virginia.[30]

In 1937, the New Deal new town of Greenbelt, Maryland, was able to capitalize on Stein and Bauer's thinking, break from the pattern of periphery shopping, and carry on the interest in planning for family and children by

85. Greenbelt, Maryland's centrally located community center (later named the Roosevelt Center), 1940, which includes the town's stores, theater, post office, and government offices in buildings 29 and 31, and the community building, 15, with the library, elementary school, and auditorium. Nearby are recreational facilities, the fire house, and a gas station. The same functions were still being carried out in 2000, although some were in different buildings (collection of the Greenbelt Public Library)

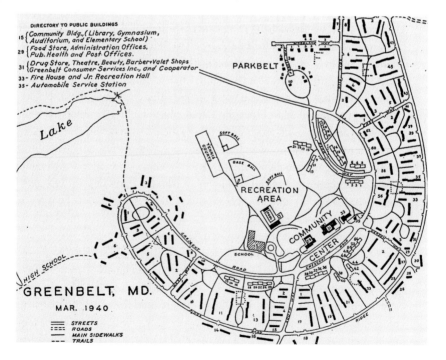

making its shopping area, called the Roosevelt Center, the civic focus of the community. Its cooperative grocery store and its drugstore, cleaners, restaurants, variety store, bank, movie theater, shoe repair shop, post office, and doctors' and lawyers' offices are all there, along with the nearby town offices, community center, library, and recreation facilities. The central and focal point of the Roosevelt Center is its rectangular open space, with benches and umbrellaed tables for socializing, a large limestone sculpture of a woman and child by WPA artist Lenore Thomas at one end, and commercial buildings on two sides. This is the town's civic plaza (fig. 85). While parking is provided, walking to the center is encouraged, with a system of footpaths and even an underpass so that shoppers would not have to cross a major street. Unlike contemporary neotraditionalists, who emphasize architecture in their developments, the designers of Greenbelt and Radburn concentrated not on appearance but on the functions that strengthened community. The modest two-story art deco buildings of Greenbelt's Roosevelt Center have been designed to frame the town's civic open space, not to make architectural statements of their own. This central shopping area–civic plaza—with one end opening up to the residential neighborhoods, giving the impression that the plaza welcomes these neighborhoods and their residents—contrasts sharply with Perry's proposal, in which the neighborhood has turned its back to the shops, which are strung along the periphery of a neighborhood with no public buildings or common spaces for socializing.

The small scale of the stores and shops in the 1930s and 1940s fit well into village centers like Greenbelt's and into shopping streets in towns and cities everywhere. But as the size of the stores expanded in the 1950s and 1960s, becoming supermarkets reaching larger numbers of customers and requiring bigger parking lots and truck loading areas, these village stores outgrew their Main Street locations and peripheral thoroughfare locations. Stores were forced to move to new, more spacious sites, sometimes on thoroughfare locations. The economic imperatives of inherent retail industry competition, automobile-dependent suburban living, and conveniences like refrigerators with freezers were transforming shopping from a local, intimate activity, where butchers were known and neighbors recognized, to a larger-scale, more impersonal style of shopping. No longer was the housewife making the daily rounds of shops; instead, she was loading the car weekly with big purchases from the supermarket.

These changes, some incremental and others more dramatic, were profoundly reshaping postwar America. They resulted from societal, economic, and political forces and decisions, which were well beyond the scope of planners' prognostications. Thus, instead of undertaking predictive programs, planners found themselves reacting to rapid and massive changes. They tried to control and shape the sprawl so that some open space would be left and the requisite social, economic, and engineering infrastructure would be provided in the burgeoning suburbs, while at the same time coping with the problems of the tired older cities and their downtowns, which were fast being abandoned. The breadth of the changes was overwhelming for the most conscientious planner, and new and strengthened concentrations of political power, such as the highway lobby, backed by high-powered industries like automobile, gas, trucking, cement, and real estate businesses, made it hard for planners to take an assertive leadership role in creating the new suburbia.

Retail-Driven Development

The powerful pressures behind postwar development were difficult enough for communities that had planning or zoning policies in place. But for the many places without either, there were no tools or policies to guide development to serve these communities' interests, often making them helpless victims of pressures beyond their control.

Paramus, New Jersey, is an example. Located seven miles from the George Washington Bridge, Paramus was a nondescript area with a population of 3,688 in 1940, with ninety-four retail establishments. It had no town center or identifying features other than acres of rich muck soils for truck farming, which helped New Jersey earn its title of the Garden State. Post–World War II market pressures, combined with highway accessibility, a weak sense of community, and no planning or zoning, made Paramus ripe for developers. The development that hit Paramus was not so much the residential sprawl oozing throughout suburbia but rather miles of intensive commercial strips with three major, early malls and one of the area's first discounters on the two major highways, Routes 4 and 17, that intersect the municipality.

In the 1950s and again in the 1980s, Paramus experienced phenomenal growth. Its population jumped from 6,268 to 23,238, and its retail activities soared. Between 1948 and 1958, its 111 retail establishments nearly tripled to 319, and sales mushroomed from almost $5.5 million to more than $112 million. During the 1970s, 100 new stores located in Paramus, so that by 1982 sales reached more than $1 billion. Both the number of stores and their sales continued to grow constantly. In 1992, Paramus could boast of having more than 800 stores with sales of over $1.7 billion. Big Boxes, Category Killers, and a helter-skelter of stores and office buildings followed, one housing the headquarters of Toys "R" Us, the country's first Category Killer and later its largest toy store, with sales of more than $9 billion and 650 stores. Tucked behind the commercial strip are residential areas where 24,738 people lived in 1992, only 1,500 more than in 1960. With this roaring retail growth in the last forty years, Paramus, for Bergen County residents and most New Yorkers, has become synonymous with shopping, and its image is of one continuous commercial strip.[31]

Although the 1931 opening of the George Washington Bridge and the widening of Route 4 and later of the north-south Route 17 made Paramus accessible to millions of people, it was not until the 1950s that massive development hit this section of northern New Jersey. Then the Paramus farmers found shopping malls a far more lucrative use of their land than growing cabbages. With the construction of the Bergen Mall in 1952, and then of the Garden State Plaza mall in 1956, Alexander's discount store in 1961, another shopping mall, Fashion Park, in 1967, and dozens of other small and large stores, restaurants, gas stations, and sundry commercial establishments, Paramus became the first stop outside New York City for shopping. Here New Yorkers could shop at New York department stores like Stern's and avoid paying New York's sales tax, as New Jersey had no sales tax. In fact, retailing "made" Paramus, as one of its planning consultants, Peter Steck, commented.[32]

Not until 1969—long after the highways were lined with nonstop commerce—did Paramus approve a master plan. Today the city has a planning board but no staff, so its work is done by outside consultants. Although the die has been cast in its massive retail developments, many problems exist for the city's consultants. Old malls need refurbishing, tenants, and new life as anchors like B. Altman and stores like Alexander's have gone out of business. The smaller strips have just become tawdry. Traffic problems are beyond the belief of the foresighted traffic engineers, whose 1931 cloverleaf at the intersection of Routes 4 and 17, designed for 30,000 cars, has a 100,000-car volume. Contributing to the traffic problems are the safety hazards created by miles of multiple and confusing entrances and exits to stores on both highways.

Paramus's transformation into a major metropolitan shopping strip is an extreme case of unfettered development. It was a developer's dream: flat, cleared land adjacent to major arterials and accessible to a growing suburban population and the country's largest city—with no planning restrictions. As suburban development stretched, the shopping developments have required more land, forcing developers to reach into what seems hinterland, where land is available with little interference from planning and zoning boards. Shopping's relationship to community has not been a priority for Paramus—or for many similar market-driven developments.

Although many places like Paramus ignored planning, others undertook comprehensive planning to direct development for the long-term benefit of their jurisdictions. States like California, regions like Minneapolis–St. Paul, and cities like New Haven, Connecticut, carried out active public planning, although they were often overwhelmed by development pressures. California's Santa Clara County, with grade A soil and acres of farms, valiantly tried to protect its natural resources so that they might coexist with the new development, but developers bulldozed right through the grade A land. The

New York Regional Plan Association promoted its *Race for Open Space* in the 1960s to show how parks, open space, and stream valleys could enhance sub-urban living and protect natural resources, such as the hydrological system, but the setting-aside of some open space in subdivisions was the most that came out of that effort.

The money, brains, and legislation in the planning field were then focused on salvaging the city through urban revitalization. Programs like Model Cities, block grants, and demonstration projects of all sorts tried to thwart flight to the suburbs and to glue the city together. Shopping was a consideration. Strengthening the downtown department stores and intro-ducing new shopping areas with supermarkets were goals of these urban renewal plans, as in Washington, D.C.'s Southwest area. But powerful social and economic forces were shrinking the role of downtown shopping and changing its customers while expanding the number, size, and nature of sub-urban shopping centers—seemingly beyond the control of the planner in a nation where free enterprise was heralded and government was considered a back-up partner.

Another Track: Planned Communities

Compared to a country like England, the United States has had limited expe-rience with planned communities. Except for some company towns, there have been few experimental communities, such as New Harmony, Indiana; Olmsted and Vaux's Riverside, outside Chicago; Radburn; the Depression Greenbelt towns; and the new towns of Reston, Virginia, and Columbia, Maryland. How these communities planned for shopping reflects the ideas and values of their promoters, as well as the social, cultural, and economic influences of the different times.

In the late nineteenth century, enlightened English industrialists such as Titus Salt, W. H. Lever, and the Quaker candy manufacturers George Cadbury and Joseph Rowntree built model villages for their workers. These villages have provided attractive, healthful housing, parks, allotment gardens, lyceums and schools, theaters, churches, and shops, all with high architectural standards and varying degrees of social paternalism. Not only were the industrialists patrons and developers of exemplary villages, but these idealistic—and realistic—businessmen actively participated in national efforts to ameliorate living conditions at a time when most workers' housing in cities was appallingly overcrowded, unsanitary, and expensive. These model communities continue to thrive, as do some of the charitable trusts of their patrons, like the Joseph Rowntree Trust and the Bournville Trust.

In Lever's Port Sunlight, founded in 1888 near Liverpool for the work-ers in his soap factory and named for his Sunlight soap, careful physical and social planning integrated shops in this community; first, at the end of a block

86. *The Post Office, originally the general store, Port Sun-light, England, 1891 (from T. Raffles Davison,* Port Sun-light *[1916])*

of cottages not far from the railroad station, and then, when the shops outgrew that space, which is now the post office, they were relocated to the ground floor of a building housing the Girls' Institute (fig. 86). These shops, consisting of "grocery and provision shop, drapery and millinery shops, and butcher's shop," were "managed by the employees themselves entirely," with capital expenditures provided by the employees, and profits divided among those employees (fig. 87).[33] Centrally located in a prominent building, these cooperative stores assumed a far more significant social role in Port Sunlight than did the typical company store in a company town. Lever, the son of a grocer, maintained an interest in successful retailing and its role in the community; in fact, the Lever Brothers house magazine, *Progress,* even had advice on store window displays, as well as on the role of "personal" attention and "goodwill" for a grocer to "appeal to the sentiment of his customers and possible customers."[34]

Bournville was started in 1895 by Cadbury so that the employees of his chocolate factory near Birmingham, as well as other working people, could own their own houses. "This factory in a garden," like the other model vil-

Collegium. Port Sunlight.

87. *The Central Shops and Girls' Institute in Port Sunlight, England, built in 1894 and destroyed by bombs in World War II*

lages of this time, offered well-designed houses, many with generous gardens, in a carefully planned community with parks, allotment gardens, schools (including the Ruskin School of Arts and Crafts), a Quaker meeting house, and shops (fig. 88). Imbued with a strong Quaker philosophy to combine a muted beauty and social concerns, this village was designed by several eminent architects-planners, all of whose plans featured a central triangle-shaped green as the civic core of the community, surrounded by the religious and educational institutions—and the shops, which remain in place almost a century later.

The Garden City movement, launched by Ebenezer Howard after the publication of his 1898 book *Tomorrow: A Peaceful Path to Real Reform* (republished as *Garden Cities of Tomorrow* in 1902), followed the model villages with more sophisticated social, economic, and physical planning for large self-sustaining towns. Howard's writings, then the Garden City Association he organized in 1899, and later the first Garden City, Letchworth, spurred international interest in Garden Cities. The movement, fueled by intellectual groups concerned with issues relating to the ownership, taxation, valuation, and nationalization of land and the impact of industrialization on society and, specifically, on urban living conditions, attracted a range of architects, planners, and professionals, as well as political leaders and industrialists, including George Cadbury, who hosted the first Garden City Association Conference. While Howard's ideal of a core central city surrounded by a greenbelt and then a ring of Garden Cities did not materialize as he envisioned, Garden Cities were built, beginning with Letchworth in 1902, Welwyn in 1920, and later Stevenage, Harlow, Hemel Hampstead, and many more. It was hoped that these Garden Cities would be self-sufficient and not dependent on a single industry, but, as the cities could not provide jobs for all their residents, many Garden City residents commuted to London for work. Far larger and more complete than the earlier model villages, these Garden Cities have built impressive downtowns, with a large range of stores, shops, offices, and restaurants lining their high streets, along with the town offices and public buildings—just like American downtowns in the early part of the twentieth century. Letchworth's commercial streets are still bustling with small shops, but they have accommodated larger-sized contemporary stores by continuing their narrow street frontages and entrances, which lead to large extensions behind.

After the devastation of World War II, England, eager to rebuild and worried about the pace of "ribbon" development, as the English call uncontrolled development unraveling along roadways, enacted ambitious planning

88. Map of Bournville, England, 1915. Note the central triangular park with nearby shops, school, library, and church

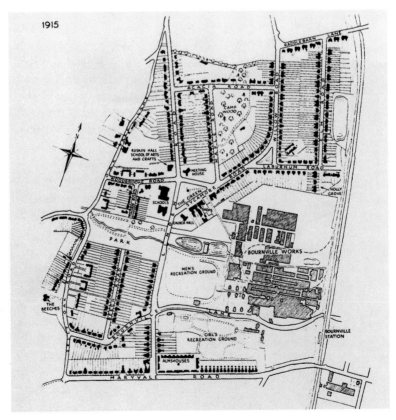

legislation to ensure that the country's limited land area would provide livable communities and beautiful countryside for present and future generations. Planning was energized with new initiatives and by the national government's vigorous role in local planning. Tight planning controls were accepted by the English, who had survived years of deprivation and government authority during the war. The government planner was in control; he called the shots, not the individual property owner, the highway contractor, the automobile lobby, or the developer. Shopping, while still a primarily small-scale and highly intimate activity with a dazzling array of small independent stores—the greengrocer, the butcher, the florist, the shoemaker—lining the high street in town after town, was subject to new planning restrictions. And in England, shopping was recognized as an important economic and social function of communities, justifying tight controls over what types of retail uses would be allowed in given sites.

The success of English planning and new towns, as well as of the Scandinavian new towns, the American Greenbelt towns, and Radburn, inspired a handful of imaginative developers and planners in the United States who were worried about the massive and uncontrolled postwar sprawl. In the 1960s, two new towns, Columbia and Reston, were developed near Washington, D.C., by private entrepreneurs seeking an alternative to galloping sprawl.

Both of these new towns, Columbia, located between Washington and Baltimore in Howard County, Maryland, and Reston, west of Washington in Fairfax County, Virginia, by the 1990s a thriving mini-Silicon Valley, recognized the importance of shopping and integrated it into their new communities. Because of the differences in the backgrounds and objectives of their founders, Columbia's James Rouse, a shopping center and mortgage finance magnate, and Reston's Robert E. Simon, an idealistic businessman interested in architectural quality and landscape integrity, these new towns developed differently. They both, however, followed the same hierarchy for stores—village centers for neighborhood shopping, a town center as the hub for the entire town, and Power Centers for discount buying.

Reston's first shopping area at the end of Lake Anne was designed to serve as a community focal point. It looks like a miniature crescent-shaped Italian fishing town filled not with boats and cafes but small shops and restaurants on the first floors of the buildings with apartments above (fig. 89). A footpath system leads to it, boaters dock there, and an adjacent parking lot serves the automobiles. All immediate commercial needs, whether food, drugs, or sundries, as well as restaurants and a church, were to be found there.

Although the original buildings in the village center today look pretty much as they did in the mid-1960s, the commercial tenants have changed many times, sometimes giving the village a bedraggled image. As appealing as that fishing village design has been to the eye, it did not allow for expan-

89. *The shops with upstairs apartments in Reston's Lake Anne Village crescent-shaped shopping area, 1989*

sion, which has been a major drawback, according to Simon. The 15,000-square-foot supermarket, adequate in the 1960s, could not be enlarged into a larger (60,000-square-foot) one-stop supermarket, so it has gone through many owners, who have tried to operate it as a midsized store. Meanwhile, a fifteen-checkout-lane supermarket several miles away but still in Reston attracts most people doing major shopping. Lake Anne's small shops have also changed hands many times as well; the drugstore, like the supermarket, has experienced the problems of limited space and new competition from the one-stop drugstores. Across from these stores, small incubator retail activities have cropped up in the first floor of townhouses, introducing new life to the area, but the viability of such independent retail in small spaces remains a problem. Since the conversion to a condominium in 1984–85 by developers who bought this shopping area as an investment, Lake Anne's village center and its multitude of condo owners have not been able to mobilize effective rehabilitation plans.

New life is being injected into some of the other early village shopping centers by Atlantic Realty Companies, headed by David Ross, a Restonian whom Simon considers the "best community worker we've had."[35] With a business and planning degree and a long involvement in Reston's community activities, Ross is well suited to resuscitate two shopping areas, Tall Oaks and Hunter's Woods, making them the vital shopping and community centers they once were.

Hunter's Woods, a run-down center with tired stores and a shabby appearance, is being redesigned with a larger Safeway and fewer smaller shops better integrated with the nearby community and senior citizens' facilities, as well as nearby townhouses. With steady traffic going to the community building, the center should be assured constant customers if the stores are where and what shoppers want. Atlantic Realty's redesign follows contemporary retail thinking by opening up the center to provide visual and physical access to all the facilities, in contrast to yesterday's shopping centers, which turned their backs to the street and pulled patrons into the centers' interiors. That internalized layout does not appeal to today's hurried shopper. The open layout for fast shopping also encourages free-standing operations—called "end caps" in the trade, such as gas stations, banks, and fast-food restaurants—in the parking lot near the street.

The redevelopment of Tall Oaks required a slightly different tack, as it did not have an existing community center. By demolishing a hodgepodge of buildings with shops and offices on one side of the supermarket, adding stores to the other side, and then developing a community facility at one end of the center, Atlantic Realty has opened up the center and made the stores and child care center more visible and accessible than they were.

Community facilities—whether child care centers, community centers, or dance, karate, or other schools—are central to Atlantic Realty's strategy. Within the limited footprint for these shopping areas Ross targeted "complementary community uses, which would continue the original Reston vision."[36] The day care facility, for example, provides a needed service to the community—and probably patrons for the nearby stores. Both developments carefully considered the access and other needs of senior citizens attending or living in nearby facilities. To assure the continued existence of neighborhood stores in the village centers, Ross has provided assistance to the mom-and-pop businesses, often newcomers to retailing, by "acclimating them to the networks, news media, and Chamber of Commerce," as well as varying their rents when necessary, as the Rouse Company also does.

Away from the villages and by the main highway, Atlantic Realty has built a shopping center–office complex, Plaza America, with a more typical 1990s shopping center, anchored by Fresh Fields, a popular chain store specializing in organic food, along with a string of other, mostly discount, stores, and a million square feet of office buildings in a parklike setting. In all of these developments in Reston, Ross understands the hierarchy of stores, the vision of Reston, and the role that shopping can play in the life of the neighborhoods and in Reston as a whole. The bagel store, hair salon, arts and crafts shop, and video place are necessary for the vitality of a neighborhood center, as are such civic facilities as senior housing, community centers, and child care centers.

Reston's Town Center is its downtown for shopping and entertainment. This hub looks like a downtown—with high-rise office buildings, a large hotel, a main street with an old-time movie theater, franchised stores like Williams-Sonoma, and a central community open area–plaza with cafes in the summer and ice skating in the winter, all within a small, walkable area. Nearby, but more accessible by car than by foot, are other communitywide civic facilities, like the central library, the hospital, local government offices, police headquarters—and Power Centers of Big Boxes. With the decentralized management since Mobil's departure in 1996 as owner, Equity Office Holding Company has acquired the Town Center and Lerner Enterprises the Power Center. This decentralization may produce a greater variety of shopping opportunities and also a chance for the citizens' group, the Reston Association, to assume a more influential role in community affairs. But whatever the opportunities, much of this spread-out institutional and commercial development near the Town Center misses the "urban feeling," according to Simon, who wanted more housing and pedestrianization. The inward-oriented Big Boxes are like "circling wagons," Simon states, turning their backs to Reston.[37]

In Columbia, James Rouse was intimately involved in developing that new town's retailing strategy, especially for its early village centers. At Wilde Lake Village, Columbia's first village center, Rouse was proud of the small-scale shops—like the butcher and cheese store—that his company subsidized with lower rents. Rouse considered these shops vital to the community, and he wanted to be sure that they had a foothold in Columbia's village shopping centers, despite the prevailing attitude that such small shopkeepers were outdated or marginal. For Rouse, this type of subsidizing is called "pre-servicing." At other times, the Rouse Company has offered subsidies to introduce new concepts or products. Such subsidizing fits the Rouse philosophy that retailing is a means to the goals of both community welfare and corporate profitability.

The Rouse Company's progressive approach to shopping has involved constant attention to the changing nature of retailing: the increasingly larger scale of stores, like large, one-stop supermarkets or discount Big Boxes, as well as changes in the lifestyles of Columbia's residents. The early village centers, with their small-scale shops, small supermarkets (small compared to today's), and social, religious, and community facilities, were designed for the housewife with time to linger in the center's inner courtyard with friends and neighbors. Today that young woman, struggling to balance job and family responsibilities, has little time for such leisurely shopping. Instead, she seeks one-stop shopping, which means larger supermarkets, fewer small shops and villages. And since 1963, the anchor supermarkets in Columbia's centers, like Safeway and Giant, have almost tripled in size. Instead of purchasing flowers at the florist, drugs at the pharmacy, or magazines at the corner store, one buys them at the 63,000-square-foot supermarket. Despite the size of these new stores, they are not as overwhelming or as bare of amenities as the big discounters. "The village centers," states Alton Scavo, the Rouse Company's vice president for community development, "are still comfortable places in which to shop and deal."[38] They continue to be community centers, as well as places to shop.

The layouts of three village centers, Wilde Lake from the 1960s, King's Contrivance from the 1980s, and River Hill from the late 1990s, show how design strategies have changed, how supermarkets have enlarged, and open space has shrunk and been reconfigured. The interior courtyard has been replaced by a linear open space at Wilde Lake, and by benches and a bulletin board at King's Contrivance. It has been reduced in length at River Hill but is accessible at both ends, so the shopper can get in and out quickly. Community facilities have also changed from a community center and ecumenical church to a community association building to a sports center (fig. 90).

Columbia's Town Center spreads over a wide area, with restaurants and office buildings, two of which house the various Rouse companies and Columbia's civic association. Also part of the town center are the public library and the Columbia Mall, the town's central shopping hub, with major anchors like Hecht's, Sears, and J. C. Penney. Unlike Reston's Town Center, which is designed with a main street for pedestrians, Columbia's suburban-scaled center is geared to the car, as its buildings are not clustered.

Columbia has not missed a beat with the trends in discount shopping and Big Boxes. Snowden Square—a line of Big Boxes, scarcely a cozy square—and Columbia Crossing are two long stretches of Big Boxes and Category Killers, but they are on an artery near I-95, away from the villages. Columbia's bargain hunters, who once had to travel out of Columbia to find Big Boxes, now can shop close to home.

While Columbia has been adapting to changing needs and to new types and scales of stores, it has not forgotten its commitment to retain shopping in the life of the community. Even as stores get larger and farther away from residential areas, many of those basic retail services, like the shoe repair shop, the video rental store, the liquor store, and the hardware store still exist side by side with the one-stop supermarket. Columbia hopes to retain that mix of scale and types of stores, but it requires day-by-day attention to the details of the hard business of retailing, as well as to the impacts of larger societal trends. Under careful management, shopping continues as a vital economic and social element in this new city of 83,000. Often large-scale developers, such as Westinghouse and Gulf, have separated retailing from the operation of their new developments. But in Columbia shopping has always been seen as not just "an income source, but as an amenity," according to Rouse's Alton Scavo.[39] In fact, Scavo goes on to state, retailing was treated as an "insurance policy" for community well-being.

The careful planning at Reston and Columbia stands out in an era of ever-expanding and often unplanned suburbia, in which ranches, split-levels,

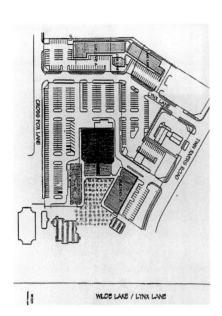

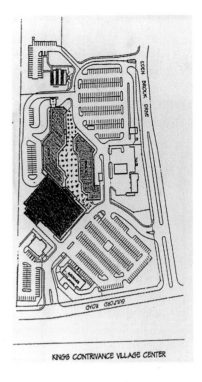

WILDE LAKE / LYNX LANE

KINGS CONTRIVANCE VILLAGE CENTER

90. Three village centers in Columbia, Maryland: Wilde Lake (1960s), King's Contrivance (1980s), and River Hill (1990s), 2000. Supermarkets marked in black, other stores and restaurants in gray, community buildings in stripes, and communal open space in dots. Note how the layouts of these centers have opened up and how communal open space has become more of a passageway than a civic meeting place associated with community buildings. Source: Columbia Management, Inc.

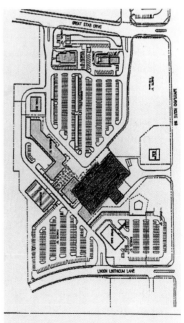

RIVER HILL VILLAGE CENTER

townhouses, colonials, monster houses, or Victorians with wrap-around porches have been planted in old potato, tomato, or corn fields, or in old orchards or woods. The fate of these suburban settlements and their shopping has been determined primarily by the marketplace. Planners, instead of guiding this development, have ended up often serving as clerks facilitating developers' permits through the bureaucratic process, except in a few places with a high level of civic consciousness and concern for short- and long-term public interests, such as Portland, Oregon, and Burlington, Vermont. But the dominant pattern has been suburban sprawl, with its shopping centers, malls, Big Boxes, and discounters, who have little regard for how this retailing relates to the welfare of nearby communities. Retailing is rarely treated as an "insurance policy" for community well-being, as it is in Columbia and Reston.

The New Traditionalism and Town Centers

As a counterpoint to the overriding sameness and remoteness of postwar suburban development and its large-scale shopping centers and malls, two overlapping movements encouraging friendlier and more communal living and shopping areas emerge. One is the interest in pedestrian-oriented town centers, where people ideally meet, shop, eat, play, work, and live, and where civic life is concentrated, with nearby town halls, post offices, performing arts centers, movie theaters, and other public buildings. Some of these centers are vital and real, while others are ersatz or simply traditional malls with new names. The other movement, known as Neo-Traditionalism or the New Urbanism, was started by a group of planners and designers in the 1980s to offer an alternative to sprawl in clustered, village-type neighborhood developments reminiscent of earlier small towns. This movement has many different roots, but its emphasis has been overwhelmingly architectural. In the early 1980s, two architects from Miami, Elizabeth Plater-Zyberk and Andres Duany, designed Seaside, a small pedestrian-oriented community in Florida's panhandle. This compact eighty-acre development of vernacularly derived wooden houses, with picket fences and wide porches, is clustered on narrow red-colored roadways and sandy walkways to the Gulf. Seaside—"The New Town. The Old Ways," as advertised on a billboard on nearby Route 98—is like yesterday's small village, and a dramatic contrast to Florida's typical coastal developments.

Although catering to an upper-end market and offering rather cutesy commerce, like the Sip and Dip refreshment stand, a restaurant named after the dachshund and cat of Seaside's developer, Robert S. Davis, and a miniaturized post office, Seaside became an overnight architectural and planning sensation. It was a welcome contrast to the usual subdivision, whose lack of community Duany blames on planners and engineers stuck on segregated zoning and free-flowing automobile traffic. Yet Duany believes that Americans are "ready for the return of the town. The signs of a revival of interest in com-

91. Neo-Traditional Big Boxes in Kentlands, Maryland, 1999

munity on a smaller scale are everywhere."[40] Since the development of Seaside, Duany and Plater-Zyberk have been called in to design developments all over the United States. These projects, varying in size, structure, and purpose, are rarely total towns. They are usually carefully designed developments with traditional architecture, but they often lack the necessary infrastructure for community survival, forcing them to rely on public authorities for services such as transportation and schools, and on the private sector for shopping.

In Gaithersburg, Maryland, a suburb of Washington, D.C., the Duany team was challenged to convert almost 1,000 acres into two communities, Kentlands and Lakeland. Kentlands, originally one large farm, was developed by the Great Seneca Development Corporation in the mid to late 1990s. By 2000, about 4,500 people lived there in a wide variety of houses, mostly detached, but also row houses, all in "traditional" yesteryear architecture. The townhouses resemble the Federal-period rows in Alexandria, Virginia, or Washington's Georgetown; some of the detached houses are pure Victorian, most are colonial, and others are a blend. To foster an urban feel and prevent the isolation of many suburbs, there are alleys as well as "granny apartments" over some of the garages. There is not much space around the houses, which consume most of their lots. For the community, there is a recreational complex, a community center in the original farmhouse, and an elementary school. An adjacent shopping center, built in 1995 in coordination with the Duany team, features a large Giant one-stop supermarket, a massive Lowe's hardware store, and a medley of shops in a conventional L-shaped shopping center encased with columns and Neo-Traditional architectural details (fig. 91).

Next to Kentlands is another large tract of land, which surrounds a high-rise building formerly owned by National Geographic. It was designed by the Duany team and developed by Natelli Communities as another Neo-Traditional community. In March 1996, the Duany–Plater-Zyberk team, along with consultants and Kentlands residents, held a charrette to evolve a design for the new community, named Lakeland. Charrettes, what architectural schools call the last-minute, all-night work programs to complete projects, are used by the Duany team to work out design concepts for their projects—whether Wolf Mountain, Utah, East Ocean View in Norfolk, Virginia, or Kentlands/Lakeland. The charrette for the Kentlands/Lakeland project lasted five days, from 9 a.m. to 11 p.m., and attracted about 300 enthusiastic participants, including county officials, the city of Gaithersburg political and professional staff, and the interested public, mostly Kentlands residents. An excitement permeated these sessions; suggestions and ideas were coming from right and left, but mostly from the middle-class residents of Kentlands who could afford to pay $100,000 to more than $300,000 for a house.

Shopping was discussed one night of the charrette, stirring a great deal of interest. What did residents want their downtown, called Midtown, to be? The charrette attendees rejected the suburban strip shopping patterns of fast-food emporia, huge parking areas, and Big Boxes and instead urged a small-town shopping ambience, with low buildings lining the street, with most of the parking out of sight behind the buildings. "I don't want it to be too impersonal and big. In a mall, you have to buy and get out," said Kentlands resident Andy Jaska. "There are no places to sit down. This should be like the city dock in Annapolis or the old village well where the women went and talked."[41] The charrette ideas were translated into a plan; forty-two of its forty-seven pages were devoted to design, with fifteen pages just on building types. The town square was pictured with a mix of buildings, some resembling eighteenth-century Massachusetts Hall at Harvard, others resembling Greek temples, 1930s banks, and eighteenth-century shops. A two-story corner store, the Lakeland Grocery, was sketched to look like an old IGA store in a small New England town. Above the store were two apartments, and adjacent was the town meeting hall. The scale is small and pedestrian-friendly.

What ultimately was built is a villagey retail-entertainment district, currently popular for small-scale developments and renovated strip malls. The district, which seems almost like a stage set, is intersected by streets with one- and two-story buildings, all with windows facing the street, and street parking, some diagonal, as on yesterday's Main Streets (fig. 92). There are no grocery stores, banks, drugstores, town hall, or public buildings, but instead a variety of small shops—a florist (Flowers and Bows), an ice cream shop (Cone Zone), restaurants with outdoor seating, and the requisite art deco diner and movie theater. Its back side houses some large discounters like Petsmart and Dress Barn, but if you want groceries, hardware, drugs, and everyday necessities, a mega-supermarket and drugstore, as well as Big Boxes like Lowe's and Kmart, are only a stone's throw away.

92. Some shops and restaurants at Market Square in Kentlands, Maryland, 2000

93. Mashpee Commons on Cape Cod, Mashpee, Massachusetts, 1998

In a shopping development on Cape Cod in a barren area near Falmouth, Massachusetts, the Duany team has tried to re-create the feeling of yesteryear's downtown with a Main Street–style development with stores, a post office, and an area for community activities. The development, Mashpee Commons, built in the late 1980s on the site of a 1960s strip mall, is a full-fledged shopping destination, with banks, a drugstore, a hardware store, a supermarket, boutiques, franchised stores, restaurants, and a few stores left over from the strip mall. This shopping center, planned to be the community center of a future new town—with a library, post office, town hall, public green, and an arts and cultural program—has some of the ingredients needed to make it more than just a shopping center. It is interesting to note that again shopping has preceded residential development in this proposed new town (fig. 93).

The message—and an important one—from Seaside and other Duany-designed developments is that communities can be designed with innovative architectural attention to scale, circulation, siting, and detail to make them humane and civilized. Many of the earlier new towns, whether Greenbelt, Maryland, or Vanport, Oregon, or Reston, Virginia, had more sophisticated planning, but they were built when planning was seen as a means of improving how many types of people live. The Neo-Traditional developments are often architecturally driven and targeted at middle- and upper-middle-income, well-educated people seeking an alternative to the sameness of suburbia. The names of the architects interested in Neo-Traditionalism read like a listing of the country's top designers, from Robert A. M. Stern and Calthorpe Associates to Alex Krieger and Jonathan Barnett. Their philosophy is trickling down as developers of all stripes try to incorporate the scale and amenities of yesterday's village into their projects.

One of the significant aspects in the planning of shopping facilities in these communities has been a resurgence of interest in communal meeting places, such as town commons, often with shopping nearby and sometimes even with public transportation. Peter Calthorpe, a San Francisco architect who came to city planning through his interest in sustainable communities and his work for former California Governor Jerry Brown on energy-saving buildings, has articulated a philosophy of compact communities, encouraging interactions between different types of people. Calthorpe is concerned with the segregation that now occurs in economically and socially differentiated, and usually bland, suburbs, as well as "chain-store architecture" and "scaleless office parks." His community designs—with "neighborhoods of housing, parks, and schools placed within walking distance of shops, civic services, jobs, and transit"—are not novel, but this approach has been lost in mainstream automobile-oriented suburban living. Like the old railroad suburbs, many of his communities have been planned around transit system stations. Pedestrians are the "catalyst," Calthorpe writes, because they "create [the] place and the time for casual encounters and the practical integration of diverse places and people," and because they "turn suburbs into towns, projects into neighborhoods, and networks into communities."[42]

Other planners have had similar thoughts, but Calthorpe conscientiously integrates social, economic, cultural, and environmental factors into his projects because he is as concerned with the loneliness, racial isolation, and land and energy consumption of the suburban landscape as he is with the inner cities' crime and economic stagnation. "Our urban/suburban split has created on one side disinvestment and economic hardship, on the other congestion and pollution. The crisis of place in America affects everyone in that it fails to fulfill the real needs of so many. But in defining an alternate we must clearly distinguish the physical problems and solutions from the social and cultural."[43]

The town center constitutes the civic, commercial, and recreational

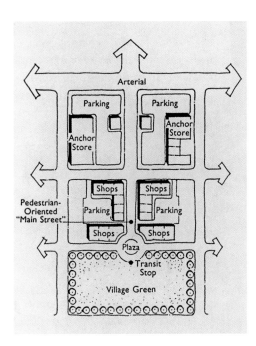

94. A 1993 Calthorpe plan for a core commercial area with small shops oriented to pedestrians and to the plaza while larger anchor stores with parking abut an arterial street

core of Calthorpe's communities. "It was what made a town a town," he says. The town common, displaced by "exaggerated private domain: shopping malls, private clubs, and gated communities," is restored by Calthorpe to its role of "centering our communities with convivial gathering and meeting places." And shopping—the marketplace—is part of the social dynamics, which makes his town commons function as the focus of the town, in contrast to conventional development, where shopping, Calthorpe contends, has been "removed from neighborhood and town, removed from the social dimension it used to play in defining a community." As commerce changed, towns lost their commercial core, along with two critical and traditional functions of shopping: its role in a community's center, and its role in providing a "unique quality of local products and services."[44]

Calthorpe's town centers mix ground-floor retail, office, and commercial space; the size and mix depend on the development's size, site, and functions. While larger, anchor-type stores are oriented to parking lots and roads, smaller shops with minimal setbacks form a Main Street for pedestrians. Office buildings, preferably with built-in parking, are proposed near transit stops. Facades, street-level windows, and building entrances are designed to offer "visual interest" to the pedestrian, and upper floors are reserved for housing or offices (fig. 94). The Calthorpe firms' projects range from revivifying the tired downtown of Derry, Pennsylvania, to redeveloping a sizable dead mall in Redmond, Washington, and an old race track in San Mateo, California, into new town centers and mixed-use developments. In North Boulder, Colorado, a twelve-acre site was transformed into the town's Safeway and Village Center—a Neo-Traditionalist's version of the shopping center—with a large Safeway supermarket in the center, and with other stores, commercial buildings with storefronts, a public library, day care center, transit stop, some housing, and a gathering place at the intersection. All are low-rise buildings connected by walkways and narrow streets to look like downtown Boulder.

The conversion of large-scale sites provides opportunities to design more complete projects for a mix of housing, retail, and public uses in pedestrian-sealed blocks. A shopping center in Mountain View, California, became the Crossings Transit-Oriented Neighborhood, as it is adjacent to a CalTrain station. Some commercial-retail uses are located near the station and the main avenue leading to the train station. The rest of the site is housing, ranging from apartments, townhouses, and row houses to single-family houses, all connected by tree-lined footpaths and side streets (fig. 95).

Not only did Mountain View get a new neighborhood at the Crossings, but it received a new downtown—both due to its imaginative city manager, Bruce Liedstrand. This city of 60,000 people, a neighbor of fancier Palo Alto, was considered a stepchild in Silicon Valley. After Mountain View was drained of life by outlying malls, its downtown was so dead that an office building, abandoned before completion in the late 1970s, had to be guarded for years by police dogs. Liedstrand, with Michael Freedman as the architect-planner, converted this dormant downtown in the late 1980s into the city's now active civic-commercial core by developing a civic center with a city hall, a performing arts center, a Chamber of Commerce office, a public library, and a public plaza with underground parking, and also reinvigorating retail and commerce while adding housing (fig. 96). The goals were "to make it a 'nice place' that people enjoyed coming to," as well as "making it the 'center' of the community," where people can live and work—and avoid ever-lengthening commutes.

All the civilizing commerce of coffee houses, outdoor cafes, and bookstores are there for round-the-clock activity, but they are paired with the places that meet one's sundry daily needs: grocery stores, cleaners, banks, shoe repair shops, garages, accountants, travel agencies, photography shops, and doctors' and lawyers' offices, as well as restaurants, brew pubs, and night clubs. Important in infusing life in this downtown has been the addition of new office buildings with ground-floor retailing and of new apartments and single-family houses. Liedstrand hopes that the "downtown will continue to grow over the years with more housing and offices." The vitality and staying power of such a city center hinges on the mix of uses, such as housing, stores,

95. A residential street with commercial space at the corner in The Crossings, Mountain View, California, 2000

96. The new civic center in downtown Mountain View, California, 2000

and offices, with the essential civic glue of the public buildings, like the
library, city hall, and performing arts center, enclosing the public plaza.[45]

Town centers, combining a traditional town green with Main
Street–type stores, are being revived by some developers in an attempt to
introduce a sense of community in smaller-scaled projects. Sometimes the
green is used just as an amenity in an upscale development, as in Williams-
burg Commons in Vienna, Virginia, with thirty-eight Williamsburg-type
houses facing a "beautifully landscaped mall bordered by brick walkways,"
according to Washington's Long and Foster real estate advertisement, or

planned as an "old fashioned" central town square to be surrounded by a church, post office, restaurants, and shops, as in the compact, pedestrian-oriented Worman's Mill development near Frederick, Maryland. In Frederick County, the concept of "livable communities," with stores you can walk to, has caught on; almost ten such communities have been approved for construction under 1986 development guidelines, which provide the flexibility of greater density, varied housing types, and more land for parks and other public amenities—flexibility that is not available under traditional zoning.

The interest in a central civic-shopping-entertainment town center and the national popularity of the Neo-Traditionalists mirror new attitudes toward community planning. Proposals for mixing uses, including housing in the town centers, downplaying the car, and emphasizing the pedestrian, all represent a departure from mainstream development. These attempts to make communities and their commercial areas friendlier will work only if they function economically, politically, and socially. For town centers to succeed, more than boutiques and cafes are needed, even though they provide a civilizing influence in such centers. It is the public buildings and activities, whether town halls, performing arts centers, post offices, libraries, or public markets that can provide stability and civic glue to such centers. While stores and cafes come and go, the town hall and library remain. Whether in new town centers or old commercial districts, assuring the survival and integration of the now precarious small-scale service retailers looms as a critical concern for communities interested in their shopping districts functioning as real places, not just stage sets.

Foreign Approaches

In Japan, France, Germany, Norway, and especially England, the role of shopping and shops has been recognized as crucial to the survival of a way of life, the vitality of town and city shopping districts, the strengthening of civic life, the provision of goods and services for the many who have no cars—and the employment of millions of people. In short, shopping has been viewed as a vital social, civic, and economic community function. Faced with recent changes in shopping patterns and lifestyles, as well as the growing number of American-scaled stores, these countries' national governments have enacted policies and directives aimed at staving off the most aggressive assaults on traditional patterns of shopping.

Japan
Japan has had a longer history than most countries in protecting the small store, for "Japan is still a country of small stores," wrote Roy Larke, a professor at the University in Kobe, in 1994. In 1991, Japan had 1.6 million stores employing almost 7 million people, making retailing the largest employment

sector of the economy (11 percent of the full-time labor force). While in 1991 the average store employed four people, the shops employing one or two people declined, often because of the advancing age of the shopkeepers. In 1991, 93 percent of the stores had under ten employees. But as the shops with one to two employees decreased by almost 20 percent from 1982 to 1991, those with one hundred or more employees grew by 82 percent.[46]

Because of the large number of small shopkeepers, who formed a powerful lobby; the fear of massive unemployment if such stores disappeared; and the Japanese consumers' dependence on and appreciation of their local stores, Japan from the mid-1950s to the mid-1990s tried to protect the small stores from the invasion of competitive larger stores. This was done by controlling the hours that stores could be open, limiting the expansion of large stores, and regulating the number of days a store could be closed. Under the Large Scale Retail Store Law (Daiten-ho, its short Japanese name), which was enacted in 1974, large stores with more than 1,500 square meters of floor space (3,000 for stores in Tokyo and other big cities) had to go through a complicated and lengthy review in order to increase business hours, open new stores, or enlarge an existing store. Most of these reviews involved the local Business Regulation Council, the local Chamber of Commerce, and finally the national Ministry of International Trade and Industry, which sought comments from local officials and residents. In essence, local approval was essential. An economic adviser at the Japanese Embassy in Washington explained that the policy was designed to prevent the unemployment that would undoubtedly occur if these small stores, usually run by extended families, disappeared.

Others expressed a concern that these stores were critical to the social life of towns and cities, which "would not be complete without them. . . . Japanese like them for their merchandise and their atmosphere," Larke reports.[47] These small stores, whose loyal customers usually shop daily, have bred a familiarity and localness, with many shops making what they sell on their premises. They not only have provided fresh ingredients for traditional Japanese cooking, but they have connected people with one another and with the community. This networking role helped stimulate the national government to protect the small store from the competitive might of large retailing companies.

However, as deregulation swept the globe in the 1990s, and as more women entered the workplace and the younger generation turned to "modern" retailing, Japan relaxed its Large Scale Retail Store Law, and its valiant protection of small stores vanished. In 1990 the U.S. government saw the 1974 law as "one of the biggest obstacles against imports," according to a Japanese expert, because, among other things, small stores did not have the space to sell American goods. Pressure from American commerce through trade negotiations was one force, and a strong one, that drove Japan to abandon its policies of protecting small businesses.

In 1992 and 1994 amendments were enacted that "released large retailers from the shackles imposed by the original law of 1974," stated the Japan External Trade Organization.[48] Instead of going through endless local reviews, a large retailer could now go directly to a national agency; the minimum size of a store requiring review was doubled, store hours were lengthened, closing days were reduced, and stores selling imports could be as large as 1,000 square meters instead of 100 square meters. This opened the door for American large-scale retailers, discounters, and warehouse clubs. Toys "R" Us led the way for mega-discounters. In the convenience store field, 7-Eleven, not a target of the 1974 Act, had had a foothold in Japan since the 1970s; in fact, it is the country's largest chain convenience store. Now many of the struggling mom-and-pop stores are 7-Eleven franchises.

This radical shift in policies reflects a convergence of sociocultural changes within Japan, difficult economic times, as well as pressures from the United States and its big retailers. Traditional daily shopping by foot to small local shops is not possible for the time-pressed working woman and young people, who like brand products at discount prices — and American ways. There is even a major shopping center chain named Cowboy. The famed department stores, known for their high-quality service, goods, and substantial entertainments — zoos, playgrounds, and museums — now are seen as boring by many younger Japanese. The price gap between Japanese and foreign goods has shaken the belief that domestic goods are best, as well as the belief that high prices mean quality. And, at the same time, aging shopkeepers, like the uncle of Zola's heroine who clung to "ridiculous old-fashioned ways," have not been able to keep up with the new ways, do not know about newfangled point-of-sale terminals, and have been unable to compete with the big stores in catching onto American business practices, like dealing directly with manufacturers rather than with middlemen.

How changes in retailing will affect the social and civic life of Japanese communities is not yet known, but it is clear that they are significant in a country with a long history of tight communities with many small, specialized stores, and large cities with all-encompassing, prestigious department stores.

France

French towns and cities bring to mind corner cafes with streetside tables filled with Gaulois-smoking locals, and women with their net shopping bags going from store to store for the daily baguette and other food staples. That picture has been accurate for many generations, as France has remained a country dotted with urban places whose streets are lined with thriving small cafes, bakeries, butchers, greengrocers, dressmakers, tailors, and brasseries — until recently. Shops, cafes, and bistros have been the social and commercial lifeblood of many towns and cities, but here, as in Japan and most advanced countries, many social and economic changes are producing a different style of living, which ineluctably affects, and alters, shopping patterns. The "hypermarket," a supermarket larger than 27,000 square feet, often located out of town, and smaller supermarkets are replacing the small, independent, specialized in-town shops.

A sign of the times is the fading interest in traditional French bread, the baguette, an ageless symbol of French life. In 1994, 1,000 of the 37,000 bakers in the country closed down, as people ate less bread and what bread they bought came more and more from supermarket bakeries. The plight of bakers aroused a $6 million national public relations campaign in 1995 to stimulate bread eating, as well as mass demonstrations urging President Chirac and Prime Minister Juppe to take emergency measures to help artisan bakers. The cabinet minister in charge of small business, Jean-Pierre Raffarin, discussed regulating the ingredients and the five steps necessary for authentic breadmaking so that high-quality breads could get an "appellation controllée" seal, which would differentiate them from supermarket bread. The decline in baguette eating has been a national tragedy, according to Lionel Poilane, a member of one of France's oldest bread dynasties. "The supermarkets have forced artisans out of business with their cheap loaves made out of frozen dough, which taste so awful that people soon stop buying it."[49] The decline in bread eating, unfortunately, has been a manifestation of a far more complicated socioeconomic and cultural mix of factors than just the quality of the baguette.

The corner cafe, another symbol of French urban life, has also been affected by changing times. Along with the proverbial socializing, people can talk on the telephone, fax messages, and watch televised news or sports. But like the bakery industry, the cafe is facing problems, for the new generations possess different attitudes and values from former generations and live with different economic institutions and influences. Paris lost more than 1,500 cafes in 1994, bringing its total number of cafes to half its 1980 total. What hurt the cafes? High real estate prices, reduced alcohol consumption (down to eleven liters per person annually from eighteen in 1960), poor service, gruff waiters, low salaries, often high prices for mediocre food, and competition from street vendors, McDonald's, and other carry-out restaurants.[50]

France has been facing the loss not just of its traditional urban shopping practices but also of critical ingredients in the character and life of town centers. The large out-of-town hypermarket, a symptom of changing economic ways, has disrupted patterns of living, shopping, and development. As Lyon's deputy mayor, Emil Azoulay, worrying over the drain of shopping from his center city, said, "A town with no retail trade 'has no soul.'"[51] While studies indicate that French household consumption for food, clothing, housing, and furniture did not vary much between 1980 and 1989, changes did occur in where, how, and what kinds of items were purchased.[52] When these shopping patterns emerged, France recognized a crisis.

Lyon, France's second most populous urban district, with a center city population just under half a million, illustrates these changes. Out of 15,000 small stores, 2,200 disappeared in fourteen years; in a suburb, Ville-franche, 121 out of the 127 grocers disappeared between 1978 and 1994, when the town had only six, of which three were independents. At the same time, Lyon merchants saw center city shops losing 50 percent of their trade by the year 2000. These losses made shopping a political issue and forced mayors to get more involved with city planning and management policies. Two kilo-meters from the center of Lyon is LaPar-Dieu, one of Europe's largest city retail developments, with 260 shops, two department stores, six big chain stores, cinemas, restaurants, discos, bowling alleys, a police station, super-markets, and even a Toys "R" Us. Although it has parking spaces for 4,600 cars, it is also accessible by Metro and several buses. Near a major highway on the edge of Lyon's metropolitan area is another large shopping develop-ment, Porte des Alpes, which has been designed "U.S. style, where shoppers drive from unit to unit."[53] In the five years from 1989 to 1994, out-of-town shopping centers like Porte des Alpes, according to studies, have taken a steady proportion of retail sales as small stores have lost out. Supermarkets accounted for two-thirds of all food sales in that period. An almost direct rela-tion exists between the decrease in center city markets and the increase in peripheral centers—the center city lost 8 percent of its markets, and the peripheral center gained 6 percent.

Because of pressures from small retailers and mayors, particularly in small towns, a national freeze (*le gel*) was placed on construction of new large retail developments from April to November 1993 to provide time to assess how to plan and manage such projects and, in some people's eyes, "to pro-tect market shares of existing traders." The planning and environmental implications of commercial development were divorced from the decision-making of the agency responsible for commercial projects. Mayors, who have had considerable power in planning matters, reviewed proposed commer-cial development with chamber of commerce chairmen and consumer rep-resentatives, but the planning application still went to the mayor in the usual way. Lyon, for example, set up a commission of the Rhîne with representa-tives of the city council, Chamber of Commerce, counsel, and Departmen-tal Observatory, "made up of statutory bodies and invited interests." A plan for long-term development, including shopping, was developed in 1994; it included a "priority to shop [retail] developments in town centers to main-tain their vitality and viability," and it froze out-of-town development.[54]

The problems of small retailers and center city retailing have aroused national concern in France. Even the large retail distribution outlets in France, increasingly involved with European and international marketing, recognize the need to "maintain a 'human' dimension and avoid the huge 'factory-market' environment" possible even in medium-sized stores.[55] But underlying changes in where, what, and how the French shop reflect shifts in societal values and powerful pressures from a sophisticated marketing and distribution industry, against which ad hoc measures like le gel and local efforts like Lyon's are lilliputian. Torn between becoming a part of the new Europe, with its different scale and its makeup of economic, political, and social activities, and holding on to traditional and distinctively French ways, France has not determined a course of action. And this affects the future of its communities—and shopping.

Germany

Americans, accustomed to shopping at all hours, whether at the twenty-four-hour supermarket, the seven-day-a-week mall, or the deli or convenience store that keeps long hours, would be surprised at the national furor over German Chancellor Helmut Kohl's legislative attempt in the mid-1990s to lengthen the hours that stores stay open. Until 1996, German store hours, controlled by some of the most restrictive regulations in Europe, were open from 7 a.m. to 6:30 p.m. on weekdays, 7 a.m. to 2 p.m. on Saturdays, and never on Sundays. There were some exceptions: Thursday closing hours were extended to 8:30 p.m. in 1990 after two decades of debate, certain Saturdays had longer hours, and barbers, bakers, and flower vendors were granted special hours. Even then store hours were extremely limited when compared with American store hours. The major exception to the store-hour restrictions had been for "travel needs," so shops in gas stations, railroad and bus terminals, and airports were open longer—and on Sundays—like American convenience stores.

In 1996 the German Parliament finally passed legislation lengthening weekday store hours to 8 p.m. and Saturdays to 4 p.m., with bakeries allowed to be open on Sunday morning—but only after a lengthy and bitter debate. This controversy over lengthening store hours, which applies nationally in contrast to more local blue laws in the United States, made the headlines in all the major newspapers and resulted in massive protests and a national debate on the issue, which struck deeply at sentiments about German cultural, economic, and social life. The legislation controlling store hours dates back to 1956, when Germany tried to regulate demand in the booming postwar period and to protect workers. With high unemployment rates and a slow economy in the 1990s, Kohl wanted to improve his country's competitiveness, stimulate more jobs and profits, and crack what appeared to him and his party to be a nagging complacency by eliminating what the *Wall Street Journal* labeled as "ossified competition laws" in its retailing.[56]

Those supporting the status quo included the retail trade association, unions, the Social Democrats, and the Greens. Lengthening store hours would benefit big businesses and knock out the mom-and-pop stores. The unions liked the hours as they were, and they saw no gains for either the present full-time employees or the potential part-time employees. Most small retailers thought that stretching workers over longer hours would kill what profits they might make during those extra hours. In late April 1996, in Bonn, 50,000 retail sales clerks vigorously protested the government's plans to lengthen store hours, some with posters reading "We aren't robots." The German Union of Commercial, Clerical, and Technical Employees backed the opposition of the store clerks, and the union's highest officer, Roland Issen, stated that "consumers don't lack the time, but rather the money for shopping."[57] Reaching deeper into the German psyche, Hermann Franzen, president of the 100,000-member German Retail Trade Association, said, "Nothing will really begin to change until Germans stop believing the workweek should end at noon on Friday. . . . Germans need rules and regulations and want a well-ordered, harmonious society, not the law of the jungle. They don't need more hours to shop, and my employees and I want time with our families."[58]

High wages, a thirty-five-hour workweek, and long vacations—firstyear employees get four-week paid vacations—helped make time for family and leisure incredibly important to German workers. If stores were open longer hours, it was feared that the German family would be at the malls on weekends, like the consumer-mad Americans—rather than walking in parks. Then the fabric of the German family would start to fray and the "triple-K" ("kinder, kuche, and kirche," or children, kitchen, and church) would no longer govern the German mother. But that triple-K pattern had already been altered, as 59 percent of German women were working, in the mid-1990s, outside the home, creating dual-income families for whom restricted store hours were inconvenient.

Mary Vance and Jeff Strange, a young American couple residing in Berlin for two years while Jeff undertook research in the mid-1990s at the Max Planck Institute, were startled to learn that they could not buy a quart of milk or a box of cereal at the local store after work, as they could at the deli around the corner from their old Manhattan apartment. Having to organize their shopping trips around the restricted store hours was a continuing annoyance for this couple, used to American stores open around the clock. They were also surprised to discover that bargain shopping was not part of German retailing, because bargaining has been as tightly controlled by the government as store hours. Under a 1933 law, German stores have been allowed to give only a 3 percent discount on the price of any item and to conduct major sales only twice a year, in the winter and in the summer. To the orderly German, bargaining smacks of the Middle Eastern bazaar. Despite efforts by consumer groups to rid Germany of its bargaining restrictions—"the last country in the world with such a law," according to Manfred Dimper of Germany's Consumer Association—the resistance of both retailers and the German public to the alien notion of bargaining has prevented that bit of deregulation from getting anywhere in the legislative process.[59] But many recent immigrants from different parts of the world, accustomed to other ways of living or to working late hours or to enjoying different kinds of shopping, like bargaining, are operating stores that disregard the current restrictions and may in fact start to crack what seems a solid system.

German traditions have been threatened as new people and values have been injected into the country, but the nation has maintained enormous opposition to flexing its store hours and allowing bargaining. Although only 27 percent of the German population favored government regulation of store hours, according to an Allensbach poll, retailers, who have been politically strong and supported by German traditions, defeated the weaker consumer movement.

Germany's store hours are more restrictive than those of most European countries (only Denmark's, Ireland's, and Holland's are more restrictive). This control of hours of business caused Germany's economic minister, Gunter Rexrodt, to proclaim that the "whole world is laughing at us." The fact is that many Germans and many German organizations prefer life as it has been.[60] The fear that American consumerism might take over was real for older people and for those who cherished the family and the small stores, and the community that both have produced. Shopping has not yet become a time-consuming and costly recreation in Germany. For an American expatriate journalist like Sarah Defty, restricted German shopping has provided a community life rarely seen in the United States, and a welcome relief from engulfing American consumerism.

Such consumerism worries some European leaders. Czechoslovakian President Václav Havel, in analyzing the history of Europe in a speech in May 1996, discussed the "beneficial and useful things such as democracy and the idea of human rights . . . to the European spirit of progress and endless searching," but he also saw "that same European spirit" as responsible "for many of its huge social inequities, its arrogant anthropocentric treatment of the planet, the cult of consumerism, as well as the enormous stockpiles of unbelievably destructive weapons."[61]

Despite Germans' deep-seated concerns about creeping consumerism and the strong opposition of the Social Democrats, Greens, and others, both houses of the German Parliament voted surprisingly in late June and early July 1996 to extend shopping hours—with the Lower House passing it by only six votes. Kohl's Christian Democrat Union persuaded Parliament to throw aside the store-closing restrictions in an effort to stimulate the sluggish economy at a time of record unemployment. Now stores can stay open until 8 p.m. on weekdays and until 4 p.m. on Saturdays, and bakeries are allowed to bake at night and on weekends. Whether these extended hours will fray the German family, increase employment, inject a new element of free enterprise into a social market economy, and stimulate more shopping will not be known for some time. However, it is pretty clear that the small independent baker, like so many independent shopkeepers around the world, will have a hard time keeping up with the larger bakeries and will certainly get less sleep and have fewer vacations, as the Association of German Retailers feared. Once again the march of progress seems to favor the larger operator.

Norway

Even in the Land of the Midnight Sun, whose deep fjords have not yet been penetrated by American superstores, there are worries that large American-style out-of-town stores may yet invade this Scandinavian country. Mounting concerns about the potential impacts of such stores and about the broader issue of urban sprawl prompted the Norwegian Parliament in January 1999 to pass legislation to cope with these problems. As in England, the initiative for the legislation came from a parliamentary committee established to study sprawl and regional planning.

The intent of the legislation is to stem urban sprawl, reduce dependence on the car, and encourage sustainable communities.[62] As out-of-town retailing has been seen as encouraging sprawl and, in turn, draining life from downtowns, this legislation established a five-year ban on construction of shopping centers with more than 17,640 square feet of retail space outside town centers. Compared with American shopping centers, which are usually measured in 100,000-square-foot increments, Norway's centers seem miniature. During the moratorium, from 1999 to 2004, the national government requires towns, urban areas, and regions to produce plans for future retailing in town centers, where public activities, transportation, and community facilities are already concentrated. These plans are to be carefully coordinated by local, regional, and national governments, with county governors having the final say on what gets approved. Through local planning and transportation policies, this act aims to reduce reliance on the car, make shopping accessible to everyone, including those who cannot drive or do not have cars, and revitalize downtowns as centers for trade and cultural activities, and important meeting places. Essentially, these plans will establish restricted zones for retailing, although there are exemptions for some types of uses and for certain urbanized areas. In Oslo, such a plan will involve the surrounding counties. Planners there already have started to identify the retailing zone for the city's metropolitan area, and, as is often the case, politicians find the zone too small. Because the legislation provides a 2004 deadline for these plans, it is too soon to predict the outcome.

However, the commitment to plan retailing that encourages compact, sustainable communities stands out as yet another example of a foreign country's forward thinking—and its recognition of the role that retailing plays in community life. Both Denmark and Sweden are closely following Norway's efforts to contain retailing.

England

Of all the European countries, England has been tackling the challenges of urban decentralization, out-of-town shopping, and troubled city centers with the most comprehensive national planning policies, which reach into every high street and town center. In England the pub and the small stores along the high street traditionally have provided a social and economic focus for towns and cities. They have been the heart of the community. "Town centres have grown, over the centuries, as places where people come together to buy and sell, close to where people live and where major routes converge," according to the government's 1993 policy statement, *Town Centres and Retail Developments*.

> Historically, markets and other activities have developed alongside each other, taking advantage of the congregation of people and opportunities for attracting visitors. The marketplace and retail function have therefore been at the heart of the evolution of today's towns and cities. . . . They provide a sense of place and community identity. As well as shopping facilities for local residents and others, they generally provide high levels of accessibility to services and facilities for all the community. Town centres provide a convenient location for developments, such as shops, leisure facilities and restaurants, entertainment and the arts, offices and residential accommodation; such a location allows development to build on earlier investments and infrastructure. The retail function should continue to underpin such centres.[63]

This commitment reflects a major difference from attitudes in France, the United States, and most other nations, since England not only has had strong planning to meet the social, economic, and cultural problems facing the nation, but its people, industries, and commerce respect planning. The level of attention to retailing, whether from the press, planners, trade, or from the public, is astounding to an American observer. In the United States, controversies over the location of a Wal-Mart have aroused loud local opposition, and the invasion of superstore sprawl has caught the attention of the National Trust for Historic Preservation, but there have been no federal commissions or policy announcements on retailing—or even much public interest in planning and management strategies on retailing.

Retailing policies and activities are headline news in England. Literature abounds; the best histories of shopping are written and published in England; several retailing institutes exist at different universities (one is in Oxford); government reports, bibliographies, conferences, commissions, and professional organizations are many and sophisticated. This intense interest in retailing may confirm the notion that England really is a nation of shopkeepers, as Napoleon stated, but more likely this interest results from passionate English concern to sustain their built and natural environments. The goal of this national attention is not to impede progress and return to a sentimental dream of the past but to examine realistically and comprehensively the options for retailing as they relate to the long-term national goals of providing vital communities. England's planners have had much tighter control over land use than America's have; in retailing that has meant that the local planning authority can determine exactly what kind of store can exist in a certain location. When Sainsbury's wanted to build a store on King's Road in Chelsea in London, the local authority's careful attention to the location and design of the store even included the requirement that Sainsbury's provide benches for its customers near the door.

"Good retailing contributes to the vitality and viability of town centres," the government states in its policy guidelines, *Town Centres and Retail Developments*, issued in 1993 and formalized in 1996 by the national Department of Environment. These guidelines, referred to as Planning Policy Guidance 6 (or PPG6), guide all local planning decisions—and they were just one of the three major government reports and national policies relating to retail developments issued in 1993 and 1994. The others were "Planning Policy Guidance: Transport" (PPG13), issued by the national Departments of the Environment and Transport, and the House of Commons' Environment Committee's report, "Shopping Centres and Their Future." The government's objectives on retailing are to:

- sustain or enhance the vitality and viability of town centres which serve the whole community and in particular provide a focus for retail development where the proximity of competing businesses facilitates competition from which consumers benefit; and
- ensure the availability of a wide range of shopping opportunities to which people have easy access (from the largest superstores to the smallest village shop), and the maintenance of an efficient and innovative retail sector.[64]

The aim has been to assure that retailing can continue to prosper and also be socially and environmentally responsible, so that the hearts of England's towns will not wither nor the fabric of its community life unravel. Car ownership, dual-wage earners, bulk shopping, and all the other aspects of stretched living mean that shoppers have not been wandering along the high street three or four times a week to pick up single items at specialized shops, as they had in the past. In 1994, almost 90 percent of car-owning households shopped by car at least once a week, according to the Automobile Association as reported to the House of Commons' Committee, but in 1968 only 10 to 12 percent of shopping trips were made by car.[65] Not surprisingly, public transport service has deteriorated. At the same time, shopping is being transformed into a "major social and leisure activity," as a 1994 House of Commons report stated on its first page. Such postmodern era consumption has become a way of expressing one's lifestyle and position.[66]

These winds of social, economic, and cultural change have battered the small shopkeeper. Small shops have shrunk (from 500,000 in 1966 to 400,000 in 1980) because of higher rents, aging proprietors, large corporations closing down small units, competition from multiples, mail-order houses, large supermarkets, and decreased business. Perhaps hardest hit were the small shopkeepers—the confectionery, tobacco, and news agents whose "lack of dynamism" prevented them from keeping up with the times. These independent shopkeepers "were usually close to their customers, often operated flexible hours, and offered the 'personal touch.' They can also offer specialised goods and services which would be uneconomic for multiples to offer." But, as noted in *The Future Pattern of Shopping*, a report by the Distributive Trade's Economic Development Committee and published by HMSO (Her Majesty's Stationery Office) in 1971, "If small shopkeepers . . . were more dynamic they would presumably not remain shopkeepers. Retailers under this kind of pressure are in fact those who are least capable of responding to it," just like H. G. Wells's Mr. Polly.[67]

While this loss of the small shops was gradual, more dramatic jolts to the shopping patterns and the life of towns—and to those concerned about quality-of-life and environment issues—have come from out-of-town stores, in the guise of hypermarkets, bulk stores, malls, and now remote shopping. Since the 1970s, out-of-town stores arrived in three waves: first, the hypermarkets and free-standing food supermarkets, then the free-standing nonfood retail warehouses (Big Boxes in the United States), which cluster in "retail parks" (Power Centers), and third, regional megamalls, or out-of-town high streets.

The third wave of decentralized megamalls stirred England to look carefully at retailing, at the structural changes in the retailing industry, at consumer attitudes, and at the impact this changed retail world has had on people, towns, and environmental quality. Although only five of these megamalls were built by the early 1990s (fifty-seven were proposed), they have aroused a remarkable amount of attention, maybe because they dramatically illustrate a quantum leap into a new era of shopping, one with greater car ownership and material expectations, along with social and personal stresses—an era already in evidence in the United States. These retailing changes provide a dramatic contrast to the image of the compact English village. Expenditures for convenience goods, which in England include food, cleaning materials, alcohol, newspapers, and magazines, were very steady from 1963 to 1987. But spending on comparison goods, such as appliances and furniture, more than doubled, still another indication of changed attitudes and expectations, as well as of the influence of advertising, television, and credit cards.[68]

The out-of-town retailing developments, whether bulk goods outlets or full-fledged malls, seem to appeal particularly to the younger generation. In assessing the impact of the large Meadowhall Shopping Centre outside Sheffield, Elizabeth Howard of the Oxford Institute of Retail Management found its "greatest success with 25–44 year olds. Meadowhall is the most popular destination for nonfood shopping trips with the 25–44 year olds (car own-ing or not)." On the other hand, Sheffield's town center was found to be the most popular destination for those over sixty, even among car owners.[69]

Lakeside, a shopping mall of more than 1 million square feet located in Essex only seventeen miles east of London, was one of the early mega-malls—a novelty to the English, but a clone of any large American mall, especially those featuring atria, domes, and an overall airiness. Americana pervades Lakeside. Its shops include American franchises, such as the Gap and Sam Goody, and its fast-food restaurants include McDonald's. Even the restaurants have American themes: the Old Orlean, a mock riverboat, and Capone, a Chicago-style speakeasy. Judging by the number of people shop-ping there, sometimes up to 350,000 a week, and the number of cars, 175,000 a week for the 9,000 parking spaces, Lakeside seems to be popular. Mean-while, nearby towns like Basildon and Dagenham have seen their high streets empty of stores and life—a familiar pattern in the United States thirty years ago, when suburban shopping centers cropped up at highway interchanges and the inner cities or nearby towns struggled with few stores and leftover populations. Seventeen percent of all English retail sales were made out of town in 1991, compared with only 5 percent in 1980.

The government's concern about the influence of megamalls like Lakeside and the new Power Centers, hypermarkets, retail warehouses, and clusters of outlet stores has focused on broad environmental impacts, includ-ing air pollution, loss of open space, and congestion, as well as on the peo-ple left behind in a car-oriented world—the elderly, the poor, the carless, the young, the disabled, and those inadequately served by public transportation. To meet this concern, the government's 1996 planning policies (Planning Policy Guidance: Town Centres and Retail Developments, or PPG6) insti-tuted a sequential approach to retail planning to encourage the siting of new stores in existing town centers and, if that is not possible, at the edge of cur-rent town centers. The local authorities are responsible for carrying out these policies, but, if serious controversies occur, the national Department of Envi-ronment, Transport, and Regions will send inspectors to review such cases and then, in highly contested situations, the department secretary may make final decisions. The government's transport policy is similar to its planning policy—and very clear. Plans should promote: 1. shopping that is accessible by foot, bicycle, and public transport; 2. convenience shopping in local and rural centers; and 3. when no suitable locations for large retail development are available in the center city, then accessible edge-of-center sites should be considered.

The food retailers, many of whom were already planning more in-town stores, generally have accepted the government's policies, as the cor-porate affairs manager of one of England's major supermarket chains, Tesco, wrote: "We have worked with the grain of PPG6 since it was introduced . . . and we have over 200 town centre stores and are planning more in the next financial year."[70] However, retailers have many complaints about the new policies' inconsistencies and inappropriate distance criteria; local authorities' excessively long planning process and their inadequate analyses of retailing needs and types; and difficult site assembly for urban sites due to multiple ownership. But even the nonfood retailers and developers have adopted PPG6 criteria in site identification.

In just four years since these government polices were formalized, a dramatic change has occurred: in 2000, the floor space of out-of-town shopping centers reached "one of its lowest-ever levels," and, at the same time, town center retail constructions exceeded the 1980s boom level of construction, according to C. B. Hillier Parker, a respected English consulting firm.[71] This impressive drop in out-of-town retail construction and a parallel increase in town center retail construction certainly indicate the influence of the government's policies, as well as the local planning authorities' response to those policies. The drop also reflects some market saturation as well—food retailers, such as Tesco and Sainsbury's, already are planning and building smaller units in center cities and developing smaller supermarkets with fewer goods.

For Americans, the British attention to the role of retailing in the cities and villages and in the life of its citizens seems staggering. This attention confirms England's efforts to treat retailing as a community service as well as an economic activity, and, more important, it confirms the country's tradition of blending social concerns into a myriad of planning activities. The elderly are housed in bungalows just behind the high street so that their ties with the community are not severed nor their independence reduced; the countryside, kept free of incompatible developments, is not treated like a museum but is used for farming, housing, and villages and is accessible through a lacework of public footpaths. Private activities, like retailing, are only part of a larger public weal.

In the United States, retailing usually has been considered a matter for private enterprise, so decisions on how retailers serve communities and their varied citizens have been left all too often to the invisible hand. England had a taste of this during its spell of unbridled private enterprise in the 1980s, when Margaret Thatcher was prime minister and the retail industry produced plans for many American-style large retail complexes in out-of-town locations, including some in the once-sacred greenbelts. The spectre of more of this American-style retailing further fraying town centers, exacerbating traffic problems, and disenfranchising those without cars no doubt helped to generate public interest in the planning controls on out-of-town retailing, which resulted in the 1996 legislation.

This legislation's sequential policy for new retail development is its most significant feature. Norwich, a medieval East Anglia market town—a city, by American standards—physically dominated by its castle, which also

97. Blending the old and new in Norwich, England, 1998

abuts High Street, has tried to fit contemporary retailing into its center city. A forty-five-acre development, Riverside Site, with "substantial retail elements," including retail warehouses, has been built next to the railroad station and River Wensum. It is connected to the city's existing shopping precinct with walkways over the river. Closer to and "plugged into" the old shopping area is the new million-square-foot and mostly underground Castle Mall shopping development, with four levels of floor space, each connected to street level, due to the sloping topography. This Castle Mall project has converted a surface parking lot into a four-acre city park (fig. 97). These projects, which take into account that 40 percent of Norwich's households are carless, promote center city retailing. The City Council "aims not to prevent choice, but to allow more people to have a choice of shopping facilities."[72] Pedestrianization, traffic calming, street entertainment, expansion by major retailers like John Lewis and Marks and Spencer, as well as Sainsbury's building a new store near the city center, have been some of the benefits of Norwich's program to cluster its retailing in and near the city center. All this modern, large-scale retailing blends with the historic nature of the city—its nearby cathedral, castle, its public markets open six days a week, the refurbished Royal Arcade—and, most important, with its existing stores, shops, and offices (fig. 98).

The government's commitment to support center city retailing and halt the spread of megamalls was evident in a 1997 decision to deny the expansion of a gigantic American-style mall, Merry Hill, near Dudley and Birmingham (fig. 99). The mall declared that it was virtually a town center and, therefore, entitled to expand. However, the government claimed that,

98. Norwich's Castle Mall, built partially under the castle grounds and partially under city streets, 1998 (photograph by Donald Skinner)

99. Merry Hill Shopping Centre, near Dudley, England, 1997

despite the mall's assertion, it was just a big shopping mall. In a more sophisticated try in 1999, Merry Hill enlarged its town center concept to include the nearby town of Brierley Hill and other adjacent areas, a proposed "high-quality" mixed-use development along the Dudley Canal, and an expanded and improved Merry Hill mall as the "primary retail centre." The proposal was backed by the Dudley Metropolitan Borough Council but objected to by many nearby jurisdictions.[73] This proposal to make the mall the core of a larger urban area, though cleverly veiled, is basically another attempt to expand the Merry Hill mall, which will test the government's commitment to concentrate retailing in existing full-fledged town centers.

British retailers' worst nightmare—Wal-Mart arriving on English soil—became a reality in 1999 when Wal-Mart took over Asda, a Wal-Mart clone already operating several hundred stores. The cannibalizing giant Wal-Mart, with its massive buying power and tight margins, can offer prices to consumers in England that are lower than those that English retailers pay their manufacturers. British retailers, planners, and many others feared that the meeting between Wal-Mart's chief and Prime Minister Tony Blair, prior to the Asda takeover, might lead to a relaxation of regulations like PPG6, allowing Wal-Mart to build stores out of town. However, Planning Minister Richard Caborn quickly dispelled that fear by reconfirming in public speeches and testimonies the government's support for policies that concentrate retailing in existing "city, town and district centres." "We have no plans to change it," Caborn said. "We are determined to take a tough line."[74] Caborn's predecessor, John Gummer, urged the government to stand by its planning regulations: "This is not America, and there is no more room for major out-of-town development, whatever the excuse."[75]

Efforts to concentrate retailing in the hearts of cities and towns are evident. Oxford connected shopping centers and parking garages with the old city and made its core pedestrian-friendly by banning cars. Smaller places, like Witney and Henley-on-Thames, have integrated contemporary-

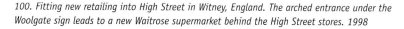

100. Fitting new retailing into High Street in Witney, England. The arched entrance under the Woolgate sign leads to a new Waitrose supermarket behind the High Street stores. 1998

101. *Witney's 35,000-square-foot Waitrose store and parking lot, a joint development by the West Oxfordshire District Council and a private developer, 1998. The design won the Royal Town Planning Institute's planning achievement award in 1988. Even the roof design was copied from a nineteenth-century brewery.*

sized supermarkets into their high streets (figs. 100, 101). Some of the major chain stores—Tesco, Sainsbury, and Marks and Spencer—are also trying to reduce the pollution and nuisances of their truck loading operations by limiting the number of trips and by using cleaner, quieter trucks. It all adds up to the fact that the English are conscious of the role that retailing plays in the social, economic, and environmental well-being of their country.

Some American Efforts

Although the Big Boxes, out-of-town malls, new suburban lifestyles, and growing dependence on the car are new challenges for many foreign countries, they are problems the United States has been coping with for decades. Dying center cities, while still a gnawing concern, have been the target of conscientious renewal efforts since the 1950s, when the suburban drain was first felt. Attention to flagging commercial areas has produced government programs, like urban renewal in the 1960s and Urban Development Action Grants in the late 1970s, and many locally driven projects—by cities, towns, Chambers of Commerce, Business Improvement Districts, and the National Trust for Historic Preservation's twenty-five-year-old Main Street projects. Initially, many of these local projects focused on physical appearances and cosmetic changes—upgrading buildings, planting trees, improving signs.

Then attention was paid to helping storekeepers run their businesses efficiently, improve accounting, and promote their merchandise, with public agencies helping to provide more parking, pedestrianized streets, policing, and services like improved garbage collection. More recently, efforts to reinvigorate comatose commercial areas have become more sophisticated and comprehensive in tackling the economic and physical problems, as well as involving a broad array of community and commercial participants crossing the divide between residents and businesspeople.

Revitalizing North High Street, the main street of Columbus, Ohio's Clintonville neighborhood, represents such an effort. Scattered over four miles on this north-south spine in Columbus were shops, restaurants, and businesses, along with vacant land and used car lots, giving the artery a generally tattered and no-there-there appearance. Moreover, the stores and businesses did not well serve this inner suburb, an economically stable community of well-educated people located near the university. Concern about the deterioration of North High Street on the part of the citizens, the local Chamber of Commerce, and public agencies led to a concerted program to improve the appearance and functioning of this important street. These diverse groups cooperated on finding ways to improve the infrastructure, as well as to provide visible projects to be tackled incrementally. To deal with the physical problems, a zoning overlay was prepared and passed (in an election year); it proposed building setbacks, drive-in uses attached to the sides of buildings, buildings facing the street with large windows, and screening parking from the street. To grapple with the social, economic, marketing, infrastructure, and maintenance problems, a panel of local experts in urban real estate finance, retailing, zoning law, and historic preservation met, focus groups were held, and a planning consultant, Hal Miksch, was hired.

The program is action-oriented. By establishing a nonprofit organization to oversee planning and "overcommunicate" the activities, and then a community development corporation, the groups set in motion the machinery to undertake projects on four nodes of intensive uses along this strip. Such nodes provide critical masses of pedestrian-friendly commercial activities, offices, and housing with opportunities to use historic buildings like a theater and public buildings like a post office as magnets. Slowing traffic, improving the perception and reality of convenient parking, and strengthening existing retailing have been part of this cooperative effort. No Urban Land Institute national taskforce nor National Trust Main Street program was involved, only local people coping with their own dysfunctional retail strip. North High Street could be an older artery in most any inner-ring suburb; in fact, its ordinariness and its dependence on local resources make it of special significance.

An easier revitalization—in fact, an almost spontaneous regeneration of commercial districts—has occurred in unique and usually historic sections of cities and towns. Here little public assistance has been needed. Such spontaneous regeneration, however, has often resulted in outright gentrification, an upgrading of shops, sometimes into boutiques, antiques stores, bars, and restaurants. In this gussying up, stores that serve a community are replaced by specialty shops appealing to outsiders and tourists. The modern histories of New Orleans's French Quarter, Washington's Georgetown, and Santa Fe's Plaza area well illustrate this gentrifying process, which prices out shops that provide local services. Carmel, California, fearing the onslaught of tourist-trap stores and their attendant congestion, has been regulating its commercial uses to prevent an excessive influx of stores catering only to tourists, such as souvenir shops, eating, and drinking establishments.

Other California cities, including San Francisco, Santa Cruz, San Diego, Berkeley, and Santa Monica, are experimenting with ways to manage their local retail in this era of Big Boxes and tourist-oriented boutiques. Berkeley has caps on the number and size of stores in four neighborhoods; San Francisco put limits on the percentage of commercial frontage of restaurants and banks in several districts, as well as design controls preventing construction of pedestrian-unfriendly blank walls and reflecting glass windows; and West Hollywood has been trying to blend community shopping with the entertainment industry on Sunset Boulevard by "encouraging" landlords to replace lost local-serving uses with new local-serving uses.[76]

Although these California cities' programs are pioneering, many other public and private experiments are needed to uncover effective ways to retain shopping oriented to a town's residents rather than to transients. Escalating rents have forced many local service stores to close. To keep these stores, intervention in the real estate market is needed, similar to that of private nonprofit groups which have bought residential buildings through revolving funds. Such funds have been used effectively and extensively by local historic preservation groups, like Historic Charleston Foundation, in residential areas to save houses, protect their physical features, and provide affordable rents for tenants with a variety of incomes. Rarely have revolving funds been used for similar purposes in commercial buildings, where rents could be scaled to sales and services needed. Several New England situations are exceptions. Portland, Maine's local historic preservation organization protected two commercial buildings, both strategically located so that their rehabilitation stimulated upgrading in adjacent areas. In Providence, Rhode Island, the Providence Preservation Society's revolving fund helped with a $30,000 loan to restore the exterior of the Hudson Street Market, a neighborhood store with upstairs living space for its owners, and is also working with other nonprofit organizations in the rehabilitation of a large house with two storefronts. The use of revolving funds is the most reliable way to assure that buildings—residential, commercial, or industrial—are not only protected, but that their rents are affordable for a mix of tenants or uses that meet public objectives, like retaining community-serving stores. That more revolving funds have not been directed toward commercial sites is yet another indicator of the deep divide between residential and commercial interests in many communities.

More Positive Signs

More and more communities are grappling with the problems of their tired commercial areas, which, aside from being eyesores and economic disappointments for their owners, employees, and the tax collector, are usually not meeting the shopping and civic needs of their residents. One operation that has been in the business of tackling dying downtowns for almost twenty-five years is the National Trust for Historic Preservation's Main Street Program. Started in 1977 with three town demonstration projects in the midwest and directed by Mary Means of the National Trust's Chicago regional office, the Main Street Project has become a major national program in resuscitating the downtowns of small and midsize cities and the neighborhood commercial areas of large cities like Boston. These community-driven projects have concentrated on the heart of the economic and social life of those communities and have been promoted by a spectrum of business and civic leaders who recognize that the vitality of their main streets has a ripple effect not just in the immediate community but in the wider region. Statistics tell the story: by 1999, 193,000 net jobs were created, $12.8 billion was reinvested in Main Street commercial districts, 51,000 net new businesses opened, and an average of $38 was generated in Main Street investment for every dollar spent on commercial revitalization.[77] These projects, while transforming downtowns physically, economically, and socially, have also changed the psyche of small-town commercial revitalization.

Historic preservation efforts are often pictured as cosmetic, but the National Trust's Main Street program has tried to take hardheaded business approaches to some of the systemic and difficult problems facing downtowns. With a glut of retail space resulting from unrealistic expectations, downtowns have to plan retail space on Main Street that can be supported. Using a simple formula, Kennedy Lawson Smith, director of the Trust's Main Street Center, calculates the money that a typical household spends per year on retail purchases, on the basis of the Bureau of Labor Statistics' *Consumer Expenditure Survey,* then multiplies that by the number of households in the community; the resulting figure can be translated into the estimated square footage needed for retailing. This formula has been part of the economic restructuring phase of each Main Street project, undertaken along with three other concerns: the production of designs enhancing the physical environment of buildings, streets, signs, lighting, and so forth; the promotion of the district to residents, tourists, and investors; and the organization of all the partnerships needed to make the Main Street project function. Each project has been overseen by a local Main Street manager, who is guided by a state Main Street manager, usually someone in the state's department of economic development, with the Trust's National Main Street Center available for help. Most of the Main Street projects have been in small places—more than 70 percent have been in towns with populations below 50,000. They range from places like Tacoma, Washington, Saratoga Springs, New York, and Port Huron, Michigan, to Corning, Iowa. Ten urban neighborhoods in Boston have signed up for the program, and other large cities, such as Providence, Philadelphia, Richmond, and Oakland, are interested in coming aboard.

Many Main Streets are getting a new lease on life in the cyberage. Competition from mail-order operations, e-commerce, malls, Big Boxes, and Category Killers has forced Main Street businesses to refocus, as they can no longer depend on a captive market of nearby customers. As these small businesses specialize so they are not competitive with remote stores and out-of-town discounters, and as they use the Internet and new postal and transportation services, they can now instantly reach customers all over the world. Some of these businesses are cyberage "location-neutral"—that is, not dependent on local markets—while others are local businesses reaching out to wider markets. In the National Trust's 1999 survey of its projects, the greatest changes from 1998 to 1999 reported by four hundred communities participating in its program were: more businesses using the Internet (84 percent), more retail businesses (58 percent), more locally owned businesses (48 percent), increased number of professional offices (48 percent), more restaurants (47 percent), more personal services businesses (39 percent), and more location-neutral businesses (24 percent). Chain stores and franchises were at the bottom of the list of Main Street changes.[78]

Strengthening this mix of activities on Main Street has hit the snag of the single-use mentality, which ever since the Chinese laundry cases has pervaded zoning regulations, building codes, and other health and safety requirements. In recycling downtowns, the National Trust's Kennedy Lawson Smith has found that these zoning and building code problems, what she calls vertical redlining, prevent mixed uses in single buildings and require parking and other facilities geared to suburban-style development. As the Neo-Traditionalists have also found in their projects, building codes in many towns and cities today make it difficult to replicate the traditional apartments over shops and offices, which have provided convenient and inexpensive housing for shopowners' families, and all the activity generated from such housing in downtowns. But some progress has been made on this front, as the Trust's 1999 survey reports that more than a third of the respondents had more "housing units" in their districts.

Even though such problems as real estate speculation, increased rents, inadequate code enforcement, out-of-town commerce, loss of movie theaters and post offices, and the difficulties of small business succession continue to plague downtowns, there are signs that the long-term health of some of these small businesses is improving. Modern communication and transportation technology have helped, but the growing interest in small-scale, independent, authentic, and livable places provides the main engine for this revival of downtowns. BeaverPrints, located in downtown Bellwood, Pennsylvania, a small town near Altoona, is a mail-order operation selling business cards, letterhead, folders, and brochures, as well as computer templates for desktop publishing. This contemporary business with forty-five employees could locate anywhere, but it opted to be near the bank, post office, stores, luncheonette, and other downtown services.[79] This trend bodes well for the future of all downtowns.

Another encouraging sign for the planning and design of commercial areas has been the growing interest in community life and the pleasurable benefits of urban living emerging in new meccas for the young, like Seattle. Seattle City Planning Commission member David Sucher shows in his book book *City Comforts* how an "urban village" can provide comfortable, friendly, "fun" areas in our cities—places where we can enjoy both community and autonomy, bustle and tranquility, familiarity and anonymity, excitement and quiet. Using design to enhance urban village qualities, Sucher offers a myriad of well-illustrated, almost how-to examples of ways to increase opportunities of "bumping into people": benches and cafes; places for chance encounters or social strolls; chess tables in parks; places for concerts; bus shelters with automatic teller machines and other services for the public; newspaper and magazine kiosks; movable chairs; pedestrianization of streets; murals on walls; raised crosswalks; narrowed streets; and much more. All very simple, constructive, and appealing but possible only in upbeat, homogeneous cities where crime, litter, and decay have not overtaken frail budgets and limp bureaucrats. Many of Sucher's examples involve shopping and commercial areas, often with a lively mixture of activities, people, and uses— far removed from the single-track mindset of zoning administrators and from people living in gated communities isolated from the verve of the outside world. The details, Sucher suggests, can transform commercial streets into places with distinctiveness and personality—places where one would like to linger. The challenge is to stretch this thinking so that a wider range of people (not just cafe attendees and bookstore patrons) and a wider range of cities can have such opportunities. But that such public concern exists for these designs for community life and commerce and that a trend-setting city like Seattle finds them popular is heartening.

Other signs of new interest in encouraging community life in cities are appearing. The Project for Public Spaces, led by Fred Kent and Stephen Davies and following in the footsteps of keen urban observer William H. Whyte, has been invigorating public spaces for twenty-five years in hundreds of cities throughout the United States and around the world by encouraging activities and uses—like cafes, sitting areas, entertainments, and public markets—that are inviting to the public. Through carefully observing and listening to citizens, the Project for Public Spaces has helped communities envision their futures, reinforce their local assets, and then implement small-scale projects with visible results. The variety of their projects has increased from an early interest in bringing people and activities into the dead office plazas of large cities to big downtown revitalization efforts, urban park initiatives, a range of projects dealing with public transit, public markets, public art, and even a cooperative program with the federal government's major property managing agency, the General Services Administration. The focus of these projects is not comprehensive planning or addressing systemic problems but rather on visible and doable tasks, and in those tasks the Project for Public Spaces has had admirable success in carrying out its mission of "rebuilding communities both in spirit and places."

In Boulder, Colorado, concern about traffic congestion stimulated the city to study and then enact new classifications of streets, all narrower and on a human scale, to try to revive street-centered communities. Other locales—Portland, Oregon, Olympia, Washington, and Bucks County, Pennsylvania—have experimented with different street standards, but few efforts have been as comprehensive as Boulder's. Traffic calming, street closings, diversions, and alleys, as well as provision for bicycling, walking, and transit, are just some of the methods of making streets more positive—community builders rather than dividers, as many of the Neo-Traditionalists have advocated.

In San Luis Obispo, California, a city with a population of 45,000 and a high level of environmental and design consciousness, an ad hoc citizen's advisory group recommended desirable features and qualities for residential development in its draft 1994 Land Use Element, an alternative to the City Planning Commission's draft plan. One suggestion featured porches, which the ad hoc group thought provided three benefits for neighborliness: encouragement of interaction between neighbors; friendlier fronts than garage doors and windowless walls; and "eyes on the street" for safety. The porch suggestion was integrated into the architectural review guidelines and development standards for all residential building, as it follows the city's policy of encouraging friendly streetfronts, which "facilitate neighborhood interaction" with not only front porches, but "front yards along the street, and entryways facing public walkways."[80]

California, the state that introduced the first grocery stores with parking lots in 1935, as well as later generations of shopping centers and malls, also produced one of the country's more interesting community-retail center infill developments in San Diego. When Sears Roebuck left its twelve-and-a-half-acre site in the Uptown District in 1986, residents worried that a shopping mall would fill the gaping hole and overwhelm the neighborhood. Instead, the city bought the property with the intention of building its central library there. But not long after, the city decided that the library should remain downtown, so the city then sought proposals from architects and developers to convert this 12.5-acre site to commercial, residential, and communal uses. Oliver McMillan/Odmark & Thelan was chosen as the developer. Working with the local Hillcrest community leaders and the city, the team devised a plan that was accepted by all parties.

The community wanted a supermarket, stores, restaurants, and housing with a minimal intrusion of cars. Ralph's Grocery Store, the key feature of the development, risked going into a "location with no street visibility and underground parking," as Bryon Allumbaugh, chairman of Ralph's Grocery Company, observes. Ralph's had just left Federated Department Stores to become a separate corporation, a move that probably gave the store the flexibility to experiment with a configuration unknown to most supermarkets. The gamble proved successful, with "the market wildly over our projections," according to Allumbaugh. He thinks that taking the mixed used route, as Uptown did, is "about the only way a supermarket is going to gain entry into established high density urban areas."[81]

The Hillcrest community also got more than 300 apartments, some over the shops near Ralph's, and a community center in the heart of the project, which "gives people the feeling that although it's a new development . . . it has a history of being associated with the community," according to Pat McLaughlin, a team member and head of the business improvement association. From the beginning, the developers approached the community with an eye to "picking our brains and doing their homework," said Tess Wilcoxson, former chair of the Uptown Community Planners. The Uptown project created "an urban village that works," according to Michael Stepner, San Diego's city architect and acting city planner in the late 1980s; it works because it provides what the community wanted: grocery shopping scaled to a community and not a larger region (fig. 102).[82]

A community looking to the larger picture of its retailing and how it relates to neighborhoods, the county, and the region has been Arlington County, Virginia, just across the Potomac River from Washington, D.C. Mostly filled with detached brick houses, row houses, and garden apartments lacking distinctiveness (and fitting Gertrude Stein's "no there there" description of Oakland, California), Arlington, with an estimated population of 189,000 in 2000, has benefited from many leaders elected from a nonpartisan political party, Arlingtonians for a Better County (ABC). The county has looked at its stores and service establishments, big and small, thriving and marginal, with the same concern it applies to other county planning problems, such as providing affordable housing for low- and middle-income residents, and programs encouraging the assimilation of the 35,000 Asian and Hispanic immigrants, as well as numerous other recent immigrants living in Arlington.

102. *The Uptown Project in San Diego, 2000. Looking toward Ralph's supermarket from the residential section*

Although major corporations like MCI, USAir, Gannett, and Marriott are located in Arlington's Manhattan-like Rosslyn and other Metro station areas, as well as big federal operations like the Pentagon, the county is vying with other jurisdictions for more corporate and high-tech firms. The county has several major malls, like Pentagon City, anchored by Nordstrom and Macy's. The county also harbors the Crystal City complex of high-rise apartment and office buildings, with an underground shopping center, as well as Big Boxes, Category Killers, and other mass marketers. At the same time, Arlington has not neglected its lower- and middle-income residents, nor its small businesses and older commercial corridors, which it has been trying to bolster with a myriad of public and private programs. In fact, the effort to "preserve and enhance neighborhood retail areas . . . that serve everyday shopping and service needs" stands out as a key land use policy.[83]

Despite the gigantic installations like the Pentagon and dense high-rise sections like Rosslyn and Crystal City, Arlington County remains a conglomeration of neighborhoods without any downtown. Nonetheless, it also has thirty-two shopping centers, some from the early days—four were built in the 1930s, six in the 1940s, and more than half before 1960. All are recognized as critical assets to the adjacent neighborhoods in the county's master plan. To ensure their sustained vitality, the county established a Business Conservation Program to stimulate public and private initiatives. An inventory of neighborhood commercial areas was prepared to provide information on uses, spaces, parking, and land values in four areas with concentrations of small businesses, many in the older shopping centers or along tired commercial-retail corridors. These areas—Ballston, Columbia Pike, Clarendon, and Rosslyn—which are targeted for special attention, have mobilized public-private partnerships to undertake a variety of design, business-bolstering, and community-supported projects.

Columbia Pike, called South Arlington's Main Street, is a three-mile stretch of 500 businesses—a hodgepodge of supermarkets, diners, car dealerships, bakeries, stationery stores, invisible weavers, doctors' offices, banks, office buildings, accountants, apartment complexes, restaurants, and early shopping centers. This aging strip serves a potential 81,000 customers, 36,000 of whom live within a mile of the Pike. To some the Pike seems rundown and tawdry, while others find it a wonderfully eclectic mix of shops and services. For ten years the Columbia Pike Revitalization Organization, working with 250 business members, adjacent neighborhood groups, and the county, has made visible improvements: utilities were placed underground; brick sidewalks, trees, and garbage bins were installed; and property owners were nudged to spruce up their holdings with new awnings, paint, and even up-to-date stores. Stores like the franchised Boston Market have produced the desired domino effect in stimulating general refurbishing nearby, resulting in a much improved image for the Pike. This reinvestment, guided by the *Columbia Pike 2000: A Revitalization Plan*, carefully prepared by the county planning staff, civic associations, business groups, and the Columbia Revitalization Organization, has focused on ways to upgrade existing businesses and to attract new ones. The goal is to improve the appearance of the corridor by "providing appropriate transitions between residential and commercial areas that strengthen the image and amenities of both areas."[84]

Preserving existing neighborhood—and destination—retailing, while also modernizing and redeveloping, is a challenge for Arlington in all its Business Conservation Program areas. The underlying premise is that neighborhood retail shops—the "drugstore, hardware stores, repair shops, cleaners, restaurants and grocery stores"—can meet community needs, enhance the livability of the areas, and contribute to the economic base of Arlington County.[85] While that may sound vague, the plan has emphasized specific sections of the Pike for concentrated efforts, the first of which promoted a "town center" for South Arlington with public improvements, business revitalization, urban design, and marketing strategies. Other areas were planned as gateways, or as improved environments for apartment buildings, housing complexes, and nearby neighborhoods.

103. A small section of Columbia Pike, Arlington, Virginia, 1999

The Pike is getting an upbeat look, but it has not lost its small shops and services, as so often happens when neighborhoods "revitalize." A guide to the Pike's shopping, services, and eating places includes the Reweave Shop, Bob and Edith's Diner, Rita's Tailoring and Altering, Brenner's Bakery, Arlington Printers and Stationers, Signs To Go, H&R Block, C. W. Fields Plumbing, and the Oriental Super Market among its approximately 250 listings. Yet Conchita Mitchell, director of the Columbia Pike Revitalization Organization for many years, tried to retain such small, individual stores by helping them expand and upgrade, attract new businesses, and prevent the franchised stores from tipping the scales to the point where they overtake the independent businesses, a worry in any successful commercial improvement program (fig. 103).

Sustaining the identity of the Pike and the individuality of the stores, restaurants, and businesses—and being conscious of all the ingredients making up a strong sense of place—has been a constant challenge. Columbia Pike has not been going it alone, for an array of help exists from Arlington County's planning department and economic development staffs, the Small Business Development Center at George Mason University, a savvy micro-business group begun as the Ethiopian Community Development Council, the Neighborhood Conservation Advisory Council, the Economic Development Commission, the Area Business Development Officials Committee, federal agencies, state minority programs, and colleges and universities. Columbia Pike, like the other targeted areas in Arlington, has been tackling the gritty problems of strengthening everyday businesses, providing services to neighborhoods and customers, and providing taxes and an ambience to the county.

Arlington is unusually conscientious in trying to help a wide range of businesses: cab drivers trying to buy their own cabs; minority groups getting accounting assistance on how to prepare a bid; incubator companies needing low-rent space; mega-corporations looking for new headquarters or room to expand; home-based businesses getting started. The county's success has hinged on its solid long-range planning, which has protected its many neighborhoods by concentrating businesses in targeted areas, such as Metro station areas and commercial arteries like Columbia Pike, and then helping those commercial areas remain healthy. The results are visible in the diverse, functional, and vital commercial areas scattered throughout the county, which serve county residents and others from all over the metropolitan area. Shopping and small commercial activities may not be top-of-the-line companies or on the cutting edge of fashion, but they have been recognized by Arlington County as integral to its planning and the future.

Aside from these on-the-ground projects, one of the most promising approaches to retail planning is being taken in Vermont. The legislature there has been trying since 1988 to tackle some of the problems deterring new retail development in town centers. Vermont, a leader in state planning, has been spurred by the reports of the Burlington-based statewide Forum on Sprawl, which outlined the reasons why retail developers have opted for outlying sites. The difficulties of site preparation, complicated environmental problems and title searches, troublesome neighborhood relations, and time-consuming permits and historic preservation regulations are among the reasons that development in town is slower and costlier than in outlying sites. To lessen these problems and make in-town development simpler, faster, and more appealing to developers, state legislators have proposed a series of incentives for towns with plans, zoning, or new downtown development districts. These incentives include reduced tax burdens, speeded-up planning funds and loans for water pollution control and water supply, asbestos and lead cleanup funds, higher rehabilitation tax credits for older buildings, limited appeals from nonadjoining property owners, and transportation aids. While some incentives have been passed and others are under consideration, the important message is that such a systemic approach grapples with the problems discouraging developers from building and rehabilitating stores in downtowns. If downtown retail development can be made as profitable as out-of-town shopping, perhaps downtowns will be able to lure developers. A similar approach worked in historic preservation. When federal tax incentives were made available for the rehabilitation of historic buildings, historic preservation took on a new life. By tackling the causes of developers' lack of interest in constructing and rehabilitating stores in downtowns, Vermont may lead the way in showing how retail development can return to the town center.[86]

These examples in Vermont, California, suburban Washington, Columbus, Seattle, new towns, and on scattered Main Streets in this country and abroad show how retailing can be guided so that it contributes to a place's economic, social, and civic vitality. Such projects indicate a sense of community empowerment, a growing interest in countering the anonymity and remoteness in our communities—and our lives. But it takes public commitment and careful planning involving the community, public agencies, and the businesses themselves—something cities and towns have often realized only after being jolted by the prospect of out-of-town Wal-Marts and Big Boxes threatening the sociability, scale, and community cohesion of their Columbia Pikes and Main Streets.

CHAPTER SIX

Shopping

A Public Concern

What Emile Zola described as "ridiculous old ways" of doing business have been replaced throughout history by new types of stores, new selling and promotion techniques, new goods, and new customers. Driven by the seemingly inexhaustible entrepreneurial engine, shopping has responded to the mercurial twists and slow, surging shifts that provide the constant excitement and volatility which have kept recharging that engine. With the latest cannibalizing competition of e-commerce, catalogue mail-order houses, Big Boxes, Category Killers, and every variety of superstore, even many large malls have had trouble staying afloat, just like yesteryear's downtown flagship department stores and Main Street's small service shops. "I shop therefore I am" may be bumped aside by reduced acquisitiveness and growing interest in simpler living. Continual changes in the objectives, commitments, and scale of mega-corporations affect what, where, and how we buy, even our simplest groceries. This is capitalism at work. Retailers have understood that "capitalism mandated growth," as Susan Strasser stated in her fascinating book on mass marketing, *Satisfaction Guaranteed*. To stay on top in that laissez-faire world, stores have had to grow — and keep up with the latest marketing and production technologies.

Despite retailing's inherent competitive laissez-faire nature, retailers have also required, sought, and enjoyed public help for services like roads, sewers, police and fire protection, tax mitigation, relief for such calamities as fires and floods, or more recently protection of the consumer and assistance to small businesses. This help has come from all levels of government. President Franklin Roosevelt even shifted the Thanksgiving holiday from the last to the fourth Thursday in November to extend the Christmas shopping season to help American business at the urging of Fred Lazarus, Jr., of Federated Stores. Much of the public assistance is highly visible—highways and access roads to reach new malls, for example—but less visible are the federal tax policies, like accelerated depreciation, which encourage retail developments, and the many financial lures inducing big retailers to locate in given jurisdictions. A 1999 southern California study for the Orange County Business Council reported that Ventura dismissed $1.5 million of development fees to attract a Kmart superstore after nearby Oxnard had already lured Price Club and Wal-Mart with similar deals. Lake Elsinore had courted Wal-Mart by agreeing to reimburse the retailer $2.2 million from the city's share of sales and property taxes.[1] Such public undergirdings have often been obscured, especially in the blurred lines of public-private partnerships, but public support of retail developments has been considerable and will undoubtedly continue. The Urban Land Institute predicts that "cities increasingly will assume a direct role in creating the preconditions for marketing urban entertainment development," the popular late twentieth-century Times Square–like developments.

The enormous public involvements—and consequences—of retailing have not been adequately recognized. Haunted by the lingering image of a low-class, peripheral trade and, no doubt, ignored partly for its very ordinariness, retailing has rarely been considered a vital economic or social influence in the United States. Although attention to consumer protection and to the plight of small businesses has spotlighted the operations and integrity of corporations, and recent locational battles of Big Boxes and mega-stores have aroused interest in community viability, the broader issues of how goods and materials are sold and distributed to consumers, and the impacts of those decisions on the welfare and civic life of communities, have not been seriously addressed. It's been a hands-off, almost "libertarian" system, as Stanley Hollander stated. "Public policy planners and high-level economic strategists in the United States, as in most countries, have not regarded retailing as a key area," Hollander wrote.[2]

In southern California, concern that towns and cities were rushing after the sales tax revenue from large new grocery-discount supercenters without adequately researching their impacts prompted a thorough study of these new mega-retailers. This study, *The Impact of Big Box Grocers on Southern California: Jobs, Wages, and Municipal Finances*, found that the negative impacts of these big grocers' low wages and poor benefits, as well as their displacement of older grocery stores, were considerable.[3] Lost wages and benefits were estimated to be almost $2.8 billion a year. Lower wages alone, which in this region affect 250,000 grocery industry employees, could create a serious multiplier effect, as those employees would have less to spend in the area. Each dollar increase in wages is estimated to generate more than two dollars in new spending. The fiscal impacts of these new stores are complicated but appeared to be less than some estimates. Although such mega-retailers often boast of the new jobs and added tax revenue they can offer communities, careful scrutiny of their figures, as in the case of southern California, may reveal quite a different picture.

If the economic aspects of shopping get little attention, the social implications of shopping on individuals and communities rarely appear on the screen. Yet how and where we shop affects not only the economic life of our communities but our personal lives and the civic life of our communities. If shopping is done at the internalized, private mall on the highway, if the post office is on the outskirts of town, if the accountants and lawyers have moved to the office park, and if the restaurants, gas stations, and stores have joined the strip highway commerce; then the commercial and civic life of a town has been fractured and there is no critical mass of social and commercial activity. As Lizabeth Cohen reflected in her article on Paramus, New Jersey's malls, "The commercializing, privatizing, and segmenting of the physical gathering places that has accompanied mass consumption has made more precarious the shared public sphere upon which our democracy depends."[4] Because shopping affects that shared public sphere and the critical mass of social capital, it is too important to be left primarily in the hands of the private, profit-making sector. It is our concern; a public concern. As consumers and citizens we can directly influence public decisions affecting the locations, sizes, and types of stores, and we can also help steer private investment and development decisions in retailing so that they reinforce the civic and commercial critical mass which is essential for the sustenance of communities.

Shopping: Its Social Benefits in the Community

Shopping, although only one aspect of community life, is important for its role in strengthening our bonds with each other and our communities, as we all have to shop, sometimes on a daily basis, and usually in real stores near where we live. Our shopping experiences, our repeated face-to-face encounters with clerks, fellow customers, neighbors, and strangers, can enlarge our worlds, strengthen our trust in each other, and help create a sense of community. Sociologists refer to "networks of social exchanges," but whatever the term, the casual, trivial encounters day after day with the same clerks, and with familiar and random customers, build a sense of familiarity and belonging. A trust develops. Robert Putnam, a scholar on the role of social capital and the author of *Bowling Alone*, describes this type of trust as a "thick trust . . . embedded in personal relations that are strong, frequent, and nested in a wider network."[5]

In this web of trust is woven the mundane negotiations and conversations between ordinary people in and near stores. For the clerk, that trust may have an economic motive to assure continued transactions, a subject that economists have long debated, but many agree with the commonsense notion that economic behavior is influenced by social relations. For the customer, shopping has a mix of predictability and randomness with expected social situations, such as certain clerks at the cash registers at certain hours, as well as random encounters with whoever happens to be in the store or on the street at that time. It was just such repeated visits by customers and the familiarity and trust they bred that made Maya Angelou's grandmother's store the "lay center of activities" in Stamps, Arkansas, and made more than half (52 percent) of Vermonters in 1998 cite "local connection" and "closeness to home" as reasons they shopped in a downtown or a town center.[6]

Shoppers' face-to-face encounters with diverse people, the words exchanged, the body language, and the facial expressions all help to engender this basic trust. In contrast, the virtual communities of the Internet connect, "create spontaneous, serendipitous bonds," and link "people of similar interests or backgrounds," as AOL's Steve Case states. But the anonymity of virtual communities, as Case thoughtfully discussed in a talk at Harvard in 1998, "can have a corrosive effect on community. When we don't really know who we're talking to, the conversation may be exciting—but can it ever be lasting? Without knowable identities, it is difficult to sustain trust. Without trust, it is difficult to sustain community."[7] Trust, indeed, is the bedrock of community.

For Jane Jacobs, that trust can be found on the city streets and in its stores from the "many, many little public sidewalk encounters" to having a beer at a bar, "getting advice from the grocer and giving advice to the newsstand man, comparing opinions with other customers at the bakery . . . hearing about a job from the hardware man and borrowing a dollar from the druggist." But as Jacobs continues, "The sum of such casual, public contact at a local level—most of it fortuitous, most of it associated with errands, all of it metered by the person concerned and not thrust upon him by anyone— is a feeling for the public identity of people, a web of public respect and trust."[8] While the scale and types of stores have changed since 1960, when Jane Jacobs wrote *The Death and Life of Great American Cities*, we still frequent real stores with clerks where we meet our neighbors, friends, and strangers. And our shopping experiences and the kinds and locations of the stores we frequent can enlarge that web of trust and enrich our community life. As John Dewey said on his discussion of the Great Community, "In its deepest and richest sense a community must always remain a matter of face-to-face intercourse."[9]

Community: Its Public Nature

The role of community should be at the heart of any discussion about shopping and its place in American towns and cities. A basic tug exists between the desire for communal interdependence and for individual self-determinism; this tug has impeded communitarianism in planning neighborhoods, cities, or regions, and in cooperative ventures, such as co-op stores. The need to connect with others to share and serve, to be part of something larger than the self, to be involved with issues and ideas, or just to have friends and companions, is common to us all. That need and the belief in its necessity were cornerstones of the earliest colonies. John Winthrop's famous "city set upon a hill" speech described this basic Puritan concept of community. "Wee must delight in eache other, make others' Condicions our owne, rejoyce together, mourne together, labour and suffer together, allwayes haveing before our eyes our Commission and Community in the worke, our Community as members of the same body."[10] And almost a century later, Benjamin Franklin indicated his commitment to community in rejecting Pennsylvania Governor Thomas's offer of a patent for the "sole vending" of his popular Franklin stove invention on the grounds "that, as we enjoy great advantages from the inventions of others, we should be glad of an opportunity to serve others by any invention of ours and this we should do freely and generously."[11]

The Oxford English Dictionary lists eleven definitions for community, all stemming from the Latin word *communis*, meaning fellowship and community of relations or feelings. These eleven definitions range from common character, ownership, and rank to bodies of people organized into a political, municipal, or social unity, a group of plants or animals growing or living together in natural conditions or inhabiting a specified area, and, most important, life in association with others, or society as a social state. In the United States the search for community has been a much more powerful force than in many older, settled countries—because here lay a tabula rasa on which early settlers created a civilized society providing freedom and independence for individuals united in an indivisible nation. Americans were bound together in a large community governed by a Constitution prepared by and for its people. That concept of an overriding whole composed of a variety of parts inherent in federalism has been one of the most enduring features of American democracy.

For a nation of pioneers, many of whom came to the United States over the centuries to escape intolerance and the oppression of structured societies, or to seek the excitement of exploring a new world, the establishment of communities has been a priority. Some of the pioneers yearned for independence, others organized tight communities, some sought an agrarian existence, still others were lured by life on the frontier. Some clustered in dense urban neighborhoods where friends and family had settled, others pursued often unknown opportunities in pristine territories, and some groups formed utopian communities bound by shared ideals, such as the Brook Farm, New Harmony, and the Shaker settlements. The endurance of the Amish and Mennonites is a testament to communities fired by commitment. More transitory are the communities of those escaping current mainstream values, whether hippie communes of the 1960s or today's anti-government colonies. Probably the most vivid image that comes to mind when community is mentioned is the small village with its security, friendship, and comfort, which may be a sentimental veneer over a stifling and insulated world. But this Norman Rockwell village is often featured in retirement magazines and lists of the most livable places.

For all these communities, one of the driving forces has been the quest for civility and public governance not only to meet common needs but also to enrich the hearts and minds of its inhabitants. The experiences of two very different people in California's rough-and-ready mining towns in the mid- to late-nineteenth century, Josiah Royce, a philosopher, and Frederick Law Olmsted, a landscape architect, reveal this urge for civilized communities. Both men, estranged in their California milieus, yearned for a community with order, discipline, and cohesion, as in the older eastern states.

Royce, born and raised after the Gold Rush in the mining town of Grass Valley, California, felt the stings of loneliness and isolation in this lawless settlement. He saw a deep need for the civilizing force of an order, which he translated into a loyalty to the great community of individuals. Teaching at Harvard in its philosophy department's golden days of William James and George Santayana, Royce became one of the country's most profound philosophers concerned with community and idealism. For him, "man the individual . . . essentially insufficient to win the goal of his own existence" needed "man the community" as the "source of his salvation," a higher order than the individual.[12] Running against the tide of pragmatism, relativism, and irrational psychology of his time—and the American intellectual mainstream—Royce made a compelling case for his idealized community in tight Hegelian terms, so much so that James predicted that Harvard would be known, in two hundred years, as the place where Royce once taught.

From 1863 to 1865, Olmsted worked for the Mariposa Estate, a 44,000-acre gold-mining operation in the foothills of the California High Sierra. He was shocked by the lack of community there, as well as by the residents' poor working habits. The "squatterations" of settlements in these mining communities lacked a "concept of civilization based on a sense of community and loyalty to law." For Olmsted, this absence of civilization and loyalty to law stemmed from a lack of "communitiveness," a term he used to express the essential qualities of communities, serve others and be served by others "in the most intimate, complete, and extended degree imaginable." Olmsted's New England background in Puritan social thinking led him to view civilization as a fraternity, a "state of dependence or assistance or of mutual offices (civil) in distinction from savage or self dependent life."[13] Olmsted's observations of the lawlessness and lack of civilization in his Sierra mining work, combined with his earlier thinking about the South, reinforced his New England intellectual underpinnings on the importance of community. Royce had come to the same conclusion, but from a different direction. Both were determined to introduce more community into American life, Royce through his writings and teachings and Olmsted through his designs of parks, suburbs, towns, institutions, and estates. The thinking and work of these two men reflect some of the basic intellectual urges for communities.

Today that quest for civilizing community is beset by paradoxes. In an ever-shrinking global village, we can communicate with people and establish connections and "communities" more quickly than ever imagined. We can join cyberspace's burgeoning discussion groups, exchange e-mail messages in minutes, talk on the telephone from any corner of the world, and share information instantly. Yet we are also isolated in our gated developments, surrounded by spreading sprawl, and we drive long, lonely commutes and deal remotely with distant mega-corporations for most of our daily commercial transactions. We have lost much of the traditional face-to-face socializing and the public trust and respect that it breeds. At the same time, a sense of helplessness grows as remote, large, and powerful forces seem to govern our lives, making it seem pointless to get involved in community affairs. The very troubled Unabomber, articulating this feeling of helplessness in his 1995 statement, described the anguished alienation that many feel about the powerful influence of forces beyond their reach: "Our lives depend on decisions made by other people; we have no control over these decisions and usually we do not even know the people who make them. The disintegration of small-scale social groups . . . promoted by the fact that modern conditions often require or tempt individuals to move to new locations, separating themselves from their communities."[14] The Unabomber saw the individual floundering as his ties to community are severed. Yet this feeling of powerlessness, felt in different degrees by many, is indeed ironic in a democratic country whose early settlers, like John Winthrop, envisioned themselves as members of an all-encompassing community.

Interest in communities, however, is reemerging from varied sources. The popular Neo-Traditionalists have introduced strong community elements into their designs. City advocates like David Sucher in his *City Comforts* forcefully elaborate the benefits of incorporating features that make neighborhoods and cities pleasant and communal places to live. Then there are advocates of what is being called the community movement; these include Scott Peck, the author of *The Road Less Traveled*, who said, "In and through community lies the salvation of the world." His message and the movement represent a pervasive late twentieth-century reaction to America's rugged individualism on a more individual and psychological basis than Royce's and Olmsted's intellectual and perhaps elitist puritanical communal benefits. For both Royce and Olmsted, the emphasis was on the whole community. Today it is on personal uplifts, rewards, and involvements that are viewed as making up the whole. "People today are intentionally joining together," stated Shaffer and Anundsen in *Creating Community Anywhere*, "to create communities based on shared intrinsic values rather than common external threats and obligations." Scott Peck talks of the "requirement of real community—such as personal commitment, honesty, and vulnerability," words indicating the permeation of psychological thinking into our society. Community is created and maintained by individual commitments, not by external forces. "One of the things a community is not," Peck states, "is a simple geographical aggregate of people."[15]

For the recent community movement, commitment is not to societal order but more often to a group and to activities supporting groups like "family, place, clear communication or the healthy working out of conflict." For Shaffer and Anundsen, community is a "dynamic whole that emerges when groups of people participate in common practices, depend upon one another, make decisions together, identify themselves as part of something larger than the sum of the individual parts, and commit themselves for the long term to their own, one another's, and the group's well-being." This is a 1990s interpretation of much that Royce and Olmsted were talking about— today's terms are those of therapy, communicating, vulnerability, and working out conflict, but the same values of "trust, honesty, compassion, and respect" persist. Steps are enumerated for creating all sorts of communities, such as friends, interest groups, workplace, electronic, residence sharing, visionary, old neighborhoods, and depressed cities.[16] The how-to guide by Shaffer and Anundsen spells out how to establish communities step by step, and it provides a helpful bibliography. The community movement capitalizes on the assumption that people want to join, to be empowered, and to be "whole," as Shaffer terms it.

The movement addresses the dislocations and remoteness and, as they say, the lack of "back home" to go to. "Divorces have fragmented the family, the friendly street has become a shopping mall, old friends have relocated thousands of miles away. Even those who return to what looks like home do not find the kind of community in which they grew up." In discussing how to turn neighborhoods and cities into communities, experts cite the role of stores in perpetuating the village quality of urban neighborhoods, where "almost every product or service was available within walking distance. Shopkeepers watched out for the kids and performed other community services."[17] These benefits have widespread appeal—far beyond those often associated with alternate styles of living, such as late-blooming flower children and injured divorcees.

Scholars have been analyzing the economic, social, and political benefits of community orientation, and several recent studies of business and political situations have yielded interesting findings on the productive nature of communitiveness. Comparing the industrial/intellectual communities of the electronic world along Route 128 near Boston and California's Silicon Valley, AnnaLee Saxenian found that the Route 128 companies' protective and possessive attitudes prevented sharing of information with nearby electronic companies, impeded their intellectual synergy, and kept them from creating the vibrant, stimulating intellectual atmosphere of the Silicon Valley.[18] A lively network of communication and a free marketplace of ideas existed in the latter, where no ideas were privileged information and employees shifted from company to company. Harvard Business School's William Sahlman describes Silicon Valley as one company, with each corporation operating as a subsidiary. If your subsidiary does badly, "you just go next door. You join another part of the 'company.' You simply restart your [employment] contract."[19] That free-flowing exchange of ideas and people provided a stimulus to the entire industry that has been absent from Route 128. Between 1975 and 1990, Silicon Valley generated three times as many jobs as Route 128 did, produced more than twice the value of electronic products, and attracted 39 of the country's fastest-growing electronics companies compared to four on Route 128. Saxenian concluded that Route 128 seems to have "ceded [its] longstanding dominance in computer production to Silicon Valley."[20]

Silicon Valley's "dense social networks and open labor markets," according to Saxenian, "encourage entrepreneurship and experimentation," so necessary in a fast-moving industry that depends on innovation. Silicon Valley's dynamic regional network—or community—with its competition and collaboration, seems to foster intellectual stimulation more often and faster than occurs in the confines of the firms along Route 128. The lesson for communities in this industrial management analysis is the importance of the interplay between local culture and the productivity of an industry, and in the case of Silicon Valley, an open community of ideas, people, and "shared understandings and practices" in defining "everything from labor market behavior to attitudes toward risk-taking."[21] Local culture—and its communal values—shapes and is shaped by economic institutions like electronic firms.

The role of community and community involvement proved to be critical predictors of both economic and political vitality in an extensive study undertaken by Robert Putnam, professor of public policy at Harvard, who analyzed how various sections of Italy established regional governments, which were mandated by the national government in 1970. This twenty-year study evolved into a fascinating investigation of the fundamental questions of civic life. The findings illustrate that the northern sections of Italy, which had a long history of communitarianism and egalitarianism, with impressive numbers involved in such communal groups as soccer teams, choral societies, the Rotary, and unions, as well as an important sense of participating in larger societal issues—adapted to regional government far faster and more effectively than did southern Italy.

In the South, a long-standing hierarchy or patron-client relationship existed for both church and state. There, dependence and dominance ruled, so instead of people being involved as common partners in enterprises—whether regional governments or industry—they tried to win favors from the powerful. The result was that most people felt exploited, powerless, and alienated. Less educated than northerners, the southerners seemed content with their way of life, as indicated in the findings that more than half of the those who attended mass rarely read the newspapers or discussed politics. The southerners seemed "more concerned about the city of God than the city of man," according to Putnam. No wonder that the Mafia has been so successful in southern Italy. In the north, "collective life . . . is eased by the expectation that others will probably follow the rules," but in the south rules were not considered binding.[22]

The mistrust and insecurity that such civic incivility breeds are essential to the success of the Mafia. "Distrust percolates through the social ladder," according to Diego Gambetta, "and the unpredictability of sanctions generated uncertainty in agreements, stagnation in commerce and industry, and a general reluctance toward impersonal and extensive forms of cooperation." Here "one feels too much the 'I' and too little the 'we,'" Pasquale Villari stated in 1883. This vertical ladder of authority and power, with its favors and tyranny, contrasts sharply with the horizontal pattern of collaboration and solidarity in the north—and it affects every aspect of life. It is a pattern with deep roots into history. Putnam found that today's most civic regions matched the "heartlands of republicanism in 1300."[23]

Not only has civic government prospered in the north, so have industry and commerce. The north's cultural climate of reciprocity, similar to that in the Silicon Valley, and its social, political, and civic networks stimulate exchange of information, provide credibility and reliability for workers, investors, and mutual trust—all essential for dynamism in commerce and industry. "Innovation depends," Putnam observes, "on continual informal interaction in cafes and bars and in the streets," for that base of "mutual trust, social cooperation, and a well-developed sense of civic duty . . . the hallmarks of the civic community" makes ideas flow, risks possible, and commitments meaningful. "It is no surprise that these highly productive small-scale industrial districts are concentrated in those very regions of north-central Italy that . . . [are] highlighted as centers of civic tradition, of the contemporary civic community, and of high performance regional government."[24]

Turning his attention to modern America, Putnam finds civic or social capital—all those networks, values, and the trust needed to produce cooperation and community involvement—at a low ebb, according to his January 1995 article "Bowling Alone." The title of this article makes his point: Putnam discovered that more than 80 million people bowled in 1993, a 10 percent increase from 1980, but in that same period there was a 40 percent drop in those playing in organized leagues. Similarly, attendance at public meetings on school or town affairs fell from 22 percent in 1973 to 13 percent in 1981, PTA attendance dropped from 12 million in 1964 to 7 million in 1994, and those who trusted Washington, D.C., "some of the time, or almost never" jumped from 30 percent in 1966 to 75 percent in 1992.[25] Coupled with this drop in civic engagement, Putnam also found a decrease in neighborliness, as measured in time spent with neighbors; figures indicated that between 1961 and 1974 those who socialized with their neighbors more than once a year fell from 72 percent to 61 percent.

This drop in civic involvement, social trust, and just "social connectedness" was seen by Putnam as resulting from multiple factors, including the increase of women in the workforce, greater mobility, technological changes in leisure—with television a major factor—demographic changes, and the large scale of economic activities. Illustrating the changes in the scale of economic activities, Putnam cites the takeover of local businesses by multinational conglomerates, and "the replacement of the corner grocery by the supermarket and now perhaps by electronic shopping at home," and the consolidation of small post offices and school districts.[26]

As he found the informal socializing in Italy's cafes and bars helpful in encouraging social interactions, so he also sees the change to larger-scale and remote patterns of shopping in the United States as an influence in reducing social capital. Although participation in the many support groups, networks, and large mass-membership organizations might be seen as counterweights to a diminishing social capital, these are not communal activities, as Putnam points out, but rather "their ties . . . are to common symbols, common leaders, and perhaps common ideals, but not to one another."[27]

To reverse the erosion of social capital, Putnam emphasizes the role of voluntary associations in his book *Bowling Alone*. He looks to "an era of civic inventiveness to create a renewed set of institutions and channels for a reinvigorated civic life"—an era in which "the twenty-first century equivalent of the Boys Scouts or the settlement house or the playground" could be reinvented. Recognizing the role of planning, he challenges planners, developers, homebuyers, and community organizers "to ensure that by 2010 Americans will spend less time traveling and more time connecting with our neighbors than we do today, that we live in more integrated and pedestrian-friendly areas, and that the design of our communities and the availability of public space will encourage more casual socializing with friends and neighbors."[28] The new interest in the community movement and in Neo-Traditional planning, as well as in simplified living, indicate support of Putnam's proposals.

But breaking through the mistrust, fears, and doubts that impede greater communality is tough, as organizers of one type of communal project, co-housing, have found. In Washington, D.C., a group of twenty people, including families, singles, and the elderly, spent three frustrating years trying to find a location in suburban Maryland for a co-housing development. Regulations like zoning, compounded by neighborhood fears of group living, made it impossible for the group to find a site. As the years went on, the group shrank as some members found conventional housing, others located in co-housing farther from traditional suburban development, and others dropped out. A new co-housing group formed years later, and members did find a site in the Takoma Park section of Washington, D.C.

Communal solidarity itself may be difficult to achieve. Overwhelming changes in scale of corporations, technology, and communication reduce or even eliminate many of the small-scale institutions inculcating communitiveness. The strong individualistic bent of Americans, and the pull of entrepreneurial free enterprise, result in people's reluctance to join communal activities. And the rules and dogma established to protect individual property can complicate and even obstruct the process of establishing community. Antipathy to government, its taxes, its welfare and health care programs, its pensions, its support of education, and its protection of the environment crescendoed in the 1990s to the point of closing down the government. All this mirrors increasing fears, anxieties, and insecurities, which erode civility and social trust.

Yet there is an equally strong strain toward union, federalism, communitiveness, and plain, open sociability. The bonds of sharing, caring, and working together for a common good have been integral in American democracy throughout history, in public and private agencies, and, most important, in the hearts and minds of the people. Americans are committed "to form a more perfect Union," as the preamble to the Constitution states.

The critical initial steps toward ameliorating deficits in the communal and social capital are being taken. First, the topic is being discussed in different ways in different forums, and its need is recognized, whether in books like Putnam's *Bowling Alone*, in community designs like the Neo-Traditionalists', or in the many communities being formed in the more progressive parts of this country.

The pace and scale of change are staggering, but several letters and op-ed pieces in the *New York Times* are reminders that community, its sociability, and its institutions are still valued. A letter writer from a Los Angeles expatriate living in New York comments that life in such a crowded city, where one is constantly mingling with varied people, produces more tolerance for diversity than in life in a sprawling area like Los Angeles, where the automobile isolates and segregates its citizens. The writer suggests that New York City's tolerance for its diverse citizens might well prevent the type of riots Los Angeles suffered in Watts in 1965. An editorial after Christmas 1995 extolled the comfort of Fifth Avenue's familiar Christmas decorations—comparing it to the "pleasure that comes from meeting an old friend," especially in a city where the "restaurant you patronized on Monday disappears by Wednesday, where shops have the life span of mayflies."[29] After the blizzard of 1996 a Cambridge, Massachusetts, writer, operating out of her "virtual office" at home, found herself talking with her neighbors, as she had not for months, when they shoveled their adjacent sidewalks and complained about the nuisances of the storm. "The weather became a costly nuisance," she wrote in an op-ed piece, "but perhaps it was a bargain."[30] Incremental incidents of neighborliness, the pleasure of familiarity, whether in Christmas decorations or in the shops we frequent, and the lessons of tolerance are steps toward creating the climate needed for the kind of community we all seek.

Consuming and Retailing: Their Public Side

"The problem is you can't take long vacations—things just change too quickly."[31] That statement by a CEO of a national property development company, who was discussing shopping malls in Witold Rybczynski's class at the University of Pennsylvania, captures the volatility of the world of shopping—where indeed "shops have the life span of mayflies." The interplay between the changing needs, desires, and tastes of consumers and new ways of selling goods and services produces that volatility, which throughout history has accounted for much of the democratization of shopping. And that will continue as long as society is fluid and open and "habits of heart" can change, as Tocqueville stated.

The glamour, grace, and luxury of the big-city department stores in the early twentieth century—opening doors to new worlds for many, both literally and figuratively, and providing an obvious democratization of luxury—have been largely replaced by an egalitarian and bare-bones style of shopping, once found only in low-end stores, like New York's S. Klein's on Union Square, but found everywhere in discount stores, Category Killers, and Big Boxes in cities, suburbs, and rural areas. Shopping at these stores, buying from mail-order catalogues, or ordering through the Internet offers none of the pleasures of dressing up, going downtown, looking with wonder at a store's windows and displays, meeting friends for lunch in the store restaurant, and discussing potential purchases with a knowledgeable sales clerk. But then modern shopping is easier, quicker, and maybe cheaper—and there are many shopping options.

While specialty stores, boutiques, and upscale markets will continue to prosper for the carriage trade, mainstream shopping seems to be heading in the very different direction of quick accessibility, bulk purchasing, and no-frills environments. As lives have changed among dual-earning families with heavy debts and looming costs of college and medical care, time and money for shopping has shrunk, as has the desire of many baby boomers to fill their closets and houses with more and more possessions. The shopping mall developer must keep his eyes and ears open to changing consumer desires, and so must manufacturers, advertising agencies, and all of the industries related to the consumer market. The yin and yang of consumer changes—some generated by deep-seated personal responses to changing directions, others influenced by superficial advertisements, and yet others by exigencies of their immediate situations—make the entire field of shopping a mirror of the mores, habits, and desires of people.

Even the meanings of the words "consume" and "consumption" have changed over time, reflecting changing societal attitudes. "Consume" has been used in English from about the fourteenth century. Derived from the French *consumer* and the Latin *consumere*, meaning to devour, waste, spend, or take up completely, it had the negative connotations of destroying, using up, and wasting, according to Raymond Williams in his fascinating book *Keywords*. That negative meaning still exists in tubercular consumption and "consumed by fire." But with the emergence of the bourgeois economy in the middle of the eighteenth century, "consume" developed a more neutral connotation. In the new industrialization and marketing, producing and using goods and services came to be paired abstractly as producer and consumer and production and consumption, according to Williams. The negative connotations of consuming continued until the middle of the twentieth century, when consuming started to be used as a popular and general word rather than just an economic one. With the development of large-scale industrialism and advertising, and with all the ramifications of marketing, the consumer became the "creation of such manufacturers and their agents." More recently, due to heightened concern for the environment and conservation of natural resources, consumer society and consumption have reclaimed some of that early negative connotation of wasting and using up. It is interesting to note that "consumer" has always projected a more abstract impression than "customer," which has "implied some degree of regular and continuing relationship to a supplier," market, stores, or shop.[32]

In the ever-changing world of consumers, shopping, and community values, the recent swing toward simplicity seems a serious switch in directions, one that may greatly influence the world of shopping and its role in communities. The confluence of the moral and environmental concerns of people turned off by the excessive materialism of the 1980s and 1990s, and new uncertainties about job security, have lowered sights and produced tighter shopping budgets. This means not only less entertainment shopping but reduced numbers of shopping trips and fewer purchases. Add to that the proliferating options of nonstore shopping—television, telephone, mail order, and the Internet, for example—and perhaps real stores will not expand as they did at the end of the twentieth century. Who would have thought fifty years ago that the downtown department stores would vanish? The same fate may hit our large private shopping malls, discount malls, Power Centers, and Category Killers. Going to the mall on Saturday for recreation may become a thing of the past, and shopping as entertainment may be difficult to sustain. The penetration of shopping into every activity, as Disney has so successfully demonstrated, may turn off consumers, who are tired of being manipulated. The Naughton family from Cresskill, New Jersey, with three children from ten to sixteen years of age, found their dream of Disney World tarnished by its materialism, which hit them at every turn during their first family visit.[33] If the simplicity movement continues to gain in popularity, its impact will be felt in more and different circles.

The future seems to hold less shopping, more remote shopping, more bargain shopping, less shopping for personal self-defining purposes, and more shopping for products that are healthful, environmentally sound, communally beneficial, and aesthetically pleasing. If shoppers are buying less, they are going to be sure that their purchases fit their budget and their personal and community needs, like the co-op purchasers of organic food whose attitudes seem to be spreading. The expansion of chain stores selling "organic" and healthful products, such as Whole Foods, proves that what had been attracting a limited market of health-conscious customers now is attracting a much more generalized market. Even the large chain supermarkets are catching on to this new market, as they now feature organically grown produce, fresh turkeys, and free-range eggs. The Schumacher pitch of "small is beautiful" of the 1960s and the "less is more" of the recent simplicity movement are being increasingly adopted by more people, including those who dwell far from alternate lifestyle centers like Amherst, Massachusetts, Berkeley, California, Missoula, Montana, and Portland, Oregon.

The continuous tension between the freedom of the individual, the appeal of the unfettered free enterprise system, the role of material objects as symbols of success, and, on the other hand, the role of the community, the values of sharing, and the urge to return to less material values, means that no matter how significant the changes are toward diminished materialism and shopping, the fantasy, excitement, and hopes of shopping will never disappear. Tidal changes of values, economics, and social mores can occur, but the emotions that overcame Virginia Woolf as she tried on the new dress will always exist—as retailers well know.

Another paradox in shopping is the role of service in the bare-bones style of discount shopping. Along with the veneer of luxury and glamour, traditional service has been eliminated from most of contemporary shopping.

Yet as shopping has become more basic, there is also recognition that people yearn for service and personal attention. The restaurant waiter's mechanical greeting—"My name is Tom and I am your waiter this evening"—is an attempt to add a personal touch to mass eating in franchised restaurants, or in any restaurant. The personalized touch has arrived at the big discounters, as Wal-Mart's greeters meet you at the door and Loehmann's provides its club members with information when sought-after items are available. While many of these attempts at service may be programmed, they indicate that business recognizes the need to treat customers like more than numbers. This trend toward more personal attention seems a logical answer to the larger scale, remoteness, impersonality, loss of loyalty, and globalization of so many businesses involved with our daily life, including retailing.

Yet another paradox directly related to shopping can be seen in the narrowing and widening of gaps between types of stores and types of customers—and incomes of customers. As the gap between moderate-priced and discount stores narrows, the gap between the "have" and "have not" shoppers widens, as upper-end stores, modern technology for shopping (like the Internet), and credit cards are available mainly to the haves. And those trends seem to be strengthening.

The changes in the "habits of heart" and pendulum swings in economic, political, and social concerns produce new directions and commitments, inducing dramatic changes in social consciousness. The civil rights movement righted past wrongs and turned the United States in what seems an inevitable direction, so that a child of today cannot comprehend that certain people had to go to the back of the bus, eat in special areas, and go to segregated schools. The environmental movement stirred interests in personal and community health to the point where overt polluting of air or water is considered irresponsible. Smoking, a habit for most people only twenty years ago, is banned in many public places and recognized as a health hazard by the majority and an addictive activity by many. So, too, many of the excessive aspects of shopping of the 1980s and 1990s may seem out of tune with mainstream values in the future.

Planning for Shopping in the Community: Public Actions

When shopping's social and economic impacts are recognized as having important public consequences in communities, shopping moves into a new arena of public attention and concern. That public significance of shopping has not yet been acknowledged. Even England, which has paid considerably more attention to shopping and its role in community life than other nations, has had trouble deciding whether shopping is a social or economic activity, according to Dorothy Davis in her 1966 history of shopping. Well, it is both, as England has admitted and as the United States is beginning to acknowledge.

Although retailing is the world's oldest activity, according to the 1967 edition of *The Columbia Encyclopedia*, it remains one of the most neglected. More courses on it in planning, design, social work, American studies, and even in business graduate programs, and more community involvement in plans for retail areas are essential if shopping is to receive careful public attention. Not until a store puts up its going-out-of-business signs does the public usually realize that it is shutting down. Then it is too late for the public to intervene. Unlike residential neighborhoods, where vocal residents are ready to thwart highway incursions or loss of parkland, commercial districts rarely have such outspoken local constituents or advocates. That typical divide between community and commerce, between residents of a neighborhood, city, or region and its shopping facilities, needs to be narrowed. Community and commerce are dependent on each other yet have not worked well together. Suspicion, mistrust, and disdain often prevent cooperative planning and activities. The public benefits from accessible, friendly, and profitable shops, as the shops benefit from supportive customers and public controls.

Recognition of the public impacts of shopping would lead to greater public planning of shopping in communities, cities, and regions. Rejection of public governance, evidenced in the conservative efforts to protect private property rights, have undermined planning and its ability to regulate land use. Fearful of government regulations reducing the values of property or restricting the uses of property, citizens and conservative groups have campaigned to block planning through legislation and litigation invalidating regulations, forcing compensation, or adding roadblocks. Should government pay a landowner not to develop a floodplain or not to build on a barrier island? The answer will hinge on the acceptance of public governance and the government's right to regulate land in the public interest for the future, as well as on the public's attitude toward the private sector. Respect for public governance and planning will return when it becomes apparent that profit-making, not public interest, is the goal of private corporations and institutions. But planners need to abandon the wimpy role of facilitating whatever development hints at creating more jobs and tax revenue; they must strengthen their backbone so that they can assert publicly shared goals and visions and enforce them imaginatively.

Careful analysis of retail needs, as a first step, might help in determining what kinds of retailing are needed where and when, as Bauer and Stein did in Radburn. In the past, planners—with the backing of the local Chambers of Commerce—have often overestimated and then overzoned the space required for commerce and retailing, so locales have often ended up with excessively long, and underused, commercially zoned streets. Also, the rigid mind-set of segregated land uses needs to be softened so that shopping can blend in with offices and housing to provide lively and accessible communities. Coming full circle, shopping has returned to the home, but, instead of shops in front of artisans' houses, as in the late Middle Ages, they are now on the computer or television screen. With remote shopping taking care of many purchasing needs, the close-to-home stores will need to be accessible, speedy, service-oriented, friendly, and rooted in a community. For those who stare at the computer monitor for hours, having a face-to-face discussion with a shopkeeper or neighbor may seem like an anachronism, but opportunities for friendly, nearby shopping will grow increasingly popular. Also, the need for planning flexibility in allowing and even encouraging unexpected and community-enhancing retailing is another area for planners. The popularity of the flea market, tag sale, and farmers' market can be provided in many ways, but the need for such unorganized and adventurous shopping will become a greater public asset in communities. A new phenomenon is the retail/wholesale operation oozing out of the cracks of warehouse and industrial districts. While not necessarily planned, such retailing must be recognized as a popular, economical way to obtain many supplies, and such activities should not be scorned because they do not fit into established zones. Instead, they should be seen as incubators for commercial activities that could benefit the community at large.

Trends in planning point to a greater intersection between the public and private sectors—and that will certainly be true as planners try to strengthen the community function of shopping. Many successful examples of these interactions already occur. Whether on Main Street or in a mall, public activities and buildings, like a city hall, community center, post office, or a performing arts center, can provide a stability that offsets the fickle nature of retailing.

Public Uses in Private Places

Public-private partnerships abound in this era of downgraded public government and elevated respect for private initiatives, but permitting public activities in the malls—the most important shopping places since World War II—has been strained. Turning malls into the new town centers, as Gruen and other early mall developers predicted, has not occurred. Certainly all sorts of activities, functions, and institutions exist in shopping malls, but their functions have been limited because they are tenants in a private place. By promoting their safety and security, in contrast to the crime and violence of the outside world, shopping malls have limited such freedoms as free speech and access, along with their potential serendipitous opportunities, traditionally available on the downtown street.

Yet for these controlled environments to survive, shopping malls must be recognized as the new town centers in many suburban areas, as the New Jersey court decisions point out. And as the big department stores vanish and shoppers turn to nonstore shopping opportunities, malls may well have to look to public institutions and activities to stay afloat. A larger infusion of public institutions—post offices, schools, town halls, libraries, community colleges, federal and state offices—will not only help to keep the malls from bankruptcy but will add useful civic institutions to these private places.

If a downtown store went out of business, just one building would be affected. But in the case of the massive malls—some with more than a million square feet of space and tens of acres of parking lots—a gigantic tract of land with gargantuan buildings would lie idle like a downed giant. Rather than becoming an economic and social loss (and eyesore), a dead shopping area could be revived with public activities into more of a civic hub. And many sprawling suburban areas with few old town centers desperately need a civic center. Such a public-private partnership will require a change in management practices for shopping malls, however: a change that will be difficult because it will mean a lessening of control and security, a key selling point of modern malls.

Private Uses in Public Places

Attracting private commercial retail activities to public places is yet another way of stimulating a community's economic and social capital. This recognition of the social role of shopping and commercial retail activities has taken many different forms. In Mill Valley, a town of 22,000 nestled outside San Francisco in up-market Marin County, an old railroad station in the center of town was bought by the city to assure that it be used for community public uses. Having turned down a proposal to operate a restaurant in the old station because it would attract tourists (referred to as "visitors" by the locals), the city decided to rent the space to a bookstore and coffeehouse. Now the Depot Bookstore and Coffeehouse and the adjacent outdoor plaza with chairs and benches have become a safe and inviting space: a major meeting place for the community. On a Sunday morning, people of many ages gather for coffee with their newspapers to just pass the time of day—the way people lolled around the country store at the crossroads. This public-private operation is indeed a friendly place (fig. 104).

Garrett Park, Maryland, a suburb of Washington, D.C., purchased in 1976 a historic 1880s building near its railroad station, which has become the town's meeting place. It has rental space for various businesses: a real estate firm, local press, restaurant, and most important, the town offices and post office. This town, named after a president of the Baltimore & Ohio Railroad, which developed this garden suburb in the late nineteenth century, has always had a strong sense of community. Now absorbed in the Washington suburban area, Garrett Park voted down home mail delivery, according to Paul Edlund, the town's ex-mayor, who lived there with his family for

104. Mill Valley, California's popular coffeehouse, bookstore, and meeting place, 1994

105. The post office, town offices, and restaurant in Garrett Park, Maryland, 1999

thirty-eight years, so that it could keep its post office and provide the towns-people "the opportunity of seeing people you might not see otherwise" (fig. 105).[34]

That was in 1976. By 1996, the U.S. Postal Service was not so sympa-thetic with small communities keeping their old downtown post offices. Mod-ernized mail service, better suited to larger, one-story buildings with truck access and plenty of parking, does not fit into the cramped older post office, argues the Postal Service. Proximity to the railroad station and downtown are no longer needed, as mail, once transported by rail and sorted on the trains, now is trucked or flown into towns. So the post offices—just like big retail-ers—leave downtown for roomier sites, often in standardized buildings on the edge of towns, near highways and airports, and in so doing nip away at the heart of civic life in communities. To the Postal Service, these locational decisions are "just business decisions, real estate decisions," states Richard Moe, president of the National Trust for Historic Preservation. But the "post office needs to understand its social function," Moe continued. It's the "glue that keeps communities together."[35]

Losing the downtown post office is a jolt to small-town civic life. After all, "downtown is a community," noted Charlene Beckett of Abbeville, Louisiana, which lost its old post office in 1996. As this worker on the town's Main Street program, operated through the National Trust, reminisced, "You wander to the post office, get your mail, and bid everyone good day. That community feeling is missing."[36]

Livingston, Montana, a town of 6,500 in the southern part of the state, learned in 1996 that the Postal Service wanted to replace its eighty-four-year-old downtown post office with a large facility (double the size of its current building) that could accommodate modernized mail service—probably out of town. Despite strip development—also out of town—and the loss of the railroad, Livingston had managed to keep a "historic downtown that is very viable," according to Councilwoman Caron Cooper. After much negotiation, Livingston retained its downtown post office for customer service while the Postal Service built an out-of-town facility for its "modernized" operations.[37] In Saratoga Springs, New York, home of James Howard Kunstler, author of *The Geography of Nowhere*, the Postal Service also compromised, after a struggle in 1994, by retaining the downtown post office for stamps and post boxes and moving the mail sorting to a building away from downtown.

Most communities, however, have not been so effective in dealing with the fast-charging Postal Service. Their concerns about post office relocations, closings, and consolidations, backed by many governors, reached Capitol Hill, where Congressman Earl Blumenauer (D-Oregon) introduced in 1997 legislation to "strengthen the voice of local citizens in decisions to relocate and rebuild post offices."[38] This bill, paired with a Senate bill, garnered strong support on Capitol Hill and among national organizations like the National League of Cities, the International Downtown Association, the American Planning Association, and the National Trust for Historic Preservation to require the Postal Service to comply with local planning and zoning, provide more public notice, and give greater consideration to community concerns.[39] This legislative initiative triggered the Postal Service to issue new community relations regulations in 1999. While these new regulations indicate an effort by the Postal Service to be more receptive to community interests, they miss the mark, as the Postal Service is not willing to totally comply with local planning and zoning. Compliance hinges on whether "doing so is consistent with prudent business practices and unique postal requirements."[40] Another loophole appeared as the Postal Service owns only 20 percent of its post offices; the rest are leased.

The post office controversy is significant because it is yet another example of Americans' deep attachment to community life. "Post offices are the heart and soul of America's small towns, drawing people to main streets and preserving the core of these communities," as Blumenauer stated. The legislative debate about the bills and all the community activism on the issue also illustrate the need for a partnership between local citizens and their government agencies, as the House bill is now aptly entitled Post Office Community Partnerships Act.[41]

Parks are another public responsibility being divided between public agencies and private nonprofit operations—and offering communal benefits. Traditionally, many parks and other public facilities have had private concessionaires to provide restaurants, shops, and hostelries. Perhaps best known for their long-term concessionaires are the national parks, where the famous hotels in Yosemite, Grand Canyon, and Yellowstone have been run by private companies under contract to the National Park Service. Some state and local parks have followed suit. New York's remarkable Central Park and Bryant Park now are managed and maintained by public/private partnerships. Both are public parks whose land is owned by the city.

The early 1990s transformation of Bryant Park, located behind the New York Public Library, from a drug-ridden, underused park in the heart of New York City to a spruced-up, well-maintained, and well-patrolled—and extremely popular—park results from the successful efforts of the Bryant Park Restoration Corporation. This nonprofit private management corporation, started in the 1970s, cooperates with a Business Improvement District of neighboring property owners and the city, whose commissioner of parks and recreation sits on its board of directors. Boasting that it uses the "best techniques of private business," the Bryant Park partnership has created an "island of civility" and "reinscribed secure middle-class values within the urban center," according to *New York Times* architecture critic Herbert Muschamp.[42] Sitting in chairs in the sun, reading the newspaper, picnicking on the welcoming grass, or just strolling along the formal walks is possible for anyone (fig. 106). It feels safe and comforting—a reminder of the days when cities seemed alive and well. Abutting the library building is a privately operated restaurant and cafe, its trellised views of the park providing an almost bucolic atmosphere for those who want to enjoy the verdant pleasures of the park along with a nice meal.

In Central Park another public-private partnership has been at work. Since 1980 the Central Park Conservancy has been coordinating with the city's Department of Parks and Recreation to restore and manage Central Park so that it can again be the beautiful and safe oasis that Frederick Law Olmsted and Calvert Vaux envisioned in 1858. This nonprofit organization has raised almost $300 million, which has enabled it to prepare a restoration and management plan following the original Olmsted/Vaux design, fund

106. Even in the dead of winter, people enjoy Bryant Park, New York, 2000

capital improvements, and offer new programs for visitors and volunteers. The effectiveness of the Central Park Conservancy was recognized in 1998 when it was awarded by the city a management contract for maintenance, public programming, and capital restoration of the entire park. The conservancy has also become one of the most highly visible role models in effective American public-private partnership in parks.

As cities and towns grapple with dire financial situations, all sorts of public-private partnerships are being constructed to meet public needs. Main Street merchants from large city downtowns like Philadelphia's to city neighborhoods like Washington, D.C.'s Georgetown and New York's Greenwich Village are turning to Business Improvement Districts to supplement municipal services like garbage collection, merchandising events, beautification efforts, and security patrols. Through a tax on participating merchants, funds are distributed by the board of the business district to its priority projects. While a general Chamber of Commerce–type of enthusiasm among merchants exists for this kind of private partnership, the small merchants sometimes feel that they are being bulldozed by the larger, more influential ones, thereby producing a small merchant–big merchant rift. In terms of community benefits, community organizations often participate as voting members of these districts, but that may not necessarily be enough of a check to assure that communal interests are met.

Difficulties in revitalizing these retailing areas are sometimes more serious and systemic than merchants realize, so the cosmetic and security responses, usually the first step in many districts, are ineffectual in tackling the real problems. As Kennedy Lawson Smith, director of the National Main Street Center, wrote, "BIDs [Business Improvement Districts] are fair and equitable—within the commercial district itself." But the critical question she asks is, "Are they fair within the broader community?" The answer is no, because attention in BIDs and other revitalization efforts is too often focused narrowly on the local downtown, not on the wider region generating the new retailing. In fact, "those businesses out on the strip are getting away with economic murder—and getting off free," Smith correctly states. "The reason that most communities need to revitalize their traditional commercial districts is because they have created too much commercial space." She suggests, "Why not make the businesses and developers who want to add more commercial space pay an assessment to offset the economic damage that will almost certainly affect existing commercial centers in the region?" Even more basic than a tax assessment is the need for broader regional planning, which could help many older commercial centers avoid some of the problems plaguing them, like out-of-town superstores—dubbed "economic blackmail" by Smith.[43]

Eighth Street between Fifth and Sixth avenues in Greenwich Village, once a street with refined bookstores, restaurants like the Jumble Shop, and stores catering to the city's intellectuals, artists, and bohemians, has deteriorated into a tawdry strip of shops selling T-shirts, metal-studded belts, jarring music, and all the sundries sold on similar strips, like New Orleans' Bourbon Street. The sounds, sights, smells, and customers of these shops are a far cry from the warm and pleasant atmosphere of yesteryear Greenwich Village. In an effort to restore some class to this Main Street of Greenwich Village, two dozen businesses along Eighth Street have formed a Business Improvement District. Graffiti removal, street sweeping, and private security patrols, along with open grill, pull-down window grates, have been the early responses of the BID to the tawdriness of this street. The window security grates stirred a fuss because they violated the landmark regulations of Greenwich Village's historic district after the BID started to use part of a $72,000 Urban Development Corporation grant for the job, which would have provided a $400 reimbursement to businesses converting to the grates. But whether there are window grates or improved signs or clean streets is irrelevant when it comes to dealing with the festering causes of the blight. The basic issues are what the shops sell and, therefore, whom they attract. New York is not tackling the problem of the uses of the stores, as have Carmel, California, and English cities and towns, including London's Chelsea on King's Road.

Certainly the concern of inner-city retail areas to project an image of safe, upbeat areas is understandable. But the problems facing such areas go far beyond image-making and maintenance and into the realm of supporting healthy retailing, which responds to the needs of changing consumer needs, to providing affordable rents and controlling uses and activities. Public-private partnerships, now so popular, can tackle some of those problems, but such partnerships often lack the breadth of interest, the sophistication, and experience to take on serious systemic problems. Also, these partnerships can be skewed by whichever partner has more clout and money; in most cases, that is the private sector. For example, the deals between cities and the Rouse Company for festival marketplaces reveal that cities have often yielded prime sites, like Baltimore's waterfront and Boston's Faneuil Hall, at ridiculously low rates in a desperate effort to renew themselves. Sometimes, because of the involvement of the private sector, the public facility or space is perceived as a totally private operation. Because Bryant Park's maintenance, restaurant, and security are operated by the Bryant Park partnership, one almost forgets that the park is owned by the city of New York. Contributors can sway decisions, fads can captivate private operators, and functions such as two week-long fashion shows a year can limit public use of the park. Such public-private partnerships are meeting some current problems, but will they do so in the long term? And will today's assumption that imagination and innovation are primarily products of the private sector continue?

Private Places and Public Interests

The basic axiom is that private places that recognize community functions will benefit themselves and the larger community. Communities will be energized when stores, downtowns, Main Streets, and malls weave in vital, face-to-face, neighborly activities, and likewise stores and commercial establishments attract business and swell their profit margins. Often such communitiveness has been automatically incorporated into small-scale retail-commercial operations, like the general store at the country crossroads and the neighborhood convenience store. On the other hand, the large department stores in the beginning of the century, like Selfridge's, Marshall Field, and the downtown flagship stores in every middling or large city, worked hard to make themselves a community fixture—a "community center," as Selfridge aptly stated.

That interest in being part of the community, being seen as a community center, faded in the latter half of the twentieth century as the ownership, management, and policies in retailing and commercial development adapted to changing times. Marvin Taubman converted Bloomingdale's from what he saw as a drab, homely store—albeit a neighborhood fixture—to a jazzy emporium that helped to jolt retailing into a new style of marketing. National chains, conglomerates, and large department store operators like Federated and May took over stores in city after city, closed center-city flagship stores, tinkered with mall stores, and removed many community features, such as community rooms and restaurants. Boutiques invaded the higher-end shopping areas, fancy malls, and festival marketplaces, adding some color and "fun" to such shopping spots. Franchised stores like the Gap, Limited, Nature Company, Laura Ashley, Crabtree and Evelyn, and The Wiz proliferated in malls, innards of buildings, and historic preservation villages.

Shopping became recreational, just as the retail marketing strategists hoped, but it also became disenfranchised from the community. It seemed that the hands of the distant mega-corporations were reaching all the way down to the neighborhood 7-Eleven, with their guidelines for pushing up short-term profits, which did not necessarily include considerations for the long-term benefits of encouraging face-to-face, or socially responsible shopping. Since the mid-1990s, however, a new concern for shopping that relates to both the local and global community has emerged.

Interest in health foods, regionally grown on family farms with respect for environmental axioms and labor laws, has spread all over the country and is evidence of a concern for the global community, the welfare of the environment, and human rights. The popularity of the colorfully arranged produce at the Korean greengrocers in inner cities is an indicator of this attention to health and ecology. Like many other cities, the upper-income section of Washington, D.C., was inundated with a rash of new up-market healthy food stores—Fresh Fields, Sutton Place Gourmet, Bread and Circus, and Dean and Deluca. A videocassette sent to neighbors when Bread and Circus (now Fresh Fields/Whole Food) opened in upper Georgetown, featured clerks and customers describing the wonders of their food, produce, and service, and a message from its manager, Chris Hitt, saying how he looked forward to being part of the community. New York City's new Uptown Fairway Market on 133rd Street has meant that Harlem residents can buy the fresh fruit, vegetables, and meat that were previously available only to customers of the West Side Fairway, known for its wide selection of gourmet items. Nagging negatives of the store's seemingly disingenuous tangles with the city's zoning regulators and its threats to the smaller businesses have been offset by the enthusiasm of the customers, the 150 jobs the store added to the local economy, and the hope that the store will stimulate more economic development and jobs in the area. Such a market meets both local and global community concerns.

The small and large, local and chain bookstores, with their cafes, lounge chairs, roaring fires, and community events show how commercial operations can capitalize on their place in a community. People hanging around reading magazines, attending readings, and meeting friends for coffee is good business for bookstores and for the neighborhood. Coffee cafes, once dotting only such friendly cities as San Francisco, Portland, Oregon, and Seattle, have appeared in every large city in every corner of the United States. They are becoming neighborhood meeting places—maybe not for the group that gathered at the fountain of the five-and-ten or the local lunchroom-cafe, but for many educated middle-class customers with few ties to their neighbors or the community. Like the bookstores, they offer opportunities for face-to-face sociability.

The arts can be another stimulant to both the sense of community as well as its economic well-being. In Cheverly, Maryland, a suburb of Washington "on the wrong side of the tracks" in Prince Georges County, the conversion of a movie theater into a community theater, the Prince Georges Publick Playhouse, raised a community spirit among the performing artists and audiences, while the nearby shops and restaurants gained new life and people converged on the once sagging downtown.

Peekskill, New York, for years a run-down Hudson River city where traditional commercial and industrial activities died or deserted the old downtown, has revitalized itself by inducing artists to live and work there. Peekskill's planner, with advice from a consultant, decided that its empty stores and upper floors might appeal to artists if the price was right. Advertising in magazines and newspapers read by artists living in Greenwich Village, SoHo, Tribeca, and other New York City enclaves of artists, Peekskill offered low rents, community support for housing, and gallery space in its downtown buildings. Though it is just thirty minutes from Pennsylvania Station by train, hugging the banks of the majestic Hudson River, Peekskill was not removed from the bright lights of the big city yet could provide a quiet community. The city's gamble worked. Artists were lured by the cheap rents. They liked the smaller community atmosphere, yet they were never far from New York. With grants from the National Endowment for the Arts and local help, the city was able to convert buildings into artists' housing and provide living space above the storefronts. Ground-floor space was transformed into galleries, and later there were artist supply stores, antiques shops, and restaurants (fig. 107). The artists energized the downtown and created a community for themselves and a new life for the city.

In Wooster, Ohio, Freedlanders' Department Store remains a downtown anchor in this county seat because of unusually enlightened private initiatives and public actions. After three generations of Freedlanders running the store, there were no Freedlanders left in the 1980s to take over. Recognizing the critical role of the store in the community, the last Freedlander owner/operator donated the store building to the city, which still has a downtown post office, functioning stores (thanks to an early and active Main Street program), a prominent county courthouse—and no malls. The responsibility for the store was transferred to the city's community improvement agency, Wooster Growth Corporation, headed by the city's attorney, Richard Benson. The city continues as the owner of the store, but the renovation of the building and the retailing operation were undertaken by a group of investors, all long-term Wooster businesspeople and residents. In 2001, the business of running the store was bought from the investors by Stanley Gault, another Wooster resident and former CEO of Rubbermaid, one of the city's major industries. This community, which boasts having the world's largest Amish population, Wooster College, a branch of Ohio State University, an agricul-

107. Galleries and housing for artists in Peekskill, New York, 1998

tural research center, several automobile parts companies, and Rubbermaid, can also be proud that it has a publicly owned, privately operated downtown department store. Although its lines of merchandise and the size of its retailing operation are more limited than they were in the days of the Freedlanders, the continuation of this important Wooster institution provides convenient shopping, bolsters the downtown economy and the community identity, and confirms Wooster's commitment to sustain a vital downtown.

Not all downtowns can spin such fairy tales. Boarded-up storefronts and vacant upper floors line many a downtown street. If the stores are not empty, then a deadening homogeneity of the franchised shops often pervades. Uses have changed, as have values, tastes, merchants, and customers. It's a new retail landscape. But such commercial property has priced out the very activities and uses that are badly needed. Rents soared in the prosperous days in these retail areas, and even when flagging, landlords often tried to match the prices of the malls. Like gamblers hoping to recoup their losses, landlords often hold out for a better day. Meanwhile, neighbors and nearby residential communities consider these problems off their turf. They are the businessmen's problems. Maybe these residential neighbors will support a Business Improvement District and beautification efforts, help with Christmas decorations, and appear at their Chamber of Commerce's Christmas parties, but they do not grapple with the jugular problems. They do not intervene in the real estate market, which is essential to tackling the commercial district's problems.

Privately supported revolving funds are needed so that commercial-retail buildings can be bought, renovated if necessary, and then rented out at varying prices to attract tenants who can supply shops, restaurants, and activities that will serve the community and offer attractive products and storefronts. For decades these revolving funds, often combined with subsidies, have worked in residential areas in such cities as Charleston, South Carolina, and Savannah, Georgia, to maintain mixed-income neighborhoods and to prevent gentrification. Such a simple, imaginative, and successful tool as the revolving fund has not been used in commercial areas. The possibilities for revolving funds in commercial buildings are endless: provision of needed services, unique and authentic retail activities, encouragement of incubator businesses and artistic ventures, and space for local organizations.

Above-the-store spaces could be occupied by people seeking low-rent housing: singles, artists, and the elderly. The elderly would like to be in central locations, where they can see and be part of the action. Warehousing them in remote retirement homes removes them from the world in which they have participated and signals that they are over the hill. Apartments on the second floors of stores are like the bungalows, which the English government provides for some of its elderly citizens, near the high street in their town or village.

Such diversity of uses and people would return life and safety to these deadened areas far more effectively than many Business Improvement District programs. Streets would no longer be lined with the franchised stores, which have come out for air from the mall, and it would again be fun to window shop, a disappearing entertainment. Despite the control of signs, paint colors, awnings, sidewalk surfaces, trees, and "street furniture," a street can be tiresome if you have seen all the shops before. Storefronts are the faces of stores and restaurants, as urban critic and University of Pennsylvania professor Witold Rybczynski stated in *City Life*. As with human faces, the expressions are meaningful only if they convey sincere emotions and thoughts. If commercial stores and their upper floors in many of our dying commercial areas could attract local, authentic, individualistic, and needy people and activities, an amazing burst of new life would emerge. This would be a public-private effort going far beyond the cosmetic and superficial solutions offered in town after town. It would return community to shopping and shopping to community.

Shopping and Consuming and the Public Sphere

Although global influences affect many of our decisions about shopping, as well as about our community life, there are innumerable ways of countering the pervading remoteness, of encouraging connections between people, and of making shopping more communally responsive.

One of the most basic challenges is to foster a greater sense of local empowerment, which could lead to greater local control. The benefits of more local control would affect not only shoppers but the overall livability of towns and cities. Communities' local institutions are being taken over by distant corporations, some with seemingly constant turnovers of remote owners. The overwhelming outpouring of national interest in Aaron Feuerstein's decision to continue the operation of his Malden Mills factory, which manufactures Polartec, in Lawrence, Massachusetts, after its devastating fire in 1995—and also pay his workers during the plant's reconstruction—indicates the strong, underlying support in America for such humane and *local* management of a company—an anomaly in today's corporate world of downsizing.

More typical is the case of the Williamstown National Bank. For more than eighty years this bank remained a locally run bank in Williamstown, Massachusetts, where it was closely connected with Williams College; it was located originally in the college's main academic building, Griffin Hall. That long local ownership ended in 1965, when the Third National Bank of Springfield bought it out, but that was only the first of seven turnovers for this bank. In nine years the bank has had four different owners. Its name changed from Williamstown National Bank to Third National Bank of Springfield, Bank of New England, First Service Bank, People's Bank of Worcester, First Agricultural Bank, and Bank of Boston. Now it is First Massachusetts Bank, a division of Banknorth Group of Portland, Maine. Only one former employee, Shirley Dushna, remained at the bank through six of its incarnations as the bank's staff dwindled to half full-time employees and half "occasional labor" with no benefits.[44]

Middletown, Connecticut's newspaper, the *Middletown Press*, owned locally by the D'Oench brothers until 1991, was bought by Eagle Publishing of Pittsfield, Massachusetts, in 1991, and then again in 1995 was taken over by the Journal Register Company, once of New Haven, Connecticut, and now of Trenton, New Jersey. By clustering small-town papers and sharing reporters, companies are able to maintain acceptable profit levels, but in the process they are losing touch with the locality. "The *Middletown Press* no longer feels like a hometown paper," said Stephen T. Gionfriddo, a councilman and former mayor of Middletown. "You wonder whether the *Middletown Press* is just going to be one of those papers that changes hands every few years when the owner can make a profit."[45] And the *Middletown Press* is dealing with a small-time operator in the Journal Register Company, compared with Gannett, which buys up newspapers by the dozen, bringing its total to eighty-two. Gannett also bought Multimedia, Inc., which owns not only newspapers but television syndicates and broadcasting. Imagine the small-town newspaper trying to make its point in that conglomerate.

It was not surprising that Vermonters mobilized a loud campaign in late 1999 to keep its well-known ice cream company Ben & Jerry's Homemade, a Vermont company after Ben Cohen and Jerry Greenfield announced that they were considering offers from outside potential buyers.

Ben & Jerry's garnered support from all corners: Governor Howard Dean considered Ben & Jerry's a "signature corporation" in Vermont being threatened by globalization; the state legislature enacted a law so that corporations could consider more than profit when investigating take-over offers; and ordinary citizens worried about this community-oriented company losing its soul to out-of-state profiteers. Aside from fitting into Vermont's environmental and idealistic image, with pre-tax profits and campaigns for such causes as literacy and peace, Ben & Jerry's has provided hard economic support of this small state in buying Vermont dairy farmers' products—$34 million worth in 1999—and making its Waterbury plant a tourist destination; in fact, the company's identification with the state is so strong that the director of Vermont Public Interest Research Group suggested that the state consider taking over the company. The cries not to sell out Vermont were heard by Unilever, which took over Ben & Jerry's in August 2000 and has stated that it intends to keep the corporation in its Vermont location, to carry on and expand its foundation work, and to use Vermont dairy products.

When the hometown newspapers, banks, and all the other local institutions—drugstores, grocery stores, neighborhood convenience stores, and ice cream companies—have been taken over by distant and ever-changing owners, customers and employees lose that important sense of loyalty and allegiance. The residents of such communities feel disenfranchised when they find that what had been important to them is treated like a pawn in a larger economic game. And tourists get little sense of a place when a generic newspaper like *USA Today*, instead of a local newspaper, is left at their hotel door, and many of their commercial dealings are with branches of some multi-state bank or store.

Today's distrust of public governance and politicians and fear of outsiders, immigrants, and foreign trade are certainly related to the loss of local control. Fears abound, crime seems to surge, welfare recipients do not seem to abide by the revered concepts of work and honor, and outsiders seem to ride high. Technology seems to be transforming the way we communicate and work, while old values appear to be disregarded. These changes, symbolizing a disintegration of the familiar world and its values, create an uneasiness and metastasize fears. When you think the ship is sinking, you hold on for dear life to that ship—to what you know and what you have trusted. So the retreat into a comfortable world of the self—and commodities and values you have known—offers a comforting haven. This retreat to the self can be seen also as a response to the pervasive changes facing communities everywhere, many promulgated by remote and shifting private entrepreneurs who operate by rules that may be flexing, but are still legitimate in the world of laissez-faire, and hard for the individual to challenge.

The government, on the other hand, is a fair target because you are part of it and have a stake in it. You can vote, you can write and lobby your legislators. So when you want to restore those time-honored principles, which many think are being ignored, you can look to the church for strength and to the government for public actions. Changing distant, even local, corporations is a daunting task, but as disparaged as government may be today, it is an avenue open to the public for expressing concerns and hoping for improvements. Individuals cannot easily alter the policies of private drug and insurance companies whose alliance affects so many health care issues, including what types of drugstores will be in your neighborhood. But they can turn to government to try to intervene so that the consumer can have free choice of drugstores for prescriptions. Ironically, the same government that has been the target of venomous attacks for more than a decade is also sought after for its help in crises of floods, fires, accidents, plane crashes, and bomb threats, as well as for its protection of individual freedoms and opportunities. The private sector alone cannot restore a sense of community to a neighborhood and assure that shopping is accessible and meets community needs; the government's help is needed.

The loss of local control and hometown pride affects every neighborhood, town, and city—and shopping is only one aspect of this pervasive trend. Shopping and interest in things or commodities, and the larger spread of "commodification" in society, are indicators of a quest for self-worth. But the irony is that absorption with shopping only fuels the very forces that produce the environment which has been disenfranchising the individual. Thus, those forces in the corporate world that seek greater and greater profits from more and different products with increasingly clever appeals to the consumer are capturing the very consumer who may be trying to retreat from the powerless state produced by those corporate actions.

The success of Disney World in Florida reveals that process. While the guests there seek an antidote to their regular life, which has shrunk their sense of power and autonomy, they also "submit to Disney's total control of the operation and to the commodification of their own experience," according to Stephen Fjellman in his book *Vinyl Leaves*. Here in this make-believe land, a tourist can find a welcome civility, safety, and an enjoyable return to American values of yesteryear—lost amid the massive forces of technology, corporate actions, and changing values and attitudes. Disney presents a world of continual progress, going back to familiar memories of the past and forward to the Magic Kingdom's promises of better times, based on glimpses of science and technology, history, and travel, all shrouded in beguiling fantasy. It is a "community of memory," Fjellman states, and "one of the reasons Disney theme parks are so successful and so ambiguous in their effects. The consummate irony . . . is that this community of memory is presented as a myriad of commodities in the interests of the corporate world that has constructed the problem of broken ontology and fractured epistemology in the first place."[46] It is also a world completely controlled by the Disney corporate

108. Main Street at Disney World, Orlando, Florida, 1999

machine, which requires strict adherence to a dress code for employees (known as hosts and hostesses), compulsive cleanliness in its maintenance, tight security, and an etiquette of the perpetual "we," referring to the corporation and the guests, Disney's term for its patrons.

Main Street and its shops provide the entry to both Disney World and Disneyland. No Big Boxes or Category Killers here. Just small-scale buildings reminiscent of the late nineteenth century, with Victorian facades, gaslights, wrought iron, porches, and carpentry details—all selling Disney souvenirs and products. Its town square is lined with the basic institutions of any community—city hall, railroad station, and bank—and in its center is the flagpole and space for band concerts and flag retreats (fig. 108). This cute street evokes all the innocence of the small town where many Americans were connected with everyone, where red, white, and blue was still important, and where the stores were all owned and run by local residents. Walt Disney himself was particularly fond of the Main Street section of his theme park and even had an apartment over the town square fire station that allowed him to see his guests entering the square. Behind the facades of these old-fashioned shops are contemporary businesses; the same businesses that existed at the turn of the century but with today's technology and corporate policies. The bank, now the Sun Bank, cashes checks and provides credit card advances in all types of currency; city hall has tourist information, including Walt Disney merchandise mail-order catalogues; and the Emporium, the largest store on Main Street, sells all the Disney souvenirs. Disney's romanticizations of the past have captured not only the pocketbooks but the hearts of his many guests, mostly middle-class people of all ages who find Disney's fabrication of yesteryear a comforting contrast to the often jarring everyday world at home.

In the real world, the need to cope with remoteness and powerlessness looms as a major societal issue, and how we deal with the planning, development, and redevelopment of shopping is just one part of the puzzle, which touches many of the forces creating today's pervasive alienation. Gentrified shops, often nationally franchised operations, in the new "villages" or malls redesigned to look like city streets are just as much a retreat to a pasteurized image of the past as are the Disney Main Streets. To encourage the development of commercial-retail activities that serve the community in practical terms is a tough task. It requires an understanding of the forces at work as well as the publics involved, and also an ability to challenge and innovate while remaining patient and persistent. Stores can be made to fit the needs of the community. Some places, like Peekskill, found the infusion of artists brought new life to their depressed city; others, like Wooster, found that locally owned companies empowered their town and residents. Different places have different needs, and it is the local residents, who know their community best, who should be involved in determining those needs and how they can be met.

Forcing remote corporations to be more responsible partners with local businesses, to respect local needs, and involve local consumers is often a major challenge. Citizens have demanded that McDonald's fit into historic downtowns, as in Portland, Oregon, and prevented Wal-Mart from deadening downtowns by having them fit into the communities, as in Rutland and Bennington, Vermont. Sometimes only local action is called for, sometimes state legislation, and other times federal regulations and legislation. But nothing happens unless the driving force for change is local. A crisis may be the initial generating charge, but the task to assure that retailing successfully serves a community requires continuous citizen involvement in local planning and economic development programs.

If communities are to function so that people do not feel alienated, unsafe, and powerless, attention must be focused on the economic and social functions of shopping—not just the exterior appearance of stores, as has often occurred in many old towns, historic districts, and Neo-Traditional developments. The Nantuckets may look quaint and romantic, but often they have lost their gritty vitality and diverse social and economic retailing in their spiffed up architectural authenticity. Similarly, that gritty vitality seems lost in the current vogue of fantasy architecture, full blown in theme parks like Disneyland and tourist-driven places like Las Vegas, but also evident in the whimsical touches of porticos pasted on supermarkets and Chippendale curves and oversized swans on the tops of buildings, all lavishly described in architectural magazines. The town center of the heralded Disney new town of Celebration near Orlando, designed by a Who's Who of contemporary American architects, has evolved into a playset of architects' fantasies as each public building, designed by a different, well-known architect, has mimicked in many ways the ageless images of such buildings: Philip Johnson the town hall, Venturi/Scott-Brown the bank, Cesar Pelli the movie house, Graham Gund the inn, Michael Graves the post office, and Robert A. M. Stern, the overseer of planning for the town, the hospital, and some of the Main Street buildings. This melange of architecture parodies real, working downtowns. The minuscule post office hardly follows current Postal Service policies, which have determined many of the much larger Depression-era buildings do not meet today's operational standards. Buildings reflect our culture, dreams, and needs; and those buildings addressing our commercial activities—shopping, banking, moviegoing, dining, and postal service—can be enlivened with touches of fantasy, but they also need to work. The current stores in Celebration, mostly locally owned, cater primarily to tourists and their appetite for silk shirts, antiques, and paintings. Only one small grocery store, Goodings, which has to order many items from its other stores, and a tiny beauty salon serve the everyday needs of the town's pioneers. It almost seems that architects and planners have forgotten the golden rule of form following function (figs. 109, 110).

Modern technology is here to stay, and although it contributes to the remoteness of contemporary living, it can work for greater communal connectedness and efficiencies. The introduction of the Internet has many parallels with the telephone, as both can reinforce existing social networks and reduce loneliness; both can complement but not replace face-to-face communication, as Robert Putnam discusses.[47] How much one's virtual world becomes private and individualized and how much involves community engagement is not clear. Certainly, though, mobilizing political action by public interest groups, a type of community engagement, has benefited from the Internet's swift means of communication.

In retailing, new technology is essential to modernized operations and improved customer services. That need not mean the death of sociable and communal shopping. The intimacy of shopping, the desire to touch and feel, to talk and listen, to see and be seen—is needed as much today as it was in Charlemagne's time—and competent retailers realize that the challenges are how to use the new technology to enhance shopping opportunities; how to retain face-to-face retailing; how to increase local store ownership; and how to encourage authenticity. We will always need to shop, and how and where it is done affects every person and every community—and involves citizens, private corporations, and community organizations, as well as local, state, and federal government. Individuals and the community need socially and economically successful shopping, and, likewise, profitable and up-to-date shopping needs us and the community.

109. Palm tree–lined main street of Celebration, Florida, 1999

110. Philip Johnson's town hall and Michael Graves's post office in Celebration, Florida's civic center, 1999

Producing that equation of socially and economically successful shopping for consumers, entrepreneurs, and communities assumes a public awareness of shopping's social—and public—functions, as well as a public commitment to creating and sustaining livable and functional communities. That may seem a daunting task in an era often rejecting public governance, especially planning controls and regulations, in favor of unfettered individual rights—from outposts in Montana refusing to recognize the legitimacy of traffic lights to major corporations fighting off government regulations. This hands-off attitude toward government and authority, coupled with prevailing self-determinism, has moved the pendulum farther and farther toward rampant materialism—a new level of consumerism. For those enjoying the money, power, and possessions of this materialism, evident in pretentious monster houses in gated communities, opulent designer clothes, and expensive cars, the rest of the world, which missed this bandwagon of material success, is seen as a laggard in the world of free enterprise. Troubling divides occur. As materialism and commercialism roared along with new highs in the stock market and multimillion-dollar salaries for corporation executives, the divide widens between the haves and have-nots, between those earning minimum wage and those earning millions, and those searching for tax deductions and those working two or three jobs. Interest in community well-being, responsibility for the common weal, or concern about the social impact of shopping are not necessarily by-products of material success in the world of free enterprise and its often ensuing self-absorption of consumerism.

On the other hand, new voices countering this consumerism are being raised. Vocal community debates are occurring on locating superstores, whether in Greenfield, Massachusetts, or New York City; towns and cities are mobilizing Main Street resuscitation projects and community-driven redevelopments, as in San Diego; and even small towns like Salem, New York, are resurrecting their local supermarkets. Such debates indicate a commitment to the survival of local commerce and, most important, to the strengthening of community life. Also, the emerging interests in a simpler and less materialistic world, combined with communitarianism of a different sort, may start to nudge the pendulum back from its far right, materialistic perch. Already the proven ability of consumers to influence the types of foods in stores is evident in the proliferation of healthful foods—whether multigrained bread or organic vegetables, formerly found only in upscale markets but now in most chain supermarkets. Changing attitudes, values, and desires can also influence where, how, and what is sold. Citizens often have more power than they realize. They have stopped the construction of nuclear power plants, restricted assault weapons, prevented the dumping of toxic wastes, and forced the display of the nutritional contents of foods, to name only a few people-power achievements. In shopping, it is not the promotion of Spartan life styles or a dampening of the vitality of free enterprise that many seek, but a notching down of today's commercialism and a renewed concern for satisfying communal life.

Commercialism and shopping, however, are inextricably intertwined. No matter what individual desires, cultural values, economic possibilities, or social pressures exist—no matter how and where shopping is done, what is bought or sold—the basic fact is that shopping is an intractable part of living and has existed ever since people could barter or sell whatever surpluses they could produce. Similarly, despite Veblen's and other critics' fears of the destructiveness of excessive commercialism, the desire for luxuries and the propensity to display superiority and wealth—conspicuous consumption— are inherent human drives going back to the earliest civilizations, tempered at times by moral constraints, availability of money, and class and mobility restraints.

In the sixteenth and seventeenth centuries, a trading city like Venice was teeming with goldsmiths, and the avarice of the church's hierarchy, with its jewels, art, sumptuous palaces, and gilded clothes, was legendary. Such conspicuous consumption was copied by the upwardly mobile—and by already established leaders throughout Europe and the Middle East. The Ottoman Sultan Suleiman, benefiting from thriving trade, reveled in visible luxuries in the sixteenth century and enjoyed impressing Western European political powers with his might and wealth. He even sported an extravagant jewel-studded helmet, which was designed to compete with Charles V's regalia for his 1529 coronation as Holy Roman Emperor.[48] Throughout the Renaissance, interest in "worldly goods," as Lisa Jardine so well describes, was rampant. However, such possessions were limited to the upper strata of society—the wealthy, the church, the mercantile and bourgeois—who could afford the jewels, art, and luxurious clothes, and could aspire to country houses like the English rising mercantile class, or city palaces like the Medicis' and Barberinis' in Italy.

In today's democracies, where rarities have indeed become commonplace, shopping and its worldly goods rank as one of the most visible symbols of freedoms stimulating rising aspirations and social mobility. The serf in the Middle Ages, the slave on American plantations, the chambermaid in eighteenth-century England, and even Cobbett's nineteenth-century farm family ventured no such hopes—or desires. Now the Bill Gateses, Donald Trumps, and Sam Waltons can amass their millions—or billions—and buy whatever they want. Similarly the young Hispanic can drive a magenta-colored "low rider" down Main Street displaying his wealth—and aspirations—just like the yuppie lawyer sporting a black BMW. Many Eastern European countries recently freed from the restrictions of Communism have come to interpret democratic freedom as freewheeling laissez-faire with its flashy cars, fancy clothes, glitzy houses, and jet-setting lifestyle. The global village's instant communications and the ever-sophisticated advertising can feed desires and hopes all over the universe, so Nike sneakers are worn in Tokyo, Bangkok, Bucharest, and Beverly Hills by those who share the same universal aspiration and have the wherewithal to purchase such in items. That drive is elemental, as every retailer knows. It fuels commerce, and it also reflects the freedoms—and dynamism—of democracy.

Despite democracy's captivating aspects, such as its social mobility and leveling, as well as the inherent belief that shopping is a way to reach a better life, faith in the power of material possessions has entrapped many in a treadmill of spending and debt. Entertainment shopping—converting a Sunday trip to the mall into a family entertainment—is just the latest means of stimulating sales by luring potential customers into flagging shopping emporia, revivifying down-at-the-heel downtowns, and perpetuating that shopping treadmill. No wonder the Germans worry that longer store hours might introduce "American commercialism" into their way of life, disrupt their family time, and prevent their Sunday family walks in the park.

Our attitudes about shopping raise questions about ourselves, our hopes and dreams, and about how we want to live as well as what kind of communities we want. Democracy provides us with seemingly never-ending opportunities to shop, reinvent ourselves, and survive the disappointments of unfulfilled dreams and unsatisfied pleasures. It also gives us the freedom to direct our lives and help to govern the places where we live. As consumers, we need not be helpless victims of manipulative advertising and selling nor powerless citizens in a capitalistic democracy. As citizens, we can participate in local government and influence local plans and land-use regulations, ensuring that the locations and types of stores meet community objectives. We can make sure that our local public institutions, like town halls, post offices, libraries, and police headquarters, are sited and operated so that they

111. Statue of woman going to market in front of Marché Maison-neuve, Montreal, 1999

112. Meeting friends at farmers' market in Arlington, Virginia, 1999

reinforce the civic core of our communities (figs. 111, 112). Our downtowns, our shopping opportunities, malls, and shopping districts need not be determined primarily by profit-making private entrepreneurs. Although usually considered private, entrepreneurial retailing decisions have profound public impact on civic life—and sociability and civility—in our neighborhoods, towns, and cities. We are consumers and citizens whose participation and votes can affect how and where we shop and what we purchase and, most important, what kind of community and world we live in. Shopping is a public concern—and our concern.

Notes

Introduction

1. Tocqueville, *Democracy in America*, pp. 256, 257.
2. Ibid.
3. Marcus Marks, *Report on Market System for New York City and on Open Markets in Manhattan*, from Project for Public Spaces and Urban Land Institute, *Public Markets and Community Revitalization*, p. 31.

Chapter 1. Shopping Through the Ages

1. Lucie Young, "Armani Opens Museum Shops Selling Clothes," *New York Times*, September 12, 1996.
2. Davis, *History of Shopping*, p. 235. A thorough and competent history of shopping published in 1966.
3. Zola, *The Ladies' Paradise*, p. 52. This provocative book benefited from Zola's careful observations and analysis, in this case of the impacts of new department stores on the life and people of Paris. Although focused on the mid-nineteenth century retailing, *The Ladies' Paradise* raises questions and exposes the tensions that can occur whenever a capitalistic society is faced with disruptive changes. Zola's picture of social and economic turmoil in Paris and of the captivating and manipulative fantasy of the new cathedrals of consumption, blended with the romance of the shop clerk and her department store tycoon, makes this a fascinating and entertaining book.
4. Child, *American Frugal Housewife*, p. 89.
5. Winstanley, *Shopkeeper's World*, p. viii. This thoughtful study of the English shopkeeper, along with Philip Nord's *Paris Shopkeepers and the Politics of Resentment*, provides an excellent picture of shopkeepers in the late nineteenth century and of their fears and resentments when facing rapid changes in retailing and in society. Winstanley focuses on the socioeconomic aspects of the shopkeeper, while Nord concentrates on the sociopolitical realm.
6. Defoe, *Complete English Tradesman*, 1: 227–247.
7. Atherton, *Frontier Merchant in Mid-America*, p. 39. Atherton's writings on merchant life in outpost communities in the Midwest and elsewhere are solid and informative.
8. Ibid.
9. Mehling, "Brief Profile of the Origins of the Retail Merchants Association of Baltimore."
10. Boddewyn and Hollander, *Public Policy Toward Retailing*, p. 395.
11. Bushman, "Shopping and Advertising in Colonial America," in *Of Consuming Interests*, p. 234. This chapter and others, like T. H. Breen's "Baubles of Britain: The American and Consumer Revolutions of the Eighteenth Century," in this volume well illustrate colonial lifestyles and the early hints of American conspicuous consumption.
12. Daniel Miller, "Could Shopping Ever Really Matter?" in *Shopping Experience*, ed. Falk and Campbell, p. 32. Miller, an anthropologist at University College, London, raises probing questions and offers new ways of looking at shopping, as does Falk and Campbell's introduction, Rachel Bowlby's article and several other articles in this book, which again confirms England's intellectual leadership in shopping studies.
13. Nystrom, *Economics of Retailing*, p. 48. Nystrom's work on the economics of retailing, fashion, and consumption in the late 1920s in this and other books is an important contribution to scholarship.
14. Wycherley, *How the Greeks Built Cities*, p. 50.
15. Aristotle, *Politics*, pp. 1293, 1294.
16. Wycherley, *How the Greeks Built Cities*, p. 67.
17. Anderson and Latham, *Market in History*, p. 57.
18. Meiggs, *Roman Ostia*, p. 272.
19. MacDonald, *Architecture of the Roman Empire*, p. 93.
20. Braudel, *Civilization and Capitalism*, vol. 2, *The Wheels of Commerce*, p. 29. The depth and breadth of this economic history, the weaving of complicated and disparate material into an evolving drama, and the well-chosen illustrations make this an indispensable source.
21. Ibid., p. 30.

22. Waddy, *Seventeenth-Century Roman Palaces*, p. 132.

23. Braudel, *Civilization and Capitalism*, vol. 2, *The Wheels of Commerce*, pp. 68, 69.

24. Cobbett, *Rural Rides*, p. 353.

25. Herman Freudenberger, "Fashion, Sumptuary Laws, and Business," *Business History Review* 37 (Spring–Summer 1963), p. 40. Interesting article on the economic role of sumptuary laws.

26. Roche, *Culture of Clothing*, trans. Jean Birrell, pp. 503, 505.

27. Forty, *Objects of Desire*, p. 47.

28. Child, *American Frugal Housewife*, p. 5.

29. Franklin, *Autobiography of Benjamin Franklin*, p. 211.

30. Tocqueville, *Democracy in America*, part II, book two, p. 211.

31. Roche, *Culture of Clothing*, p. 514.

32. Veblen, *Theory of the Leisure Class*, pp. 33, 87–88, 120.

33. Ibid., pp. 180, 53.

34. Ibid., pp. 167, 168.

35. Davis, *History of Shopping*, p. 235.

36. Exhibit, Canadiana Gallery, Royal Ontario Museum, Toronto, Canada, 1995.

37. Pevsner, *History of Building Types*.

38. Davis's *History of Shopping* and Pevsner's *History of Building Types* are sources for the information on Lipton.

39. Davis, *History of Shopping*, p. 290.

40. Ibid., p. 292.

41. Marshall Field, like A. T. Stewart's, grew from an earlier store.

42. This new mass consumption and the Parisian department stores are well discussed by Kristin Ross in her introduction to Zola, *Ladies' Paradise*, pp. vi, vii, and in Williams, *Dream Worlds*, pp. 3, 4. They detail how these stores functioned and transformed shopping into a spectacle where the mundane became fascinating, and how the middle-class woman shopper gained greater freedom as she found her way in this new permissible public sphere.

43. Zola, *Ladies' Paradise*, pp. 231, 378.

44. Ibid., pp. 52, 38.

45. Bridenbaugh, *Cities in the Wilderness*, p. 97.

46. Sarah Booth Conroy, "Mount Vernon's Avid Shoppers," *Washington Post*, April 3, 1995.

47. Sweeney, "High-Style Vernacular," p. 5.

48. Bailyn, *New England Merchants in the Seventeenth Century*, p. 9.

49. Bridenbaugh, *Cities in the Wilderness*, p. 42.

50. Stokes, *Iconography of Manhattan Island*, vol. 2, pp. 209–348. A rare source of data on New York.

51. Bridenbaugh, *Cities in the Wilderness*, p. 36.

52. Ibid., pp. 41–43.

53. Whitehill, *Boston*, p. 48.

54. Gilchrist, "Market Houses in High Street," p. 304; Bridenbaugh, *Cities in the Wilderness*, p. 193.

55. Gilchrist, "Market Houses in High Street," p. 304.

56. Marks, *Report on Market System for New York City*, p. 31.

57. Ibid., p. 52.

58. Hawke, *Everyday Life in Early America*, p. 26.

59. Carson, *Country Stores in Early New England*, pp. 2, 15.

60. Tocqueville, *Democracy in America*, pp. 213, 211, 210.

61. Atherton's research and writings, especially *Frontier Merchant in Mid-America*.

62. Atherton, *Southern Country Store*, p. 193.

63. Strasser, *Satisfaction Guaranteed*, provides excellent, well-researched material on the advent of parcel post and its impact on retail stores and on many other areas in American marketing.

64. Helpful sources of information on the rise of retail giants are Nystrom, *Economics of Retailing*; Pevsner, *History of Building Types*; Strasser, *Satisfaction Guaranteed*; John K. Winkler, *Five and Ten*; *Chain Store Age Executive*, Spring 1994 issue.

65. Ressequie, "Decline and Fall of the Commercial Empire of A. T. Stewart," p. 256.

66. Twyman, *History of Marshall Field & Co.*, and Pound, *Selfridge*, are major sources of information on these early department stores.

67. Twyman, *History of Marshall Field & Co.*, and Pound, *Selfridge*.

68. Pound, *Selfridge*, is an authoritative source of information.

69. *Boston Globe*, September 4, 1912, p. 13.

70. Babette Gorman, *All About Filene's and the People Who Made It Grow*, Filene's Public Relations Department, no date, p. 15.

71. Jackson, "All the World's a Mall," p. 1117.

72. Riverside Improvement Company, *Riverside in 1871, with a Description of Its Improvements*, pp. 18, 40.

73. Many sources used, including Longstreth's excellent "Neighborhood Shopping Center in Washington, D.C.," pp. 5–34. Longstreth's important *City Center to Regional Mall* discusses the development of Los Angeles and the roles that retail stores played in that city's history.

74. Worley, *J. C. Nichols and the Shaping of Kansas City*, p. 248.

75. Ibid., p. 263.

76. Hoyt, "Sales in Leading Shopping Center Districts in the United States," p. 5.

77. Gillette, "Evolution of the Planned Shopping Center," p. 452. A well-researched and thoughtful article on how the internalized mall has and has not adapted in suburban and urban settings.

78. Longstreth, "Neighborhood Shopping Center in Washington, D.C.," p. 17.

79. Sources for shopping areas in planned communities and the early shopping center may be found in many sources, including Richard Longstreth, Clarence Stein, and Catherine Bauer.

80. Bell, *Cultural Contradictions of Capitalism*, p. 70.

81. Sternlieb and Hughes, eds., *Shopping Centers: USA*, p. 76.

82. Regional Plan Association of New York and Its Environs, "Central Retail Shopping District of New York and Its Environs," p. 24.

83. Hoyt, "Sales in Leading Shopping Center Districts in the United States," p. 3.

84. Jonassen, *Shopping Center vs. Downtown*, p. 40.

85. Crimmins and White, *New Georgia Guide*, p. 255.

86. Whitwell, *Making the Market*, pp. 11, 12.

87. Stanley C. Hollander, paper presented at a symposium published in *Public Policy Toward Retailing*, ed. Boddewyn and Hollander, p. 396.

88. Bluestone et al., *Retail Revolution*, p. 149.

89. Alexander and Muhlebach, *Shopping Center Management*, p. 8.

90. Grupe, "How a Neighborhood Center Grew into a Community Center," p. 6.

91. N.a., *Urban Land* 55 (February 1996), p. 10.

92. "Wired Society," p. 48. Interesting reflections on the cyberage by Harvard Business School professors, whose broad interests allow them to see an expansive and very human side of this new computer era.

93. Bluestone et al., *Retail Revolution*, p. 85.

94. Traub and Teicholz, *Like No Other Store*, pp. 44, 43.

95. Ibid., pp. 113, 144, 145.

96. Ross, in introduction to Zola, *Ladies' Paradise*, p. x.

97. Traub and Teicholz, *Like No Other Store*, pp. 381–382.

98. Hoover, Campbell, and Spain, *Hoover's Handbook of Business 1995*, pp. 287, 534, 691,

1035, and John Tagliabue, "Enticing Europe's Shoppers: Dressing and Selling the U.S. Way Catches On," *New York Times*, April, 24, 1996.

99. U.S. Department of Commerce, Bureau of the Census, 1992 Census of Retail Trade, RC92-S-1, pp. 1–27, Current Business Reports, Monthly Retail Trade, 1977–1997, County Business Patterns, 1982–1995.

100. U.S. Department of Commerce, Bureau of Census, County Business Patterns 1997, Table 1b.

Chapter 2. Shopping: A Community Activity

1. Pound, *Selfridge*, p. 107.

2. Otten, *Corner Grocery Store*, p. 9. This book was mentioned in Beasley, *Corner Store*, which accompanied her show on Galveston's corner stores at the National Building Museum in the winter and spring of 2000. Beasley brought out the significance of these overlooked stores, so important in community life.

3. Angelou, *I Know Why the Caged Bird Sings*, pp. 4, 5.

4. Pirenne, *Economic and Social History of Medieval Europe*, p. 11.

5. Nord, *Paris Shopkeepers and the Politics of Resentment*, pp. 133, 265.

6. U.S. Department of Commerce, Bureau of the Census, *County Business Patterns, 1948*, SIC Code #573; idem, *County Business Patterns*, 1997, SIC Code #525.

7. Idem, *County Business Patterns, 1948*, SIC Code #539; idem, *County Business Patterns*, 1997, SIC Code #539.

8. Idem, *County Business Patterns, 1948*, SIC Code #533; idem, *County Business Patterns*, 1997, SIC Code #533.

9. Idem, *County Business Patterns, 1948*, SIC Code #573; idem, *County Business Patterns*, 1997, SIC Code #525.

10. All the statistics on hardware stores are from idem, *County Business Patterns*, SIC Code #525 and #573, for the years 1948–98.

11. Gallup Poll, *Poll Releases*, November 16, 1999.

12. National Public Radio, "Morning Edition," May 7, 1996, transcript, pp. 19, 20.

13. U.S. Department of Commerce, Bureau of the Census, *County Business Patterns, 1948*, SIC Code #572; idem, *County Business Patterns*, 1997, SIC Code #591. *Census of Retail Trade, 1992*, Table 6.

14. *Chain Drug Review*, October 11, 1999, p. 93.

15. *Drugstore News*, August 30, 1999, p. 13.

16. Interview with James Virgoina, December 13, 1999.

17. Interview with Harold Sugar, September 26, 1995.

18. *New York Times*, April 16, 1994.

19. U.S. Department of Commerce, Bureau of the Census, *County Business Patterns, 1948*, SIC Code #572; idem, *County Business Patterns, 1997*, SIC Code #591.

20. Interview with Georges Jacob, July 25, 1995.

21. *Georgetowner*, August 1995, p. 11.

22. Beaumont, *How Superstore Sprawl Can Harm Communities*, pp. 10, 11. An excellent guide for citizens concerned about retail sprawl by a National Trust for Historic Preservation expert.

23. Gans, *Urban Villagers*, p. 117.

24. Otten, *Corner Grocery Store*, p. 11.

25. *New Jersey Coalition Against War in the Middle East v. J. M. B. Realty Corporation et al.*, 138 N.J. 326, 400 (1994).

26. Jacobs, *Death and Life of Great American Cities*, pp. 4, 63.

27. Ibid., p. 37.

28. Von Hoffman, *Local Attachments*, p. 102. Neighborhood stores, although only a small part of the large picture of Boston's Jamaica Plain in this thorough and readable history, reveal much about the nature of the community, its residents, and their upward mobility.

29. Ibid.

30. Goodwin, *Wait Till Next Year*, pp. 66, 68, 67.

31. The Jewish storekeeper is an important topic that I do not explore here because it deserves more careful attention than I can give it. I hope that scholars will study the Jewish merchant in the same depth as scholars have plumbed the role of shopping for women. Several books discuss different aspects of the Jewish shopkeeper: Eli N. Evans, *The Provincials: A Personal History of Jews in the South* (Evans's father ran a department store in Durham, North Carolina); Harris, *Merchant Princes*; and Suberman, *Jew Store* (Suberman's father also ran a department store in the South).

32. Soderberg, "Nineteenth-Century General Store," p. 370.

33. Hebron Preservation Society, *Hebron: A Century in Review*, p. 46.

34. Thompson, "Country Store," pp. 15, 16.

35. Ownby, *American Dreams in Mississippi*, p. 72. A significant and compelling study of consumer culture and the broader sociocultural picture of life in Mississippi, which shows the role of shopping in the lives of rich and poor, blacks and whites, men and women, and urban and rural populations.

36. Thompson, "Country Store," p. 15.

37. Taylor, *William Cooper's Town*, p. 18. A fascinating history of the rise and fall of a striving early American.

38. Historic marker at town square in Carlisle, Pennsylvania.

39. Atherton, *Main Street on the Middle Border*, pp. 29, 52.

40. Crimmins and White, *New Georgia Guide*, pp. 254, 255.

41. Sales figures from Woodward and Lothrop's SEC Form 10-K, 1982, in Woodward and Lothrop Collection, Historical Society of the District of Columbia Archives, Washington, D.C.

42. "Woodward and Lothrop: Portrait of a Washington Institution," in ibid.

43. Doris S. Bruffey, "Washington Has Lost More Than a Store," *Washington Times*, December 8, 1995.

44. Rebecca Johnston, "When Woodies Finally Closes, Christmas Will Never Be the Same Again," *Washington Post*, September 26, 1995. The tradition of Christmas windows was reintroduced in 1999 and 2000 in the otherwise empty Woodward & Lothrop building in downtown Washington, indicating the enduring popularity of such displays.

45. Trish Thomas, "When Price Wasn't Everything," ibid., July 2, 1995.

46. Statement by Woodward and Lothrop Public Relations Department entered in the 1953 American Public Relations Association contest, Woodward and Lothrop Collection, Historical Society of the District of Columbia Archives, Washington, D.C.

47. Woodward and Lothrop announcement of October 1964 opening of its Annapolis store, ibid.

48. Woodward and Lothrop, *Washington of the Future*, booklet celebrating the store's golden anniversary in 1950, p. 1, back page, ibid.

49. "Our Adaptable Merchants," Editorial, *Washington Post Times Herald*, September 18, 1956, p. 12.

50. Jonassen, *Shopping Center vs. Downtown*, p. 40.

51. Ibid., pp. 2, 95, 100.

52. Urban Land Institute, *Remaking the Shopping Center*, pp. 2, 4.

53. Hoyt, "Sales in Leading Shopping Center Districts," p. 3.

54. Sternlieb and Hughes, *Shopping Centers: USA*, p. 77.

55. Gillette, "Evolution of the Planned Shopping Centers in Suburbs and City," p. 450.

56. Bluestone et al., *Retail Revolution*, pp. 109, 85.

57. U.S. Department of Commerce, Bureau of the Census, *Census of Retail Trade, 1997*, "Subject Series Establishment and Firm Size," table 3, NAICS Code 4521102.

58. Arthur Kopkind, "High Life Playground, a Theme-Park of Nostalgia, and a Theater of Consumption," *Real Paper*, February 19, 1977.

59. *Boston Globe*, February 1, 1958, p. 5.

60. Jack Frank, lecture presented at the American Planning Association Conference, San Francisco, Calif., April 1994.

61. Lieder, "Planning for Housing," p. 365.

62. Albrecht, *World War II and the American Dream*, pp. 192, 154.

63. *Newsday*, August 15, 1947. Clipping courtesy of Levittown Archives, Levittown Public Library, Levittown, N.Y.

64. Kelly, *Expanding the American Dream*, p. 44. A thoughtful and well-researched discussion and analysis of the development of Levittown and post–World War II suburbanization.

65. *Newsday*, October 2, 1947. Clipping courtesy of Levittown Archives, Levittown Public Library, Levittown, N.Y.

66. Riesman, "Suburban Dislocation," p. 241.

67. Levitt, "A House Is Not Enough," p. 59.

68. Barbara M. Kelly, letter to author, May 3, 1996.

69. Ibid.

70. Sternlieb and Hughes, *Shopping Centers: USA*, p. 76.

71. Howard and Davies, *Change in the Retail Environment*, p. 59.

72. Fairfax County, Va., Planning Commission, "Draft Tysons Corner Urban Center Plan," p. 1.

73. Ibid., pp. 9, 8.

74. U.S. Department of Commerce, Bureau of Census, *County Business Patterns, 1948*, SIC Code #539; idem, *County Business Patterns, 1997*, SIC Code #539; idem, *Census of Retail Trade, 1948*, SIC Code #539; idem, *Census of Retail Trade, 1997*, SIC Code, #539.

75. Telephone interview with Home Depot public relations department, May 1998.

76. Ibid.; U.S. Department of Commerce, Bureau of Census, *County Business Patterns, 1948*, SIC Code #5912; idem, *County Business Patterns, 1997*, SIC Code #5912.

77. Ibid.; idem, *County Business Patterns, 1948*, SIC Code #5651; idem, *County Business Patterns, 1997*, SIC Code #5651.

78. National Research Bureau, *NRB Census—14 Year Trends*, p. 1.

79. Rybczynski, "New Downtowns," p. 106.

80. Rhees, "Mall Wonder," p. 23.

81. Margaret W. Pressler, "The Not-So-Far-Out-Outlets," *Washington Post*, March 6, 1995.

82. Information from the Corporate Communications Department, Mills Corporation.

83. Michael D. Shear, "More Than They Bargained For," *Washington Post*, May 12, 1995.

84. Ibid.

85. Interview with Robert E. Simon, February 25, 1997.

86. Gruen, *Heart of Our Cities*, pp. 203, 204.

87. *Shopping Centers Today*, November 1993, p. 17.

88. Ibid., May 1991, p. 73, 70.

89. Telephone conversation with Tom Cabot, National Association of Mall Walkers, June 2000.

90. U.S. Department of Commerce, Bureau of the Census, *Statistical Abstract of the United States, 1999*, table 17.

91. International Council of Shopping Centers, *Research Bulletin* 4 (December 1993), p. 5.

92. *Shopping Centers Today*, May 1994, p. 91.

93. Rand Youth Poll, Teen-Age Research Unlimited, *New York Times*, March 14, 1998.

94. "Are Teenagers Treated Fairly at the Mall?" in "Fresh Voices," *Parade Magazine*, February 12, 1995, p. 10.

95. *Shopping Centers Today*, May 1994, p. 91.

96. "Plan To Bar Buses at Mall Is Put on Hold," *New York Times*, September 1, 1994.

97. *Shopping Centers Today*, May 1994, p. 122.

98. Ibid., April 1994, p. 3.

99. *New Jersey Against War in the Middle East v. J. M. B. Realty Corporation et al.*, 138 N.J. 326, 391 (1994).

100. Ibid., see evidence k14, k90.1 (1.1).

101. Ibid., 337, 339, 338.

102. Ibid., 333.

103. Ibid.

104. *Green Party of New Jersey and James Mohn v. Hartz Mountain Industries, Inc., d/b/a The Mall at Mill Creek*, 2000 N.J. Lexis 656 (1999–2000).

105. Ibid., sections VI, IV.

106. Ibid., section IV, and *New Jersey Against War in the Middle East v. J. M. B. Corporation et al.*, 138 N.J. 333.

107. *Green Party of New Jersey and James Mohn v. Hartz Mountain Industries, Inc., d/b/a The Mall at Mill Creek*, section IV.

108. de Avila, "Back to the Future," p. 40.

Chapter 3. Shopping:
Matching Dreams with Realities

1. Garry B. Trudeau, "Doonesbury," *Washington Post*, March 6 and 7, 1995.
2. Advertisement for Forest City Ratner Development, *New York Times*, November 8, 1996.
3. Ambry, *Consumer Power*, p. 141.
4. U.S. Department of Commerce, Bureau of the Census, *Statistical Abstract of the United States, 1963*, table 435; idem, *Statistical Abstract of the United States, 1982/83*, table 698.
5. Idem, *Statistical Abstract of the United States, 1999*, table 1223.
6. Interview with Judy Bonderman, February 22, 1996.
7. Wendy Wasserstein, "The Anatomy of a Shopping Jag," *New York Times Magazine*, November 12, 1989.
8. Interview with Gerry Medley, March 5, 1996.
9. Jennifer Steinhauer, "Shopping as a Competitive Sport," *New York Times*, October 26, 1996.
10. eBay website, March 9, 2001.
11. Bushman, "Shopping and Advertising in Colonial America," p. 251.
12. Kara Swisher, "Boom or Bust," *Washington Post*, March 6, 1994.
13. Featherstone, *Consumer Culture and Postmodernism*, p. 85.
14. Woolf, "The New Dress," in *A Haunted House and Other Short Stories*, p. 50.
15. Campbell, *Romantic Ethic and the Spirit of Modern Consumerism*, p. 87. The interrelated social-cultural-psychological factors in the history of modern consumerism, especially the constant tension between utilitarianism and romanticism, are well discussed in this interesting book. The research and writings of Ewen, Davis, Forty, McCracken, and Williams also cover this and related subjects with different but complementary perspectives.
16. Bushman, "Shopping and Advertising in Colonial America," p. 243.
17. Veblen, *Theory of the Leisure Class*, p. 167.
18. McCracken, *Culture and Consumption*, was helpful on this topic.
19. Forty, *Objects of Desire*, pp. 199, 207, 119.
20. Veblen, *Theory of the Leisure Class*, pp. 176, 88.
21. Dreiser, *Sister Carrie*, pp. 17, 51.
22. Robinson, "Importance of Fashions in Taste to Business History," p. 13.
23. Barth, *City People*, p. 144.
24. Davis, *Fashion, Culture, and Identity*, p. 155.
25. Kristin Ross, in introduction to Zola, *Ladies' Paradise*, p. x.
26. Featherstone, *Consumer Culture and Postmodernism*, p. 104.
27. Pound, *Selfridge*, p. 107.
28. Barth, *City People*, p. 147.
29. Trish Thomas, "When the Price Wasn't Everything," *Washington Post*, July 2, 1995.
30. Roxanne Roberts, "Once There Was a Woodie's," ibid., June 23, 1995.
31. Thomas, "When the Price Wasn't Everything."
32. Roberts, "Once There Was a Woodie's."
33. Ann B. Colcord, letter to author, January 1997.
34. Patten, *Consumption of Wealth*, p. 51.
35. Boorstin, *The Americans*, p. 107.
36. Peterson, *Future of U.S. Retailing*, p.157; Michael Schnudson (1984) said "it democratized envy" in ibid.
37. Veblen, *Theory of the Leisure Class*, p. 182.
38. Campbell, *Romantic Ethic and the Spirit of Modern Consumerism*, p. 205.
39. Bowlby, *Just Looking*, p. 31.
40. Veblen, *Theory of the Leisure Class*, pp. 180, 182.
41. Bowlby, *Just Looking*, p. 20.
42. Ross, introduction to Zola, *Ladies' Paradise*, p. xv.
43. Rappaport, *Shopping for Pleasure*, pp. 143, 167. Rappaport, by blending an amazing array of cultural, economic, and social history, shows how commerce, and particularly department stores, helped enable late nineteenth-century middle-class English women to enter the public sphere, start to become emancipated, and evolve into active participants in civic and welfare projects.
44. Stanton, *Eighty Years and More*, pp. 9, 205–207.
45. Faber, "Money Changes Everything," p. 809.
46. Ann B. Colcord, letter to author, January 1997.
47. *New York Times*, November 11, 1999, Money and Business section.
48. Ownby, *American Dreams in Mississippi*, p. 29.
49. Hutzler's Department Store, "Your Smile Means a Lot to Your Customer," p. 16.
50. Linden, *Affluence and Discontent*, p. 171.
51. Strasser, *Satisfaction Guaranteed*, pp. 6, 7.
52. Edward L. Bernays, introduction to "Crystallizing Public Opinion," p. 29b, Papers of Edward L. Bernays, Manuscript Division, Library of Congress, Washington, D.C.

53. Curti, "Changing Concept of 'Human Nature' in the Literature of American Advertising," p. 340.

54. Bernays, "Crystallizing Public Opinion," Papers of Edward L. Bernays, Manuscript Division, Library of Congress.

55. E. L. Bernays, letter, December 15, 1989, ibid. I focused only on Bernays's papers relating to his work for the American Tobacco Company, as that was one of his most prominent projects and also one that well illustrates the clever manipulation of the consumer by this father of public relations.

56. Bernays, "Crystallizing Public Opinion," ibid.

57. E. L. Bernays to George W. Hill, American Tobacco Company, January 15, 1929, ibid.

58. E. L. Bernays to Ethel R. Peyser, January 14, 1929, ibid.

59. E. L. Bernays to G. W. Hill, January 15, 1929, ibid.

60. Letter, May 10, 1929, ibid.

61. E. L. Bernays to Dunhill, February 21, 1929, ibid.

62. Letter, April 2, 1929, ibid.

63. Document, February 7, 1929, ibid.

64. Document, April 29, 1929, ibid.

65. Letter from G. H. D. Sutherland, ed., *Ludington Daily News*, Winter–Spring 1929, ibid.

66. Postcard from *Stevens Point Journal*, Winter–Spring 1929, ibid.

67. E. L. Bernays, "Crystallizing Public Opinion," ibid.

68. Schmookler, *Illusion of Choice*, p. 234.

69. Letter, March 12, 1929, Papers of Edward L. Bernays, Manuscript Collection, Library of Congress.

70. McCracken, *Decoding Women's Magazines*, pp. 4, 38, 49, 50.

71. France, "Letter from the Editor," p. 17.

72. Schmookler, *Illusion of Choice*, p. 233.

73. Fromm, "Psychological Aspects of the Guaranteed Income," p. 179.

74. U.S. Department of Commerce, Bureau of the Census, *Statistical Abstract of the United States, 1998*, table 820.

75. Ibid., table 799; idem, *Statistical Abstract of the United States, 1987*, table 824.

76. Idem, *Statistical Abstract of the United States, 1998*, tables 822, 820.

77. Benjamin Franklin, "The Way to Wealth," in *The Autobiography of Benjamin Franklin and Selections from his Writings*, p. 225.

78. Nystrom, *Economics of Retailing*, pp. 26, 27.

79. Nystrom, *Economic Principles of Consumption*, p. 403.

80. Bartos, *Moving Target*, p. 27.

81. Ewen and Ewen, *Channels of Desire*, pp. 78, 178.

82. Schor, *Overworked American*, p. 158. Schor's research in this well-written book as well as in her more recent, equally well-written *The Overspent American: Upscaling, Downshifting, and the New Consumer*, provide comprehensive data and extremely thoughtful analyses of today's consumerism, its impacts on our lives, and the need for downshifting.

83. Scitovsky, *Joyless Economy*, p. 178.

84. Maddox, *D. H. Lawrence*, p. 325.

85. Trump, "What My Ego Wants, My Ego Gets," *New York Times*, September 17, 1995.

86. Riverside Improvement Company, *Riverside in 1871, with a Description of Its Improvements*, p. 15.

87. Mayer and Wade, *Chicago*, p. 422.

88. Blakely, *Shaping the American Dream*, p. 8.

89. Sternlieb and Hughes, *Shopping Centers: USA*, pp. 76, 34.

90. Whyte, *Organization Man*, pp. 8, 39.

91. Kelly, *Expanding the American Dream*, p. 149.

92. Goodwin, *Wait Till Next Year*, p. 57. Although this fascinating and readable account of Goodwin's childhood describes Rockville Centre on Long Island after World War II, her description could apply to many other suburbs of major cities at that time.

93. Ibid., p. 52.

94. Whyte, *Organization Man*, p. 346.

95. Seeley et al., *Crestwood Heights*, pp. 52, 4.

96. U.S. Department of Commerce, Bureau of the Census, *Statistical Abstract of the United States, 1999*, tables 650, 653, and 659.

97. U.S. Department of Labor, Bureau of Labor Statistics, "News," pamphlet 91–547, October 28, 1991.

98. U.S. Department of Commerce, Bureau of the Census, *Statistical Abstract of the United States, 1999*, tables 668 and 669.

99. Idem, *Statistical Abstract of the United States, 1994*, p. 391; idem, *Statistical Abstract of the United States, 1999*, table 659.

100. Idem, *Statistical Abstract of the United States, 1994*, table 13; idem, *Statistical Abstract of the United States, 1999*, table 14.

101. U.S. Department of the Treasury, Internal Revenue Service, *Statistics of Income Bulletin*, Winter 1999–2000, p. 70, tables 4 and 5.

102. Interview with Janet Swart, March 1998.

103. U.S. Department of the Treasury, Internal Revenue Service, *Statistics of Income Bulletin*, Winter 1999–2000, table 1.

104. U.S. Department of Commerce, Bureau of the Census, *Statistical Abstract of the United States, 1994*, table 691.
105. Idem, *Statistical Abstract of the United States, 1999*, tables 753, 669.
106. Idem, *Statistical Abstract of the United States, 1994*, tables 771 and 797.
107. Idem, *Statistical Abstract of the United States, 1999*, table 822.
108. Standard and Poor's, *Industry Surveys: Retailing*, February 5, 1998, p. 1.
109. Franklin, *Autobiography of Benjamin Franklin*, pp. ix, 223, 224, 225.
110. Klein, "Consumer Credit and the Institutionalization of Consumerism," pp. 50–54.
111. Ibid., pp. 57, 274.
112. U.S. Department of Commerce, Bureau of the Census, *Statistical Abstract of the United States, 1998*, table 722.
113. Idem, *Statistical Abstract of the United States, 1994*, table 694.
114. Idem, *Statistical Abstract of the United States, 1998*, table 722.
115. Chinitz, "Framework for Speculating about Future Urban Growth Patterns in the United States."
116. U.S. Department of Commerce, Bureau of the Census, *Statistical Abstract of the United States, 1994*, table 1035; John Herbers, *The New Heartland*, p. 79.
117. U.S. Department of Commerce, Bureau of the Census, *Statistical Abstract of the United States, 1994*, table 1035.
118. *American Demographics* 16 (February 1994), pp. 33, 27, 29.
119. Fairfax County, Va., Planning Commission, "Draft Tysons Corner Urban Center Plan," p. 9.
120. *American Demographics* 16 (February 1994), p. 28.
121. Fairfax County, Va., Planning Commission, "Draft Tysons Corner Urban Center Plan," p. 8.
122. *Washington Post*/Kaiser Family Foundation/Harvard University Survey Project, *Why Don't Americans Trust the Government?* p. 27.
123. Regional Plan Association, *Region at Risk*, pp. 14, 15.
124. Jura Koncius, "At Home, at Work. Lexis-Nexis Sent Them Home: Now Office Politics Collide With Domestic Issues," *Washington Post*, October 19, 1995.
125. Telephone interview with Russ Blackburn, April 1996.
126. E-mail correspondence with Julie Withrow, January 2001.
127. Hahn and Stout, *Internet Complete Reference*, p. xix, xx.
128. Paul Goldberger, "Cyberspace Trips to Nowhere Land," *New York Times*, October 5, 1995.
129. Tawney, *Acquisitive Society*, p. 161.
130. Kathleen Day, "Now the 'Virtual Company,'" *Washington Post*, October 29, 1995.
131. Whyte, *Organization Man*, p. 448.
132. National Public Radio, "Morning Edition," February 25, 1997, transcript, p. 6.
133. Harwood Group for the Merck Family Fund, *Yearning for Balance*, pp. 1, 5, 16.
134. Ibid., pp. 1, 2.
135. Ibid., p. 12.
136. Ibid.
137. Telephone interview with Ann Huntington at Yankelovich, January 2001.
138. Harwood Group for the Merck Family Fund, *Yearning for Balance*, p. 18.
139. National Public Radio, "Morning Edition," February 25 and 26, 1997.
140. Tocqueville, *Democracy in America*, p. 211.

Chapter 4. Shopping in the Future

1. PricewaterhouseCoopers and Lendlease Real Estate Investments, *Emerging Trends in Real Estate*, 2000, p. 55.
2. Standard and Poor's, *Industry Survey. Retailing: General*, May 25, 2000, p. 2. Standard and Poor's surveys are informative and well written.
3. Ibid., May 20, 1999, p. 3.
4. Ibid., May 25, 2000, p. 9.
5. Wal-Mart, Press Release, February 20, 2001, p. 2.
6. Wal-Mart, *Annual Report*, 1995, p. 4.
7. Walton with Huey, *Sam Walton*, pp. 49, 50.
8. Beaumont, *How Superstore Sprawl Can Harm Communities*, p. 12.
9. Wal-Mart, "Securities and Exchange Commission, Report 10-K," April 21, 1995, p. 8.
10. Beaumont, *How the Superstore Sprawl Can Harm*, p. 8.
11. Wal-Mart, *Annual Report*, 1999, p. 14.
12. Wal-Mart press release September 14, 1995.
13. Standard and Poor's, *Industry Survey. Retailing: Basic Analysis*, May 9, 1996, p. R86.
14. Interview with Elizabeth Clark, March 20, 1996.
15. Margaret W. Pressler, "The Not-So-Far-Out-Outlets," *Washington Post*, March 6, 1995.
16. Telephone conversation with the Town of Freeport Chamber of Commerce, June 2000.
17. Amy Argetsinger, "A Little Bit of Maine Moves to the Beach," *Washington Post*, May 27, 1995.

18. Interview with Lee Krohn, Town of Manchester Planner, July 5, 2000.

19. Telephone interview with Jay Clog, commercial real estate agent in Montgomery County, Md., 1998.

20. Telephone interview with staff of the Maryland National Capital Park and Planning Comm., Montgomery County, Md., 1998.

21. Frances Turchiano, "The (Un)Malling of America," *American Demographics* 12 (April 1990), p. 38.

22. Standard and Poor's, *Industry Survey. Retailing: Specialty*, January 27, 1998, p. 12.

23. Urban Land Institute, *Urban Land Institute Forecast: Urban Land Supplement*, May 1999, p. 40.

24. Turchiano, "The (Un) Malling of America," *American Demographics* 12, p. 38.

25. Urban Land Institute, *Remaking the Shopping Center*, p. 2.

26. U.S. Department of Commerce, Bureau of the Census, *Statistical Abstract of the United States, 1990*, table 1368; idem, *Statistical Abstract of the United States, 1991*, table 9; idem, *Statistical Abstract of the United States, 1995*, table 1293.

27. Judith Waldrop, "Mall Shoppers Want the Basics," *American Demographics* 13 (October 1991).

28. Standard and Poor's, *Industry Survey. Retailing*, February 5, 1998, p. 1.

29. PricewaterhouseCoopers and Lendlease Real Estate Investments, *Emerging Trends*, p. 57.

30. Standard and Poor's, *Industry Survey. Retailing*, February 5, 1998, p. 1.

31. Urban Land Institute, *Remaking the Shopping Center*, p. 1.

32. National Trust for Historic Preservation, "Main Street Project," unpublished study, May–June 1996, p. 1.

33. Urban Land Institute, *Remaking the Shopping Center*, p. 6.

34. Ibid., p. 1.

35. International Council of Shopping Centers, *Scope of the Shopping Center Industry in the United States, 1996*, p. 1.

36. Telephone interview with John Collich of B. F. Saul Co.; Christopher Martin, "Seven Corners Shopping Center and the Transformation of Fairfax County," paper presented at 22nd Annual Conference of Washington, D.C., Historical Studies, October 14, 1995.

37. Regional Plan Association, *A Region at Risk: The Third Regional Plan for the New York/New Jersey/Connecticut Metropolitan Area*, p. 137.

38. *Shopping Center World*, December 1999, p. 42.

39. U.S. Department of Commerce, Bureau of the Census, *Statistical Abstract of the United States, 1999*, table 659.

40. Urban Land Institute, *Dollars and Cents of Shopping Centers*, 1998, p. 10.

41. U.S. Department of Commerce, Bureau of the Census, *Statistical Abstract of the United States, 1999*, table 1284.

42. Interview with Mark Schoifet, November 17, 1995.

43. Urban Land Institute, *Remaking the Shopping Center*, p. 2.

44. Chip Walker, "Strip Malls: Plain but Powerful," *American Demographics* 13 (October 1991), pp. 48, 50.

45. Lori Ann Pristo, "A Process for Determining the Most Marketable Strip Shopping Center Design" (Arch.D. diss., University of Michigan, 1984), p.164.

46. U.S. Department of Commerce, Bureau of the Census, *Statistical Abstract of the United States, 1994*, p. 787.

47. Marshall D. Dowdy, "The Grocery Shopping Attitudes and Behavior of Convenience Store Patrons" (Ph.D. diss., Virginia Polytechnic Institute and State University, 1994), p.180.

48. Beasley, *Corner Store*, p. 11.

49. Seven-Eleven Mid-Atlantic Division Markets Report, February 8, 2000.

50. *New York Times*, November 11, 1995.

51. Clayton M. Christensen and Richard S. Tedlow, "Patterns of Disruption in Retailing," *Harvard Business Review* 78 (January–February 2000), p. 43. An interesting discussion of types of changes in retailing.

52. U.S. Department of Commerce, Bureau of the Census, *Census of Retail Trade*, SIC Code 5961; idem, *Statistical Abstract of the United States, 1999*, table 1275.

53. Direct Marketing Association, *Catalog Industry Statistics*, pp. 1–4, telephone conversation February 23, 2001.

54. Lands' End, *Fact Sheet*, 1999, p. 1; telephone interview with Anna Schryver, Media Relations, Lands' End.

55. Lands' End, *Fact Sheet*, 1999, pp. 1, 2.

56. Idem, *Annual Report*, 1996; idem, *Annual Report*, 1999; idem, *Fact Sheet*, 1997; idem, *Fact Sheet*, 1999.

57. *Fact Sheet*, 1999, pp. 1, 2.

58. Idem, *Annual Report*, 1996, p. 2.

59. Idem, *Fact Sheet*, 1999, p. 1.

60. L. L. Bean, *Fact Sheet*, 2000, p.1.

61. *New York Times*, February 23, 1998.

62. Laurie Petersen, "Twenty-First Century Supermarket Shopping," *Adweek's Marketing Week* 30 (1989), p. 9.

63. Davies and Reynolds, *Teleshopping and Teleservices*, p. 57.

64. Stuart Elliott, "Advertising: A New Campaign Will Spread the Word That QVC Is Much More Than Cubic Zirconia Jewelry," *New York Times*, June 20, 1995.

65. Christensen and Tedlow, "Patterns of Disruption in Retailing," pp. 42, 43.

66. Standard and Poor's, *Industry Survey. Retailing: General*, February 5, 1998, p. 4; ibid., May 27, 1999, p. 7; ibid., May 25, 2000, p. 2.

67. Shelley Morrisette, Kenneth Clemmer, and William M. Bluestein, "The Retail Power Shift," *Forrester Report* 1 (April 1998), p. 7.

68. Margaret Stafford, Associated Press, America Online News, November 3, 1999.

69. U. S. Department of Commerce, National Telecommunications and Information Administration, *Falling Through the Net: Toward Digital Inclusion*, October 2000, pp. 1, 2.

70. Meeker, *Internet Advertising Report*, pp. 1–5; Meeker and DePuy, *Internet Report*, pp. 1–5.

71. Standard and Poor's, *Industry Survey. Retailing: Specialty*, May 27, 1999, p. 8.

72. Press release, "Statement by Commerce Secretary William M. Daley on First E-Retail Sales," March 2, 2000, p. 1. These statistics represent the most reliable e-commerce statistics.

73. U.S. Department of Commerce, National Telecommunications and Information Administration, *Falling Through the Net*, Executive Summary, p. 2.

74. Josh Bernoff, Shelley Morrisette, and Kenneth Clemmer, "Consumer eCommerce Readiness," *Forrester Report* 1 (March 1998), p. 8.

75. U.S. Department of Commerce, National Telecommunications and Information Administration, *Falling Through the Net*, pp. 1–3.

76. Interview with Richard Sabot, December 19, 1999.

77. Frances Cerra Whittelsey, "Getting the Goods," *Working Women* 24 (March 1999), p. 92.

78. "Survey Finds Resistance to E-shopping for Clothing," *New York Times*, November 22, 1999.

79. Sales figures from *Amazon.com Annual Report*, 1999, p. 1, and employee figures from Public Relations Department, Amazon.com, June 2000.

80. Nielsen Netratings, reported in "Holiday Lessons in Online Retailing," *New York Times*, January 2, 2000.

81. eBay, "Company Overview," April 13, 2000, p. 1, February 24, 2001.

82. Reuters, "eBay Visitors," *America Online News*, December 2, 1999.

83. eBay, "Company Overview," p. 1.

84. Correspondence with Jeffrey Strange, November, 19, 1999.

85. David Cay Johnston, "Advisory Panel on Internet Taxes Unlikely to Reach Consensus," *New York Times*, March 20, 2000.

86. Press release, "Statement by Commerce Secretary William M. Daley on First E-Retail Sales," March 2, 2000, p. 3.

87. "The Wired Society," *Harvard Magazine*, May–June 1999, p. 47.

88. Adrian J. Slywotzky, "The Age of the Choiceboard," *Harvard Business Review* 78 (January–February 2000), p. 40.

89. *Shopping Centers Today*, November 1999, p. 65.

90. L. L. Bean, *Fact Sheet*, n.d., p. 1.

91. "The Wired Society," *Harvard Magazine*, May–June 1999.

92. National Trust for Historic Preservation, "Main Street News," newsletter, May–June 1996, pp. 2, 3, 10.

93. Correspondence with Esther Dyson, March 9, 1999.

94. Standard and Poor's, *Industry Survey. Retailing: Specialty*, May 27, 1999, pp. 7, 8.

95. "Wired Society," p. 48.

96. Amy M. Jaffe, "Retailing's New Strategy: I Can Get It for You Personal," *New York Times*, August 13, 1995.

97. Interview with Robert Glass, senior vice president and chief financial officer, Loehmann's, November 16, 1995.

98. Historical Society of Washington, D.C., *Metro History News*, Winter 1995–96, p. 2.

99. Love, *Colonial History of Hartford*, p. 296.

100. DeVoe, *Market Assistant*, pp. 7, 8. DeVoe, a butcher, has compiled a fascinating research document—a staggeringly comprehensive list of the food sold in public markets in major East Coast cities in the mid-nineteenth century (p. 113).

101. Urban Land Institute and Project for Public Spaces, *Public Markets and Community Revitalization*, p. 1. A very solid and well-documented and illustrated report on how public markets operate and serve communities.

102. Highsmith and Holton, *Reading Terminal and Market*, p. 41.

103. Interview with Betty Kaplan, March 25, 1997.
104. U.S. Department of Agriculture, "Agricultural Marketing Service (AMS) Farmers' Markets," February 16, 2000, pp. 1, 2.
105. Maureen Atkinson and John Williams, "Farmers Markets: Breathing New Life into Old Institutions," *Public Management* 76 (January 1994), pp. 17, 20.
106. Robert Sommer, John Herrick, and Ted R. Sommer, "The Behavioral Ecology of Supermarkets and Farmers' Markets," *Journal of Environmental Psychology* 1 (1981), pp. 13, 16. Sommer, a psychologist at the University of California-Davis, has undertaken some of the most interesting research in this country on farmers' markets. See his "Farmers' Markets as Community Events" in *Public Places and Spaces*, ed. Altman and Zube.
107. Molly O'Neill, "A City's Dreams Go to Market," *New York Times*, August 17, 1994.
108. Michael deC. Hinds, "Inner City Market Blossoms," *New York Times*, May 14, 1994; correspondence with the Reading Terminal Farmers' Market Trust, June and July 1997.
109. Stephen M. Soiffer and Gretchen M. Herrman, "Visions of Power: Ideology and Practice in the American Garage Sale," *Sociological Review* 35 (February 1987), p. 51.
110. Michelle Lebovitz, "The Garage Sale," unpublished undergraduate paper for Art 201, Williams College, 1972, p. 4.
111. Gretchen M. Herrman and Stephen M. Soiffer, "For Fun and Profit: An Analysis of the American Garage Sale," *Urban Life* 12 (January 1984), p. 412.
112. Lebovitz, "Garage Sale," p. 12.
113. Soiffer and Herrman, "Visions of Power," p. 65.
114. Robert Maisel, "The Flea Market as an Action Scene," *Urban Life and Culture* 2 (January 1974), p. 488.
115. *The Economist*, April 23, 1994, p. 31.
116. Megan Garvey, "The Last Sale of a Faded Urban Market," *Washington Post*, April 12, 1994.
117. R. C. Longworth, *Chicago Tribune*, n.d.
118. Urban Land Institute and Project for Public Spaces, *Public Markets and Community Revitalization*, p. 58.
119. Ownby, *American Dreams in Mississippi*, p. 167.
120. International Council of Shopping Centers, *Research Quarterly* 2 (Fall 1995), p. 15.
121. Ibid., p. 2.

122. Beyard et al., *Developing Urban Entertainment Centers*, p. 4.
123. Dave and Buster's, *A Navigational Guide to the Largest Dining and Entertainment Extravaganza in Maryland*, cover page.
124. Alan Snel, "Mall Will Help See Justice Done," *Denver Post*, August 18, 1996.
125. Interactive Downtown Task Force Committee, *A Vision and Action Plan to Revitalize the Heart of Washington, D.C.*, December 1996, pp. 2, 8, 10, 11.
126. William Fulton, "City of Fun," *Governing* 10 (April 1997), p. 24.
127. Letter to author from Nina Gruen, November 30, 1999.
128. Bill Moskin and Sandy Guettler, "Exploring America Through Its Culture," President's Committee on the Arts and Humanities, p. 5.
129. U.S. Department of Commerce, Bureau of the Census, *Census of Retail Trade, 1992*, table 1 for 5942; idem, *Census of Retail Trade, 1997*, table 1 for 451211.
130. Idem, *County Business Patterns, 1959*, table 1; idem, *County Business Patterns, 1997*, table 1, all bookstores' figures for SIC Code 5942.
131. Idem, *Census of Retail Trade, 1992*, table 1 for 5942; idem, *Census for Retail Trade, 1997*, table 1 for 451211.
132. Idem, *County Business Patterns, 1959*, table 1; idem, *County Business Patterns, 1997*, table 1.
133. Idem, *Census of Retail Trade, 1992*, table 5 for 451211 replacing 5942.
134. Book Study Industry Group, Inc., Press Release, June 2, 2000, and August 21, 2000.
135. Politics and Prose, "15th Anniversary," unpublished pamphlet [1999], p. 5.
136. Interviews with Carla Cohen, March 5, 1996, and March 17, 2000, and Politics and Prose *15th Anniversary*, p. 5.
137. Barnaby J. Feder, "A One-Stop Bookseller Challenges the Giants," *New York Times*, February 27, 1995.
138. *Publishers Weekly*, September 19, 1994, p. 17.
139. Telephone conversation with Ann Brinkley and Kandra Smith, Borders Public Relations Department, October 14, 1999.
140. Correspondence with Nancy Levy, marketing director, community relations coordinator, Borders Bookstores, Ann Arbor, Mich. Her statement is from an August 25, 1994, fax communication.
141. Jason Epstein, "The Rattle of Pebbles," *New York Review of Books*, April 27, 2000, p. 59.

Chapter 5. Planning for Shopping

1. Vermont Forum on Sprawl, "The Causes and Costs of Sprawl in Vermont Communities," report 3, in "Exploring Sprawl," 1999, p. 9; idem, "The Costs of Development Downtown vs. Open Spaces," in ibid., pp. 1–6. An unusually competent study that investigates why developers select out-of-town sites for stores. The costs of downtown vs. open space development, including time, land values, environmental and historic preservation regulations, neighborhood involvement, and space considerations, are explored.

2. *Barbier v. Connolly* 113 U.S. 27 (1884), p. 357.

3. Cases on Chinese laundry restrictions: *Barbier v. Connolly* 113 U.S. 27 (1884); *Soon Hing v. Crowley* 113 U.S. 730 (1885); *Yick Wo* 9 Pac. 139 (1885); *Sam Chung* 105 Pac. 609 (1909); *Hang Kie* 69 Cal. 149 (1886); *Quong Wo* 161 Cal. 220 (1911).

4. Higham, *Strangers in the Land*, p. 25.

5. Pollard, "Outline of the Law of Zoning in the United States," p. 18.

6. *Yick Wo* 9 Pac. 139 (1885).

7. *Sam Chung* 105 Pac. 609 (1909).

8. Williams, *Law of City Planning and Zoning*.

9. *Ignaciunas v. Town of Nutley* 99 N.J. 389 (1924).

10. *Steerman v. Oehmann, Washington Law Reporter*, vol. 53, no. 28, (1925), p. 437.

11. Hearing Before the Committee on the District of Columbia, 61st Congress, 2nd Session (1910); Seymour I. Toll, *Zoned America*, p. 126.

12. Ibid., p. 29.

13. Ward and Zunz, *Landscape of Modernity*, p. 29.

14. Toll, *Zoned America*, p. 176.

15. Ibid., p. 177.

16. Bassett, *Zoning*, p. 50.

17. John C. Olmsted, *Report to the Kirkwood Land Company*, November 24, 1903, p. 1. Olmsted Associates Records, Manuscript Division, Library of Congress, Washington, D.C.

18. Bassett, *Zoning*, p. 54.

19. Pollard, "Outline of the Law of Zoning in the United States," p. 26.

20. Gordon Whitnall, "History of Zoning," *Annals of American Academy of Political and Social Science* 45 (March 1931), p. 3.

21. Fries, *Urban Idea in Colonial America*, p. xvii.

22. Bartholomew, "Business Zoning," p. 10.

23. Perry, "Planning a Neighborhood Unit," pp. 124, 125.

24. Ibid., p. 125.

25. Longstreth, "Neighborhood Shopping Center in Washington, D.C.," p. 14.

26. Stein and Bauer, "Store Buildings and Neighborhood Shopping Centers, *Architectural Record* 75 (February 1934), p. 11.

27. Ibid., p. 13.

28. Ibid., p. 1.

29. Ibid., pp. 1, 3.

30. Ibid., p. 11.

31. Data from U.S. Department of Commerce, Bureau of the Census, *Census of Retail Trade* and *Statistical Abstract of the United States, 1994*.

32. Telephone interview with Peter Steck, June 4, 1996.

33. Lever, "Villages of Port Sunlight and Thornton Hough," p. 442.

34. *Progress*, December 1906, p. 368.

35. Interview with Robert E. Simon, February 25, 1997.

36. Interview with David Ross, January 16, 1997.

37. Interview with Robert E. Simon, February 25, 1997.

38. Interview with Alton Scavo, November 12, 1996.

39. Ibid.

40. Duany and Plater-Zyberk, "Second Coming of the American Small Town," p. 47.

41. Stephen C. Fehr, "A Downtown of Their Own," *Washington Post*, March 25, 1996.

42. Calthorpe, *Next American Metropolis*, pp. 16, 17.

43. Ibid., p. 20.

44. Ibid., pp. 22–24.

45. Bruce Liedstrand provided useful information on Mountain View.

46. Larke, *Japanese Retailing*, pp. 236, 71.

47. Ibid., p. 236.

48. Japan External Trade Organization, *Changing Face of Japanese Retail*, p. 6.

49. William Drozdiak, "France's New Rallying Cry: Let Them Eat Bread!" *Washington Post*, October 28, 1995

50. *Economist* 335:7918, June 10, 1995, p. 10.

51. U.K. House of Commons Environment Committee, *Shopping Centres and their Future*, vol. 1, p. lxiv. Based on research of English, French, and German shopping centers, this House of Commons report explains England's concerns about the future of shopping centers and provides a justification for England's planning regulations for retail developments.

52. Invest in France Agency, "Large Retail Distribution Outlets in France," p. 10.

53. U.K. House of Commons Environment Committee, *Shopping Centres and their Future*, pp. lxiv.

54. Ibid., lxii, lxi, lxiii, lxiv.

55. Invest in France Agency, "Large Retail Distribution Outlets in France," p. 2.

56. "Kohl's Bill to Allow Price Bargaining Isn't in Store for German Customers," *Wall Street Journal*, September 20, 1994.

57. "Retail Workers Protest Against Proposal to Expand Shopping Hours," *This Week in Germany*, May 3, 1996, p. 13.

58. Craig R. Whitney, "Comfortable Germans, Slow to Change," *New York Times*, January 16, 1995.

59. Daniel Benjamin, "Germany Considers Legalizing the Ancient Art of Haggling," *Wall Street Journal*, February 19, 1994.

60. Alan Cowell, "Germany's Anguish: History, Identity and Shopping," *New York Times*, May 19, 1996.

61. Václav Havel, "The Hope for Europe," *New York Review of Books*, June 20, 1996 (italics added).

62. Title of legislation: Central Government Regulation pursuant to Section 17–1, Subsection 2 of the Planning and Building Act Dealing with Temporary Suspension of the Establishment of Shopping Centers Outside Town Centres and Densely Populated Areas.

63. U.K. Department of the Environment, *Planning Policy Guidance: Town Centres and Retail Developments* [PPG 6 revised], p. 2.

64. Ibid.

65. U.K. House of Commons Environment Committee, *Shopping Centres and Their Future*, p. xix; U.K. National Economic Development Office, *Future Pattern of Shopping*, p. 27.

66. U.K. House of Commons Environment Committee, *Shopping Centres and Their Future*, p. xiii.

67. *Future Pattern of Shopping*, p. 21.

68. Royal Town Planning Institute, *Planning for Shopping into the Twenty-First Century*, p. 17.

69. Howard, "Assessing the Impact of Shopping Centre Development," p. 108.

70. Letter from Nicole Lander, corporate affairs manager, Tesco, to author, July 1, 1999.

71. CB Hillier Parker, "Shopping Centres in the Pipeline," p. 1.

72. U.K. House of Commons Environment Committee, *Shopping Centres and Their Future*, pp. lvii, lxiii.

73. David Lock Associates, "Brierley Hill Town Centre," pp. 1, 2.

74. Caborn, "Food and Supermarkets," pp. 1, 3.

75. Gummer, "Afterthought," p. 5.

76. Skinner, "Maintaining Retail Balance in California," pp. 3–10.

77. National Trust for Historic Preservation, "Reinvestment Statistics, 1999," p. 1.

78. Idem, "National Main Street Trends Survey, 1999," pp. 1–9.

79. Telephone conversation with Beaverprints staff, June 19, 2000.

80. City of San Luis Obispo, Calif., *Land Use Element*, Section 2.2.12 I, p. 29, as quoted in a letter from Glen Matteson, San Luis Obispo Planning Department.

81. Fillip, "Uptown District, San Diego," p. 6.

82. Ibid., pp. 4, 7.

83. Arlington County, Virginia, Department of Community Planning, Housing and Development, "Year Review of Arlington County's Comprehensive Plan," p. 3.

84. Idem, "Columbia Pike 2000," pp. 39, 47.

85. Ibid., p. 12.

86. Vermont State Legislature, bills H. 408, H. 475, and H. 659 (2000 Session), and act 120 [H. 278] (1998 Session).

Chapter 6. Shopping: A Public Concern

1. Boarnet and Crane, "Impact of Big Box Grocers," pp. 81, 82. By analyzing the hidden and sometimes significant public costs of large, superstore grocers, this study contributes solid statistics to an often emotion-driven field.

2. Stanley C. Hollander, "United States of America," in *Public Policy Toward Retailing: An International Symposium*, ed. Boddewyn and Hollander, pp. 395, 368.

3. Boarnet and Crane, "Impact of Big Box Grocers," pp. 1, 2.

4. Cohen, "From Town Center to Shopping Center," pp. 1080–81. A thoughtful discussion of the changes in retailing after World War II, with particular attention to Paramus, New Jersey.

5. Putnam, *Bowling Alone*, p. 136. In this book, his article "Bowling Alone: America's Declining Social Capital," and in his earlier study of Italian reactions to regionalism, Putnam forcefully expounds on the importance of social capital in civic life. His statistics, wide-ranging research, and overarching thesis make this an important contribution

to the study of community life.

6. Vermont Forum on Sprawl, "Vermonters' Attitudes on Sprawl," report 5, in "Exploring Sprawl," 1999, p. 5.

7. Steve Case, presentation at the Harvard University Conference on the Internet and Society, May 29, 1998. An articulate, thoughtful, and frank discussion of the problems and potential of the Internet.

8. Jacobs, *Death and Life of Great American Cities*, p. 56.

9. Dewey, *Public and Its Problems*, p. 211.

10. Winthrop, *Life and Letters of John Winthrop*, 2: 19.

11. Franklin, *Autobiography of Benjamin Franklin*, p. 132.

12. Royce quotations from author's "Josiah Royce, Neglected Philosopher," unpublished undergraduate honors thesis, Radcliffe/Harvard University, 1953.

13. Ranney, *Papers of Frederick Law Olmsted*, vol. 5, *The California Frontier, 1863–1865*, pp. 2, 659.

14. Unabomber, Statement in the *Washington Post*, September 19, 1995, p. 2.

15. Shaffer and Anundsen, *Creating Community Anywhere*, pp. vii, 8, 10.

16. Ibid., pp. 10, 57.

17. Ibid., pp. 6, 92.

18. Saxenian, *Inside-Out*, p. 2. An updating of this concise and incisive study, completed in 1993, would be interesting.

19. "Wired Society," p. 106.

20. Saxenian, *Inside-Out*, p. 2.

21. Ibid., pp. 6, 5.

22. Putnam, Leonardi, and Nanetti, *Making Democracy Work*, pp. 107, 111.

23. Ibid., pp. 146, 144, 133.

24. Ibid., p. 161.

25. Putnam, "Bowling Alone," pp. 68, 69.

26. Ibid., pp. 75, 77.

27. Ibid., p. 71.

28. Putnam, *Bowling Alone*, pp. 401, 407.

29. "A Still Point, Still There," *New York Times*, December 30, 1995, editorial.

30. Rose Moss, "No Space Like Shared Space," *New York Times*, January 15, 1996.

31. Rybczynski, "No Place Like Home," p. 140.

32. Williams, *Keywords*, pp. 78, 79. This is a gem of a book. Williams explores how the meanings of keywords have changed over time.

33. Interview with Esther Naughton, January 1994.

34. Telephone interview with Paul Edlund, February 1998.

35. Jim Robbins, "Montana Town Says Post Office Move Would Take Heart Out of Main Street," *New York Times*, December 3, 1996.

36. Ibid.

37. Ibid.

38. *Congressional Record*, January 21, 1997, p. H503.

39. The House bill, H.R. 1231, was titled Post Office Relocation Act of 1997 and renamed Post Office Community Partnership Act of 1998; the Senate bill, S. 2025, was Community and Postal Participation Act of 1998.

40. U.S. Postal Service, "Community Relations Regulations for the United States Postal Service Facilities Projects," 2nd ed., 1999, p. 4.

41. *Congressional Record*, January 21, 1997, p. H503.

42. Herbert Muschamp, "Remodeling New York for the Bourgeoisie," *New York Times*, September 24, 1995.

43. Kennedy Lawson Smith, "Director's Column," *Main Street News* 122 (May–June 1996), p. 9.

44. Telephone interview with Shirley Dushna, April 1998.

45. William Glaberson, "Newspaper Owners Do the Shuffle," *New York Times*, February 19, 1996.

46. Fjellman, *Vinyl Leaves*, pp. 403, 57.

47. Putnam, *Bowling Alone*, p. 179.

48. Jardine, *Worldly Goods*, pp. 380, 381.

Bibliography

Published and Unpublished Sources

Albrecht, Donald, ed. *World War II and the American Dream*. Cambridge, Mass.: MIT Press and the National Building Museum, 1995.

Alexander, Alan A., and Muhlebach, Richard F. *Shopping Center Management*. Chicago: Institute of Real Estate Management, 1992.

Alexander, Laurence A. *Strategies for Stopping Shopping Centers: A Guidebook on Minimizing Excessive Suburban Shopping Center Growth*. New York: Downtown Research and Development Center, 1980.

Ambry, Margaret. *Almanac of Consumer Markets, 1989*. Ithaca: American Demographics Press, 1990–91.

———. *Consumer Power: How Americans Spend*. Chicago: Probus, 1991.

American School of Classical Studies at Athens. *The Athenian Agora*. Princeton, N.J.: Princeton University Press, 1971.

Anderson, B. L., and Latham, A. J. H. *The Market in History*. London: Croom Helm, 1986.

Angelou, Maya. *I Know Why the Caged Bird Sings*. New York: Bantam, 1993.

"Are Teenagers Treated Fairly at the Mall?" *Parade Magazine*, February 12, 1995, p. 10.

Arlington County, Virginia, Department of Community Planning, Housing and Development. "Columbia Pike 2000: A Revitalization Plan." Published report, 1991.

———. "Year Review of Arlington County's Comprehensive Plan." Published report, 1995.

Atherton, Lewis E. *Main Street on the Middle Border*. New York: Quadrangle/New York Times, 1978.

———. *The Frontier Merchant in Mid-America*. Columbia: University of Missouri Press, 1971.

———. *The Southern Country Store, 1800–1860*. Baton Rouge: Louisiana State University Press, 1949.

Atkinson, Maureen, and Williams, John. "Farmers Markets: Breathing New Life into Old Institutions." *Public Management* 75 (January 1994), pp. 16–20.

Bacon, Robert W. *Consumer Spatial Behavior: A Model of Purchasing Decisions Over Space and Time*. Oxford: Clarendon, 1984.

Bailyn, Bernard. *The New England Merchants in the Seventeenth Century*. Cambridge, Mass.: Harvard University Press, 1955.

Baldassare, Mark. *Trouble in Paradise: The Suburban Transformation in America*. New York: Columbia University Press, 1986.

Barnett, Jonathan. *The Fractured Metropolis*. New York: Icon Editions/HarperCollins, 1995.

Barth, Gunther. *City People: The Rise of Modern City Culture in Nineteenth Century America*. New York: Oxford University Press, 1980.

Bartholomew, Harland. "Business Zoning." *Annals of American Academy of Political and Social Science* 45 (March 1931), pp. 101–4.

Bartos, Rena. *The Moving Target: What Every Marketer Should Know About Women*. New York: Free Press, 1982.

Bassett, Edward M. *Zoning: The Laws, Administration, and Court Decisions During the First Twenty Years*. New York: Russell Sage, 1936.

BDD Planning/Oxford Institute of Retail Management. *The Effects of Major Out of Town Retail Development: A Literature Review*. London: Her Majesty's Stationery Office (hereinafter cited as HMSO), 1992.

Beasley, Ellen. *The Corner Store: An American Tradition, Galveston Style*. Washington, D.C.: National Building Museum, 1999.

Beaumont, Constance E. *How Superstore Sprawl Can Harm Communities and What Citizens Can Do About It*. Washington, D.C.: National Trust for Historic Preservation, 1994.

Bell, Daniel. *The Cultural Contradictions of Capitalism*. New York: Basic Books, 1976.

Bellah, Robert N.; Madsen, Robert N.; Sullivan, William M.; Swidler, Ann T.; Tipton, Steven M. *Habits of the Heart: Individualism and Commitment in American Life*. Berkeley: University of California Press, 1985.

Benson, John, and Shaw, Gareth, eds. *The Evolution of Retail Systems, c. 1800–1914*. Leicester: Leicester University Press, 1992.

Benson, Susan Porter. *Counter Cultures: Saleswomen, Managers, and Customers in American Department Stores. Urbana: University of Illinois Press, 1986.

Berger, Peter; Berger, Brigitte; and Kellner, Hansfried. The Homeless Mind: Modernization and Consciousness. New York: Vintage, 1974.

Bernoff, Josh; Morrisette, Shelley; and Clemmer, Kenneth. "Consumer eCommerce Readiness." Forrester Report 1 (March 1998), pp. 1–16.

Berry, Brian J. L. Geography of Market Centers and Retail Institutions. Englewood Cliffs, N.J.: Prentice-Hall, 1967.

Beyard, Michael D.; Braun, Ray; McLaughlin, Herb; Phillips, Patrick L.; and Rubin, Michael. Developing Urban Entertainment Centers. Washington, D.C.: Urban Land Institute, 1998.

Blakely, Edward J. Shaping the American Dream: Land Use Choices for America's Future. Berkeley: University of California Press, 1993.

——. Transporting and Transforming a Nation. Berkeley: University of California Press, working paper no. 588, 1993.

Bloch, Herbert A. The Concept of Our Changing Loyalties: An Introductory Study into the Nature of the Social Individual. New York: Columbia University Press, 1934.

Bloom, Paul N., and Smith, Ruth Belk. The Future of Consumerism. Lexington, Mass.: Lexington Books, 1986.

Bluestone, Barry; Hanna, Patricia; Kuhn, Sarah; and Moore, Laura. The Retail Revolution: Market Transformation, Investment, and Labor in the Modern Department Store. Boston: Auburn House, 1981.

Boarnet, Marion, and Crane, Randall. "The Impacts of Big Box Grocers on Southern California: Jobs, Wages, and Municipal Finance." Prepared for the Orange County, Calif., Business Council, September 1999.

Boddewyn, J. J., and Hollander, Stanley C., eds. Public Policy Toward Retailing: An International Symposium. Lexington, Mass.: Lexington Books, 1972.

Bonner, Simon J., ed. Consuming Visions: Accumulation and Display of Goods in America, 1880–1920. New York: W. W. Norton, 1989.

Bookchin, Murray. Urbanization Without Cities: The Rise and Decline of Citizenship. Montreal: Black Rose, 1992.

Boorstin, Daniel J. The Americans: The Democratic Experience. New York: Vintage, 1974.

Bowlby, Rachel. Just Looking: Consumer Culture in Dreiser, Gissing, and Zola. New York: Methuen, 1985.

——. Carried Away: The Invention of Modern Shopping. New York: Columbia University Press, 2000.

Branch, Mark Alden. "Where Do Wal-Marts Come From?" Progressive Architecture, September 1993.

Braudel, Fernand. A History of Civilization. Translated by Richard Mayne. New York: Penguin Books, 1993.

——. Civilization and Capitalism, Fifteenth-Eighteenth Century. Vol. 2, The Wheels of Commerce. Translated by Siân Reynolds. Berkeley: University of California Press, 1992.

Bridenbaugh, Carl. Cities in the Wilderness: The First Century of Urban Life in America, 1625–1742. New York: Knopf, 1955.

Bronner, Simon J., ed. Consuming Visions: Accumulation and Display of Goods in America 1880–1920. New York: W. W. Norton, 1989.

Brown, Frederick. Zola: A Life. New York: Farrar Straus Giroux, 1995.

Bruchey, Stuart W., ed. Small Business in American Life. New York: Columbia University Press, 1980.

Bushman, Richard L. From Puritan to Yankee: Character and the Social Order in Connecticut, 1690–1765. New York: W. W. Norton, 1970.

——. "Shopping and Advertising in Colonial America." In Of Consuming Interests: The Style of Life in the Eighteenth Century. Edited by Cary Carson. Charlottesville: University Press of Virginia, 1994.

Businessmen's Conference on Urban Problems. "Better Cities . . . Better Business." September 13–14, 1948. Washington, D.C.: U.S Chamber of Commerce, 1948.

Caborn, Richard. "Food and Supermarkets." Opposition Day Debate in Parliament, June 24, 1999.

Cahill, Jane. Can a Smaller Store Succeed? New York: Fairchild, 1966.

Calthorpe, Peter. The Next American Metropolis: Ecology, Community, and the American Dream. Princeton, N.J.: Princeton Architectural Press, 1993.

Campbell, Colin. The Romantic Ethic and the Spirit of Modern Consumerism. Oxford: Basil Blackwell, 1987.

Carson, Gerald. Country Stores in Early New England. Old Sturbridge, Mass.: Old Sturbridge Booklet Series, 1955.

Case, Steve. Presentation at the Harvard University Conference on the Internet and Society, May, 29, 1998.

CB Hillier Parker. "Shopping Centres in the Pipeline." London: CB Hillier Parker, May 2000, pp. 1–4.

Centers: Upscale Specialty and Festival: Filling the Important Niche Between Conventional Malls and Strip Centers. Spring Valley, N.J.: MJJ & M Publication Corp., 1989.

Child, Mrs. *The American Frugal Housewife.* Boston: Carter, Hendee, 1833.

Childress, Herb. "No Loitering: Some Ideas About Small Town Hangouts." *Small Town* 24 (September–October 1993), pp. 20–25.

Chinitz, Benjamin. "A Framework for Speculating About Future Urban Growth Patterns in the United States." *Urban Studies* 28 (December 1991), pp. 939–59.

Christensen, Clayton M., and Tedlow, Richard S. "Patterns of Disruption in Retailing." *Harvard Business Review* 78 (January–February 2000), pp. 42–45.

Clark, Thomas D. *Pills, Petticoats, and Plows: The Southern Country Store.* Indianapolis: Bobbs-Merrill, 1944.

Cobbett, William. *Rural Rides.* New York: E. P. Dutton, 1932.

Cohen, Lizabeth. "From Town Center to Shopping Center: The Reconfiguration of Community Marketplaces in Postwar America." *American Historical Review* 101 (October 1996), pp. 1050–81.

Coogan, Matthew A., and Karash, Kasla H. "Policy Issues in the Management of Downtown Crossing Project: A Demographic Context for Policy Analysis." Prepared for the Sixty-first Annual Meeting of the Transportation Research Board, January 1982.

Cowell, Deborah K., and Green, Gary P. "Community Attachment and Spending Location: The Importance of Place in Household Consumption." *Social Science Quarterly* 75 (September 1994).

Crimmins, Timothy J., and White, Dana F. *The New Georgia Guide.* Athens: University of Georgia Press, 1996.

Curti, Merle. "The Changing Concept of 'Human Nature' in the Literature of American Advertising." *Business History Review* 41 (Winter 1967), pp. 335–57.

David Lock Associates. "Brierly Hill Town Centre: Dudley Metropolitan Borough Council, UDP Inset," November 1999, pp. 1–56.

Davies, Ross L. *Retail and Commercial Planning.* London: Croom Helm, 1984.

———, and Reynolds, Jonathan. *Teleshopping and Teleservices.* Harlow, U.K.: Longman, 1988.

Davis, Dorothy. *The History of Shopping.* London: Routledge and Kegan Paul, 1966.

Davis, Fred. *Fashion, Culture, and Identity.* Chicago: University of Chicago Press, 1992.

Dawson, John A. *Retail Geography.* New York: John Wiley and Sons, 1980.

de Avila, Edward. "Back to the Future: Retail and Theater Development Trends." *Urban Land* 55 (August 1996).

Defoe, Daniel. *The Complete English Tradesmen in Familiar Letters.* New York: Burt Franklin, 1970.

DeVoe, Thomas F. *The Market Assistant, Containing a Brief Description of Every Food Item Sold in the Public Markets in the Cities of New York, Boston, Philadelphia, and Brooklyn.* New York: Hurd and Houghton, 1867.

Dewey, John. *The Public and Its Problems: An Essay in Political Inquiry.* Chicago: Gateway, 1946.

Direct Marketing Association. *Catalog Industry Statistics.* New York: Direct Marketing Association, 1996.

Distributive Trades Economic Development Commission. *The Future of High Street.* London: HMSO, 1988.

Dobriner, William M. *The Suburban Community.* New York: G. P. Putnam's, 1958.

Dowdy, Marshall D. "The Grocery Shopping Attitudes and Behaviors of Convenience Store Patrons." Ph.D. diss., Virginia Polytechnic Institute and State University, 1994.

Dower, Dennis. "Escaping the City: New Deal Housing and Gustave King's Garden Apartment Villages." In *Urban Forum, Suburban Dreams.* College Station: Texas A&M University Press, 1993.

Dreiser, Theodore. *Sister Carrie.* New York: W. W. Norton, 1970.

Duany, Andres, and Plater-Zyberk, Elizabeth. "The Second Coming of the American Small Town." *Wilson Quarterly* 16 (Winter 1992), pp. 19–62.

Dubester, Henry J. *Catalog of U.S. Census Publications, 1790–1945.* Washington, D.C.: 1950.

Dunne, Patrick; Lusch, Robert F.; and Gable, Myron. *Retail Management.* Cincinnati: South-Western, 1990.

Ehrlich, George. *Kansas City, Missouri: An Architectural History, 1826–1990.* Columbia: University of Missouri Press, 1992.

Enchin, Ervin. *The Great Shopocracy: The Professionalization of the Independent Shopkeepers.* Guelph, Ontario: Alexis, 1990.

Estates Gazette. London, Janary 20, 1994, April 23, 1994, May 14, 1994, and May 28, 1994.

Etzioni, Amitai. *The Spirit of Community: The Reinvention of American Society*. New York: Simon & Schuster, 1993.

Evans, Eli N. *The Provincials: A Personal History of Jews in the South*. New York: Free Press Paperbacks, Simon & Schuster, 1973.

Everton, Ann R., and Hughes, David. *Public Law and the Retail Sector*. Harlow, U.K.: Longman Group, 1988.

Ewen, Stuart, and Ewen, Elizabeth. *Channels of Desire: Mass Images and the Shaping of American Consciousness*. New York: McGraw-Hill, 1992.

Faber, Ronald J. "Money Changes Everything: Compulsive Buying from a Biopsychosocial Perspective." *American Behavioral Scientist* 35 (July 1992), pp. 809–19.

Fairfax County, Virginia, Planning Commission. "Draft Tysons Corner Urban Center Plan." Published report, April 1994.

Falk, Pasi, and Campbell, Colin, eds. *The Shopping Experience*. London: Sage, 1997.

Featherstone, Mike. *Consumer Culture and Postmodernism*. London: Sage, 1991.

Fillip, Janice. "Uptown District, San Diego." *Urban Land* 49 (June 1990), pp. 2–7.

Fishman, Robert. *Bourgeois Utopias: The Rise and Fall of Suburbs*. New York: Basic Books, 1987.

Fite, Gilbert C. *Farm to Factory: A History of Consumers Cooperative Association*. Columbia: University of Missouri Press, 1965.

Fitzgerald, Francis. *Cities on a Hill: A Journey Through Contemporary American Cultures*. New York: Simon & Schuster, 1987.

Fjellman, Stephen N. *Vinyl Leaves: Walt Disney World and America*. Boulder, Colo.: Westview, 1992.

Forty, Adrian. *Objects of Desire*. New York: Pantheon Books, 1986.

France, Kim. "Letter from the Editor." *Lucky* (Spring–Summer 2000), p. 17.

Frank, Jack. Lecture presented at American Planning Association Conference, San Francisco, April 1994.

Franklin, Benjamin. *The Autobiography of Benjamin Franklin and Selections from his Writings*. Introduction by Henry Steele Commager. New York: Modern Library, 1944.

Frantz, Douglas, and Collins, Catherine. *Celebration, U.S.A.: Living in Disney's Brave New Town*. New York: Henry Holt, 1999.

Freudenberger, Herman. "Fashion, Sumptuary Laws and Business." *Business History Review* 37 (Spring–Summer 1963), pp. 37–48.

Fries, Sylvia P. *The Urban Idea in Colonial America*. Philadelphia: Temple University Press, 1977.

Fromm, Erich. "The Psychological Aspects of the Guaranteed Income." In *The Guaranteed Income: Next Step in Economic Evolution?* Edited by Robert Theobald. Garden City, N.Y.: Doubleday, 1966.

——. *The Sane Society*. Greenwich, Conn.: Fawcett, 1969.

Fulmer, O. Kline. *Greenbelt*. Washington, D.C.: American Council on Public Affairs, 1941.

Fulton, William. "City of Fun." *Governing* 10 (April 1997).

Gallagher, Winifred. *The Power of Place: How Our Surroundings Shape Our Thoughts, Emotions, and Actions*. New York: Poseidon, 1993.

Gans, Herbert J. *The Urban Villagers: Group and Class in the Life of Italian-Americans*. Glencoe, Ill.: Free Press, 1962.

Garreau, Joel. *Edge City: Life on the New Frontier*. New York: Anchor, 1988.

Gilchrist, Agnes A. "Market Houses in High Street." In *Historic Philadelphia: From the Founding Until the Early Nineteenth Century*. Philadelphia: American Philosophical Society, 1953.

Gillette, Howard, Jr. "The Evolution of Planned Shopping Centers in Suburbs and City." *Journal of the American Planning Association* 51 (Autumn 1985), pp. 449–59.

Goe, W. Richard. "The Producer Services Sector and Development Within the Deindustrializing Urban Community." *Social Forces* 72 (June 1994), pp. 971–1009.

Goodman, Paul, and Goodman, Percival. *Communities: Means of Livelihood and Ways of Life*. New York: Vintage, 1960.

Goodman, Robert. "The Dead Mall." *Metropolis Magazine*, November 1993.

Goodwin, Doris Kearns. *Wait Till Next Year: A Memoir*. New York: Simon & Schuster, 1997.

Gorman, Babette. *All About Filene's and the People Who Made It Grow*. Boston: Filene's Public Relations Department, n.d.

Government Employees Insurance Company. *GEICO Direct*. Spring 1995.

Gratz, Roberta Brandes. *The Living City: How Urban Residents Are Revitalizing America's Neighborhoods and Downtown Shopping Districts by Thinking Small in a Big Way*. New York: Simon & Schuster, 1989.

Green, Anne. "Geography of Changing Female Economic Activity Rates: Issues and Implications for Policy and Methodology."

Regional Studies 28 (October 1994), pp. 633–45.

Green, Gordon, and Welniak, Edward. "The Nine Household Markets." *American Demographics* 13 (October 1991).

Gruen, Victor. *The Heart of Our Cities: The Urban Crisis, Diagnosis and Cure.* New York: Simon & Schuster, 1964.

Grupe, Greenlaw. "How a Neighborhood Center Grew into a Community Center." *Urban Land* 20 (January 1961), pp. 6–7.

Gummer, John. "Afterthought: Out of Town and Over There." *Planning,* March 5, 1999, p. 5.

Haar, Charles M. *Land Use Planning: A Casebook on the Use, Disuse, and Re-use of Urban Lands.* Boston: Little, Brown, 1959.

Hagan, Charlene Hughes. "Factors Influencing the Store Patronage of a Selected Group of Women Employed in Managerial and Professional Occupations in Northern Louisiana." Ph.D. diss., Texas Woman's University, 1987.

Hagman, Donald G. *Public Planning Control of Urban and Land Development.* St. Paul, Minn.: West Publishing, 1980.

Hahn, Harley, and Stout, Rick. *The Internet Complete Reference.* Berkeley, Calif.: Osborne McGraw-Hill, 1994.

Hall, Peter. *Cities of Tomorrow.* Oxford: Basil Blackwell, 1988.

Hanchett, Thomas W. "United States Tax Policy and the Shopping Center Boom." *American Historical Review* 101 (October 1996), pp. 1082–1110.

Harris, Leon. *Merchant Princes: An Intimate History of Jewish Families Who Built Great Department Stores.* New York: Kodansha, 1994.

Harwood Group for the Merck Family Fund. *Yearning for Balance: Views of Americans on Consumption, Materialism, and the Environment.* Takoma Park, Md.: Merck Family Fund, 1995.

Hawke, David F. *Everyday Life in Early America.* New York: Harper & Row, 1988.

Hebron Preservation Society. *Hebron: A Century in Review.* Hebron, N.Y.: Hebron Preservation Society, 1987.

Herbers, John. *The New Heartland: America's Flight Beyond the Suburbs and How It Is Changing Our Future.* New York: Timesbook, 1978.

Herndon, Booten. *Satisfaction Guaranteed: An Unconventional Report on Today's Consumers.* New York: McGraw-Hill, 1972.

Herrman, Gretchen M., and Soiffer, Stephen M.

"For Fun and Profit: An Analysis of the American Garage Sale." *Urban Life* 12 (January 1984), pp. 397–421.

Hester, Randolph T. "It's Just a Matter of Fishheads Using Design as a Means of Building Community." *Small Town* 24 (September–October 1992), pp. 4–9.

Hetherington, John C. *Mutual and Cooperative Enterprises: An Analysis of Customer-Owned Firms in the United States.* Charlottesville: University of Virginia Press, 1991.

Higham, John. *Strangers in the Land: Patterns of American Nativism, 1860–1925.* New York: Atheneum, 1975.

Highsmith, Carol M., and Holton, James L. *Reading Terminal and Market: Philadelphia's Gateway and Grand Convention Center.* Washington, D.C.: Chelsea, 1994.

Hirschman, Albert O. *Exit, Voice, and Loyalty Responses to Decline in Firms, Organizations, and States.* Cambridge, Mass.: Harvard University Press, 1970.

———. *Rival Views of Market Society.* Cambridge, Mass.: Harvard University Press, 1992.

Historical Society of Washington, D.C. *Metro History News,* Winter 1995–96, pp. 1–4.

Hollander, Stanley C. *Discount Retailing, 1900–1952: An Examination of Some Divergences from the One-Price System of American Retailing.* New York: Garland, 1986.

Homberger, Eric. *The Historical Atlas of New York City: A Visual Celebration of Nearly 400 Years of New York City's History.* New York: Henry Holt, 1994.

Hooper, Kevin G. *Travel Characteristics of Large-Scale Suburban Activity Centers.* National Cooperative Highway Research Program Report, no. 323. Washington, D.C.: National Research Council, 1989.

Hoover, Gary; Campbell, Alta; and Spain, Patrick J., eds. *Hoover's Handbook of Business, 1995.* Austin, Tex.: Reference Press, 1996.

Howard, Elizabeth B. "Assessing the Impact of Shopping Centre Development: The Meadowhall Case." *Journal of Property Research* 19 (September 1993), pp. 97–119.

———. *Leisure and Retailing.* Harlow, U.K.: Longman, 1990.

———, and Davies, Ross L. *Change in the Retail Environment.* Harlow, U.K.: Longman, 1988.

Hoyt, Homer. "Sales in Leading Shopping Center Districts in the United States." *Urban Land* 20 (September 1961), pp. 1–7.

Hughes, James W. *Retailing and Regional Malls.* New Brunswick, N.J.: Rutgers University Press, 1991.

Hummon, David M. *Commonplaces: Community Ideology and Identity in American Culture*. Albany: State University of New York Press, 1990.

Hutzler's Department Store. "Your Smile Means a Lot to Your Customer." *Tips and Taps*, August 1973. Courtesy of Maryland Historical Society, Baltimore.

Interactive Downtown Task Force Committee. *A Vision and Action Plan to Revitalize the Heart of Washington, D.C.* Washington, D.C.: Interactive Downtown Task Force Committee, 1996.

International Council of Shopping Centers. *The Best of the Retail Challenge Tips for Shopping Center Retailers*. New York: International Council of Shopping Centers, 1991.

———. *Issues in Downtown Retail Development: An Overview of Recent Experiences*. New York: International Council of Shopping Centers, 1984.

———. *Research Bulletin*, March 1992, February 1993, May 1993, July 1993, December 1993, and July 1994.

———. *The Scope of the Shopping Center Industry in the United States, 1996*. New York: International Council of Shopping Centers, 1996.

———. *Shopping Centers Today*, May 1991, May 1992, August 1992, December 1993, January 1994, April 1994, May 1994, June 1994, July 1994 and August 1994.

Invest in France Agency. "Large Retail Distribution Outlets in France." Unpublished survey, c. 1994.

Jackson, John Brinckerhoff, *American Space: Centennial Years 1865–1876*. New York: Norton, 1972.

———. *Sense of Place, Sense of Time*. New Haven: Yale University Press, 1996.

———. *The Necessity for Ruins and Other Topics*. Amherst: University of Massachusetts Press, 1980.

Jackson, Kenneth J. "All the World's a Mall: Reflections on the Social and Economic Consequences of the American Shopping Center." *American Historical Review* 101 (October 1996), pp. 1111–21.

———. *Crabgrass Frontier: The Suburbanization of the United States*. New York: Oxford University Press, 1985.

Jacobs, Jane. *The Death and Life of Great American Cities*. New York: Random House, 1961.

Jacobs, Jerry. *The Mall: An Attempted Escape from Everyday Life*. Prospect Heights, Ill.: Waveland, 1984.

Japan External Trade Organization. *The Changing Face of Japanese Retail*. Tokyo: Japan External Trade Organization, 1995.

Jardine, Lisa. *Worldly Goods: A New History of the Renaissance*. New York: Doubleday, 1996.

Jarrell, Randall. *A Sad Heart at the Supermarket: Essays & Fables*. New York: Atheneum, 1967.

Johnson, Jan Thomas, and Broughton, Grace. "1996 Great American Street Awards." *Main Street News* 122 (May–June 1996), pp. 1–11.

Jonassen, C. T. *The Shopping Center vs. Downtown: A Motivation Research on Shopping Habits and Attitudes in Three Cities*. Columbus: Ohio State University, 1955.

Jones, Fred M. *Retail Management*. Homewood, Ill.: Richard D. Irwin, 1967.

June, Ray, and Roberts, Bruce. *American Country Store*. Chester, Conn.: Globe Pequot, 1991.

Kelly, Barbara M. *Expanding the American Dream: Building and Rebuilding Levittown*. Albany: State University of New York Press, 1993.

———, ed. *Suburbia Re-examined*. New York: Greenwood, 1980.

Klein, Lloyd. "Consumer Credit and the Institutionalization of Consumerism." Ph.D. diss., City University of New York, 1993.

Kunstler, James Howard. *The Geography of Nowhere: The Rise and Decline of America's Man-Made Landscape*. New York: Simon & Schuster, 1993.

Langdon, Philip. *A Better Place to Live: Reshaping the American Suburbs*. Amherst: University of Massachusetts Press, 1994.

Larke, Roy. *Japanese Retailing*. New York: Routledge, 1994.

Lasch, Christopher. *The Culture of Narcissism: American Life in an Age of Diminishing Expectation*. New York: W. W. Norton, 1979.

Leach, William. *Land of Desire: Merchants, Power, and the Rise of a New American Culture*. New York: Vintage, 1993.

Lebovitz, Michelle. "The Garage Sale." Unpublished undergraduate paper, Williams College, 1972.

Legergott, Stanley. *Pursuing Happiness: American Consumers in the Twentieth Century*. Princeton, N.J.: Princeton University Press, 1993.

Leinberger, Paul, and Tucker, Bruce. *The New Individualists*. New York: HarperCollins, 1991.

Lever, W. H. "The Villages of Port Sunlight and

Thornton Hough." *Building News*, March 1902.

Levitt, William J. "A House Is Not Enough." In *Business Decisions That Changed Our Lives.* Edited by Sidney Furst and Milton Sherman. New York: Random House, 1964.

Lieder, Constance. "Planning for Housing." In *The Practice of Local Government Planning.* Edited Frank So. Washington, D.C.: International City Managers Association, 1988.

Linden, Eugene. *Affluence and Discontent: The Anatomy of Consumer Societies.* New York: Viking, 1979.

Linder, Staffan B. *The Harried Leisure Class.* New York: Columbia University Press, 1970.

Longstreth, Richard. *City Center to Regional Mall: Architecture, the Automobile, and Retailing in Los Angeles, 1920–1930.* Cambridge, Mass.: MIT Press, 1997.

———. "The Neighborhood Shopping Center in Washington, D.C., 1939–1941." *Journal of the Society of Architectural Historians* 51 (March 1992), pp. 5–34.

Love, William DeLoss. *The Colonial History of Hartford.* Hartford, Conn.: Centinel Hill, 1974.

MacDonald, William L. *The Architecture of the Roman Empire.* New Haven, Conn.: Yale University Press, 1982.

McConnell, Gloria E. "A VALS Overview of U.S. Shopping Patterns and Attitudes." Stanford Research Institute, unpublished report, June 1990.

McCracken, Ellen. *Decoding Women's Magazines from Mademoiselle to Ms.* New York: St. Martin's, 1993.

McCracken, Grant. *Culture and Consumption: New Approaches to the Symbolic Character of Consumer Goods and Activities.* Bloomington: Indiana University Press, 1988.

McKeon, Richard, ed. *Aristotle: The Basic Works.* New York: Random House, 1941.

Maddox, Brenda. *D. H. Lawrence: The Story of a Marriage.* New York: Simon & Schuster, 1994.

Maisel, Robert. "The Flea Market as an Action Scene." *Urban Life and Culture* 2 (January 1974), pp. 488–505.

Malloy, Enid. *Over the Counter: The Country Store in Canada.* Markham, Ontario: Fitzhenry & Whiteside, 1985.

Manchester, Vermont, Town of. "Town Plan, 1997," n.d.

Marcus, Stanley. *Minding the Store.* Boston, Mass.: Little, Brown, 1974.

"Marketplace." June 15, 1999. Tape distributed by Public Radio International, Los Angeles.

Marks, Marcus. "Report on Market System for New York City and on Open Markets in Manhattan." In *Public Markets and Community Revitalization.* New York: Project for Public Places and Urban Land Institute, 1995.

Martin, Christopher. "Seven Corners Shopping Center and the Transformation of Fairfax County, Virginia." Paper presented at the Twenty-Second Annual Conference of Washington, D.C., Historical Studies, October 14, 1995.

Marty, Martin E. *Religion and Republic: The American Circumstance.* Boston: Beacon, 1987.

———, and Appleby, R. Scott. *Accounting for Fundamentalism.* Chicago: University of Chicago Press, 1991.

Mayer, Harold M., and Wade, Richard. *Chicago: Growth of a Metropolis.* Chicago: University of Chicago Press, 1969.

Meeker, Mary. *The Internet Advertising Report.* New York: Harper Business, 1997.

———, and DePuy, Chris. *The Internet Report.* New York: Harper Business, 1996.

Mehling, Richard J. "A Brief Profile of the Origins of the Retail Merchants Associations of Baltimore." Unpublished paper, Johns Hopkins University, May 1962.

Meiggs, Russell. *Roman Ostia.* Oxford: Oxford at the Clarendon Press, 1960.

Michman, Ronald D. *Lifestyle Market Segmentation.* New York: Praeger, 1991.

Miller, Arthur. *The Price.* New York: Viking, 1968.

Mishan, Ezra J. *The Costs of Economic Growth.* New York: Praeger, 1967.

Mollenkopf, John Hull, ed. *Power, Culture, and Place.* New York: Russell Sage, 1988.

Morrisette, Shelley; Clemmer, Kenneth; and Bluestein, William M. "The Retail Power Shift." *Forrester Report* 1 (April 1998), pp. 1–15.

Moskin, Bill, and Guettler, Sandy. "Exploring America Through Its Culture." President's Committee on the Arts and Humanities, 1995.

National Public Radio. "Morning Edition." May 7, 1996, and February 25, 1997.

National Trust for Historic Preservation. "Main Street Project." Newsletter, May–June 1996.

———. "National Main Street Trends Survey, 1999." Unpublished report, n.d.

———. "National Reinvestment Statistics, 1999." Unpublished report, n.d.

Nelkin, Dorothy. *Science Textbook Controversies*

and the Politics of Equal Time. Cambridge, Mass.: MIT Press, 1978.

Noel, C. L. Retail Impact Assessments: A Practical Appraisal. Oxford: Oxford Polytechnic School of Planning, working paper no. 118, 1989.

Nord, Philip G. Paris Shopkeepers and the Politics of Resentment. Princeton, N.J.: Princeton University Press, 1986.

Nystrom, Paul N. Economic Principles of Consumption. New York: Ronald Press, 1929.

———. Economics of Fashion. New York: Ronald Press, 1928.

———. Economics of Retailing. New York: Ronald Press, 1930.

O'Brien, Larry, and Harris, Frank. Retailing, Shopping, Society, and Space. London: David Fulton, 1991.

Oldenburg, Ray. The Great Good Place. New York: Paragon, 1991.

Osborne, G. Scott. Electronic Direct Marketing. Englewood, N.J.: Prentice Hall, 1984.

Otten, Catherine. The Corner Grocery Store. Milwaukee, Wis.: T/D, 1980.

Ownby, Ted. American Dreams in Mississippi: Consumers, Poverty, and Culture, 1830–1998. Chapel Hill: University of North Carolina Press, 1999.

Oxford English Dictionary. Oxford: Clarendon, 1989.

Packard, William. Evangelism in America from Tents to TV. New York: Paragon, 1988.

Park, Robert E.; Burgess, Ernest W.; and McKenzie, Roderick D. The City. Chicago: University of Chicago Press, 1925.

Parker, Florence E. History of Distributive and Service Cooperatives in the United States, 1829–1954. Superior, Wis.: Cooperative Publishing, 1956.

Patten, Simon N. The Consumption of Wealth. Philadelphia: Boston, Ginn, 1901.

———. The New Basis of Civilization. Edited by Daniel M. Fox. Cambridge, Mass.: Harvard University Press, 1968.

Peck, W. Scott. The Different Drum: Community-Making and Peace. New York: Simon & Schuster, 1987.

Perin, Constance. Belonging in America: Reading Between the Lines. Madison: University of Wisconsin Press, 1988.

Perry, Clarence A. "Planning a Neighborhood Unit: Principles Which Would Give Added Character, Convenience, and Safety to Outlying Sections of Cities." American City 41 (September 1929), pp. 124–26.

Petersen, Laurie. "Twenty-First Century Super-market Shopping." Adweek's Marketing Week 30 (1989).

Peterson, Robert A., ed. The Future of U.S. Retailing: An Agenda for the Twenty-First Century. New York: Quorum, 1992.

Pevsner, Nikolaus. A History of Building Types. London: Thames & Hudson, 1976.

Pfueller, Lisa M. "The Spread of the Supermarket in the Washington Area, 1936–1956." Paper presented at the Twenty-Second Annual Conference of Washington, D.C., Historical Studies, October 14, 1995.

Pirenne, Henri. Economic and Social History of Medieval Europe. New York: Harcourt Brace, n.d.

Politics and Prose Bookstore-Coffeehouse. "Fifteenth Anniversary." Washington: Politics and Prose Bookstore-Coffeehouse, 1999.

Pollard, W. L. "Outline of the Law of Zoning in the United States." Annals of American Academy of Political and Social Science 45 (March 1931), pp. 15–33.

Pound, Reginald. Selfridge. London: Heinemann, 1960.

PricewaterhouseCoopers and Lendlease Real Estate Investments. Emerging Trends in Real Estate, 2000. New York: Pricewaterhouse Coopers and Lendlease Real Estate Investments, 1999.

Pristo, Lori Ann. "A Process for Determining the Most Marketable Strip Shopping Center Design." Arch.D. diss., University of Michigan, 1984.

Putnam, Robert D. "Bowling Alone: America's Declining Social Capital." Journal of Democracy 6 (January 1995), pp. 66–78.

———. Bowling Alone: The Collapse and Revival of American Community. New York: Simon & Schuster, 2000.

———; Leonardi, Robert; and Nanetti, Raffaella Y. Making Democracy Work: Civic Traditions in Modern Italy. Princeton, N.J.: Princeton University Press, 1993.

Ranney, Victoria P., ed. The Papers of Frederick Law Olmsted. Vol. 5, The California Frontier, 1863–1865. Baltimore: Johns Hopkins University Press, 1990.

Rappaport, Erika D. Shopping for Pleasure: Women in the Making of London's West End. Princeton, N.J.: Princeton University Press, 2000.

Rathsur, Robert Davis, ed. Shopping Centers and Malls. New York: Retail Reporting, 1992.

Regional Plan Association. A Region at Risk: The Third Regional Plan for the New York/New

Jersey/Connecticut Metropolitan Area. New York: Regional Plan Association, 1996.

Regional Plan of New York and Its Environs, "The Central Retail Shopping District of New York and Its Environs: A Consideration of the Factors Affecting Location," *Regional Survey of New York and Its Environs*. New York: Regional Plan of New York and Environs, 1928.

Reps, John W. "Requiem for Zoning." In *Planning, 1964*. Chicago: American Society of Planning Officials, 1964.

Ressequie, Harry E. "The Decline and Fall of the Commercial Empire of A. T. Stewart." *Business History Review* 36 (Autumn 1962), pp. 255–86.

Reuters, "eBay Visitors." *American Online News*, December 2, 1999.

Rhees, Suzanne S. "Mall Wonder." *Planning* 60 (October 1993), pp. 18–23.

Riesman, David. "The Suburban Dislocation." In *Abundance for What? and Other Essays*. Garden City, N.Y.: Doubleday, 1964.

———; Denney, Reuel; and Glazer, Nathan. *The Lonely Crowd: A Study of Changing American Character*. New Haven, Conn.: Yale University Press, 1977.

Ritzer, George. *The McDonaldization Thesis: Explorations and Extension*. Thousand Oaks, Calif.: Sage, 1998.

———. *The McDonaldization of Society*. Thousand Oaks, Calif.: Pine Forge, 1996.

Riverside Improvement Company. *Riverside in 1871, with a Description of Its Improvements*. Chicago: D. & C. H. Blakeley, 1871.

Robinson, Dwight E. "The Importance of Fashions in Taste to Business History." *Business History Review* 37 (Spring–Summer 1963), pp. 5–36.

Robinson, John P. "The Time Squeeze." *American Demographics* 12 (February 1990), pp. 30–33.

Roche, Daniel. *The Culture of Clothing*. Translated by Jean Birrell. Cambridge: Cambridge University Press, 1994.

Rogers, David S. *Developments in U.S. Retailing*. Harlow, U.K.: Longman, 1990.

Royal Town Planning Institute. *Planning for Shopping into the Twenty-First Century*. London: Royal Town Planning Institute, 1988.

———. "Shopping Centres and Their Future." Evidence submitted to the House of Commons Environment Committee on its Inquiry, London, June 1994.

Rybczynski, Witold. "The New Downtowns." *Atlantic Monthly* 271 (May 1993), pp. 98–106.

———. "No Place Like Home." *Public Interest* 122 (Winter 1996), pp. 140–43.

Sandel, Michael J. "America's Search for a New Public Philosophy." *Atlantic Monthly* 277 (March 1996), pp. 57–74.

Satterthwaite, Ann. "Josiah Royce, Neglected Philosopher." Unpublished undergraduate honors thesis, Radcliffe/Harvard University, 1953.

Saxenian, AnnaLee. *Inside-Out: The Industrial Systems of Silicon Valley and Route 128*. Berkeley: University of California Press, 1993.

Schmookler, Andrew B. *The Illusion of Choice: How the Market Economy Shapes Our Destiny*. Albany: State University of New York Press, 1993.

Schor, Juliet B. *The Overspent American*. New York: Basic Books, 1998.

———. *The Overworked American: The Unexpected Decline of Leisure*. New York: Basic Books, 1991.

Schwartz, Barry. *The Changing Face of the Suburbs*. Chicago: University of Chicago Press, 1976.

Scitovsky, Tibor. *The Joyless Economy: The Psychology of Human Satisfaction*. Rev. ed. New York: Oxford University Press, 1992.

Scott, Rosemary. *The Female Consumer*. New York: John Wiley and Sons, 1976.

Seeley, John R.; Alexander, R.; Sim, R.; and Loosley, Elizabeth W. *Crestwood Heights*. New York: Basic Books, 1956.

Sennett, Richard. *The Conscience of the Eye: The Design and Social Life of Cities*. New York: W. W. Norton, 1990.

———. *The Fall of Public Man*. New York: W. W. Norton, 1992.

Shachtman, Tom. *Around the Block: The Business of a Neighborhood*. New York: Harcourt Brace, 1997.

Shaffer, Carolyn R., and Anundsen, Kristin. *Creating Community Anywhere*. New York: Jeremy R. Tarcher/Perigee, 1993.

Shapiro, Benson P., and Sviokla, John J., eds. *Seeking Customers*. Cambridge, Mass.: Harvard University Press, 1993.

Skinner, Donald J. "Maintaining Retail Balance in California Cities, or Mom and Pop Meet 'Big Box.'" Report for the Panel on Maintaining Retail Balance, California Chapter of the American Planning Association Annual Conference, Monterey, Calif., October 12–15, 1997.

Slywotzky, Adrian J. "The Age of the Choice-board," *Harvard Business Review* 78 (January–February 2000), pp. 40–41.

Smith, Kennedy Lawson. "Main Street at 15." *Historic Preservation Forum* 9 (Spring 1995), pp. 49–64.

———. "Director's Column." *Main Street News*, May–June 1996, p. 9.

Soderberg, Susan C. "The Nineteenth-Century General Store in Montgomery County." *Montgomery County Story* 39 (February 1996), pp. 369–80.

Soiffer, Stephen M., and Herrman, Gretchen M. "Visions of Power: Ideology and Practice in the American Garage Sale." *Sociological Review* 35 (February 1987), pp. 48–83.

Sommer, Robert. "Farmers' Markets as Community Events." In *Public Places and Spaces*. Edited by I. Altman and E. Zube. New York: Plenum, 1989.

———; Herrick, John; and Sommer, Ted R. "The Behavioral Ecology of Supermarkets and Farmers' Markets." *Journal of Environmental Psychology* 1 (1981), pp. 13–19.

———; Wynes, Marcia; and Brinkley, Garland. "Social Facilitation Effects in Shopping Behavior." *Environment and Behavior* 24 (May 1992), pp. 285–97.

Sorenson, Helen. *The Consumer Movement*. New York: Harper & Row, 1941.

Spitzer, Theodore M., and Baum, Hilary. *Public Markets and Community Revitalization*. Washington, D.C.: Urban Land Institute, 1996.

Stanton, Elizabeth Cady. *Eighty Years and More, 1815–1897: Reminiscences of Elizabeth Cady Stanton*. New York: Source Book, 1970.

Starbeck, Thomas M., Jr. *The New Suburbanization: Challenge to the Central City*. Oxford: Westview, 1991.

Stein, Clarence S. *Toward New Towns in America*. Cambridge, Mass.: MIT Press, 1971.

———, and Bauer, Catherine. "Store Buildings and Neighborhood Shopping Centers." *Architectural Record* 75 (February 1934), pp. 175–87.

Sternlieb, George, and Hughes, James W., eds. *Shopping Centers: USA*. New Brunswick, N.J.: Rutgers University Press, 1988.

Stilgoe, John R. *Borderland: Origins of the American Suburb, 1820–1939*. New Haven, Conn.: Yale University Press, 1988.

Stokes, Isaac Newton Phelps. *The Iconography of Manhattan Island, 1498–1909*. New York: Robert H. Dodd, 1918.

Stoneall, Linda. *Country Life, City Life: Five Theories of Community*. New York: Praeger, 1983.

Strasser, Susan. *Never Done*. New York: Pantheon Books, 1982.

———. *Satisfaction Guaranteed: The Making of the American Mass Market*. New York: Pantheon, 1989.

Suberman, Stella. *The Jew Store*. Chapel Hill, N.C.: Algonquin, 1998.

Sucher, David. *City Comforts: How to Build an Urban Village*. Seattle: City Comforts Press, 1995.

Sweeney, Kevin M. "High-Style Vernacular: Lifestyles of the Colonial Elite." In *Of Consuming Interests: The Style of Life in the Eighteenth Century*. Edited by Cary Carson. Charlottesville: University of Virginia Press, 1994.

Sweet, William Warner. *The Story of Religion in America*. New York: Harper & Brothers, 1950.

Tawney, R. H. *The Acquisitive Society*. New York: Harcourt & Brace Jovanovich, 1948.

Taylor, Alan. *William Cooper's Town: Power and Persuasion on the Frontier of the Early American Republic*. New York: Knopf, 1996.

Thompson, Edgar T. "Country Store." In *Encyclopedia of Southern Culture*. Edited by Charles R. Wilson and William Ferris. Chapel Hill: University of North Carolina Press, 1989.

Tides Foundation. *Redefining the American Dream: The Search for Sustainable Consumption*. Unpublished conference report, April 1995.

Time-Life Book Editors. *The Rise of Cities*. Alexandria, Va.: Time-Life, 1990.

Tocqueville, Alexis de. *Democracy in America*. New York: New American Library, 1956.

Toll, Seymour I. *Zoned America*. New York: Grossman, 1969.

Tomlinson, Alan, ed. *Consumption, Identity, and Style: Marketing, Meanings, and the Packaging of Pleasure*. New York: Routledge, 1990.

Traub, Marvin, and Teicholz, Tom. *Like No Other Store*. New York: Random House, 1993.

Tse, K. K. *Marks & Spencer: Anatomy of Britain's Most Efficiently Managed Company*. Oxford: Pergamon, 1985.

Turchiano, Francesca. "The (Un)Malling of America." *American Demographics* 12 (April 1990), pp. 36–39.

Twyman, Robert W. *History of Marshall Field & Co., 1852–1906*. New York: Arno, 1976.

Underhill, Paco. *Why We Buy: The Science of Shopping.* New York: Simon & Schuster, 1999.

Urban Land Institute. *Dollars and Cents of Shopping Centers, 1998.* Washington, D.C.: Urban Land Institute, 1998.

——. *Remaking the Shopping Center.* Washington, D.C.: Urban Land Institute, 1994.

——. *Shopping Center Development Handbook.* Washington, D.C.: Urban Land Institute, 1995.

——. *Urban Land Institute Forecast: Urban Land Supplement.* Washington, D.C.: Urban Land Institute, 1999.

——, and Project for Public Spaces. *Public Markets and Community Revitalization.* Washington, D.C.: Urban Land Institute, 1995.

Veblen, Thorstein. *The Theory of the Leisure Class.* New York: Reprints of Economic Classics, Augustus M. Kelly, 1975.

Vermont Forum on Sprawl. *Exploring Sprawl.* Issues 1–6. Burlington: Vermont Forum on Sprawl, 1999.

von Hoffman, Alexander. *Local Attachments: The Making of an American Urban Neighborhood, 1850–1920.* Baltimore: Johns Hopkins University Press, 1994.

Wachtel, Paul L. *The Poverty of Affluence: A Psychological Portrait of the American Way of Life.* Philadelphia: New Society, 1989.

Waddy, Patricia. *Seventeenth-Century Roman Palaces: Use and the Art of the Plan.* Cambridge, Mass.: MIT Press, 1990.

Waldrop, Judith. "Mall Shoppers Want the Basics." *American Demographics* 13 (October 1991), p. 16.

Walker, Chip. "Strip Malls: Plain but Powerful." *American Demographics* 13 (October 1991).

Walton, Sam, and Huey, John. *Sam Walton: Made in America.* New York: Doubleday, 1992.

Ward, David, and Zunz, Olivier, eds. *The Landscape of Modernity: Essays on New York City, 1900–1940.* New York: Russell Sage, 1992.

Washington Post/Kaiser Family Foundation/Harvard University Survey Project. "Why Don't Americans Trust the Government?" Menlo Park, Calif.: Henry J. Kaiser Foundation, 1996.

Way, James, ed. *Encyclopedia of Business Information Sources, 1993–1994.* Detroit, Mich.: Gale Research, 1994.

Weber, Max. *The City.* New York: Collier, 1962.

Weinberg, Zy. *No Place to Shop.* Washington,

D.C.: Public Voice for Food and Health Policy, 1996.

Wells, H. G. *The History of Mr. Polly.* New York: Press of the Readers Club, 1941.

Whitehill, Walter Muir. *Boston: A Topographical History.* 2nd ed. Cambridge, Mass.: Harvard University Press, 1968.

Whitnall, Gordon. "History of Zoning." *Annals of American Academy of Political and Social Science* 45 (March 1931), pp. 1–14.

Whittlesey, Frances Cerra. "Getting the Goods." *Working Woman,* March 1999.

Whitwell, Gregory. *Making the Market: The Rise of Consumer Society.* Melbourne, Australia: McPhee Gribble, 1989.

Whyte, William H., Jr. *City: Rediscovering the Center.* New York: Doubleday, 1988.

——. *The Organization Man.* New York: Doubleday, 1957.

Williams, Brett. *Upscaling Downtown: Stalled Gentrifications in Washington, D.C.* Ithaca, N.Y.: Cornell University Press, 1988.

Williams, Frank Backus. *The Law of City Planning and Zoning.* New York: Macmillan, 1922.

Williams, Raymond. *Keywords.* London: Flamingo, Fontana Paperbacks, 1984.

Williams, Rosalind H. *Dream Worlds: Mass Consumption in Late Nineteenth-Century France.* Berkeley: University of California Press, 1982.

Williamson, Judith. *Consuming Passions: The Dynamics of Popular Culture.* New York: Marion Boyars, 1980.

Winkler, John F. *Five and Ten: The Fabulous Life of F. W. Woolworth.* New York: Bantam Books, 1957.

Winstanley, Michael J. *The Shopkeeper's World, 1830–1914.* Manchester: Manchester University Press, 1983.

Winthrop, Robert C. *Life and Letters of John Winthrop.* 2 vols. Boston: Ticknor and Fields, 1864–67.

"The Wired Society." *Harvard Magazine,* May–June 1999, pp. 42–53, 106, and 107.

Wood, Robert C. *Suburbia: Its People and Their Politics.* Boston: Houghton Mifflin, 1959.

Woods, Walter A. *Consumer Behavior: Adapting and Experiencing.* New York: North Holland, 1981.

Woolf, Virginia. *A Haunted House and Other Short Stories.* New York: Harcourt, Brace, 1944.

Worley, William S. *J. C. Nichols and the Shaping of Kansas City: Innovation in Planned Residential Communities.* Columbia: University of Missouri Press, 1990.

Worthy, James C. *Shaping an American Institution: Robert E. Wood and Sears Roebuck.* Urbana: University of Illinois Press, 1984.

Wycherley, Richard Ernest. *How the Greeks Built Cities.* London: Macmillan, 1949.

Zukin, Sharon. *Landscapes of Power.* Berkeley: University of California Press, 1991.

Manuscript Collections

Papers of Edward L. Bernays, Manuscript Division, Library of Congress, Washington, D.C.

Olmsted Associates Records, Manuscript Division, Library of Congress, Washington, D.C.

Woodward & Lothrop Collection, Historical Society of the District of Columbia Archives, Washington, D.C.

Government Documents

U.K. Department of the Environment. *Planning Policy Guidance: Town Centres and Retail Development.* [PPG 6 revised.] London: HMSO, July 1993.

U.K. House of Commons Environment Committee. *Shopping Centres and Their Future.* London: HMSO, 1994.

U.K. National Economic Development Office. *The Future Pattern of Shopping.* London: HMSO, 1971.

U.S. Department of Agriculture. "Agricultural Marketing Service (AMS) Farmers' Markets Facts." Washington, D.C.: Government Printing Office, February 16, 2000.

U.S. Department of Commerce. Bureau of the Census. *Census of Population Supplementary Reports.* Washington, D.C.: Government Printing Office, for the year 1990.

——. *Census of Retail Trade.* Washington, D.C.: Government Printing Office, for the years 1987, 1992 and 1997.

——. *County Business Patterns.* Washington, D.C.: Government Printing Office, for the years 1948–98.

——. *County and City Data Book.* Washington, D.C.: Government Printing Office, for the years 1940, 1962, and 1972.

——. *Current Business Reports, Monthly Retail Trade.* Washington, D.C.: Government Printing Office, for the years 1977–97.

——. *Statistical Abstract of the United States.* Washington, D.C.: Government Printing Office, for the years 1963, 1982, 1983, 1984, 1987, 1990, 1991, 1994, 1995, 1998, and 1999.

——. National Telecommunications and Information Administration. *Falling Through the Net.* Washington, D.C.: Government Printing Office, 1999.

U.S. Department of Labor. Bureau of Labor Statistics. "News." Pamphlet 91–547. October 28, 1991.

U.S. Department of the Treasury. Internal Revenue Service. *Statistics of Income Bulletin.* Washington, D.C.: Government Printing Office, for the year 1995.

U.S. Postal Service. "Community Relations Regulations for the United States Postal Service Facilities Projects." Washington, D.C.: Government Printing Office, 1999.

Vermont State Legislature. Bills H. 408, H. 475, and H. 659 (2000 Session). Act No. 120 [H. 278] (1998 Session).

Legal References

Barbier v. Connolly. 113 U.S. 27 (1884).

Green Party of New Jersey and James Mohn v. Hartz Mountain Industries, Inc., d/b/a The Mall at Mill Creek. 2000 N.J. Lexis 656 (1999–2000).

Hang Kie. 69 Cal. 149 (1886).

Ignaciunas v. Town of Nunley. 99 N.J. 389 (1924).

New Jersey Coalition Against War in the Middle East v. J. M. B. Realty Corporation et al. 138 N.J. 326 (1994).

Quong Wo. 161 Cal. 220 (1911).

Sam Chung. 105 Pac. 609 (1909).

Soon Hing v. Crowley. 113 U.S. 730 (1885).

Steerman v. Oehmann. Washington Law Reporter, vol. 53, 28 (1925).

Yick Wo. 9 Pac. 139 (1885).

Company and Corporation Annual Reports and Statements

Amazon.com. *Annual Report,* 1999.

eBay. "Company Overview." April 13, 2000.

Lands' End. *Annual Report* for the years 1996, 1997, 1998, and 1999.

Lands' End. *Fact Sheet* for the years 1996, 1997, and 1999.

L. L. Bean. *Fact Sheet* for the year 2000.

7-Eleven. "Mid-Atlantic Division Markets Report." February 8, 2000.

Wal-Mart. *Annual Report* for the years 1994, 1995, 1996, and 1999.

Wal-Mart. Press releases for September 14 and October 10, 1995, and February 27, 1996.

Wal-Mart. "Securities and Exchange Commission Report 10-K," April 21, 1995.

Newspapers and Periodicals

Adweek's Marketing Week
Albuquerque Journal
American Behavioral Scientist
American City
American Demographics
Annals of American Academy of Political & Social
    Science
Architectural Record
Atlantic Monthly
Boston Globe
Brandweek
Business History Review
Chain Store Age Executive with Shopping Center
    Age
Chicago Tribune
Christianity Today
Denver Post
Drug Store News
Economist
Estates Gazette
Gallup Poll
Georgetowner
Governing
Grocer
Harvard Magazine
Independent Business
International Council of Shopping Centers
    Research Bulletin
Journal of the American Planning Association
Journal of Democracy
Journal of Property Research
Lever Co., Progress
Magazine of National Federation of Independent
    Business
Metro History News
Metropolis Magazine
Monitor
New York Review of Books
New York Times
Parade Magazine
Planning
Progressive Architecture
Public Interest
Public Management
Publishers Weekly
Regional Studies
Shopping Center Age: The Newsletter for Retail
    Management
Shopping Center Directory
Shopping Center World
Shopping Centers Today
Small Town
Social Forces
Social Science Quarterly
Sociological Review
Standard and Poor's Industry Surveys
This Week in Germany
Urban Land
Urban Life
Urban Studies
Wall Street Journal
Washington Post
Washington Times
Wilson Quarterly
Wired

Personal Interviews

Kris Abrahamson, Fairfax County Office of
    Comprehensive Planning, Fairfax, Va.
Robert Atkinson, Arlington County Department
    of Economic Development, Arlington, Va.
Michael Bach, Department of Environment,
    Transport and Regions, U.K.
Jonathan Baldock, CB Hillier Parker, London.
Tanya Barvenik, Arlington County Department
    of Economic Development, Arlington, Va.
Ellen Beasley, Galveston, Tex.
Judy Bonderman, Washington, D.C.
Elizabeth Clark, Washington, D.C.
Carla Cohen, Politics and Prose, Washington,
    D.C.
Sarah Bixby Defty, Berlin
Fay Dorsett, Bureau of the Census, Suitland, Md.
Robert Glass, Vice President and Chief Financial
    Officer, Loehmanns, New York
Georges Jacob, French Market, Washington, D.C.
Betty Kaplan, Philadelphia, Pa.
Lee Krohn, Town Planner, Manchester, Vt.
Janet Landfair, Arlington County, Va.
Gerry Medley, Arlington, Va.
Conchita Mitchell, Columbia Pike Revitalization
    Organization, Arlington, Va.
Esther Naughton, Cresskill, N.J.
David Rose, Royal Town Planning Institute,
    London.
David Ross, Atlantic Realty Company, Reston, Va.
Richard Sabot, Lycos and eZiba Officer,
    Williamstown, Mass.
Thomas H. Sander, Saguaro Seminar, Kennedy
    Institute, Cambridge, Mass.
Alton S. Scavo, Rouse Company, Columbia, Md.
Mark Schoifet, Director of Communications,
    International Council of Shopping Centers,
    New York
Michael Shippobottom, Architect, London.
Robert E. Simon, Reston, Va.
Kennedy Lawson Smith, National Mainstreet
    Program, National Trust for Historic Preser-
    vation, Washington, D.C.

Harold Sugar, Dumbarton Pharmacy, Washington, D.C.

Janet Swart, Tenafly, N.J.

Telephone Interviews and Other Correspondence

Richard Benson, Wooster Growth Corporation, Wooster, Ohio.

Russ Blackburn, Leesburg, Va.

Patricia Boudrot, Filene's Basement, Wellesley, Mass.

Ann Brinkley, Border's Bookstores, Ann Arbor, Mich.

Tom Cabot, National Association of Mall Walkers.

Jay Clog, Montgomery County, Md.

Ann B. Colcord, London.

John Collich, Washington, D.C.

Ralph diBart, Peekskill, N.Y.

Shirley Dushna, Williamstown, Mass.

Esther Dyson, ICANN.

Paul Edlund, ex-Mayor, Garrett Park, Md.

Nina Gruen, San Francisco, Calif.

Kathy Hamor, L. L. Bean, Freeport, Me.

Sandra Hull, Main Street Wooster, Inc., Wooster, Ohio.

Barbara M. Kelly, Hofstra University, Hempstead, N.Y.

Nicole Lander, Tesco, U.K.

Nancy Levy, Borders Bookstores, Ann Arbor, Mich.

Bruce Liedstrand, City Manager, Mountain View, Calif.

Glen Matteson, Planning Department, San Luis Obispo, Calif.

Kelly Pennock, Simon DeBartolo Group, Albuquerque, N.M.

John Rector, National Community Pharmacists Association, Alexandria, Virginia.

Anna Schryver, Lands' End, Dodgeville, Wis.

Kandra Smith, Borders Bookstores, Ann Arbor, Mich.

John Sorenson, U.S. Postal Service, Washington, D.C.

Peter Steck, Paramus, N.J.

Jeffrey Strange, Portland, Ore.

James Virgoina, Bower's Pharmacy, Tenafly, N.J.

Acknowledgments

The most enduring influences for this book have been the encounters and associations I have had over the years with different shops, stores, and markets and their staffs. From my New Jersey suburban childhood I have fond memories of cheerful Mr. Ryan at Demarest's Hardware, the serious Mr. Bower at the drugstore, the skinny and fat Katzes, cousins who ran two separate stores, one a novelty shop and the other the local department store, almost side by side, and jolly Mr. Fitzpatrick at his taxi stand. For "good" clothes, there were the trips to Best's in New York and often lunch at Schrafft's. Then in Cambridge I discovered a more sophisticated shopping world: the Square, with its many bookstores, where you could browse to your heart's content, Hayes-Bickford's, for lingering over a cup of coffee with friends, the wonderfully stocked five-and-ten, Sage's on Brattle Street for fancy food treats, the funky antique store upstairs on Church Street, and the service shops up on Mass. Ave. In my Greenwich Village neighborhood there were an Italian market and a restaurant around the corner, which always had deliciously rich tomato soup ready for me.

In New Haven I became friendly with the nearby Chinese laundryman, who was continuously constructing a five-foot-high waterfall contraption from half-pint milk containers, and with the older Italians making the best pizza in town at The Spot, situated in an alley near Wooster Square. In Washington my world has been enriched by the always upbeat Mrs. Trotter, Mrs. Simmons, and Mr. Williams at the post office; my house repair advisers at Cherrydale Hardware; Mort, with all his problems, at the corner store; knowledgeable Harold Sugar and Bob Royce at the Dumbarton Pharmacy, and Herman, their cheerful driver; Virginia Garrett and all the busy yet chatty vendors at the Arlington Farmers' Market; and Gerard Pain and the waiters at my favorite restaurant, La Chaumière, which I call my club. These are just a few of the shopkeepers who have been part of my life and have helped me feel—and appreciate being—part of a community.

My only direct experience in retailing was a Christmas season job in Lord and Taylor's New York store as a clerk in the men's underclothes and sleepwear department, where the store was promoting men's sleep shirts. What surprised me most in that job was how Lord and Taylor seduced my fellow clerks with a modest discount to spend much of their meager salaries on Lord and Taylor goods. In the end, Lord and Taylor benefited from both cheap labor and increased sales.

I am grateful for stimulation and guidance from my family. The intellectual curiosity, the analytical ways, and the fascination with economic history of my late father, J. Sheafe Satterthwaite, a Wall Street municipal bond analyst, helped stir my interest in how social and cultural events shape economic behavior. The incisive mind, the interest in vernacular landscape and architecture, and the social conscience of my late mother, Margaret H. Speer Satterthwaite, a journalist, sharpened my eye and spurred me to look beyond research. My brother, Sheafe Satterthwaite, who teaches landscape history and cultural geography at Williams College, has been my most constant support. His thoughtful and perceptive criticisms, encouragement, and advice have bolstered me at every step. He has suggested new approaches, ideas, and sources of information, has pointed out oversights and exaggerations, and has even organized several discussion groups with diverse retailers.

I decided to write this book without any grants or an institutional base, partly to allow myself flexibility and freedom and partly to avoid the hassles and red tape so often connected with grants and organizations. As a result of that decision I have been on my own, which has had many advantages. However, that freedom has meant that I depended on my own initiatives, background, connections, and interests, which may have limited my exposure to diverse ideas, points of view, and quests for information. It also meant that I had to seek advice, data, ideas, help, and support from more people than I can ever adequately acknowledge and thank.

In my academic and professional work I have been guided by many confreres, especially several who are now deceased but are of continuing intellectual influence: John E. Sawyer, a good friend who ignited my interest in economic history at Harvard and later went on to Yale, Williams, and the Mellon Foundation; Christopher Tunnard, who at Yale broadened my approach to planning to include man-made and natural amenities; the landscape historian J. B. Jackson, a dear friend whose refreshing independence and egalitarian outlook—and wit—were always welcome; and many others, including the urban observer and writer William H. Whyte, William Wheaton, dean of the College of Environmental Design at the University of California at Berkeley, and Washington planner David Hartley.

I could not have undertaken this book without the incredible resources of innumerable libraries, here and abroad. My research was launched with a magic card from my alma mater, Radcliffe/Harvard, enabling me to use all of Harvard's libraries, some of which were off-limits to women when I was an undergraduate. In Washington, D.C., the rich collections and helpful and courteous staff at Georgetown University's Launinger Library were a constant source of help. The accessible and well-stocked Sawyer Library at Williams College also met many research needs. I was helped, time and time again, by the staff in all sorts of libraries: those in towns like Levittown, Long Island, and in cities like London, New York, and Washington; those belonging to organizations like the National Association of Chain Drug Stores and the National Trust for Historic Preservation; and those in government agencies like the Census Bureau. The quiet and competent librarians who staff these libraries have been the unsung heroes for me.

My friend and literary agent, Katharine Kidde, offered professional and constructive advice and welcome support at the most needed times. I depended on the thoughtful, professional advice about publishing offered by another friend, Margot Backas. Many other friends and associates helped me in many ways: Carolyn F. Hoffman, editor of the Olmsted Papers, who helped with copy editing, indexing, and computer tutoring; Nora Sayre, who helped with early editing; Charles Beveridge, editor-in-chief of the Olmsted Papers, who did most of the copy photography; and Tina Hummel, a resourceful researcher, who could locate the most obscure facts and also resolve computer problems. Fellow planners Ruth Eckdish Knack, editor of *Planning*, and California consultant Donald Skinner provided me with ideas, books, reports, and photographs. Kennedy Lawson Smith of the National Trust for Historic Preservation's Main Street Program supplied helpful information on that project. Charles Saunders simplified legal matters for me, and both he and his wife, Marcia Saunders, took photographs. Eugene J. Johnson of the Williams College art department and his wife, Leslie, sent me useful information and photographs; Roger Bolton of the economics department at Williams bolstered my knowledge of the economic side of retailing by exposing me to ideas and publications that I would not have stumbled upon; Edward Straka provided me with data on his hometown of Riverside, Illinois; Sarah Harbaugh and Dana White sent me information on Atlanta; and Stephen Davies of the Project for Public Spaces helped with photographs. The insights and experience of economic consultant

Nina Gruen of San Francisco, Ellen Beasley, author of an excellent book on corner stores, writer Philip Langdon of New Haven, and City Manager Bruce Liedstrand of Mountain View, California, were all helpful. Carla Cohen of the Washington bookstore Politics and Prose gave me insights into the operation of that successful store.

For the business side of retailing I am grateful for the help given me by Robert Glass, chief financial officer of Loehmann's; Richard Sabot, chairman of e-Ziba and board member of Lycos; Alton J. Scavo, vice president of the Rouse Company; Wayne Christmann, general manager, Columbia Management, Inc.; Robert E. Simon, "father" of Reston, Virginia; and all the corporate public information and other staffs who answered many questions and sent me useful material. Sometimes people went out of their way to provide me full and forthright information, look up data for me, and steer me to new ideas and material. For this I thank Nancy Levy of Borders, Anna Schryver of Lands' End, John Rector of the National Community Pharmacists Association, and Patricia Boudrot of Filene's Basement.

In England, Jonathan Baldock of CB Hillier Parker; Michael Bach of the Department of Environment, Transport, and Regions; Ann Colcord, Christopher Hall, Daniela Karakasheva, Brenda Maddox, and David Rose of the Royal Town Planning Institute; Michael Shippobottom; and many others helped me with research. Sarah B. Defty was my German adviser, and Rannheid Sharma was my Norwegian translator and adviser. The Japanese Embassy in Washington and its New York economic trade office were among the most helpful of all the foreign legations I interviewed.

In most of the places that I visited or wrote about, I interviewed or corresponded with the local planners, who were both interested in my topic and also very helpful—from Nassau County, New York, to San Luis Obispo, California, to Palm Beach, Florida, to Manchester, Vermont. Although there are too many to acknowledge individually, I do want to express my appreciation for their willingness to share their intelligence, experience, and thoughts with me. As an independent planning consultant, I respect these planning practitioners, who have been been working in the trenches at a time when planning has not been in public favor.

The staffs and publications of the American Planning Association and the Royal Town Planning Institute, along with my daily reading of the *New York Times*, were indispensable sources of information and ideas. In the 1970s and 1980s two grants from the National Endowment for the Arts enabled me to undertake research that helped focus my attention on how to retain the authenticity of certain commercial activities and the livability of residential areas threatened with rapid urban change. My first grant on fish market districts in major cities, "Fishmongers in the Concrete Jungle," led me to study how these districts, deemed marginal by many cities and targeted for urban renewal, could be economic, social, and cultural assets for cities. In exploring these fish districts and the phenomenon of cultural tourism, I looked at ways to balance the drive to move ahead with the seeming efficiencies of new capitalistic ventures with the need to sustain the human and social benefits of long-held customs.

In this era of word processing, I depended on the late Neil Rappaport of West Pawlet, Vermont, Lee Suppowit of Troy, New York, Kathleen Brunner of Bowie, Maryland, and Tara Devereux of Hartland, Vermont, to extricate me from innumerable computer problems.

Even with all this help and stimulation, I fear there are omissions and misinterpretations, which I trust will not diminish my overall thesis. Nor should any of the people I have acknowledged here, or neglected to acknowledge, be held responsible for these omissions and misinterpretations.

Index

Protestant work ethic, 51
Providence Preservation Society (Providence, R.I.), 295
Public markets, 4, 34, 214–20
Public/private partnership, 327–29, 332–33
Public relations. *See Bernays, Edward L.*
Public spaces, private uses of, 324–30
Puritanism, 25, 35, 37
Pushcarts, 248
Putnam, Robert, 314–16

Quakers, 35, 258
Queen Elizabeth I, 23
Queens Center Mall (NYC), 188
QVC, 200

Radburn, New Jersey, 255, 258; planned community, 252–53
Radburn Plaza Building (Radburn, N.J.), 49
Ralph's Grocery Company, 300–1
Reading Railroad, 218
Reading Terminal Market (Philadelphia, Pa.), 34, 217, 218–20, 222
Regional fairs, 20–21
Regional Planning Association, 191–92
REI (Seattle, Wash.), 229
Reston, Virginia, 108, 109, 254, 258, 262–65
Retailers, 90
Retailing, attitudes toward, 12; changes in, 318; and corporations, 55; and customer loyalty, 129–30; democratization of, 63, 143; discount, 185; entertainment in, 59; future of, 172, 239; history of, 2, 13; incubator, 184; and individualism, 147; mail-order, 40; respectability of, 211; role of government in, 11, 307; in rural areas, 35–41; and technological innovations, 171, 340; and women, 42, 44. *See also shopping*
Revco, 70
Revolving funds, 334
Rich's Department Stores (Atlanta, Ga.), 65, 83
Riesman, David, 162
Rite-Aid, 69
Riverside, Ill., 46–47, 108, 148, 258
Riverside Stores (Riverside, Ill.), 49
Roland Park (Baltimore, Md.), 46, 108
Roland Park Building (Baltimore, Md.), 49
Roman Empire, 14–17
Romanticism, 26, 131
Rome, Italy, 18, 21
Rosemary Lane's Rag Fair (London, England), 28
Rouse, James, 48, 59, 109, 265
Rouse Company, 92, 108, 217, 228
Rowntree, Joseph, 258
Royce, Josiah, 311; and community, 313

Rural free delivery, 39, 40, 171
Rural Retreat, Virginia, 72
Russia, 127
Rutland, Vermont, and Wal-Mart, 180
Rybczynski, Witold, 105

Safeway, 70, 82
Saks Fifth Avenue (NYC), 214
Salt, Titus, 258
Sam's Clubs, 176, 180
San Diego, California, Uptown District in, 299–300, 301
San Francisco, California, 94; and Chinese laundry cases in, 243; coffee cafes in, 331; discount shopping in, 61; warehouse clubs in, 181
San Luis Obispo, California, 299
Santa Clara County, California, 68; planning in, 257
Saturday Market (Portland, Ore.), 227
Savannah, Georgia, 334
Saxenian, AnnaLee, 314
Schor, Juliet, 119
Scottsdale, Arizona, 17
Sears Roebuck, 39, 40, 58–59, 62, 197
Seaside (Miami, Fla.), 268–69
Seattle, Washington, coffee cafes in, 331; markets in, 35; planning in, 298
Selfridge, Gordon, 42, 44, 51, 64, 89, 117, 128
Selfridge's (London, England), community role of, 44; role of in emancipation of women, 134
Self-service stores, 40, 41
Seven Corners (northern Va.), 189–90
7-Eleven, 194, 195
Shakespeare & Co. (NYC), 234
Shopaholics, Ltd., 135
Shopkeepers, 10–11; negative views of, 11
Shopko, 70
Shoppers, debt of, 120; demographics of, 112–13, 155; fantasies of, 123
Shopping, 131; addiction to, 120, 135; American attitudes toward, 344; and American character, 6, 7; as areas in community activity, 64–66; as areas of public concern, 345; bargain, 173, 175; and benefits to communities, 308–10; and commercialism, 342; and communities, 75, 109, 330–31; and convenience, 192–96; and democratizing effects of, 7, 35, 58, 131, 209, 343–45; discount, 106–7; as entertainment, 93, 227–31; and fantasies, 123; and fashion, 23–24, 124, 125; future of, 320; guild control of, 21; history of, 4–5, 9, 9–10, 11–12, 21–22, 63; and installment payment, 157; by Internet, 200–5; local control of, 334–37; motivations for, 117, 123, 124,

Photo Credits